OPENING THE BLACK BOX

NEW FRONTIERS OF SOCIAL POLICY

OPENING THE BLACK BOX

THE CONTEXTUAL DRIVERS OF SOCIAL ACCOUNTABILITY

Helene Grandvoinnet, Ghazia Aslam,
and Shomikho Raha

WORLD BANK GROUP

ISBN (paper): 978-1-4648-0481-6
ISBN (electronic): 10.1596/978-1-4648-0482-3
DOI: 10.1596/978-1-4648-0481-6

Cover image: Bill Pragluski, Critical Stages LLC.

Cover design: Naylor Design, Inc.

Library of Congress Cataloging-in Publication Data has been requested.

In many developing countries, the mixed record of state effectiveness, market imperfections, and persistent structural inequities has undermined the effectiveness of social policy. To overcome these constraints, social policy needs to move beyond conventional social service approaches toward development's goals of equitable opportunity and social justice. This series has been created to promote debate among the development community, policy makers, and academia, and to broaden understanding of social policy challenges in developing country contexts.

The books in the series are linked to the World Bank's Social Development Strategy. The strategy is aimed at empowering people by transforming institutions to make them more inclusive, responsive, and accountable. This involves the transformation of subjects and beneficiaries into citizens with rights and responsibilities. Themes in this series include equity and development, assets and livelihoods, citizenship and rights-based social policy, and the social dimensions of infrastructure and climate change.

Titles in the series:

- *Assets, Livelihoods, and Social Policy*
- *Building Equality and Opportunity through Social Guarantees: New Approaches to Public Policy and the Realization of Rights*
- *Delivering Services in Multicultural Societies*
- *Inclusion Matters: The Foundation for Shared Prosperity*
- *Inclusive States: Social Policy and Structural Inequalities*
- *Institutional Pathways to Equity: Addressing Inequality Traps*
- *Institutions Taking Root: Building State Capacity in Challenging Contexts*
- *Living through Crises: How the Food, Fuel, and Financial Shocks Affect the Poor*

- *Opening the Black Box: The Contextual Drivers of Social Accountability*
- *Social Dimensions of Climate Change: Equity and Vulnerability in a Warming World*
- *Societal Dynamics and Fragility: Engaging Societies in Responding to Fragile Situations*

All books in the New Frontiers of Social Policy series are available for free at: https://openknowledge.worldbank.org/handle/10986/2170

CONTENTS

Boxes

Figures

Tables

In 2014, the World Bank Group adopted the Strategic Framework for Mainstreaming Citizen Engagement in WBG Operations. The framework offers a roadmap for the ways we as an institution mainstream and scale up citizen engagement across our operations to improve results. Central to this commitment is achieving the target of beneficiary feedback from 100 percent of World Bank Group projects with clearly identifiable beneficiaries.

When governments engage with their citizens it provides opportunities to meet the World Bank's twin goals of ending extreme poverty and boosting shared prosperity in a sustainable way. With this spirit in mind, Bank experts took stock of existing evidence in this field with a focus on the role of context (this includes broad social and political factors, and factors linked to specific interventions such as accessibility).

The authors further assess how contextual factors have a pivotal impact on how citizens engage with their governments to bring about accountability (a process also referred to as social accountability). In this way the framework provides a systematic method to assess both opportunities and risks in citizen engagement. It also gives policy makers new tools to help prioritize entry points to support improved public services, transparency, and accountability, and broader institutional outcomes such as state legitimacy.

An important point to underscore is that social accountability is not about state against citizens, but about bridges between stakeholders. Information as well as civic mobilization and the interface of governments and citizens are necessary to support such engagement. The authors also explore how constructive citizen engagement operates in challenging contexts—namely fragile and conflict-affected countries—as well as countries where the space for citizen-state engagement is formally constrained.

This book took shape through multiple interactions and enriching partnerships with numerous civil society organizations, academics, and practitioners who champion transparency and accountability initiatives and reforms all over the world. We offer them our heartfelt thanks for their help and support.

By providing much needed guidance for our colleagues within the institution, as well as practitioners in other organizations, we hope this book will present a convincing case for citizen engagement as a game changer for sustainable development.

Ede Jorge Ijjasz-Vasquez	Mario Marcel Cullell
Senior Director	Senior Director
Social, Urban, Rural, and	Governance Global Practice
Resilience Global Practice	The World Bank
The World Bank	

> An approach which only asks the question of the impact of transparency and accountability initiatives [TAIs] in an abstract or de-contextualized sense has limited value. A more nuanced question is needed: What are the factors—enabling and disabling—that shape the possibility of TAIs achieving their goals in a particular context? Such an approach binds the analysis of impact both to the broad contexts in which transparency and accountability initiatives exist and to the theory of change underpinning their application in a particular setting. (McGee and Gaventa 2011, 19)

Developments around the world over the past several years provide arguments for greater and more effective citizen-state engagement. The World Bank Governance and Anti-Corruption 2011 strategy update notes that a groundswell of citizens' movements has signaled frustration with the seeming inability of governments to handle increasingly complex global problems of poverty, joblessness, fiscal crises, and environmental vulnerability (World Bank 2012). In parallel to these calls for a "new social contract" in many development contexts, the information and communication technology (ICT) revolution has provided additional space for new forms of enhanced citizen-state engagement. By allowing individuals and organizations both to generate and to disseminate information cheaply and on a mass scale, ICT is providing extensive and innovative avenues for states and citizens to engage with each other.

The World Bank's guidance on its two overarching goals—ending extreme poverty and boosting shared prosperity—highlights the critical role of accountability, participation, and empowerment in realizing them:

> Ending poverty and promoting shared prosperity are unequivocally about ... *enhancing voice and participation of all segments of society in economic, social, and political spheres.* ... Increasing the welfare of

the poor in low-income countries will *require complex institutional and governance reforms that enhance the accountability of the state*, raise the quality of service delivery, and improve the overall economic and social environment. An inclusive society must have the institutions, structures, and processes that *empower local communities, so they can hold their governments accountable*. It also requires the *participation of all groups in society*, including traditionally marginalized groups such as ethnic minorities and indigenous populations in decision-making processes.[1]

Beginning in fiscal 2015, the World Bank Group will implement its framework for mainstreaming citizen engagement (CE). The "Strategic Framework for Mainstreaming Citizen Engagement in World Bank Group Operations" (World Bank 2014) calls for incorporating citizen engagement in World Bank Group–supported policies, programs, projects, knowledge, and advisory services to improve their development results and, within the scope of these operations, to strengthen engagement processes between governments and the private sector and citizens. The framework proposes an approach that focuses on results, is context specific, is gradual, and emphasizes partnership. It encompasses, as a subset, the presidential mandate to achieve beneficiary feedback in 100 percent of World Bank–funded investment projects with clearly identifiable beneficiaries.

The components that make up CE—citizen voice and participation through consultation, collaboration, and empowerment—are closely related to social accountability (SA).

Although the emphasis on accountability makes SA distinct from CE, the two terms share many commonalities, and the present report provides a strong framework for analyzing the contextual elements of accountability-enhancing CE approaches.

This report focuses on SA, a form of citizen engagement defined in World Bank reports as the "extent and capability of citizens to hold the state accountable and make it responsive to their needs" (World Bank 2012, 30–31). Accountability and SA are concepts that apply not only to public officials such as service providers, policy makers, and elected officials, but also to donors, private sector organizations, and nongovernmental organizations. This report focuses solely on the accountability of public officials.

SA has gained prominence not only for its intrinsic value, but also for its potential to bring about a range of development outcomes. Most development agencies have invested in promoting forms of SA labeled in various ways, including demand for good governance, greater voice, and increased transparency and accountability, among others.

How policy makers, practitioners, and development agencies can best support development outcomes through SA, however, is still subject to debate, and knowledge gaps persist. This report aims to fill three specific knowledge gaps and provides guidance on how to assess contextual drivers of SA effectiveness. Its principal contribution is to provide a framework for thinking and operationalizing SA.

First, conceptually, there is a lack of clarity about the notion of SA, with no generally agreed definition of the range of actions that it comprises. At the same time, there is inadequate understanding of how SA activities yield different outcomes. Moreover, the outcomes that SA activities can achieve are poorly defined. This report analyzes the various schools of thought underpinning the concept of SA and their implications for operationalizing the concept. It conceptualizes SA as the interplay of five constitutive elements: citizen action and state action, as well as information, interface, and civic mobilization (chapter 1).

Second, while there is a growing body of empirical evidence regarding the impact of SA, it is difficult to make sense of the information because it is often incomplete or mixed and does not refer to the same expected outcomes. In part, this is because evaluations often focus on specific tools in specific settings, and it is difficult to generalize over broader contexts. It is also because practitioners have different views and objectives regarding the type of impacts they expect from SA approaches. In addition, evaluation methods are not necessarily able to capture complex processes, and, while fundamental to the concept of SA, some outcomes are difficult to measure. This report reviews the range of outcomes that can be associated with SA, points to reasons for this mixed body of evidence, and summarizes some key findings (chapter 2).

Third, there is little understanding of how and under what circumstances various processes of SA lead to various outcomes. That context matters for the success of an SA intervention is undisputed, but how and in which ways it does so are inadequately understood. Based on the existing evidence, chapters 3 and 4 address the knowledge gaps surrounding these relationships. In particular, chapter 3 considers how broad political and social conditions affect the design and outcomes of SA in a given context. Chapter 4 enriches the analysis of chapter 3 by incorporating intervention-based factors into an analytical framework for "opening the black box" of SA. This framework explores the contextual drivers of SA's five constitutive elements, their relationships, and the enabling or disabling factors that can affect them.

The last three chapters use the framework at two levels. Chapters 5 and 6 map archetypes of challenging country contexts along this framework. Challenging contexts are those where there is low willingness or capacity to support or engage with SA approaches. There is a poor understanding of the potential and effectiveness of SA in such contexts. Nevertheless, these may well be the contexts most in need of greater accountability. For many observers, SA represents an advance in thinking about ways in which citizens can exercise control over public authority in contexts where traditional mechanisms of political accountability do not exist. In the case of fragile and conflict-affected situations (FCSs), it might also encourage renewed trust between citizens and the state. Chapters 5 and 6 use the analytical framework to discuss two archetypes of challenging contexts: FCSs and countries where space for citizen-state engagement is formally constrained. These chapters highlight what we know about SA's potential and its outcomes in such contexts. To illustrate how to use the framework for a specific SA intervention, chapter 7 gives examples from SA activities in the Kyrgyz Republic, Pakistan, Sierra Leone, and the Republic of Yemen.

Methodology

This report builds on literature reviews, wide-ranging consultations with practitioners, and select operational engagement.

Reviews of SA evidence and literature across different disciplines (economics, sociology, political science, and others) informed the reorganization of the existing state of knowledge and supported the construction of the analytical framework (see the acknowledgments for the authors of the background papers used).

In parallel, practitioners, academics, and representatives of donor agencies provided useful advice and insights, through partnerships with select individuals, presentations at various conferences, brainstorming sessions with internal and external audiences, and interviews of practitioners (see the acknowledgments).

Selected operational engagement and empirical exploration made it possible to refine the analytical framework and test its applicability. In particular, the team benefited from a Nordic Trust Fund grant to support the work of World Bank teams in designing SA interventions in the Kyrgyz Republic, Pakistan, and the Republic of Yemen (see chapter 7 and forthcoming full-fledged case studies).

Note

1. Parts of the original document that are relevant to this report have been italicized. In the original document, they are not italicized. See World Bank (n.d.)

References

McGee, R., and J. Gaventa. 2011. "Shifting Power? Assessing the Impact of Transparency and Accountability Initiatives." IDS Working Paper 383, University of Sussex, Institute of Development Studies, Brighton, U.K. http://www.ids.ac.uk/files/dmfile/Wp383.pdf.

World Bank. 2012. "Strengthening Governance, Tackling Corruption: The World Bank's Updated Strategy and Implementation Plan." World Bank, Washington, DC, March 6. http://siteresources.worldbank.org/PUBLICSECTORANDGOVERNANCE/Resources/285741-1326816182754/GACStrategyImplementationPlan.pdf.

———. 2014. "Strategic Framework for Mainstreaming Citizen Engagement in World Bank Group Operations (Draft)." Draft from the decision meeting on July 8, World Bank Group, Washington, DC.

———. n.d. "The World Bank Group Goals: End Poverty and Promote Shared Prosperity." World Bank, Washington, DC. http://siteresources.worldbank.org/EXTPOVERTY/Resources/WB-goals_final.pdf.

ACKNOWLEDGMENTS

Helene Grandvoinnet is the task team leader and lead author. The team comprised Sanjay Agarwal, Ghazia Aslam, Saki Kumagai, Tiago Peixoto, Janelle Plummer, Shomikho Raha, and Daniela Villacres. Gracie Ochieng provided invaluable administrative support to the team throughout. Maria Amelina, Ezgi Canpolat, Asli Gurkan, Shruti Majumdar, Simon O'Meally, Caroline Rusten, Janmejay Singh, and Warren Van Wicklin also contributed inputs for this report. Maria Amelina, Sandra Boekman, Jennifer Gandhi, Margaux Hall, Anuradha Joshi, Shruti Majumdar, Nicholas Menzies, Simon O'Meally, Caroline Rusten, and Warren Van Wicklin drafted background papers.

The principal contributors to the report are listed below (including the principal authors of each chapter and the authors of the background papers and literature reviews).

Chapter	Principal author(s)	Author(s) of background papers
Chapter 1 (concept)	Helene Grandvoinnet, Shomikho Raha, Saki Kumagai	Anuradha Joshi
Chapter 2 (evidence)	Helene Grandvoinnet	Maria Amelina (methodology), Anuradha Joshi
Chapter 3 (political and social context)	Helene Grandvoinnet	Simon O'Meally, Badru Bukenya, Sam Hickey, Sophie King
Chapter 4 (analytical framework)	Helene Grandvoinnet, Ghazia Aslam, Shomikho Raha	Shruti Majumdar (impact evaluations)
Guiding tables	Shomikho Raha	Simon O'Meally, Badru Bukenya, Sam Hickey, Sophie King, Shruti Majumdar
Chapter 5 (constrained environments)	Janelle Plummer, Ghazia Aslam, Helene Grandvoinnet	Jennifer Gandhi, Warren Van Wicklin
Chapter 6 (fragile and conflict-affected situations)	Ghazia Aslam, Helene Grandvoinnet	Caroline Rusten, Sandra Boekman, Warren Van Wicklin
Chapter 7	Ghazia Aslam, Margaux Hall, Nicholas Menzies, Daniela Villacres, Helene Grandvoinnet	Daniela Villacres (Kyrgyz Republic case study), Ghazia Aslam (Pakistan and the Republic of Yemen case studies), Margaux Hall and Nicholas Menzies (Sierra Leone case study)

The team is grateful to Anuradha Joshi for a sound partnership on the "causal chain" approach and her careful review of drafts of this report. The team also thanks Jonathan Fox, Varja Lipovskek, Audrey Sachs, Fletcher Tembo, and Leni Wild for their helpful comments on early drafts.

We also thank the task teams of the village investment project 3 (VIP3) in the Kyrgyz Republic, co-led by Asli Gurkan and Mark Woodward, and the governance support project in Pakistan, led by Sher Shah Khan as well as Balakrishna Menon Parameswaran and Kanishka Balasuriya (working on the Yemeni decentralization dialogue), for their support for the case studies.

We also thank World Bank staff and other development practitioners for the insights they shared in structured interviews on lessons learned from their work in challenging contexts.

Thanks go to participants in the Nordic Trust Fund annual workshop in Stockholm, the Social Accountability Community of Practice meeting (in February 2014), the Jakarta Transparency and Accountability Initiative 2014 annual conference, the Jakarta Brown Bag Lunch at the World Bank and Australian Agency for International Development, and the brainstorming session in Washington, DC, in April 2014, for their insights on earlier versions of the framework.

Background papers and field research for this report in the Kyrgyz Republic, Pakistan's Khyber Pakhtunkhwa Province, and the Republic of Yemen were funded in part by a Nordic Trust Fund grant. Practitioners' interviews were partly financed by a Global Partnership Facility grant.

Last but not least, we thank our peer reviewers for their detailed and extremely useful comments, which have been incorporated into this final version of the report. Peer reviewers are Hana Brixi (program leader, MENA Strategic Cooperation Department), Jonathan Fox (professor, School of International Services, American University), Stuti Khemani (senior economist, Development Economics Vice Presidency/Human Development), Balakrishna Parameswaran (program leader, MENA Djibouti, Egypt, Yemen Country Management Unit), Caroline Sage (senior social development specialist, Social, Urban, Rural, and Resilience Global Practice), Jeff Thindwa (practice manager, Governance Global Practice), and Joel Turkewitz (lead public sector specialist, Governance Global Practice).

ABOUT THE AUTHORS

Ghazia Aslam is currently with the Global Partnership for Social Accountability at the World Bank and a policy fellow at the School of Public Policy, George Mason University. She has also worked with the Social Development Department and the Development Economics Research Group at the World Bank. She held a visiting faculty position at the economics department, Lahore University of Management Sciences, where she taught constitutional political economy. She received a doctorate in public policy from George Mason University in 2011 and a master's degree in economics from Lahore University of Management Sciences in 2004. Her main research interests include local governance, citizen participation, social movements, political transitions, and theories of dictatorships.

Helene Grandvoinnet is a governance expert with 19 years of experience in research, policy dialogue, and project design and management on a gamut of governance areas: transparency and accountability, decentralization, public finances, justice reform, anticorruption, and civil service reform. In her current position at the World Bank, she provides managerial and strategic support to the Governance Global Practice in the Africa region. Previously, she worked in low-capacity and fragile countries in the Africa region and spearheaded implementation of the governance and anticorruption strategy as the Africa coordinator. She led the work on this book as the cluster leader of the social accountability team in the Social Development Department, where she built a very active Community of Practices on Social Accountability, expanded training and capacity-building activities, and task-managed the Civil Society Fund.

Prior to joining the Bank, she worked for the Organisation for Economic Co-operation and Development's Development Centre and the Legal and Financial Division of the Ministry of Culture in France and did volunteer work in Calcutta, India.

An American and French national, she holds a degree in public administration from the Paris Institute of Political Science and a postgraduate degree in international administration from the University of Paris II, Pantheon-Assas.

Shomikho Raha is a governance and public sector specialist in the Governance Global Practice of the World Bank. He previously worked in the South Asia Human Development Unit of the Bank and for the demand for good governance and social accountability cluster within its Social Development Department. He has been a consultant to the Asia Foundation and the government of India and a governance adviser for the U.K. Department for International Development on its operational projects in India, covering reform of public administration and public services in health, education, and water and sanitation. His work relates to the political economy of public policy reform, human resource management for organizational performance, and transparency and accountability initiatives. He has published peer-reviewed articles, book chapters, and policy reports. He holds a doctorate, a master of arts, and a master of philosophy with a focus on politics and economic history from Trinity College, Cambridge University.

AK	*aiyl kenesh* (the Kyrgyz Republic)
AO	*aiyl okmotu* (the Kyrgyz Republic)
ARIS	Community Development and Investment Agency (the Kyrgyz Republic)
ARVIN	association, resources, voice, information, and negotiation
CBO	community-based organization
CS	civil society
CSO	civil society organization
DPL	development policy lending
EITI	Extractive Industry Transparency Initiative
FCS	fragile and conflict-affected situation
FHCI	free health care initiative (Sierra Leone)
GRM	grievance redress mechanism
GSP	governance support project (Pakistan)
ICT	information and communication technology
IT	information technology
J4P	Justice for the Poor Program
KP	Khyber Pakhtunkhwa (Pakistan)
LIC	local investment union executive committee (the Kyrgyz Republic)
NCDD	National Committee for Sub-National Democratic Development (Cambodia)
NGO	nongovernmental organization
RCT	randomized controlled trial
RTI	right to information
RTS	right to services
SA	social accountability

SDPK	Social Democratic Party of Kyrgyzstan (the Kyrgyz Republic)
VIC	village investment union executive committee (the Kyrgyz Republic)
VIP3	Village Investment Project 3 (the Kyrgyz Republic)
WDR	*World Development Report*

Overview

Opening the Black Box: Contextual Drivers of Social Accountability Effectiveness focuses on social accountability (SA), a form of citizen engagement defined in World Bank reports as the "extent and capability of citizens to hold the state accountable and make it responsive to their needs" (World Bank 2012). Accountability and SA are concepts that apply not only to public officials (such as service providers, policy makers, and elected officials), but also to donors, private sector organizations, and nongovernmental organizations. This report focuses on the accountability of public officials.

SA has steadily gained prominence for its intrinsic value as well as for its potential to bring about a range of development outcomes. Most development agencies have invested in promoting forms of SA labeled in various ways: demand for good governance, voice, transparency, and accountability initiatives, among others.

Yet how policy makers, practitioners, and development institutions can best support development outcomes through SA is still open to debate and subject to several knowledge gaps. This report aims to fill some of the knowledge gaps and provides guidance on how to assess contextual drivers of SA effectiveness and constructs a framework for thinking and operationalizing SA.

Origin of SA and Common Biases

SA mechanisms rely on civic engagement in which ordinary citizens, civil society organizations, or both participate directly or indirectly in exacting accountability, including efforts by government and other actors (media, private sector, and donors) to support these actions. The World

Bank's Governance and Anti-Corruption strategy update defines SA as the "extent and capability of citizens to hold the state accountable and make it responsive to their needs"—in other words, "accountability-enhancing actions that citizens can take beyond elections" (World Bank 2012).

The SA concept derives from distinct intellectual roots that have led to some biases in interpretations of the approach (chapter 1). Its two main intellectual roots are the principal-agent model and the voice and participation model.

The principal-agent model treats SA as an extension of new public management, introducing the idea of "client power" as conceptualized in the *World Development Report* (WDR) *2004* (World Bank 2004). It also frames users as individuals rather than as collective actors. The influential WDR 2004's "short route" to accountability puts reducing information asymmetries at the core of "client power" that enables citizens to hold service providers directly accountable.

A contrasting view emphasizes the value of "voice" and "transparency" and frames SA as an intrinsic "good" and as a way of creating "active citizens." This relates to a definition of poverty that focuses not only on instrumental gains but also on poor people's opportunities and capabilities to exercise influence in the public sphere (Sen 1999; Narayan et al. 2000; World Bank 2001). The intrinsic contribution of SA also lies in its promotion of transparency, which differs markedly from a focus on correcting information asymmetries.

In part because of these diverse origins, common biases are observed in current interpretations and implementation of SA:

- *A support centered on the technical application of standardized "tools."* A set of well-developed tools can support SA approaches. Yet the application of these tools needs to be embedded in an analysis of the opportunities and constraints in a given context. Approaching SA from a tool-specific perspective might also divert attention from the need to engage across the "supply" chain.
- *A focus on information and transparency as sufficient for SA.* In the case of "visible" weaknesses (such as poor school infrastructure, lack of equipment, and teacher absenteeism), the main bottleneck to accountability is not information asymmetry, but the low or absent civic mobilization of citizens to act on what they see and know (Khemani 2014). But when information asymmetry is an issue, information needs to be "clear" (Fox 2007) and "targeted" (Fung, Graham, and Weil 2007) to trigger action.

- *A conflation of SA with "participation."* What is important with regard to the notion of social accountability is not whether citizens have an opportunity to participate with public officials in decision making at the beginning of the policy process, but whether citizens can demand that their officials explain their actions after policies or outcomes have been produced.
- *A focus on citizen action without giving commensurate attention to state action.* The "supply-demand" dichotomy is not helpful. Most observers and practitioners of SA emphasize the fact that SA interventions will only achieve their aims if equal attention is paid to improving the state's capacity and willingness to respond as is paid to enhancing the role of citizens.

SA as the Interplay of Five Constitutive Elements

Building on these facts, this study proposes a novel conceptualization of SA in five constitutive elements as the interplay of both citizen and state action, supported by three "levers": information, interface, and civic mobilization, with the aim of supporting SA mechanisms more strategically (box O.1).

BOX O.1

What Are the Five Constitutive Elements of Social Accountability?

Citizen action. As the central constitutive element of social accountability (SA) and the basis for citizen-led engagement, citizen action has been a primary focus of the SA concept and its mechanisms or tools. Citizen action can comprise diverse activities, depending on the context and the stage in the process. It typically includes making demands (for information, justification, or sanctions), protesting against injustice, or claiming better public goods. The citizen action element within this framework also unpacks the collective action problem—a problem rarely acknowledged enough by SA tools or mechanisms.

State action. A primary element of SA, state action needs to be understood within a specific context. The drivers of state action have not been an adequate focus of SA mechanisms, even though the role of the state is pivotal to the SA concept. In order to ensure a "response" from the state, understanding—and sometimes changing—the incentives facing politicians or nonelected officials is necessary. State action can be in the form of

(continued next page)

BOX O.1 *(continued)*

pos tive responses (for example, improved public services and reduced corruption) or repression and backlash. The extent to which responses are organizational actions, based on prevailing cultures, norms, and standard operating procedures, as opposed to individual actions, based on personal preferences and degrees of discretion, matters.

Information. In an accountable and responsive state that engages citizens in decision making, information flows are needed—from citizens to the state, from the state to citizens, between the various parts of civil society, and within the state apparatus. The range of information needed for accountability purposes is vast and often highly technical, and in many cases, the information that is needed for engagement and social accountability may not exist. Informational constraints need to be considered in terms of information generation, simplification, presentation, accuracy, access, and, most important, use. Information asymmetry is rarely an accident of history; rather it is the result of authorities or other individuals in charge who intentionally withhold information or resist attempts to make it accessible. Thus improving citizens' and civil society's access to information as well as their understanding and use of information requires considerable effort and skills. Information intermediaries are almost always necessary, either to simplify or to explain the content and implications of information.

Citizen-state interface. SA is a comprehensive process that includes a complex locus of interaction between state and citizen actors. What matters are not only the interactions occurring through the interface, but also the processes that lead up to it and those that follow as well as the level of citizen representation, if any. Interlocution between the state and civil society actors is key to bringing state officials, whether nonelected or elected officials at different levels, and citizens, whether individuals or collectives, together in the interface.

Civic mobilization. One of the key elements within this framework stems from the fact that information or the existence of a citizen-state interface does not necessarily spur citizen or state action on an issue. In most cases, SA implies actions by intermediaries to spur citizens into action. Civic mobilization is often necessary to trigger and facilitate citizen "voice," especially for vulnerable or marginalized individuals and groups. On the state side, officials need to be mobilized to seek out and engage with citizens. Thus, mobilization is not confined to the community realm. Rather, it is better conceptualized as creating accountability coalitions with pro-accountability actors from both within communities and within states.

This conceptualization, which is presented in figure O.1, reflects two key findings. First, it integrates state action to show that the relationship across state and citizen actors is inherent to any SA approach. However, figure O.1 highlights a fundamental "power imbalance" of SA interventions by placing the state and its institutions *above* the citizens. Second, without undermining the importance of information for accountability, it gives equal emphasis to civic mobilization and interface as core elements of SA. Information, interface, and civic mobilization are the three "mobile" elements, acting as levers on the other two (citizen action and state action).

Links between these constitutive elements are not straightforward, and there is no generic sequence among them. To take some examples: SA may be spurred by citizens, but also by the state, and both state and citizens may initiate any of the three "levers." Information may be made available through state action or through civic mobilization and may be generated or exposed by citizen action. Mobilization may be spurred by information

Figure O.1 Social Accountability as the Interplay of Five Elements

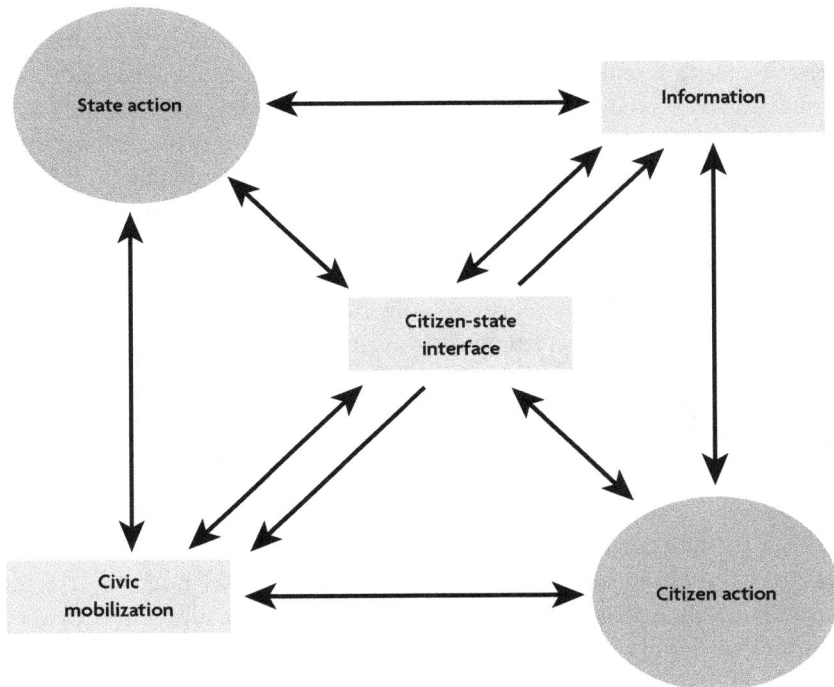

or precede it. Creation of the interface may be the starting or ending point of an SA approach.

In addition to the complexity of the multiple pathways of interaction between these five constitutive elements, the nature of the element itself matters. The content of information, how it is communicated, and what types of citizen action are targeted to be the drivers of change do matter; all civic mobilization or citizen action is not the same; and all official responses cannot be seen as enhancing accountability (Joshi 2013). In addition to defining each of these elements, the report addresses the need to identify the nature of each of these five elements for a specific accountability issue.

This conceptualization needs to be nuanced to highlight two important elements: (1) neither the state nor civil society is a homogeneous or exclusive category, and (2) SA approaches are iterative and generally must dynamically reassess entry points and trajectories, support building blocks for future SA interventions, and carefully assess risks and trade-offs.

Neither State Nor Citizens Are Homogenous or Exclusive Categories

In this analytical framework, neither "citizen action" nor "state action" presupposes a monolithic homogeneous group of citizens on one side and state officials on the other. Within the state, elected and nonelected officials respond to different sets of incentives and might have divergent attitudes toward fostering or responding to SA. Society (that is, individuals and civil society groups) can be equally heterogeneous. Depending on the context and issue, the chasm between elites and others and among diverse segments within society can run deep. As important, within these broad categories, diverse interests and preferences of individuals or the specific organizations to which they belong can trump their institutional affiliations.

Depending on the given context and the focus of the intervention, actors within "state" and "society" categories may overlap. There is a need to go beyond the supply-demand, principal-agent, and state-citizen dichotomies in order to understand the more progressive and regressive coalitions that cut across the state and citizen divide and to support those that are conducive to state-citizen engagement and that drive greater accountability. Success—however broadly defined—often depends on political engagement (and sometimes alignment) with various social groups and coalitions of reformists and sympathetic organizations within the state (for example, courts and ombudsmen's offices).

At the same time, it is useful to distinguish individuals or groups who support "public" interest versus those who support "special" interests and to recognize that state and citizen actions often take place along a continuum, which can work for or against accountability. SA interventions are only as pro-poor as one makes them, and it is important to analyze which groups benefit from a specific issue and which do not and also which ones are more prone to mobilize around the issue. Individuals can also have "layered" identities in which they are perceived as members of civil society groups in one role and as state employees or public service providers in another.

The Iterative Nature of the SA Process

SA approaches are iterative. Social accountability mechanisms primarily stem from the potential of the citizen-state interface, which is itself a dynamic, iterative engagement between citizen groups and state officials, with the flow of information acting as both a driver and an output of this engagement and further spurring citizen and state action via civic mobilization.

Acknowledging the iterative nature of citizen-state engagement can foster approaches that aim to monitor more realistic incremental changes and use them as milestones for periodically revisiting the pathway or theory of change underlying an SA intervention. It takes into account the fact that "progress" along one pathway is a catalyst to progress along another. The different pathways for a successful SA intervention may function with different time horizons, depending on the context. Factoring in the iterative nature of citizen and state engagement suggests that pathways "build" on each other or—in the case, for instance, of an absence of response from the state—unravel.

Figure O.2 thus points to the risks of SA approaches, which can result in reduced accountability or have a negative impact on development results. Numerous studies show the risks of instrumentalization or perversion of SA processes, such as elite capture, tokenistic participation, apathy, disappointment or disengagement, and retaliation.

The Puzzling Evidence

While the evidence on SA is growing, the data on various interventions in various contexts are fragmented, and the puzzling evidence base invites partisan readings (chapter 2). Consequently, it is tempting

Figure O.2 The Iterative Nature of Social Accountability

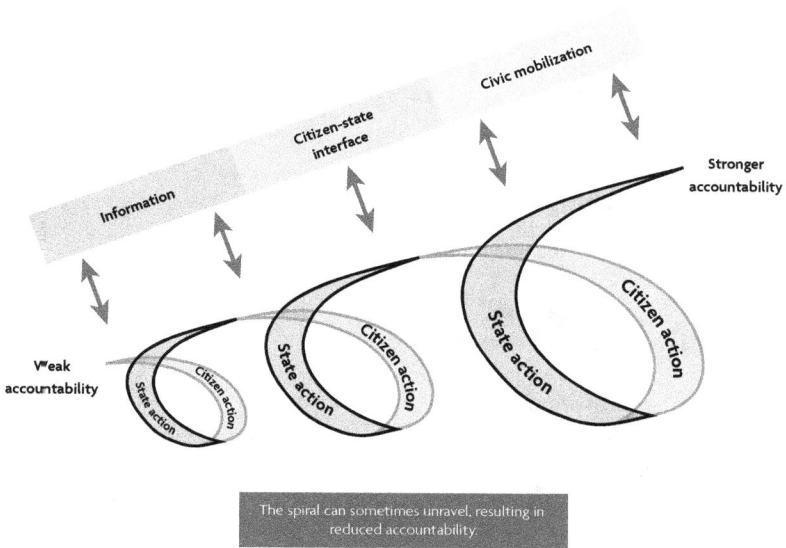

simply to ask, Does SA work or not? However, this is not helpful without sufficiently examining evidence on the multidimensionality of SA interactions, the encompassing role of context, and the difficulty of capturing impact for some of the most complex potential outcomes from SA processes.

Indeed, the range of potential outcomes is wide, including benefits in the *state* (better governance), in *state-society relationships* (increased legitimacy), and in *society* (improved provision of public goods) as well as *instrumental* benefits (improved provision of public goods) and *institutional* benefits (state building), as shown in table O.1.

Perspectives on whether SA "works" or not are partly determined by the value attributed to its outcomes, including its intrinsic value. Impact evaluations have been commissioned principally for SA's more measurable impacts on service delivery.

Biases in methodological choices and implementation of SA impact evaluations can stem from how decisions are made with regard to three challenges (1) determining the type of expected or sought-after SA outcomes,

Table O.1 Expanded Impact of Social Accountability

	States ⟺	State-society relationships ⟺	Social actors
Instrumental ↑ ↓ **Institutional**	• Reduced corruption • Responsive public officials • Better policy design • Good governance	• Institutional channels for interaction • Trust • Legitimacy • State building • Democratic deepening	• Improved provision of public goods • Empowered citizens • Social cohesion • Inclusive social norms

(2) isolating attribution within complex processes involving multiple actors and strategies, and (3) determining the time horizon covered. The preferred choice of experimental and quasi-experimental methods, especially randomized controlled trials, can have distinct advantages in specific cases, but they can be very weak in regard to information about change mechanisms or trajectories that are often critical to understanding the success or failure of SA mechanisms.

Three lessons stem from the existing evidence: (1) contextual conditions matter for understanding why interventions have the impacts they do, (2) the universe of impacts needs to be expanded and systematically traced, and (3) closer attention needs to be paid to the mechanisms through which SA initiatives are expected to have an impact.

SA entails risks and trade-offs. The costs and benefits from the perspectives of both citizens and the state also need to be included in designing and evaluating SA interventions, and deterrent factors such as "unearned revenues" or exit options need to be taken into account.

SA and a Country's Social and Political Characteristics

SA is shaped by the two institutional spheres of political and civil society and their interactions (state-society and intra-society). Three additional factors cut across these spheres and need to be given special attention: cultural norms, global factors, and the prevailing political settlement, a concept described in box 3.1 (see figure O.3).

Figure O.3 Main "Macro" Contextual Factors for Social Accountability Effectiveness

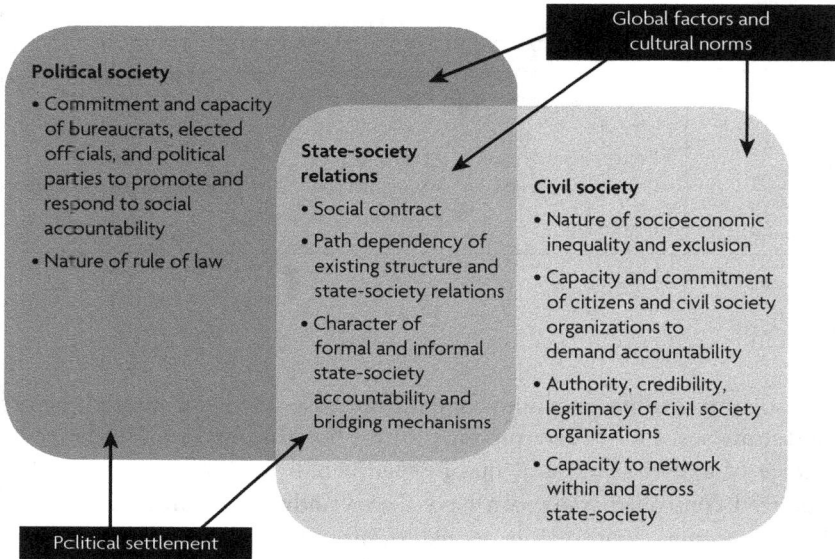

Three major findings emerge from reviewing the broad contextual determinants of SA effectiveness: (1) political and power relations are at the forefront of understanding and operationalizing SA, (2) linkages and networks between pro-accountability state and society actors have to be built, and (3) a sharper focus is needed on inequality and exclusion dynamics.

Several messages are important:

- Actors and dynamics in political society might be the most important factors in explaining the form and effectiveness of SA in a given context.
- The role of civil society for SA is fundamental, but taking an overly simplistic view of civil society as an autonomous arena free from the logic of how power and politics operate needs to be avoided. Civil society organizations and the media need to be understood as politically

embedded institutions and supported beyond their technical capacities to influence SA.

- The history of state-society relations and the nature of the existing "social contract" shape SA mechanisms and outcomes. One goal of SA mechanisms could be to change the perceptions of the responsibilities of the state as well as the perceived entitlements of citizens, both of which are fundamental to any "social contract."
- Distinct from the notions of political society, civil society, or state-society relations are cultural factors that can profoundly influence the relationships among individuals within groups, among groups, and between ideas and perspectives.
- The role of external actors (especially donor agencies) and external processes (for example, trade) or international initiatives (for example, the Extractives Industries Transparency Initiative) can influence SA processes with both positive and negative consequences.

The Analytical Framework: Contextual Drivers of SA Effectiveness

Building on the fact that SA outcomes are derived from an iterative engagement between broad sociopolitical contexts (the subject of chapter 3) and elements of the intervention, chapter 4 incorporates intervention-based factors with sociopolitical ones in an analytical framework for "opening the black box" of contextual factors for SA effectiveness (figure O.4).

This analytical framework builds on a careful remapping of the available evidence along SA's five constitutive elements. This mapping helped to identify a set of factors that will have an impact on the effectiveness of SA. The factors were then clustered into a set of "drivers" (for instance, elements around type of information, novelty, or consistency of the information were clustered under "framing" of information) and mapped to each of the five constitutive elements of the framework. These "drivers" of contextual effectiveness take into account a broad range of contextual factors (social, political, and intervention-based factors including elements of information and communication technology).

The five constitutive elements of SA respond to variable drivers that can assume different permutations to influence specific change paths leading to SA outcomes.

Figure O.4 The Analytical Framework and Its Contextual Drivers

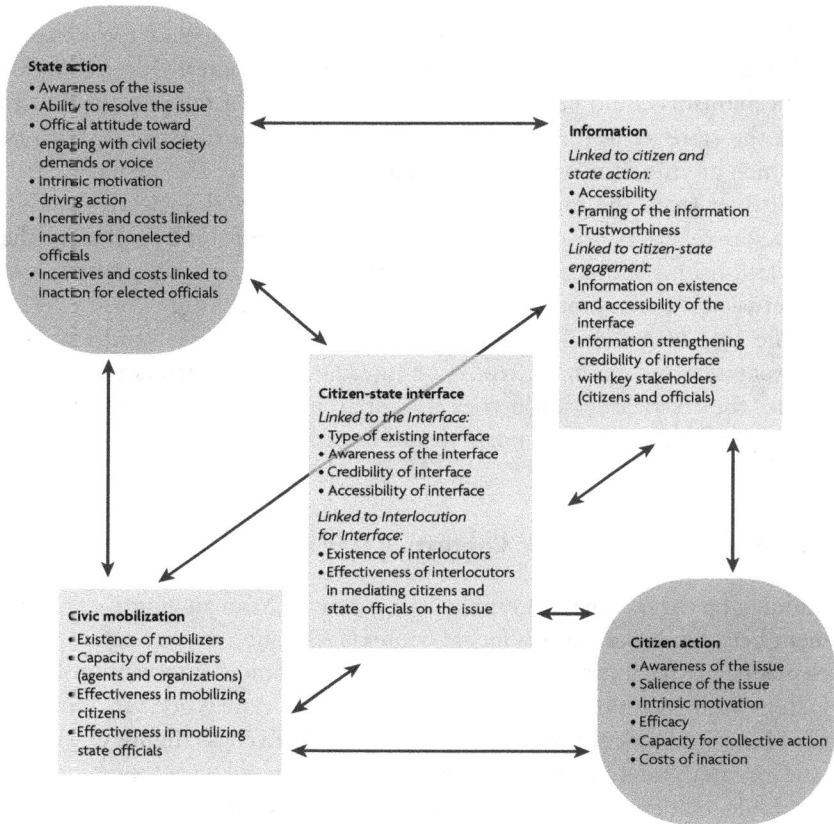

State action
- Awareness of the issue
- Ability to resolve the issue
- Official attitude toward engaging with civil society demands or voice
- Intrinsic motivation driving action
- Incentives and costs linked to inaction for nonelected officials
- Incentives and costs linked to inaction for elected officials

Information
Linked to citizen and state action:
- Accessibility
- Framing of the information
- Trustworthiness
Linked to citizen-state engagement:
- Information on existence and accessibility of the interface
- Information strengthening credibility of interface with key stakeholders (citizens and officials)

Citizen-state interface
Linked to the Interface:
- Type of existing interface
- Awareness of the interface
- Credibility of interface
- Accessibility of interface

Linked to Interlocution for Interface:
- Existence of interlocutors
- Effectiveness of interlocutors in mediating citizens and state officials on the issue

Civic mobilization
- Existence of mobilizers
- Capacity of mobilizers (agents and organizations)
- Effectiveness in mobilizing citizens
- Effectiveness in mobilizing state officials

Citizen action
- Awareness of the issue
- Salience of the issue
- Intrinsic motivation
- Efficacy
- Capacity for collective action
- Costs of inaction

SA in Countries Where Space for Citizen-State Engagement Is Formally Constrained

Designing and implementing SA in countries where space for citizen-state engagement is formally constrained confronts specific constraints and risks. Although such countries are far from identical, they share various attributes that distinguish them from other contexts in relation to social accountability approaches. Figure O.5 summarizes these constraints and risks.

It is possible to overcome the constraints to information, interface, and civic mobilization in various ways.

Figure O.5 Summarizing an Archetypical Institutional Landscape in Countries Where Space for Citizen-State Engagement Is Formally Constrained

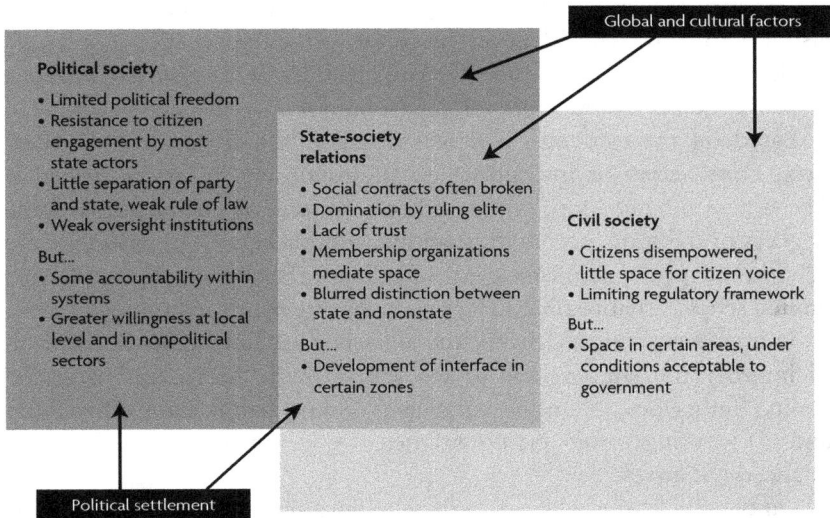

Global and cultural factors

Political society
- Limited political freedom
- Resistance to citizen engagement by most state actors
- Little separation of party and state, weak rule of law
- Weak oversight institutions

But...
- Some accountability within systems
- Greater willingness at local level and in nonpolitical sectors

State-society relations
- Social contracts often broken
- Domination by ruling elite
- Lack of trust
- Membership organizations mediate space
- Blurred distinction between state and nonstate

But...
- Development of interface in certain zones

Civil society
- Citizens disempowered, little space for citizen voice
- Limiting regulatory framework

But...
- Space in certain areas, under conditions acceptable to government

Political settlement

Governments may strictly regulate civil society organizations, but evidence suggests that they can also open up space for citizen engagement—for instance, by supporting particular associations that mobilize citizens to help the state to address deficiencies in service delivery. Information and communication technologies (ICTs) can also play a role to create spaces that help to aggregate individual "voices" into collective citizen action by, for instance, supporting mobilization through cyber-coordination.

Secrecy and asymmetry of information are fundamental attributes of constrained environments, and this is often compounded by the fact that the media are heavily regulated, state owned, or state controlled. Nevertheless, governments may have motives to seek information generated by citizens. Evidence suggests that civil society organizations and citizens have been able to provide useful information or forums for verification, public scrutiny, and feedback to governments that open spaces for citizen-state interface.

Even though state-society interface is formally constrained in these contexts, many governments operate with representative institutions that provide some form of state-society interface. Understanding the historical and political context of the interface between the state and civil society is particularly critical. The space and nature of the interface may also differ greatly depending on the sector or the level (national or local). Evidence seems to suggest that effective channels of state-society interface in such contexts generally are not confrontational.

Based on the evidence, several entry points and approaches incentivize state actors or institutions to be responsive to citizen feedback. The accountability loop, which either sanctions or encourages responsiveness of the state, occurs through five approaches: (1) appealing to the personal or professional integrity of public officials, which may have a limited scope, (2) appealing to a government's existing instrumental interest in improving service delivery and efficiency, (3) linking SA mechanisms to improve the effectiveness of the state's own "horizontal" accountability framework, (4) using existing diversity within state institutions, and (5) working within the boundaries of government-endorsed, donor-financed initiatives.

On the whole, the evidence in these polities shows that SA activity may be possible, but its scope and mechanisms are constrained, and its impact is often limited to the domains in which it operates. The gains might be partial and project based, with SA efforts running the risk of further strengthening existing power structures.

SA in Fragile and Conflict-Affected Situations

Lack of accountability is one of the main characteristics of fragile and conflict-affected situations (FCSs). Although the evidence on the impact of SA in such situations is sparse, there are indications that such citizen-engaged accountability initiatives could be effective, provided they overcome significant constraints.

FCSs differ more than any other category of states, and the caveats and limitations of using an SA approach in an FCS "archetype" need to be acknowledged. But FCSs share some similarities with regard to the "macro" contextual factors influencing SA effectiveness:

- *Weak state-society relations.* The "social contract" in FCSs tends to be in flux, and both the expected role of the state and the responsibilities of citizens may differ across social groups, making SA approaches particularly controversial and sensitive in such contexts.

- *Divided political society and the constraints to state action.* Political society in FCSs is often divided, and the state has a low capacity to deliver basic services, respond to demand, and impose sanctions. The ability of the state to engage with SA mechanisms can be curtailed in FCSs because it often does not have full or exclusive authority over its territory and is competing with other groups for legitimacy to exercise state powers.
- *Intra-society conflicts and constraints on citizen action.* Conflict and fragility divide civil society in two ways: they hamper an individual's capacity to participate in collective action, and they damage the collective, weakening its ability to coordinate collective action when individual agency might exist. Space for participation, when it exists, risks reproducing existing inequalities and exclusions. Further, when social networks exist, they usually strengthen bonds within tribal or ethnic social groups rather than "bridging" existing tensions between such groups in society.
- *Importance of local engagement.* Civil society organizations and nongovernmental organizations often have low capacity and legitimacy, but indigenous local associations and, in some cases, traditional or customary institutions play an especially important role in FCS contexts as channels for information and civic mobilization.

Nevertheless, it is possible to overcome the constraints to information, interface, and civic mobilization in FCSs. Accurate and neutral information essential for rebuilding trust between citizens and the state is particularly hard to access in FCSs. (Re)building an information ecosystem that emphasizes inclusive information flows (that reach all groups within society) is a pressing agenda that SA interventions may enable.

The basis for creating an interface is unclear, with the "social contract" in flux or its credibility not uniformly accepted across groups. SA interventions, however, may help to create local-level citizen interfaces at which constructive citizen engagement can occur, thus providing an entry point for service delivery, conflict resolution, and other issues.

Civic mobilization can be a more daunting task in FCSs than in other contexts, with the need to identify a mobilizer able to transcend identity lines being of paramount importance. Civil society organizations, tribal organizations, and media institutions often serve as mobilizers for SA interventions, but in FCS contexts, it is essential to analyze social networks carefully to identify legitimate mobilizers above and beyond their technical capacities to mobilize citizens.

What are the implications of these findings for efforts to support SA interventions?

- It is important to assess the trade-offs between the importance of citizen engagement to improve services or trust in the state and the high risks that SA interventions will fail given "macro" contextual constraints.
- SA approaches in FCSs need to be adapted and adjusted constantly to the complex and fluid local environment, perhaps more so than in any other context.
- SA "levers" of information, interface, and civic mobilization may be more sustainable in FCSs "working with the grain" of existing imperfect institutional structures.
- Engaging with local-level facilitators is paramount.
- SA approaches may use a more opportunistic approach of responding to a "window of opportunity." SA interventions may need to be small, proceeding gradually and iteratively, given the instability within political society, civil society, and, consequently, state-society relations.

Application of the Framework to Concrete Cases: Sierra Leone, Pakistan, the Republic of Yemen, and the Kyrgyz Republic

In order to understand how the framework can be used for a specific SA intervention, four case studies were carried out. In Sierra Leone, the framework was used retrospectively to map an intervention already completed, which was the subject of an impact evaluation. The intervention took the form of community participation in local health compacts. In the other three cases, the framework was used prospectively to assess bottlenecks and opportunities for SA interventions with the goal of (a) designing and implementing SA mechanisms to support the vision of the new government of Khyber Pakhtunkhwa (KP) Province in Pakistan in support of an ongoing World Bank–financed governance support project, (b) exploring challenges and opportunities for SA in the context of local governance reforms in the Republic of Yemen, and (c) introducing and strengthening SA mechanisms for a new phase of a community-driven development project in the Kyrgyz Republic.

Sierra Leone

The retrospective application of the framework highlighted the importance of building mutual incentives for improved services vertically (between frontline service providers and their supervisors) and horizontally (between local authorities such as chiefs and councilors). The original aim of initiating health compacts between citizens and service providers was to boost the level of local health services, absent improvement in the broader health system. The focus on mutual accountability between service providers and users proved successful in a context marked by distrust and limited state capacity. Nevertheless, because health care workers have the potential to evade or shape attempts by "normal" users to improve accountability, the additional need to engage vertically became evident. Building mutual incentives across various levels of administration and authorities might also increase the chances that improved accountability will become embedded and survive without continued external support.

Pakistan

The application of the framework in KP Province aimed to provide support to various interventions within the World Bank governance support project, including implementation of a citizens report card and a right to information law (spearheaded by the state's ombudsman). The analysis highlighted some characteristics of the overall political environment, such as the patron-client relationship, limited horizontal accountability, and limited state capacity, that may weaken the effectiveness of SA interventions. It led to the following recommendations: (a) focus on initiatives that aim to inculcate a sense of civic responsibilities to motivate citizens to take action, along with providing them with information regarding how the government works and how to contact government officials regarding various problems, because a sense of apathy and lack of knowledge often prevent citizens from registering complaints with the government, (b) use media and information and communication technology to achieve these goals, in addition to employing traditional associational structures (for example, *hujra* or nightly meetings of community members), (c) train tribal leaders and tribal networks to act as mobilizers, (d) make special efforts to mobilize women and target information dissemination to them, and (e) involve government officials in designing and implementing SA interventions to enable and motivate them to understand accountability relations with the citizens.

The Republic of Yemen

The case study of the Republic of Yemen was based on the continuing dialogue regarding decentralization reforms. One of the main factors behind the push for local governance is the desire to enhance engagement with citizens, bolster the legitimacy of the state, and strengthen its authority. The analysis suggests that, following the 2011 Arab Uprising, citizens were willing to forge a new relationship with the state that extends beyond tribal affiliations. This willingness needs to be harnessed quickly to avoid resentment among citizens if their motivation is not channeled effectively. SA interventions should focus on providing interfaces where citizens can communicate with the government. Since tribal leaders have traditionally been intermediaries between the state and citizens, and since this role has become stronger during times of conflict, they have to remain an integral part of any SA activity and governance reform. At the same time, in light of citizens' evolving perceptions of their tribal leaders, using these institutions as mobilizers could be counterproductive.

The Kyrgyz Republic

This case study focused on the preparation of the next phase of a community-driven village investment project. The analysis led to the following recommendations: (a) provide training on legislation, legal rights and responsibilities, and local processes of budgeting, among other training, to mitigate citizen's low level of knowledge regarding their rights and responsibilities, (b) use information and communication technology and community radios to ensure that information channels are inclusive and accessible by everyone, (c) nurture local leadership and factor in local power dynamics in doing so, and (d) foster partnerships among existing nongovernmental organizations and civil society organizations.

Conclusion

The framework and guiding tables for unpacking contextual drivers are intended to support the operationalization of the World Bank's corporate goal of "mainstreaming citizen engagement in World Bank Group operations." The framework's five interconnected elements offer a convenient framing for mapping "archetypal" contexts (discussed in chapters 5 and 6). For a particular intervention, the framework and its set of drivers can be used iteratively to analyze contextual opportunities and constraints and to identify change paths that will allow accountability demands to advance (see chapter 7 for case studies).

The framework can be applied operationally at different levels of analysis to assess opportunities and challenges for SA from the country level, to the sector level, and down to a specific frontline service delivery unit. As such, it can support the following:

- *Strategic, country-level, analytical, and engagement products* such as systematic country diagnosis or development policy lending instruments, with the objective of providing information on the main elements that can support or hinder SA in a given country or sector context. This is especially important to support a more encompassing use of SA approaches in challenging contexts such as FCSs.
- *Sector and subsector analysis* to determine the scope and likelihood of an SA engagement to improve the effectiveness of a select service (for example, curative health care or urban networked water supply) within a sector. For this purpose, the framework is being teased out to map specific sector and context characteristics to the five constitutive elements of SA.
- *Specific operations* to assist task teams and country counterparts in critically assessing various entry points for social accountability work—and their feasibility.
- *Stronger monitoring and evaluation* of Bank operations engaging citizens to improve governance and accountability, thus expanding and deepening our understanding of the mechanisms through which SA leads to outcomes. By ensuring proper documentation of cases through a combination of methods, with the right level of details, the framework should prompt intensified efforts at documenting contextual factors so far missing from program design and evaluation.

References

Fox, J. 2007. *Accountability Politics: Power and Voice in Rural Mexico.* Oxford: Oxford University Press.

Fung, A., M. Graham, and D. Weil. 2007. *Full Disclosure: The Perils and Promise of Transparency.* Cambridge, U.K.: Cambridge University Press.

Joshi, A. 2013. "The Impact of Social Accountability Initiatives on Improving the Delivery of Public Services: A Systematic Review of Four Intervention Types: Protocol." Unpublished mss., Institute of Development Studies, London.

Khemani, S. 2014. "Transparency, Citizen Engagement, and the Politics of Development." Concept Note for a policy research report on governance, World Bank, Development Research Group, Washington, DC.

Narayan, D., R. Patel, K. Schafft, A. Rademacher, and S. Koch-Schulte. 2000. *Can Anyone Hear Us? Voices of the Poor*. Washington, DC: World Bank.

Sen, A. 1999. *Development as Freedom*. Oxford, U.K.: Oxford University Press.

World Bank. 2001. *World Development Report 2000/01: Attacking Poverty*. New York: Oxford University Press.

———. 2004. *World Development Report 2004: Making Services Work for the Poor*. New York: Oxford University Press.

———. 2012. "Strengthening Governance, Tackling Corruption: The World Bank's Updated Strategy and Implementation Plan." World Bank, Washington, DC, March 6. http://siteresources.worldbank.org/PUBLIC SECTORANDGOVERNANCE/Resources/285741-1326816182754/GAC StrategyImplementationPlan.pdf.

CHAPTER 1

Social Accountability:
A Popular yet Fuzzy Concept

There is a lack of clarity around the notion of social accountability (SA) and no universally accepted definition of the range of actions that fall within its remit (box 1.1).[1] SA mechanisms rely on civic engagement, whereby ordinary citizens, civil society organizations (CSOs), or both directly or indirectly exact accountability. It also includes efforts by government and other actors, for example, the media, the private sector, and donors, to support these actions. The World Bank's Governance and Anti-Corruption strategy update defines SA as the "extent and capability of citizens to hold the state accountable and make it responsive to their needs" (World Bank 2012).

According to another conventional definition, SA constitutes the actions that citizens can take—beyond elections—to enhance accountability. Nevertheless, while the relationship of SA to broader notions of voice, political participation, and empowerment is acknowledged, this relationship has not been adequately explored. Consequently, it becomes difficult to assess what difference SA makes when the evidence is mixed across these two definitions.

SA is understood broadly as engaging the principles of transparency (information) and citizen participation to yield accountability (both answerability and enforcement). The conventional wisdom is that transparency generates social accountability by triggering participation. The chapters that follow show how this linear logic does not always match the reality of SA design or implementation. The conceptual boundaries of SA may be drawn broadly to cover all three principles of transparency, accountability, and participation, with equal emphasis on each, or they

BOX 1.1

Relationship between Different Types of Accountability

Simply defined, accountability is the obligation of power holders to take responsibility for their actions. Defined more extensively, it is a "process by which public officials inform about and justify their plans of action, their behavior and results, and are sanctioned accordingly" (Ackerman 2005b).

Scholars of public accountability generally distinguish between horizontal and vertical relationships of accountability (O'Donnell 1999). Vertical accountability is generally considered as voters exercising control over politicians through electoral systems (Mainwaring and Welna 2003). Horizontal accountability focuses on the conventional internal forms of government accountability—political, fiscal, administrative, and legal—that underpin the institutional checks and balances of the state (Peruzzotti 2011).

Social accountability comprises some form of direct vertical accountability between citizens and the state (but does not include elections). Two features of SA are important to note. First, social accountability actions can target both elected politicians and appointed state officials (or service providers). Second, SA is generally expected to work through two routes—by directly affecting either politicians or state officials and by eliciting responsiveness (usually by exacting reputational costs) or by indirectly triggering formal accountability mechanisms, including internal investigations, legislative oversight, and legal action. It is important to track the links between SA and these other accountabilities, both vertical and horizontal, to understand how these processes might work.

Society-driven horizontal accountability—also known as hybrid or diagonal accountability (Goetz and Jenkins 2001)—refers to a form of SA that supports horizontal accountability mechanisms, such as citizen groups working with human rights ombudsmen or supreme audit organizations, in order to strengthen their role and make them more responsive to social demands. SA strategies combining civic mobilization, legal action, and media exposure to support judicial impartiality in the face of entrenched vested interests are examples of such "hybrid" or "diagonal" accountability (Smulovitz and Peruzzotti 2000).

can be drawn more narrowly and focus on answerability and the power to sanction. Both of these definitions are vague, however, and as a consequence, the concept tends to be a "catch-all" term that encompasses a descriptive label with a desirable value.

This chapter tackles the fuzzy definitional terrain and proposes that the concept of SA should be understood in terms of five constitutive elements, with the aim of supporting SA mechanisms more strategically. The first section argues that, as a concept, SA has diverse intellectual roots that allow for different and even conflicting interpretations. The second highlights the common biases within current interpretations and implementation of SA. Building on these sections, the third section presents a new conceptualization of SA around five constitutive elements (citizen action, state action, information, interface, and civic mobilization). The conceptualization around these five elements is used throughout the report to support a better understanding of SA in its relation to context.

Diverse Intellectual Roots

In this section, we compare the intellectual roots of the concept of SA: the principal-agent model and the voice and participation model.[2] We also highlight two important distinctions in SA modes of engagement: individual versus collective and confrontational versus collaborative.

Principal-Agent Model

The principal-agent model treats SA as an extension of new public management (NPM), introducing the idea of "client power" as conceptualized in the *World Development Report* (WDR) *2004* (World Bank 2004).

NPM emphasizes the importance of market principles in reforming public service delivery systems, with citizens viewed principally as "clients" who reward good service with loyalty or punish poor performance by choosing to "exit" and opting for other alternatives (Ackerman 2004; Batley 1999; Manning 2001; Peters 2001). This approach takes as its premise that public officials are not to be trusted and attempts to improve their performance by subjecting them to the discipline of the market. Drawing on Hirschman's notions of exit, loyalty, and voice, NPM is concerned only with the first two, exit and loyalty (Hirschman 1970). These notions are used to assess service delivery. Through them, citizens provide information to promote better upward accountability in terms of administrative performance and efficiency. A more participative school of thought within NPM extends to the exercise of citizen "voice" through devices like clients' charters, which set minimum standards of service that clients can expect. This school of thought also grounds demands for effective service delivery in a rights-based discourse (as "citizens") rather than exclusively in the language of consumer protection. Despite these notable differences, NPM relies on SA tools such as grievance redress mechanisms, which are top-down creations of very structured and controlled bottom-up mechanisms, to address information asymmetries in managing public administration and delivering public services. It also frames users as individuals rather than as collective actors.

The influential WDR 2004's "short route" to accountability is also based on the principal-agent theory and puts reducing information asymmetries at the core of SA. The principal-agent issue arises because information asymmetry prevents principals from monitoring agents effectively in situations where their aims differ. Accordingly, the solution is to promote transparency and increase the monitoring of agents. The accountability framework in WDR 2004 describes the "long route" as a nested set of principal-agent relationships, from citizens to politicians, from politicians to policy makers, from policy makers to organization managers, and, finally, from organization managers, via middle managers, to frontline workers. The report draws attention to the "short route" to accountability between citizens as principals and providers as agents, calling it the expression of "client power." Client power is presented as weak, principally owing to a lack of information and awareness among citizens that would otherwise enable them to hold service providers directly accountable. Strengthening the short route therefore focuses on tools to promote the dissemination of information and enable citizens to demand their entitlements more forcibly.

Voice and Participation Model

In stark contrast to the principal-agent model, which promotes SA mechanisms for instrumental gains, proponents of SA as an intrinsic "good" value "voice" and "transparency." Viewed in this way, SA is a means of creating "active citizens" and strengthening democracy. In this connection, it is related to a definition of poverty that does not focus solely on instrumental gains such as higher incomes and improved access to services, but instead embraces poor people's opportunities and capabilities to exercise influence in the public sphere (Narayan et al. 2000; Sen 1999; World Bank 2000).

When viewed as an intrinsic good, addressing social exclusion as a primary source of poverty through greater citizen participation and voice is at the core of SA. It also draws attention to the need to deepen the direct participation of people in political processes. Understood in this way, SA includes a wide range of activities, from street protests and unruly politics to the creation of institutions for direct participation ranging from local-level school management committees to subnational and national participatory planning processes. Direct participation compensates for the failure of formal democracies to "listen" to the voices of the poor and underserved.

At the same time, rights-based approaches to development have taken root among certain constituencies (the 2003 United Nations Statement of Common Understanding on Human Rights–Based Approaches to Development Cooperation and Programming).[3] In order to strengthen democracy, social activists have argued that governments have an obligation to guarantee not only civil and political rights, but also socioeconomic rights. The latter are constitutionally protected. They are not simply "needs" subject to official interpretation and discretion. These rights-based, direct democracy approaches to SA emphasize the collective and public good dimensions of accountability (box 1.2).

BOX 1.2

Rights-Based Approaches, Legal Empowerment, and Social Accountability

Rights-based approaches (RBAs) and legal empowerment approaches are citizen focused. Both approaches aim to improve development processes and outcomes for the poorest. In this regard they have much in common with SA.

SA initiatives and RBAs both focus on citizen agency, a link with national policies and programs, and the accountability of public institutions. If one uses the broadest definition of SA, both approaches are concerned with targeting political and administrative institutions to ensure political, civil, and socioeconomic rights. Moreover, more political forms of SA often use a "language of rights" to articulate demands and inform citizens of their entitlements and at the same time to demand explanations and redress from authorities.

(continued next page)

BOX 1.2 *(continued)*

RBAs seek to shift the discourse from beneficiaries to citizens with rights. Beyond the discursive function of law in framing claims, direct engagement with the legal system is a key aspect of RBAs. They seek to gain recognition for claims and to institutionalize them in law, test the robustness of a legislated right or rights-based discourse, and, using the courts, challenge the legality of some policies on the basis of rights. Seeking and establishing legal rights leads to greater mobilization of citizen action and articulation of the voice of the poor. Rights (civil, political, as well as social and economic) are not hierarchical, but interrelated and interdependent. Ultimately, gaining legislatively defined rights is an important step for RBAs. In practice, they have progressed further in changing the development discourse by legitimizing rights-based claims than in changing the law or ensuring substantive realization of formally recognized rights—with notable exceptions such as India's Right to Education (2009) and Right to Information (2005).

SA can be a natural partner of RBAs. One difference between the two is that RBAs aim to change the discourse of development by resetting the standards, while SA efforts often aim to hold states to account for their failure to achieve promised standards.

Legal empowerment is "the use of rights and laws, specifically to increase disadvantaged populations' control over their lives" (Golub 2013). Five principles characterize legal empowerment approaches: (1) they attempt to demonstrate that, even in environments marked by unfairness and arbitrariness, justice (vis-á-vis the state, but also in connection with intra-community disputes, with traditional authorities, and between citizens and private firms) is possible; (2) they combine litigation and high-level advocacy with flexible grassroots tools; (3) they offer a pragmatic approach to plural legal systems, focusing on respect for traditional institutions and seeking solutions that combine the positive aspects of both; (4) they move away from treating people as clients to working to strengthen people's agency; and (5) they focus equally on the rights and responsibilities of citizens.

Actors who take the legal empowerment approach have moved away from pursuing formal litigation and toward working with the poor to help them to access services by understanding the administrative rules and procedures that ensure them their rights. By focusing on the empowerment of citizens and related awareness-raising and mobilizing strategies, legal empowerment approaches closely parallel SA approaches that attempt to build direct links with frontline providers.

(continued next page)

BOX 1.2	*(continued)*

Nevertheless, to date, the application of legal empowerment has differed from SA approaches in two ways. First, while redress and justice are at the heart of legal empowerment approaches, they have not featured prominently in SA initiatives. Second, legal empowerment approaches focus primarily on individual cases and remedies, as opposed to the largely collective social processes that SA initiatives most often tend to engage.

Sources: Ackerman 2005a; Eyben 2003; Gauri and Gloppen 2012; Golub 2013; Maru 2010; Maru and Moy 2013; Molyneux and Lazar 2003; Moser and Norton 2001; Nyamu-Musembi 2005.

The unique contribution of SA also lies in its promotion of transparency, which differs markedly from a focus on correcting information asymmetries. Seen from this point of view, SA builds on the normative notions that "transparency is always good" and that "information is power" for citizens (Björkman, de Walque, and Svensson 2014; Kosack and Fung 2014). This is different from treating information as a way to remedy a specific problem. It is linked to recognition that access to information is a human right, according to the United Nations human rights framework (Article 19)[4] and the related concept of "duty to publish" (Fung, Graham, and Weil 2007).

Contrasting Modes of Engagement and the Limitations of These Distinctions

Two distinctions cut across these different SA approaches. One of them emphasizes different types of actors (individual versus collective), and the other emphasizes different modes of engagement (confrontational versus collaborative). In practice, however, approaches cut across these boundaries.

A common distinction in SA approaches and mechanisms relates to a difference in emphasis on the types of actors to be engaged. Some SA mechanisms are tailored principally to individual action, while others focus more on collective action. For instance, grievance redress mechanisms (GRMs) target citizens as individuals, which may address individual grievances, but does not necessarily address systematic failures or intrinsically promote collective awareness and action. Citizen report cards also aggregate individual data, but do not integrate elements around collective action. By contrast, community scorecards or social audits consider a level of civic mobilization and collective action on the part of citizens to be an essential component.

Furthermore, SA mechanisms use different modes of citizen engagement with the state, which can be mapped along an axis ranging from collaborative to confrontational. For example, SA tools such as community scorecards initially assume a collaborative approach and are used to facilitate local-level "compacts" between citizens and frontline service providers (see box 2.6 in chapter 2 on health in Uganda and the case of Sierra Leone in chapter 7). In contrast, tools such as social audits (see box 2.4 in chapter 2) or others that publicly record grievances of citizens against officials rely more on the logic of "naming and shaming" to foster greater accountability. These tools follow a more confrontational logic grounded in the contestation between citizens and state officials. Nevertheless, although different from the logic of "co-production" documented in the literature, these tools can also entail collaboration with officials higher up in the hierarchy who can better monitor corrupt local officials (Joshi and Moore 2004; Lam 1996; Ostrom 1996; Tendler 1997).

While useful, these distinctions are not particularly clear-cut. For instance, when used as part of an SA strategy, "individual" tools can also be used collectively. Rights-based advocacy campaigns often use individual GRM cases to raise awareness of a more widespread problem, for example. Similarly, SA approaches often adopt simultaneous strategies of confrontation and collaboration, while engaging with different levels of the state. The right to information movement in India is another example of how social actors use different strategies to pursue their goals (see box 1.3).

BOX 1.3

Right to Work and Information Laws in India: Moving between Confrontational and Collaborative Strategies and Engaging with Various Levels of Government

Public hearings (jan sunwais) in the Indian state of Rajasthan that the local workers' and farmers' civil society group Mazdoor Kisan Shakti Sangathan (MKSS) facilitated in the early 1990s were a precursor to the SA tool of social audits. Social audits create a space for villagers to challenge village and local state authorities through public dialogue. This was usually a confrontational space of engagement or interface between citizens and state representatives.

(continued next page)

BOX 1.3 *(continued)*

It brought to the fore the need for greater transparency with regard to employment records (referred to as muster rolls) and the wages that local officials owed workers. When the local state and elected village council *(panchayat)* members resisted the demand for greater transparency, MKSS activists redirected their strategy to the national level. The national campaign for right to information drew inspiration from the MKSS right to information struggle in Rajasthan.

Unlike the confrontational stance that characterized the public hearings, the social movement activism for right to information (RTI) legislation drew on a network of predominantly middle-class "eminent citizens," among them, government officials, academics, artists, journalists, judges, and lawyers, many of them embedded in the state. The coalition supporting RTI therefore blurred the divide between state and civil society. "Cultivating links" with state actors and co-opting them for more effective civic mobilization in the cause of greater transparency legislation was particularly important. The "symbolic capital" of this coalition of eminent citizens strengthened the RTI movement more than their numbers alone would have commanded.

Following passage of the Right to Information Act in 2005, the commitments made by the federal government with regard to transparency were embedded in legislation, the National Rural Employment Guarantee Act, assuring minimum employment to rural workers. This institutionalization transformed the "public hearings" of Rajasthan into "social audits" at the local level (see box 2.4 on social audits in India, showing how the specific contexts influenced enforcement in states). Local governments, in Andhra Pradesh, for example, continued to oppose the social audits, claiming they were undemocratic and "anti-*panchayat*" because they created an alternative to existing channels (village councils) for voicing citizen demands.

Three findings are of note: (a) the iterative nature of SA, which can build on the failures or successes of past citizen action and citizen-state engagement, (b) the possibility of using innovative trajectories and taking advantage of the heterogeneity of the state, strategically shifting from one level of the state to another at crucial moments to overcome obstacles at one level and take advantage of openings at another, and (c) the need to adapt the mode of engagement (collaborative or confrontational) to the context. While an SA strategy of confrontation was successful in mobilizing citizens and state at one level (public hearings, social audits), the same social movement pursuing the same SA cause succeeded through collaboration with state officials and institutions at another.

Sources: Baviskar 2007; Pande 2013.

Common Biases in Current Interpretations of SA

This section highlights four common biases in current interpretations and implementation of SA and the need to go beyond them: (1) SA applied as a tool-based approach, (2) a focus on information and transparency as sufficient for SA, (3) a conflation of SA and participation, and (4) an unhelpful divide between supply- and demand-side approaches to governance.

Depoliticization

A tool-based approach "depoliticizes the very political processes through which poor people access services" (Joshi and Houtzager 2012). Much of the support for SA is still centered on the technical application of standardized "tools." This shortcoming is not specific to SA, and there is growing recognition that this tool-based approach to development needs to be abandoned. The "problem-driven iterative adaptation" is getting traction in doing so (see the Sierra Leone case study in chapter 7).

There are two important drawbacks in taking a tool-based approach to SA: inadequate attention is paid to (a) political realities and (b) the state's capacity and willingness to respond to voice and to previously existing social demands and practices with regard to a particular accountability issue.

A set of well-developed tools can support SA approaches. SA mechanisms cover a broad range of actions that citizens, communities, and civil society organizations can take to hold government officials accountable, among them, participatory budgeting, independent budget analysis, public expenditure tracking, citizen report cards, community scorecards, social audits, citizens' charters, public hearings, e-governance and e-procurement, citizens' juries, and community radio. Over the past decade, several of these mechanisms have been transformed into "tools," with clearly defined conceptual boundaries and standardized steps in their design and implementation.[5] For a brief description of a broad set of common SA tools, see appendix A.

The application of these tools needs to be embedded in an analysis of the opportunities and constraints associated with a given context. An understanding of the political economy of the accountability issue at stake is most important (and the subject of chapter 3).

Existing social demands and practices surrounding a particular accountability issue are stronger entry points for SA, and some SA tools are better suited to local practice than others. In recent years, a growing interest in SA among donor agencies has translated into funding for tools that induce citizen participation, sometimes in contexts with limited collective voice of citizens or social movements on which to build. The nature of citizen participation can vary significantly depending on whether it is induced or takes shape organically (Mansuri and Rao 2013). There are several examples of successful organic movements that have served a watchdog function and held the state to account. One example is the participatory budgeting initiative in Porto Alegre, Brazil, initially proposed by the Union of Residents Association. The actions of Mazdoor Kisan Shakti Sangathan (MKSS) social activists that led to the creation of social audits in India are another.[6] Both stand in sharp contrast to the application of SA tools or "widgets" (Ackerman 2005b; Joshi and Houtzager 2012).

Approaching SA from a tool-specific perspective can reduce the number of entry points for any intervention. Such an approach diverts attention from the need to engage with different levels of government across the "supply chain" (Ackerman 2004; Gaventa and McGee 2010). As Fox (2014, 2001) notes, the vertical integration of public monitoring of policy or service delivery may be needed at all levels of government to make SA more effective. Focusing on a specific tool, rather than pursuing a comprehensive strategy, can close off opportunities for action on the part of citizens and limit their action to the oversight of local, frontline service providers or local-level budgets. Efforts should be made to identify problems at different levels of government and, where possible, to cultivate the allies needed to lobby higher levels of government.

Transparency, Information, and Accountability

Transparency and information are not necessarily sufficient to yield accountability. Information alone does not guarantee accountability. Fox (2007) distinguishes between "clear" and "opaque" transparency. Clear transparency refers to policies and programs that result in the disclosure of reliable information about institutional performance, responsibilities, and spending.[7] Fung, Graham, and Weil (2007) make the same point in their description of the "action cycle," whereby information triggers individual or collective action. Information itself and the transparency of information need to be targeted to generate the "steps" that lead to calls for accountability by citizens under specific conditions.[8] Hence the need, recognized by many proponents of the "open data" movement, to simplify, demystify, and disseminate the information once it is made public.

Information, even when effectively targeted, might serve no purpose without collective action and might not produce incentives powerful enough to stimulate action. Following the logic of the principal-agent model, citizens, as principals, must have the ability to organize in order to monitor and appropriately incentivize state officials to ensure good performance by their agents. The ability to organize among citizens is fundamental because, if principals fail to coordinate and make clear their preferences, their agents can evade accountability. Collective action entails more than prioritizing interests and preventing free riding, however. It also involves setting common goals, forming strategic alliances, and developing a cultural narrative that encourages civic mobilization.

Even "clear" or "targeted" transparency can go only so far. The nature of the state, the political settlement,[9] and the characteristics of society dictate civil society's capacity and incentives to act on information.

At the same time, there are many cases where information asymmetry is not the main impediment to accountability. In the case of "visible" weaknesses (for example, poor school infrastructure, insufficient equipment, or teacher absenteeism), a lack of information is not the most serious problem. Rather, it is the failure of citizens to mobilize adequately to act on what they see and know (Khemani 2014).

Differences between Participation and SA

Although both participation and SA entail interaction between citizens and the state, they are distinct from one another. Participation in policy making enables citizens to express their opinions about what should be done or how something should proceed, but it does not offer any guarantee that officials will heed or follow through on the basis of these views. In contrast, accountability is concerned with public officials having to account for their actions. Bovens (2007), for example, emphasizes that accountability is "the obligation to explain and justify conduct," including informal obligations and the optional imposition of rewards or sanctions. With the notion of social accountability, then, what is important is not whether citizens have an opportunity to participate with public officials in decision making at the beginning of the policy process, but whether they can demand that their officials explain their actions after policies have been formulated and the outcomes have been seen.

The assumption that "voice" generated through transparency measures or community monitoring will be heard is not borne out in practice. While some social accountability interventions build channels of communication with state actors, others—for example, information campaigns—do not. When they do (for example, in social audits), these channels must be credible if citizens are going to use them to articulate their voice. Without credible pathways linking citizens with the state for the aggregation and mediation of voice, accountability will not be achieved. The same is true of grievance redress mechanisms and the sanctions associated with them.

State Action, Citizen Action, and the Supply-Demand Dichotomy

For SA, state action is as important as citizen action, and the supply-demand dichotomy is not helpful. Most observers and practitioners of SA emphasize the fact that it will only reach its aims if equal attention is paid to improving the capacity and willingness of the state to respond as is paid to the role of citizens. Citizen-based demands rarely work on their own (Booth 2012). As Fox (2007) puts it, citizens' "influence over the really shameless could be quite limited." Insufficient attention has been paid to Ackerman's suggestion that, in addition to answerability and enforcement, the concept should also include receptiveness on the part of the state or the capacity and willingness of state officials to take into account the knowledge and opinions of citizens (Ackerman 2005b). Fox (2014) points out that, after "reviewing the SA evaluation evidence, a decade after the 2004 WDR, the short route to accountability may not be so short after all, and its success may depend on making the long route more responsive as well."[10] Social accountability is not an alternative to administrative accountability. Instead, it complements other pro-accountability governance reforms. It creates mechanisms that strengthen direct interactions between citizens and public officials to yield better development outcomes, potentially strengthening political accountability. Many SA interventions interact with other accountability mechanisms or trigger them. These mechanisms include internal investigations, legislative oversight, and legal action.

Alternatively, the state can initiate and formalize SA approaches. These approaches occur at three levels. First, accountability mechanisms based on citizen participation can be built into the strategic plans of government agencies, with rules and procedures mandating low-level bureaucrats to consult or otherwise engage with citizens. Second, specific government agencies can be created to ensure that citizens are able to participate in government and monitor its work or to create links with citizens. Third, participatory mechanisms can be built into law, requiring individual agencies or the government as a whole to involve members of society at specific points in the public policy process to ensure accountability to citizens (Ackerman 2005b). As is true of many similar processes, institutionalization has pros and cons, and some of these are discussed in chapter 4.

SA as the Interplay of Five Constitutive Elements: A Conceptual Framework

This section proposes conceptualizing SA as the interplay of five constitutive elements: citizen action, state action, information, interface, and civic mobilization (box 1.4). The identification of the five constitutive elements has benefited from a schematization of SA tools into their constitutive elements (box 1.5).

In this section, the five elements are defined. The heterogeneous character of state and citizens, the areas where they overlap, and the iterative nature of SA processes are then discussed.

BOX 1.4

Key Terms for the Conceptual and Analytical Frameworks

SA has five constitutive elements:

- Citizen action
- State action
- Information
- Interface
- Civic mobilization

Information, interface, and civic mobilization act as *levers* on the other two elements: citizen action and state action. In addition, *drivers* are contextually specific factors that can influence a constitutive element—either supporting or hindering the SA intervention that relies on it. In our analytical framework, drivers are clusters of various "steps" or factors that lead to a pro-accountability action. See chapter 4 for a detailed review of these drivers.

This conceptual framework rests on three fundamental insights:

1. SA results from the interplay of state action and citizen action, and three factors leverage it: information, interface, and civic mobilization.
2. The state and citizens are neither homogeneous nor exclusive categories.
3. Because SA processes are iterative (a fact that must be acknowledged at the start), SA approaches generally will be required to (a) dynamically reassess entry points and trajectories, (b) support building blocks for future SA interventions, and (c) carefully assess risks and trade-offs.

BOX 1.5

Schematizing Popular Social Accountability Tools along Five Elements

Schematizing some of the main steps of SA tools was critical in narrowing down the set of constitutive elements for SA. Although the implementation and replication of SA tools have suffered at times from a lack of adaptation or "fit" to a particular context, many SA tools have originated from grassroots civic mobilization and CSO initiatives and reflect key principles of SA approaches.

The schematic in figure B1.5.1 provides an overview of four SA tools along the five constitutive elements. It also illustrates a fundamental difference between tools that rely on individual feedback and tools that call for collaborative engagement (GRM in particular stands out for its focus on individual transactions and the absence of civic mobilization). For more specific information on SA tools, see worldbank.saeguide.org.

Figure B1.5.1 Schematic Overview of Key Social Accountability Tools

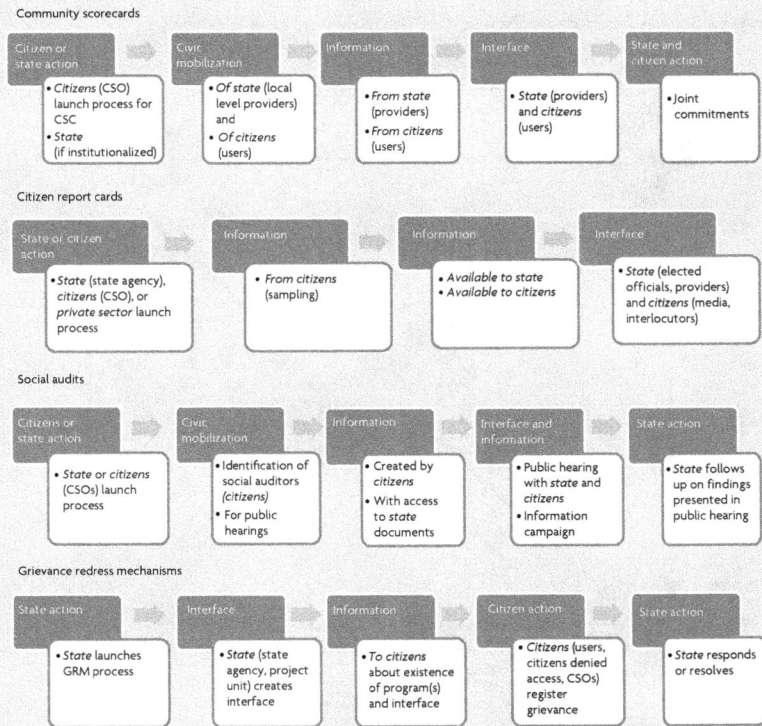

Community scorecards

Citizen or state action	Civic mobilization	Information	Interface	State and citizen action
• *Citizens* (CSO) launch process for CSC • *State* (if institutionalized)	• *Of state* (local level providers) and • *Of citizens* (users)	• *From state* (providers) • *From citizens* (users)	• *State* (providers) and *citizens* (users)	• Joint commitments

Citizen report cards

State or citizen action	Information	Information	Interface
• *State* (state agency), *citizens* (CSO), or *private sector* launch process	• *From citizens* (sampling)	• *Available to state* • *Available to citizens*	• *State* (elected officials, providers) and *citizens* (media, interlocutors)

Social audits

Citizens or state action	Civic mobilization	Information	Interface and information	State action
• *State or citizens* (CSOs) launch process	• Identification of social auditors *(citizens)* • For public hearings	• Created by *citizens* • With access to *state* documents	• Public hearing with *state* and *citizens* • Information campaign	• *State* follows up on findings presented in public hearing

Grievance redress mechanisms

State action	Interface	Information	Citizen action	State action
• *State* launches GRM process	• *State* (state agency, project unit) creates interface	• *To citizens* about existence of program(s) and interface	• *Citizens* (users, citizens denied access, CSOs) register grievance	• *State* responds or resolves

Overall Conceptual Framework

Figure 1.1 depicts two important elements: power imbalances between state actors and citizens and the equal importance of civic mobilization and interface with information. State action is integrated within this conceptualization of SA to highlight the importance of the relationship across state and citizen actors inherent in any SA approach. But the figure reflects a fundamental "power imbalance" of SA interventions, placing the state and its institutions above the citizens.[11] Second, without undermining the importance of information for accountability, equal emphasis is given to civic mobilization and interface as core elements of SA. Information, interface, and civic mobilization act as levers on the other two (citizen action and state action).

Links between these constitutive elements are not straightforward, and there is no generic sequence among them. For example, SA may be spurred by citizens but also by the state, and both state and citizens may initiate any

Figure 1.1 Social Accountability as the Interplay of Five Elements

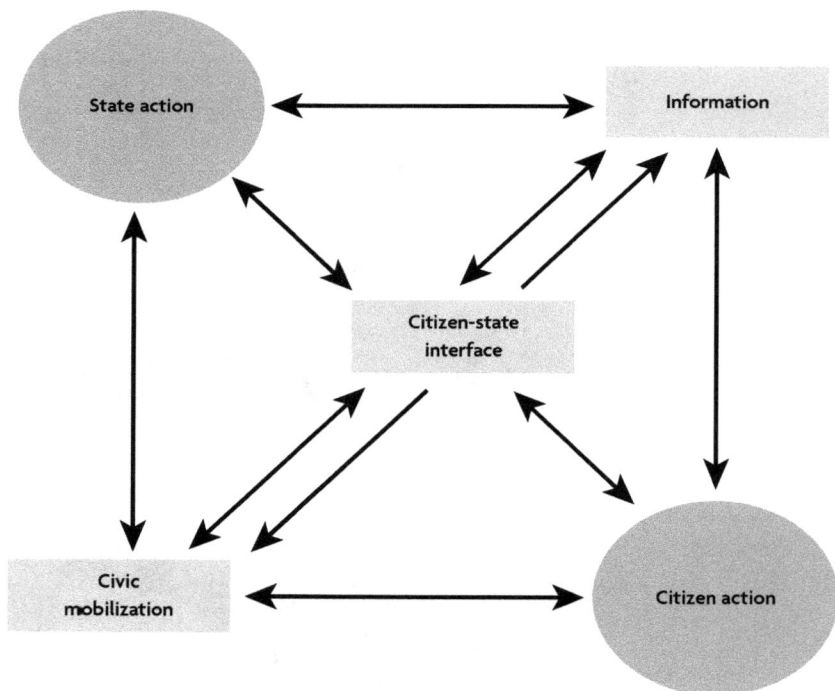

of the three "levers": information may be made available by state action or through civic mobilization, and it may be generated or exposed by citizen action; mobilization may be spurred by information or precede it. Creation of the interface may be the starting point or the ending point of an SA approach.

In addition to the complexity of the multiple pathways of interaction between these five constitutive elements, the nature of the element itself matters. The content of information, how it is communicated, and what types of citizen action are targeted to be the drivers of change matter (Khemani 2014). Not all forms of civic mobilization or citizen action are alike, and not all official responses enhance accountability (Joshi 2013). Besides defining each of these elements, the report addresses the need to identify, for a particular accountability issue, the specific nature of each of these five elements.

Citizen Action and State Action

SA results from the interplay of state action and citizen action.

Citizen Action

By its nature, citizen action is central to SA. It is the basis for citizen-led engagement, and, accordingly, it has been a primary focus of the concept of SA and its mechanisms and tools. Citizen action can comprise several diverse activities, depending on the context and the stage it has reached. Typically, it includes demands, whether for information, justification, or sanctions, protests against injustice, or claims for better public goods. The citizen action element within this framework also unpacks the collective action problem that SA tools or mechanisms have been less satisfactory in acknowledging.

State Action

Along with citizen action, state action is another key element of SA, and it must be understood within its specific context. As noted earlier, the drivers of state action have not been an adequate focus of SA mechanisms, even though the role of the state is pivotal to the concept of SA. In order to ensure a response from the state, it is important to understand and, at times, change the incentives of politicians or nonelected officials. State action can take the form of a positive response (improved public services or reduced corruption) or the form of repression and backlash. It is important to distinguish between organizational responses that are based on organizational culture, norms, and standard operating procedures and individual responses that are based on personal preferences and discretion.

Information, Interface, and Civic Mobilization

Information, interface, and civic mobilization act as "levers" on the other two elements (citizen action and state action). What matters is not only their presence, but also the interactions among them in driving citizen action or state action.

Information

Information is a fundamental element of social accountability. In an accountable and responsive state that engages citizens in decision making, information flows are needed from citizens to the state, from the state to citizens, between the various parts of civil society, and within the state apparatus. A wide range of information is needed to ensure accountability, and it is often highly technical in nature (for example, laws, policies, standards, targets, performance, assets, budgets, revenues, and expenditures). In many cases the information needed for social accountability may not even exist. Informational constraints need to be considered in terms of information generation, simplification, presentation, accuracy, access, and, most important, use. Information asymmetry is rarely an accident of history, as is sometimes inferred from principal-agent models; rather, it is the result of authorities or other individuals in charge who intentionally withhold information or resist attempts to make it accessible. Ensuring that citizens and civil society have access to information, understand it, and make good use of it takes considerable efforts and skills. For these reasons, intermediaries—whether a person, an organization, or the media—are almost always needed to improve access to information, simplify it, clarify it, and point out its implications.

Interface

Citizen-state interface is at the core of SA as a concept and a key feature in all its mechanisms. When SA is thought to be synonymous with the tools used to achieve it, the tools themselves, whether community scorecards, citizen report cards, social audits, or a grievance redress mechanism, can be mistaken for the interface. SA is a process, however, and it comprises complex interactions between the state and citizens. What matters are not only the interactions occurring through the interface, but also the processes that lead up to it and those that follow, as well as the level of citizen representation (if any).

In any given context, the citizen-state interface draws on two dynamic processes: (1) people's "imaginaries" of the state (how people "see" the state) and (2) how the state "sees" people and shapes what it means to be a citizen (Corbridge et al. 2005; Scott 1998).

Some SA interfaces emerge or are created to address a particular issue, while others are linked to existing formal mechanisms for accountability. The latter may provide more viable and sustainable entry points for action. In many societies, citizens look to the courts to adjudicate their demands for better performance on the part of the executive, trusting the judiciary to be impartial and independent of the executive (see box 1.2 on legal empowerment). Increasingly, supreme audit institutions (SAIs) are another point of entry, allowing citizens to participate in formal audit processes (see box 1.6).

Civic Mobilization

Civic mobilization is a central element within the SA framework because information or the existence of a citizen-state interface alone does not necessarily spur citizen or state action on an issue. Most often, intermediaries are needed to spur citizens to action. Civic mobilization is often necessary to trigger and support citizen voice, especially among vulnerable or

---

BOX 1.6

Citizen Participation Strengthening "Horizontal Accountability":
Supreme Audit Institutions (SAIs) Open Up to Citizen Inputs

Increasingly, supreme audit institutions are exploring innovative ways to engage citizens and leverage the capacity of civil society, breaking with a tradition of working in relative isolation. Space can be created for SAIs and citizens to interact and work together to ensure public oversight and accountability in all phases of the audit cycle:

- *Audit planning.* Using SA tools, CSOs can uncover evidence of mismanagement or inefficiency that SAIs can use in formal audits. For instance, the Republic of Korea's Board of Audit relies on citizens for advice and encourages them to report instances of fraud or misuse of public funds. Citizens can petition the board, lodge complaints with it, and request audits.

(continued next page)

BOX 1.6 *(continued)*

- *Audit process.* CSOs can undertake joint performance audits without compromising the independence of SAIs. For instance, the Commission on Audit of the Philippines has launched a Citizen Participatory Audit Program.
- *Dissemination of audit reports to a broader audience.* CSOs can collaborate with SAIs to help them to produce simplified "citizen-friendly" audit reports. For example, a World Bank–financed program, Advancing Public Participation in the Budget and Audit Process, supports a multistakeholder working group, comprising representatives from Tanzania's National Audit Office and CSOs, that co-produces citizen-friendly audit reports
- *Monitoring the status of SAI recommendations.* CSOs can monitor the status of SAI recommendations and advocate that they be acted on. For instance, Public Service Accountability Monitor, a South African think tank, used the report of the auditor general to launch an advocacy campaign that resulted in having service delivery agencies incorporate in their strategic plans the "action taken" on the auditor general's recommendations.

In countries where there is openness to build formal mechanisms of participation between SAIs and citizens, the primary challenge has been to ensure that neither the autonomy of SAIs nor the independence of civil society is undermined through the process.

Below are two examples where citizen participation and partnerships with SAIs led to improved results.

Korea's Board of Audit and Inspection has an institutionalized process to seek feedback and engage citizens in the audit process. The country's Anti-Corruption Act of 2002 created the legal foundation for participatory audits under the title of citizen audit requests. Each year, the board plans and conducts more than 150 audits, while an additional 20 to 30 audits are undertaken at the request of citizens, CSOs, local councils, or the heads of public agencies. For example, following the request of a civic group, the Board of Audit and Inspection conducted an audit of the Masan City government following allegations that a contractor involved in a water reclamation project had benefited inappropriately. The audit concluded that excessive payments had been made to the contractor and recommended that the city government seek compensation for the losses and discipline the responsible officials for their mismanagement.

(continued next page)

BOX 1.6   *(continued)*

In the Philippines, inputs from citizens to the audit process produced information about program implementation that otherwise would have been quite challenging to access and gather given the existing capacities and array of audit tools of the Commission on Audit. A pilot audit of a solid waste management program was conducted to confirm whether the Quezon City government had complied with the country's solid waste management law. The participation of "citizen auditors" resulted in more comprehensive audit findings by going beyond the standard auditing tools to check for program compliance with policy. Citizens brought to the audit greater awareness of local factors related to poor service. For example, they reported the concerns of garbage collectors regarding their health and complaints about their pay, which was below the minimum wage. Synergies between local cleanliness campaigns and the government's waste management initiative were also identified. The citizens' insights were included in the official audit report, and the city government agreed to act on its recommendations. Subsequent audits will monitor progress on these additional dimensions influencing service delivery.

Sources: Commission of Audit 2013; United Nations DESA 2013.

---

marginalized individuals and groups. Civic mobilization plays a pivotal role in bringing about organizational change and strengthening leadership capacity. Citizen action can be individual: a case in point is the use of GRM systems. The expansion of platforms enabled by information and communication technology that can be accessed directly by individuals is also increasing the scope of individually based actions. Yet individual action can face significant risk of repression or limited impact. Civic mobilization is important to ensure safety in numbers and to garner the public support and collective action needed for an interface through which citizens engage with state authorities. Collective civic mobilization of civil society might occur through external intervention (through state or CSO efforts) or through organic political processes. The role of CSOs in fostering SA is often a critical part of civic mobilization. Mobilizers can also include lawyers and paralegals who help to prepare and represent citizens in the interface, addressing, to some degree, power asymmetries between the state and citizens. Civic mobilization can also build on existing organizations and social capital and often draws on moral economy arguments and cultural repertoires to catalyze collective action.

On the government side, state officials also need to be mobilized to seek out and engage with citizens. State mobilization can occur at the instruction of elected officials or supervisors or through direct interaction and possible embeddedness with civil society actors. Thus mobilization is not confined to the community realm. Rather, it is better conceptualized as creating accountability coalitions where pro-accountability actors both within communities and within states create a common front (Fox 2007).

Civic mobilization may require a change in attitudes and behavior on the part of citizens for them to engage the state constructively and successfully in a citizen-state interface. Attitudinal changes may entail changing existing perceptions on the issue, if, for social and cultural reasons or due to other incentives, these perceptions tend to maintain the status quo and prevent stakeholders from being informed and aware. Behavioral change can be the focus of civic mobilization when the stakeholders are informed and aware, but hesitant to act—set in their ways due to either limited incentives to act on their knowledge or limited knowledge of the ways they can act on the issue either as individuals or as a collective.[12]

Beyond the function of civic mobilization, interlocution between the state and civil society is key in bringing elected and appointed government officials and citizens, whether individually or collectively, together in the interface. Different from mobilizers, interlocutors mediate two-way communications, and their role is often crucial for bridging power or culture gaps between citizens and state officials and creating a credible interface (Fox 2014; Tembo 2012).

Interlocution is different from facilitation, but in some cases these roles are merged. Facilitation is a broader concept than the interlocution between groups (between citizens and state officials in our framework). The process of facilitation is a way of providing leadership without taking control, which can be required temporarily in particular contexts and is often provided in SA interventions. Interlocutors can have a more facilitative role of getting citizens and state officials to engage in an interface when there is weak leadership, particularly among citizens.[13]

The Heterogeneous, Overlapping Categories of State and Citizens

In the analytical framework, neither "citizen action" nor "state action" presupposes a monolithic or homogeneous group of citizens, on the one side, or state officials, on the other (figure 1.2 depicts a possible configuration of SA actors; this is a partial view since even subcategories of actors are not homogeneous).

Figure 1.2 Heterogeneous Categories of the State and Civil Society

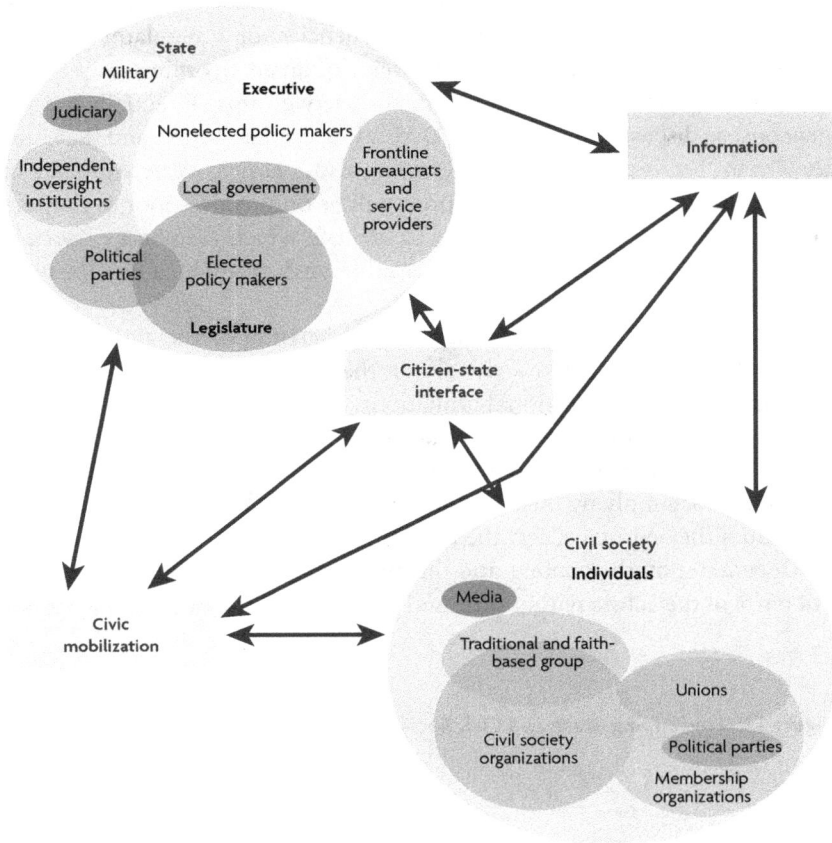

Depending on the context, figure 1.2 will vary, with various configurations of organizations and groups across the state-society divide. Yet some distinctions can be particularly meaningful insofar as they provide opportunities and entry points to support pro-accountability networks and actions.

Within the state, elected and appointed state officials respond to different incentives, and, for this reason, they might not be equally inclined to endorse SA or respond to it. The state's institutional structure, including its checks and balances institutions, can also create entry points for SA. Some state agencies or different levels of government can be more amenable than others to partnering with civil society to ensure the accountability of other state actors—for example, oversight institutions, a central government eager to monitor local governments or agencies, or a regulatory agency partnering with citizens to check the policy of an energy ministry.

Society—that is, individuals and civil society groups—is equally heterogeneous, as discussed in chapter 3. Depending on the context and the issue, the chasm between elites and others, but also among diverse segments of society, can run deep. SA interventions will be only as pro-poor as they are designed to be, and it is important to identify which members of society stand to benefit or not if an issue is addressed and which are likely to mobilize around it.

Equally important, within these broad categories, the diverse interests and preferences of individuals or the organizations to which they belong can trump institutional affiliations. While legislators, for example, may constitute a block, they may not be unified in their attitude toward accountability. Furthermore, the "champions" or proponents of SA can be identified not simply by their affiliations, but also by their way of thinking, the values they embrace, and the positions they take on issues.[14]

Depending on the context and the aim of an intervention, the constituent parts of the actors within state and civil society may overlap. Figure 1.3

Figure 1.3 Overlapping State and Civil Society Institutions

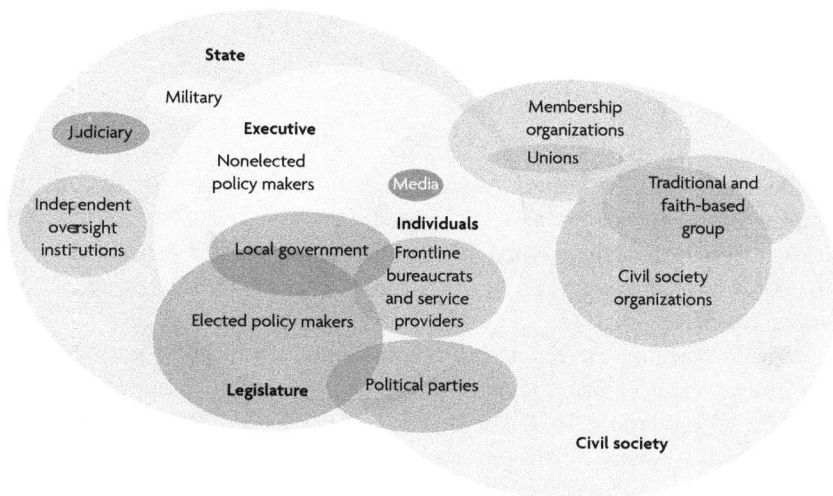

depicts the complex relationships that may exist between state and civil society and how membership in one group can coincide with membership in another.

There is a need to go beyond the supply-demand, principal-agent, and state-citizen dichotomies and instead to understand the more progressive and regressive coalitions that cut across the state and citizen divide and to foster those that can best support state-citizen engagement and elicit greater accountability. Success (however broadly defined) will often depend on political engagement (and sometimes alignment) with various social groups and coalitions of reformists and sympathetic state organizations, such as law courts or an ombudsman's office.

Individuals can also have "layered" identities, so that in one role they are participants in civil society and in another they are state employees or public service providers. As Abers and Keck (2009) state, "Especially relevant is the role of activists within the state who are committed to the goals espoused by civil society groups—indeed, who upon coming home from work at the end of the day may even be members of the civil society groups in question." Links are made through both formal and informal networks, for instance, belonging to the same temple (Tsai 2007) or an old boys' network or changing jobs over the course of a career.

At the same time, it is useful to distinguish individuals or groups who support "public" interest versus those who support "special" interests and to recognize that state and citizen actions often take place along a continuum, which can work for and against accountability. In many countries, unions and frontline bureaucrats or service providers are closely connected. For example, the state can be aligned with teachers unions, at the expense of the shared interests of citizens with regard to student achievement and teaching standards. Similarly, the media play a crucial role but nevertheless also represent specific interests (see chapter 3).[15]

The Iterative Nature of SA Approaches

Social accountability mechanisms primarily stem from the potential of the citizen-state interface, which is itself a dynamic, iterative engagement between citizen groups and state officials. The flow of information is simultaneously a driver and an output of this engagement that spurs citizen and state action through civic mobilization.

Acknowledging the iterative nature of citizen-state engagement can foster approaches that aim to monitor more realistic incremental changes, which can serve as milestones for periodically revisiting the pathway or theory of change underlying an SA intervention. It also allows us to take into account the fact that "progress" along one pathway is a catalyst to progress along another. The different pathways for a successful SA intervention may have different time horizons depending on the context. Providing information to citizens can take less time than supporting civic mobilization to articulate a demand. Similarly, the state can readily agree to engage in the interface but prevaricate when it comes to taking action. Factoring in an iterative nature of citizen and state engagement suggests that pathways "build" on each other or, conversely, unravel in the absence of response from the state (see figure 1.4).

Figure 1.4 highlights the risks associated with SA approaches in the form of less accountability or poor development results. The following section summarizes some of these risks.

Engaging or Not in Supporting SA: Balancing Potential Outcomes with Risks

SA is not a "silver bullet" for all development issues. Engaging in SA approaches needs to be done based on an analysis of the specific problem or issue that is at stake and that the SA intervention would contribute to solving.

Figure I.4 The Iterative Nature of Social Accountability

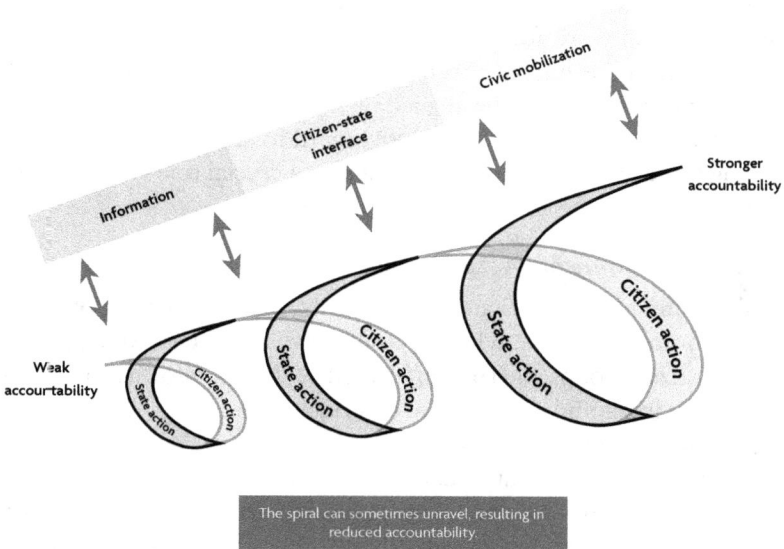

The spiral can sometimes unravel, resulting in reduced accountability.

The relevance of SA to solving a particular issue, its opportunity cost, and the potential risks of engaging in SA need to be assessed.

The first step in operationalizing the analytical framework is indeed to determine whether efforts to promote SA are worth making. The decision will depend on the outcomes expected (see chapter 2 for the different kinds of intended outcomes) from a specific involvement and the likelihood of it being achieved under specific circumstances. The five elements of the analytical framework and the guiding tables (presented in chapter 4) provide a useful structure for tailoring an assessment of the likelihood that SA efforts will deliver results and, if so, what the likely entry points may be for a viable SA strategy grounded in the realities of the existing context.

SA activities entail costs. Time and resources are invested in providing information, creating or improving the interface, and mobilizing individuals and groups. Yet measuring the cost-effectiveness of SA activities is a difficult undertaking (see chapter 2 for a discussion of the value of SA and the difficulties in measuring its impact). For both reasons, SA should be weighed against other means that have the potential to achieve the same goals.

In some cases, relying on SA to resolve a problem resulting from a lack of accountability can have negative externalities. Especially if it is "projectized," SA can displace existing, perhaps more legitimate or sustainable, structures and undermine existing mechanisms for accountability that may not be appreciated.

A problem can also be solved to the benefit of special interests rather than the public good. As is discussed in chapter 3, the risks of elite capture, misrepresentation of special interests, and manipulation abound. SA can exacerbate existing power asymmetries and perpetuate perceptions of injustice among certain groups. This may inadvertently close the space for citizen engagement instead of opening it. Elites may also mediate the relationship between the state and citizens, preventing citizens from engaging directly with state structures.

Furthermore, new SA structures run the risk of fragmenting communities, ultimately weakening their collective power. This is particularly true when state institutions are weak, and information can be easily manipulated to serve special interests.

If SA fails to elicit state response to a particular problem, the consequences can be grave. If state institutions are weak or deaf to the concerns of citizens, the iterative process breaks down, resulting in inertia, apathy, and mistrust. This can reduce people's willingness to engage in the future. These expectations may not be created by SA activities alone, but also by the state if it rhetorically promotes transparency and accountability without a genuine commitment to follow through. Frustration and grievances will mount as a consequence (McGee and Kroesschell 2013).

If the state is reluctant to engage on these issues, SA can also lead to personal risks and reprisal for individuals engaging in SA activities.

Box 1.7 presents the key takeaways from this chapter.

BOX 1.7

Key Takeaways: Social Accountability as a Concept

- There is a lack of clarity around the notion of SA and no universally agreed definition.
- The fuzzy definitional terrain stems partly from the two main intellectual origins of SA: the principal-agent model and the voice and participation model.
- Definitional clarity is also influenced by some common biases within current interpretations and implementation of SA: (1) SA is often understood primarily as a tool-based approach, which depoliticizes it, (2) the emphasis on information and transparency is not necessarily sufficient to yield accountability, (3) SA is often conflated with participation, yet they are distinct processes, and (4) when SA is focused on the demand side of a supply-demand dichotomy, too little importance is given to state action.
- Here, SA is conceptualized as the interplay of five constitutive elements, with the aim of supporting SA mechanisms more strategically: citizen action, state action, information, interface, and civic mobilization. Information, interface, and civic mobilization act as *levers* on the other two (citizen action and state action).
- This conceptual framework rests on three important observations: (1) SA results from the interplay of state action and citizen action with three levers—information, interface, and civic mobilization, (2) neither the state nor citizens are homogeneous or exclusive categories, and (3) because SA processes are iterative (a fact that must be acknowledged at the start), to be successful, SA approaches must dynamically reassess entry points and trajectories, support building blocks for future SA interventions, and carefully assess risks and trade-offs.

Notes

1. This chapter draws from Joshi (2014).
2. In doing so, we do not ignore other schools of thought that are relevant to an understanding of SA such as public choice theory, social choice theory, or behavioral economics but choose to focus on what we consider the two most influential roots in this field. Other intellectual roots and applications are discussed in the text and guiding tables in chapter 4.
3. See http://hrbaportal.org/the-human-rights-based-approach-to-development -cooperation-towards-a-common-understanding-among-un-agencies#sthash .VSlnnpw2.dpuf.
4. Article 19, Universal Declaration of Human Rights (1948) and Article 19, International Covenant of Civil and Political Rights (1966).
5. See the "How-to Notes" series published by the World Bank's Social Development Department as well as the Social Accountability E-Guide website for support in applying some of these tools (https://saeguide.worldbank.org/). Links to the how-to notes are provided in the references at the end of this chapter.
6. As discussed in box 2.4, replicating social audits across India has been difficult, in part because it has not benefited from the same momentum associated with an organic social movement.
7. *Opaque transparency* involves the dissemination of information that does not reveal how institutions actually behave in practice (how they make decisions) or the results of their actions. It also refers to information that is nominally divulged or turns out to be unreliable.
8. In their work, targeted transparency is defined as "the use of publicly required disclosure of specific information in a standardized format to achieve a clear public policy purpose" (Fox 2014; Fung, Graham, and Weil 2007; Kosack and Fung 2014).
9. See chapter 3 for a discussion of political settlement.
10. For example, Bangalore's famed citizen report cards had their most significant impact on public sector performance when a responsive chief minister was in power—combining teeth with voice (Fox 2014; Paul 2006).
11. Thanks to Jonathan Fox for this suggestion.
12. This distinction between attitudinal change and behavioral change draws on "the stairway to mobilization" process discussed in Arnold and Garcia (2009).
13. A facilitator's role is to persuade others to assume responsibility and take the lead.
14. Thanks to Jeff Thindwa for these points.
15. Thanks to Hana Brixi and Jeff Thindwa for these points.

References

Abers, R. N., and M. E. Keck. 2009. "Mobilizing the State: The Erratic Partner in Brazil's Participatory Water Policy." *Politics and Society* 37 (2): 289–314. http://pas.sagepub.com/content/37/2/289.

Ackerman, J. 2004. "Co-Governance for Accountability: Beyond 'Exit' and 'Voice.'" *World Development* 32 (3): 447–63.

———. 2005a. "Human Rights and Social Accountability." Social Development Paper: Participation and Civic Engagement 86, World Bank, Washington, DC.

———. 2005b. "Social Accountability in the Public Sector: A Conceptual Discussion." Social Development Paper: Participation and Civic Engagement 82, World Bank, Washington, DC.

Arnold, A.-K., and H. R. Garcia. 2009. "Generating Genuine Demand for Accountability: Public Opinion, Persuasion, and the Public Sphere." Learning module presented on behalf of the World Bank, Johannesburg, South Africa, May 28–June 10.

Batley, R. 1999. "The New Public Management in Developing Countries: Implications for Policy and Organizational Reform." *Journal of International Development* 11 (5): 761–65.

Baviskar, A. 2007. "Is Knowledge Power? The Right to Information Campaign in India." Paper presented to the workshop on social movements and national policy, University of Sussex, Institute of Development Studies, Brighton, U.K., September.

Björkman, M., D. de Walque, and J. Svensson. 2014. "Information Is Power: Experimental Evidence of the Long-Run Impact of Community-Based Monitoring." Policy Research Paper 7015, World Bank, Washington, DC.

Booth, D. 2012. *Development as a Collective Action Problem: Addressing the Real Challenges of African Governance.* APP Synthesis Report. London: Overseas Development Institute, Africa Power and Politics Programme.

Bovens, M. 2007. "Analysing and Assessing Public Accountability: A Conceptual Model." *European Law Journal* 13 (4, July): 447–68.

Commission of Audit, Philippines. 2013. "Citizen Participatory Audit (CPA) Report: Pilot Audit 2, Quezon City Solid Waste Management Program." CPA Report 2013-001, Commission of Audit, Quezon.

Corbridge, S., G. Williams, M. Srivastava, and R. Veron. 2005. *Seeing the State: Governance and Governmentality in India.* Cambridge, U.K.: Cambridge University Press.

Eyben, R. 2003. "The Rise of Rights." IDS Policy Briefing 17, University of Sussex, Institute of Development Studies, Brighton, U.K.

Fox, J. 2001. "Vertically Integrated Policy Monitoring: A Tool for Civil Society Policy Advocacy." *Nonprofit and Voluntary Sector Quarterly* 30 (3): 616–27.

————. 2007. *Accountability Politics: Power and Voice in Rural Mexico.* Oxford, U.K.: Oxford University Press.

————. 2014. "Social Accountability: What Does the Evidence Really Say?" Global Partnership for Social Accountability Working Paper 1, World Bank, Washington, DC, July.

Fung, A., M. Graham, and D. Weil. 2007. *Full Disclosure: The Perils and Promise of Transparency.* Cambridge, U.K.: Cambridge University Press.

Gauri, V., and S. Gloppen. 2012. "Human Rights–Based Approaches to Development: Concepts, Evidence, and Policy." *Polity* 44 (4): 485–503.

Gaventa, J., and R. McGee, eds. 2010. *Citizen Action and National Policy Reform: Making Change Happen.* London: Zed Books.

Goetz, A. M., and R. Jenkins. 2001. "Hybrid Forms of Accountability: Citizen Engagement in Institutions of Public Sector Oversight in India." *Public Management Review* 3 (3): 363–83.

Golub, S., ed. 2013. "Legal Empowerment's Approaches and Importance." *Justice Initiatives* (Autumn): 5–14.

Hirschman, A. 1970. *Exit, Voice, and Loyalty: Responses to Decline in Firms, Organizations, and States.* Cambridge, MA: Harvard University Press.

Joshi, A. 2013. "The Impact of Social Accountability Initiatives on Improving the Delivery of Public Services: A Systematic Review of Four Intervention Types: Protocol." Unpublished mss., Institute of Development Studies, London.

————. 2014. "On Social Accountability: An Issue Paper." Background paper prepared for this book, World Bank, Social Development Department, Washington, DC.

Joshi, A., and P. Houtzager. 2012. "Widgets or Watchdogs? Conceptual Explorations in Social Accountability." *Public Management Review, Special Issue: The Politics and Governance of Public Services in Developing Countries* 14 (2): 145–62.

Joshi, A., and M. Moore. 2004. "Institutionalized Co-production: Unorthodox Public Service Delivery in Challenging Environments." *Journal of Development Studies* 40 (4): 31–49.

Khemani, S. 2014. "Transparency, Citizen Engagement, and the Politics of Development." Concept Note for a policy research report on governance, World Bank, Development Research Group, Washington, DC.

Kosack, S., and A. Fung. 2014. "Does Transparency Improve Governance?" *Annual Review of Political Science* 17 (May): 65–87.

Lam, W. F. 1996. "Institutional Design of Public Agencies and Coproduction: A Study of Irrigation Associations in Taiwan." *World Development* 24 (6): 1039–54.

Mainwaring, S., and C. Welna. 2003. *Democratic Accountability in Latin America.* Oxford: Oxford University Press.

Manning, N. 2001. "The Legacy of the New Public Management in Developing Countries." *International Review of Administrative Sciences* 67 (2): 297–312.

Mansuri, G., and V. Rao. 2013. *Localizing Development: Does Participation Work?* Policy Research Report. Washington, DC: World Bank.

Maru, V. 2010. "Allies Unknown: Social Accountability and Legal Empowerment." *Health and Human Rights in Practice* 12 (1): 83–93.

Maru, V., and A. Moy. 2013. "Legal Empowerment and Public Administration: A Map of the Landscape and Three Emerging Insights." *Justice Initiatives* (Autumn): 59–74.

McGee, R., and C. Kroesschell. 2013. "Local Accountabilities in Fragile Contexts: Experiences from Nepal, Bangladesh, and Mozambique." IDS Working Paper 422, University of Sussex, Institute of Development Studies, Brighton, U.K.

Molyneux, M., and S. Lazar. 2003. "Doing the Rights Thing: Rights-Based Development and Latin American NGOs." Colchester, U.K.: Intermediate Technology Development Group.

Moser, C., and A. Norton. 2001. "To Claim Our Rights: Livelihood Security, Human Rights, and Sustainable Development." Overseas Development Institute, London.

Narayan, D., R. Patel, K. Schafft, A. Rademacher, and S. Koch-Schulte. 2000. *Can Anyone Hear Us? Voices of the Poor.* Washington, DC: World Bank.

Nyamu-Musembi, C. 2005. "An Actor-Oriented Approach to Rights in Development." *IDS Bulletin* 36 (1): 41–51.

O'Donnell, G. 1999. "Horizontal Accountability in New Democracies." In *The Self-Restraining State: Power and Accountability in New Democracies,* edited by A. Schedler, L. Diamond, and M. F. Plattner, 29–51. Boulder, CO: Lynne Rienner.

Ostrom, E. 1996. "Crossing the Great Divide: Co-production, Synergy, and Development." *World Development* 24 (6): 1073–87.

Pande, S. 2013. "The Right to Know, the Right to Live: Grassroots Struggle for Information and Work in India." Ph.D. thesis, University of Sussex, Brighton, U.K.

Paul, S. 2006. "Public Spending, Outcomes, and Accountability: Citizen Report Card as a Catalyst for Public Action." *Economic and Political Weekly* 41 (4): 333–40.

Peruzzotti, E. 2011. "The Workings of Accountability: Contexts and Conditions." In *Accountability through Public Opinion: From Inertia to Public Action,* edited by S. Odugbemi and T. Lee. Washington, DC: World Bank.

Peters, B. G. 2001. *The Politics of Bureaucracy,* 5th ed. London: Routledge.

Scott, J. C. 1998. *Seeing Like a State: How Certain Schemes to Improve the Human Condition Have Failed.* New Haven, CT: Yale University Press.

Sen, A. 1999. *Development as Freedom.* Oxford: Oxford University Press.

Smulovitz, C., and E. Peruzzotti. 2000. "Societal Accountability in Latin America." *Journal of Democracy* 11 (4): 147–58.

Tembo, F. 2012. "Citizen Voice and State Accountability: Towards Theories of Change That Embrace Contextual Dynamics." Working Paper 343, Overseas Development Institute, London.

Tendler, J. 1997. *Good Governance in the Tropics.* Baltimore, MD: Johns Hopkins University Press.

Tsai, L. L. 2007. *Accountability without Democracy: Solidarity Groups and Public Goods Provision in Rural China.* New York: Cambridge University Press.

United Nations DESA (Department of Economic and Social Affairs). 2013. *Citizen Engagement Practices by Supreme Audit Institutions: Compendium of Innovative Practices of Citizen Engagement by Supreme Audit Institutions for Public Accountability.* New York: United Nations.

World Bank. 2000. *World Development Report 2000/2001: Attacking Poverty.* New York: Oxford University Press.

———. 2004. *World Development Report 2004: Making Services Work for the Poor.* New York: Oxford University Press.

———. 2012. "Strengthening Governance, Tackling Corruption: The World Bank's Updated Strategy and Implementation Plan." World Bank, Washington, DC, March 6. http://siteresources.worldbank.org/PUBLICSECTORAND GOVERNANCE/Resources/285741-1326816182754/GACStrategy ImplementationPlan.pdf.

The following are links to the How-to Notes published by the World Bank's Social Development Department:

Citizen Charters: http://www-wds.worldbank.org/external/default/WDSContent Server/WDSP/IB/2011/08/24/000386194_20110824014624/Rendered/PDF /638900BRI0Citi00Box0361531B0PUBLIC0.pdf.

Citizen Report Cards: http://www-wds.worldbank.org/external/default/WDS ContentServer/WDSP/IB/2013/08/16/000333037_20130816130736/Rendered /PDF/804490WP0Citiz0Box0379805B00PUBLIC0.pdf).

Citizen Service Centers: http://www-wds.worldbank.org/external/default/WDS ContentServer/WDSP/IB/2011/08/24/000386194_20110824023201/Rendered /PDF/638910BRI0Citi00Box0361531B0PUBLIC0.pdf.

Feedback Matters, Part 1: http://www-wds.worldbank.org/external/default /WDSContentServer/WDSP/IB/2012/06/01/000426104_20120601162556 /Rendered/PDF/692060ESW0P1250Effective0Governance.pdf.

Feedback Matters, Part 2: http://www-wds.worldbank.org/external/default /WDSContentServer/WDSP/IB/2012/06/01/000426104_20120601163112 /Rendered/PDF/692060ESW0P1250Effective0Governance.pdf.

How, When, and Why: http://www-wds.worldbank.org/external/default/WDS ContentServer/WDSP/IB/2011/08/24/000356161_20110824025657/Rendered /PDF/639040BRI0Dema00Box0361531B0PUBLIC0.pdf.

Interactive Community Mapping: http://www-wds.worldbank.org/external/default /WDSContentServer/WDSP/IB/2014/06/27/000442464_20140627091841 /Rendered/PDF/890870WP0Box380munity0Mapping0final.pdf.

Participatory and Third-Party Monitoring: http://www-wds.worldbank.org/external /default/WDSContentServer/WDSP/IB/2013/08/16/000333037_201308161355 15/Rendered/PDF/804520WP0Monit0Box0379805B00PUBLIC0.pdf.

Rapid Feedback: http://www-wds.worldbank.org/external/default/WDSContent Server/WDSP/IB/2014/06/09/000442464_20140609160236/Rendered/PDF /884970WP0Rapid00Box385225B00PUBLIC0.pdf.

Right to Information: http://www-wds.worldbank.org/external/default/WDSContent Server/WDSP/IB/2013/08/07/000445729_20130807145156/Rendered/PDF/800 480WP0P11830Box0379800B00PUBLIC0.pdf.

Using Demand-Side Approach to Identify and Manage Risks in Projects: http://www-wds.worldbank.org/external/default/WDSContentServer /WDSP/IB/2012/07/18/000333037_20120718013845/Rendered/PDF /712610WP00PUBL0DFGG0Final07.17.2012.pdf.

CHAPTER 2

The Puzzling Evidence

The evidence on social accountability (SA) is growing. But making sense of it is difficult because the data on various interventions in various contexts are fragmented and the resulting picture is mixed (see, for instance, McGee and Gaventa 2011).[1] Such a puzzling evidence base invites partisan readings. Some promoters tout SA as the latest "silver bullet," embodying fundamental values while leading to clear instrumental outcomes. In contrast, opponents can be vocal about the opportunity costs, risks, and possible counterproductive effects of SA. Depending on the viewpoint, even robust and seemingly unequivocal findings can be reinterpreted (see box 2.1).

Asking simply, Does SA work or not? is tempting, but it is not helpful. Such a simplistic question obscures the multidimensionality of SA interactions, the encompassing role of context, and the difficulty of capturing impact for some of the most complex potential outcomes. Recognizing this complexity, observers have increasingly conducted SA impact evaluations while intensifying their efforts to interpret the existing evidence. Beyond conventional studies assessing impact (including Agarwal, Heltberg, and Diachok 2009; Gaventa and Barrett 2010; McGee and Gaventa 2010; O'Neill, Foresti, and Hudson 2007; and Rocha Menocal and Sharma 2008), meta-analyses have begun to survey impact evaluations systematically, comparing them across regions and sectors (Lodenstein et al. 2013; Lynch et al. 2013; Molina et al. 2013; Westhorp et al. 2013). These recent meta-analyses ask whether, and through what processes, SA might be working. Annex B provides an overview of the findings from selected studies.

BOX 2.1

Top-Down and Bottom-Up Approaches for Anti-Corruption: Dichotomous or Synergistic?

In a well-quoted study—using a randomized controlled trial (RCT) conducted in 608 Indonesian villages—Olken compares two distinct approaches taken to curb corruption in a road construction project: top-down, centrally administered audits and community monitoring. A 2012 J-PAL brief summarizes the findings as follows: "Top-down audits effectively reduced corruption in Indonesian village road projects, but community-level monitoring had no effect unless pains were taken to prevent control by elites" (J-PAL 2012). Indeed, Olken concludes that the top-down approach, which entailed an increased probability of external audits, substantively reduced missing funds, while the bottom-up approach—increasing community participation in village accountability meetings and using forms to report corruption anonymously— reduced missing expenditures if elite capture was mitigated, but only for the cost of labor, not the cost of construction materials.

Fox (2014) shows that, in line with Olken's paper, there is more to the story. These two approaches are actually not dichotomous but synergistic. Villagers were told that audit reports would not only be shared with the central government and project officials, but also presented to villagers in a special village meeting, which could bring village retribution. In light of the very low rate of reporting and even lower rate of prosecuting corrupt offenses in the top-down audits, holding project officials accountable for lost funds via community monitoring—that is, making the findings of the external audits public in communities—"gave teeth" to the top-down approach and complemented it.

Influenced by Olken's findings, the Indonesian government scaled up its application of top-down audits by the central government audit agency to more than 80 percent of the local development projects in 70,000 villages. Interestingly, the project's official reports do not indicate whether these audit findings are also being disseminated at the community level.

Sources: Fox 2014; Olken 2007, 2009.

Three lessons clearly emerge from the available literature: (1) contextual conditions matter for understanding why interventions have the impacts they do, (2) it is important to expand the universe of impacts and trace them systematically, and (3) closer attention is needed to the mechanisms through which SA initiatives are expected to have impact. These three lessons are discussed in the rest of the report.

Chapters 3 and 4, by building on and aggregating the growing body of evidence in a new way along SA's five constitutive elements, provide an analytical framework for systematically assessing and documenting contextual factors that mediate SA effectiveness. They also synthesize the existing evidence related to context, broadly defined (including through the guiding tables presented in chapter 4).

This chapter does not attempt to summarize the existing evidence. Instead, it aims to clarify the problems encountered when trying to determine whether or not SA is effective and why. The chapter's first section identifies a range of potential SA outcomes, not all of them consistently distinguished or even acknowledged in the design of impact evaluations. The second section discusses the range of impacts and change, and provides examples. The third section discusses the difficulties encountered in measuring outcomes. In part, these difficulties reflect a bias toward efficiency outcomes such as improved service delivery. They also reflect real methodological challenges. The last section then summarizes some of the important findings relating to the effectiveness of SA.

Mapping Potential Outcomes of SA

Different observers have different understandings of the outcomes that might be attributed to SA and of the value attributed to these outcomes. The range of potential outcomes is wide. As one recent paper puts it, the "expected results of social accountability include a reduction in corruption, better governance and policy design, enhanced voice, empowerment, and citizenship of marginalized groups, responsiveness of service providers and policy makers to citizens demands, and ultimately the achievement of rights, health, and developmental outcomes" (Lodenstein et al. 2013).

Taking into account the diverse intellectual origins of SA (discussed in chapter 1), Anuradha Joshi charts the impacts that have been expected from SA activities along two dimensions (see table 2.1; Joshi 2014). On the x-axis is the location of the benefits to the polity—whether in the *state*, which may benefit from better governance; in *state-society relationships*, which may benefit from increased legitimacy; or in *society*, which may benefit from improved provision of public goods. On the y-axis is the nature of the activity's value for development—from *instrumental*, as in

Table 2.1 Expanded Impact of Social Accountability

	States	State-society relationships	Social actors
Instrumental ↕ Institutional	• Reduced corruption • Responsive public officials • Better policy design • Good governance	• Institutional channels for interaction • Trust • Legitimacy • State building • Democratic deepening	• Improved provision of public goods • Empowered citizens • Social cohesion • Inclusive social norms

improved provision of public goods, to *institutional,* as in state building. Such outcomes can be expected from SA, but are rarely achieved in isolation from other reforms or actions that support building more capacity and responsiveness.

Perspectives on whether SA "works" or not are determined in part by the value attributed to its outcomes, including its intrinsic value. If voice and empowerment are fundamental to SA—and if they count as development objectives in themselves—then participation in an SA process may yield positive results even when service delivery remains poor. Rather than labeling an intervention "unsuccessful" simply because a service delivery outcome was not achieved, one might consider outcomes such as citizens who are empowered or parents who are more aware (Pradhan et al. 2011). Ultimately, and especially when one of the stated goals of many SA approaches is to empower citizens, one can argue that the question of the intrinsic value of SA would be best answered by the actors who are involved in trying to facilitate social accountability. As Samuel Paul eloquently puts it,

> Those who champion demand-side governance would argue that citizens coming together to engage in demand-side governance is a significant outcome in itself. ... Through these interventions, they are discharging the basic civic duties of citizens ... Even if a specific campaign or a demand for change fails to achieve its goals, ... such failures do not imply a negative outcome; rather, they enhance civil society's capacity to organize collective action and act as a stimulus to recast and repeat demand-side initiatives. (Paul 2002)

Range of Impacts of SA with Examples

This section provides a short definition of each of these outcomes together with references to examples in which SA contributes to each. As mentioned, providing successful examples only goes so far. The next section focuses on the measurement challenges to support SA understanding and then highlights some important overall findings on SA.

Scholars and practitioners have observed or proposed the following as potential impacts of SA approaches, divided into impacts on the state, impacts on the state-society relationship, and the impacts on society.

The following are the impacts on the state:

- *Reduced corruption.* In some SA interventions, reduced corruption is the main expectation and potential. For example, community monitoring often uncovers corruption and puts an end to extortion, fraud, embezzlement, bribery, and misappropriation of funds. It can also result in formal sanctions and, occasionally, the return of embezzled funds (de Renzio, Andrews, and Mills 2011; Gauthier 2006). Similarly, exposing malfeasance is one of the expected outcomes of social audits (Singh and Vutukuru 2010).

- *Responsive public officials.* Ultimately, SA interventions seek to shift the incentives facing public officials—to increase either the potential reputational costs or the fears of triggering traditional accountability mechanisms and subsequent sanctions. This is the main route to achieving some of the key outcomes of social accountability, such as improved public services and reduced corruption. Behavioral change of providers is often measured as the reduction in absentee rates (Duflo, Hanna, and Ryan 2012; see also Clark, Fox, and Treakle 2003). Some studies focus on performance indicators, for example, the equipment used in treating patients (Björkman and Svensson 2009). Systematically disaggregating and tracking specific behavioral responses—for example, absenteeism, quality of services, or empathy on the part of public servants—is important to assessing the impact of social accountability on different types of behavior.

- *Better policy design and governance.* The operation of SA over time is intended to improve policy design and governance. Governance will improve overall, removing the need for regular SA action (much as the law exerts a deterrent function, needing to be enforced only occasionally). See examples from Brazil (World Bank 2008), South Africa (International

Budget Partnership 2010), and a multicountry study focusing on Brazil and Latin America (Goldfrank 2006).

Second are the impacts on the state-society relationship:

- *Institutional channels for state-society interaction.* Such channels are fundamental, even though they are rarely spelled out as a distinct expectation of SA. Nevertheless, social accountability action usually involves the creation (or rejuvenation) of a transparent and credible public interface between states and citizens that is missing or is not being used in various contexts. For example, social audits create a new institutional space where citizens can interact directly with the state. As they get used over time, they enter the institutional repertoire in people's minds, and the practice of participating in these spaces becomes an accepted part of civic life (Aiyar and Walton 2014). Institutionalization of this kind can represent a success even if other impacts are not fully achieved. See the examples in a multicountry study (Rainbow Insight 2009).
- *Legitimacy (and ultimately state building).* Legitimacy is often defined as a willingness to defer to authority, and trustworthiness is defined as one's belief that a given actor will carry out a certain action. State legitimacy is tied to agreed rules and processes that make it accountable to its citizens, whether through participation or patronage. The various sources of legitimacy have been identified in the literature on state building. See Brinkerhoff, Wetterberg, and Dunn (2012) for an example from Iraq. Most important in building legitimacy are the following:
  - *Political legitimacy (accountability) and inclusion.* This entails the use of credible political processes in reaching decisions that reflect shared values and preferences and, above all, give equal voice to all citizens and require accountability for these decisions. Providing citizens with information and mechanisms for legal recourse to resolve disputes and air complaints, including complaints against the state, is another requirement for legitimacy.
  - *Performance legitimacy (capacity).* Performance legitimacy is earned through the effective discharge by the state of the duties assigned to it, particularly with regard to security, economic oversight, public services, and justice (World Bank 2011).

Expectations relating to trust and legitimacy figure more prominently in efforts to promote accountability in fragile states, especially when compared to narrow instrumental objectives such as improved service delivery, which might be more difficult to achieve in any case given the limited capacity of these states.

- *Deepening democracy.* Social accountability can also be expected to contribute to deepening democracy and creating a polity where active citizens interact with responsive states. Yet studies so far have failed to determine the extent to which social accountability has moved polities from low-level accountability traps to more dynamic, virtuous accountability cycles (Fox 2014).

Finally are the impacts in society:

- *Improved provision of public goods.* Almost universally, one of the expectations of social accountability is improvements in service delivery and therefore developmental effectiveness. Clearer articulation of citizen demands and transparency in delivery processes are expected to lead to responsive states and, ultimately, better policy design and improved services. Depending on the action taken to promote social accountability, the channels that lead to these results differ. Most often, improved service delivery constitutes the evidence of what social accountability can achieve. On India, see Caseley (2003); Duflo, Hanna, and Ryan (2008); and Ravindra (2004). On Tanzania and Uganda, see Sundet (2008); on Uganda, see Björkman and Svensson (2009); and for a multicountry study, see Clark, Fox, and Treakle (2003).
- *Empowered citizens.* Empowerment refers to the expansion of freedom of choice and action to shape one's life (Rayan 2002). It is the second most common expectation of efforts to promote accountability. The idea is that, by making information available and getting feedback, social accountability amplifies the voice of the poor and enables them to become active citizens (Gaventa and McGee 2013). There is a lively debate in the literature over whether empowerment is a means to an end or an end in itself. Despite the popularity of the expectation, few studies trace it as an impact, partly owing to definitional difficulties. For a few exceptions, see Goodwin and Maru (2014). For a multicountry study and India, see Mansuri and Rao (2013); for India, see Banerjee et al. (2010) and Pandey, Goyal, and Sundararaman (2009).
- *Social cohesion.* Although not widespread, there is sometimes the expectation that the processes of participating in social accountability will bring diverse groups together into a cohesive collective (Boeckmann 2012).

Given the cleavages that exist in many of the poorest societies, whether processes that are often of short duration can produce such cohesion is an open question. Any such expectation is more challenging in fragile and conflict-affected situations (see chapter 6), since accountability programs run the risk of exacerbating existing tensions rather than resolving them.

Challenges to SA Evaluation and Methodological Issues

Impact evaluations have been commissioned principally for SA's more measurable impacts on service delivery. They are rarely conducted for outcomes such as voice and empowerment, which are harder to capture or attribute to a particular approach. The outcomes that are most difficult to pinpoint may fall entirely off the radar screen for evaluators—if not for practitioners. Furthermore, the interrelation of SA approaches is not captured.

This limits the assessment of SA approaches, since it may miss important outcomes, as well as the iterative nature of SA approaches. By declaring "failure" when service delivery objectives are not met, the iterative nature of SA processes is not acknowledged. For example, in Indonesia, the parents who protested publicly to demand accountability for free education were the same parents who had formerly been members of school-based management—an approach that, itself, was found to be relatively unsuccessful (Rosser and Joshi 2012). This suggests how SA approaches can be successful as intermediate steps, both intrinsically and instrumentally.

There are two reasons for the imbalance in the design of impact evaluations. One is a bias toward a certain conception of SA stemming from the principal-agent model and the focus on reducing information asymmetries. Another is the fact that attempts to measure institutional impact are likely to encounter real methodological difficulties.

There are several major difficulties in measuring SA outcomes. First, many potential SA outcomes refer to concepts that are somewhat loosely defined—or contested. For example, empowerment is not as easily defined and bounded as service delivery outcomes: one study lists 32 definitions of empowerment used in the past decade (Ibrahim and Alkire 2007). Some studies define accountability as an ingredient in empowerment (Narayan 2002), while others define empowerment as an ingredient in accountability or at least as a prerequisite for it.[2] In addition, changes in societal attitudes (increased awareness, shifting incentives) and relationships (improved state-society relations) are inherently harder to quantify than improved service delivery, so in general they are tested much less rigorously.

Second, complex processes involving multiple actors and strategies are notoriously difficult to evaluate, with attribution a major challenge. According to Guijt (2007, 27), attribution is "a recurring headache for those engaged in multi-actor, multi-location, multi-level and multi-strategy change work." The civil society activism on which many citizen-led and social accountability initiatives are premised constitutes a set of dynamics that are very hard to disentangle from other social, political, structural, or institutional factors or the actions of other state or nonstate actors, and the sustainability of which is contingent on many extraneous factors.

Third, the time horizon of SA approaches constitutes a distinct challenge for evaluation. Most organizations have neither the resources nor the institutional continuity to measure what is happening two or three years after a project has ended. Yet to be successful, many SA approaches follow long-term, iterative pathways that experience both successes and failures (see box 2.2 on participatory budgeting in Brazil).

BOX 2.2

Participatory Budgeting in Brazil: No Quick Fix

Participatory budgeting in Brazil emerged in the late 1980s in the wake of the country's democratization and decentralization movements (Gonçalves 2009, 2013; World Bank 2008; Zamboni 2007). The larger push for greater participation in decision making, accountability, and equal access to public services leant support to the idea. An end to patronage, the 1988 constitution, and subsequent decisions by most state capitals to reform their finances made the novel process possible (World Bank 2008). Since then, participatory budgeting has spread within Brazil and elsewhere. It takes place at the municipal and state levels as well, and it varies in scope, scale, and methodology (Schneider and Goldfrank 2002; World Bank 2008; Zamboni 2007).

The potential development outcomes of participatory budgeting, which allows for direct citizen participation in budgetary decision making, range from improvements in budget allocation and management of service delivery and living conditions to democracy and political power sharing among the main stakeholders.

(continued next page)

BOX 2.2   *(continued)*

The effectiveness and impact of the process in Brazil have been uneven. Not surprising, they depend by and large on which development outcome is evaluated and the time allotted for evaluating it.

Touchton and Wampler's recent study presents findings different from the earlier findings of Boulding and Wampler on participatory budgeting's impact on citizens' well-being (Boulding and Wampler 2010; Touchton and Wampler 2013). While both studies use the same sampling techniques and methodology, the more recent study is based on data collected over a 20-year period (1989 to 2008), almost twice as long as the earlier one (1991 to 2000). In contrast to some of the 2010 findings (which found no impact on the well-being of citizens, their quality of life, infant mortality rates, or inequality), the 2013 study associates the presence of participatory budgeting with increased spending on health care and sanitation and lower infant mortality rates, proof of improved well-being. The different conclusions highlight an important point—namely, that the outcomes of participatory budgeting are associated with long-term institutional and political change rather than a short-term fix.

Consistent with the findings of Touchton and Wampler (2013), Gonçalves (2009, 2013) shows that the process leads to increased municipal spending on basic sanitation and health services and a significant reduction in infant mortality rates.

Biases in methodological choices and implementation are related to all three sources of difficulty. Experimental and quasi-experimental methods, especially RCTs, continue to be preferred over other potential sources of knowledge about SA interventions. This preference can direct disproportionate attention to more easily measurable, time-bound, transparency-based induced interventions.

There are many good reasons for using RCTs, and these methods have distinct advantages, especially when they allow policy makers to test rigorously the impact of a distinct change in policy. Yet they have some shortcomings in measuring the impact of complex SA approaches.

In measuring impacts, RCTs treat process as a black box. They yield no information about change mechanisms or trajectories. Woolcock's compelling figure on the "uncharted trajectory of change" in complex interventions (figure 2.1) highlights that the assessed impact depends on (a) the timing of the evaluation and (b) the trajectory of impact (Woolcock 2009).

Figure 2.1 Trajectories of Social Accountability Outcomes

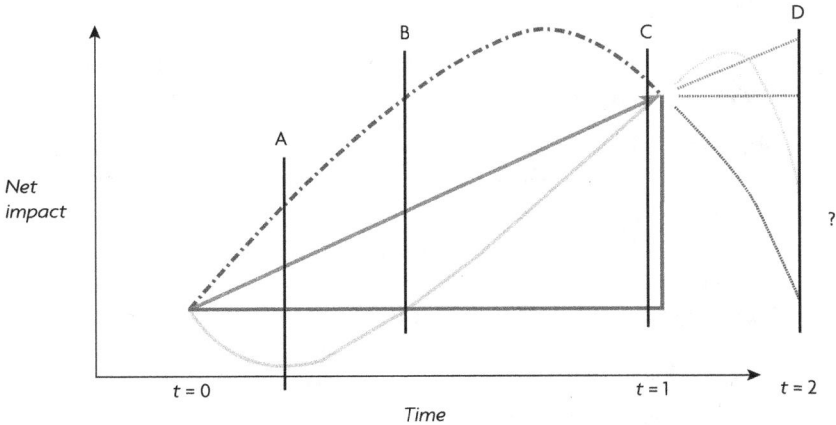

Source: Woolcock 2009.

Nevertheless, we know very little about the change trajectories that SA practices can follow in response to an intervention—thus we run the risk of missing some effects entirely.

SA impact evaluations often do not capture the intricacies of context and fail to examine a longer trajectory of citizen-state engagement or the broader political-economy context that determines the nature and contours of SA. The tendency to examine SA initiatives in a "snapshot" fashion, when the purpose and focus of the evaluation are specifically a test of the intervention itself, does not acknowledge broader contextual factors (Banerjee et al. 2010; Nguyen and Lassibille 2008). For example, Reinikka and Svensson (2005) convincingly argue that the success of Public Expenditure Tracking Surveys in Uganda was linked to better transmission of funds where information was more available. Joshi and Houtzager (2012) point out that less emphasis is given to the fact that this SA intervention did not work in isolation and that parallel reforms of the public administration contributed to the improvements in fund transmission (see also Hubbard 2007). Box 2.3 contrasts the relative success of the implementation of social audits in the state of Andhra Pradesh in India to its uneven replication in other Indian states, showing the importance of the origin and organizational and political support provided to such an implementation.

BOX 2.3

Reducing Corruption through Social Audits in Andhra Pradesh, India, and the Difficulty in Replicating Success

In 2005, India's parliament passed the Mahatma Gandhi National Rural Employment Guarantee Act (NREGA) to promote livelihood security. NREGA guarantees 100 days of employment to adults in rural households willing to perform unskilled work in development projects in their villages. The act includes provisions for social audits at regular intervals to monitor and curb corruption.

As part of the program, individuals are trained in conducting social audits in villages. Field visits to beneficiaries are used to obtain feedback on the program and to verify information obtained from official records. Public hearings are held to disseminate reports and bring citizen and state actors together.

NREGA's success in reaching the poor has varied from state to state. In Andhra Pradesh, the program, which started in February 2006, has been particularly successful, demonstrating how social audits can be scaled up effectively to monitor and evaluate public services and combat corruption.

The Andhra Pradesh program benefited from the state government's firm and continued commitment to the process. Its willingness to work with grassroots organizations and mechanisms and to partner with civil society organizations, such as the Association for the Empowerment of Workers and Farmers, were key factors in the program's success. The government also established the administrative and technical structures needed to ensure the program's success. The support given to Andhra Pradesh's Rural Development Department by the Mazdoor Kisan Shakti Sangathan (MKSS), a grassroots organization that pioneered the use of social audits in Rajasthan, was instrumental to the program's success in Andhra Pradesh. The MKSS had lobbied for social audits to become a mandatory part of NREGA and actively supported their rollout. A former MKSS activist ultimately became head of the Society for Social Audit, Accountability, and Transparency, which conducts regular social audits in 22 districts in India concurrently. In fiscal 2012–13, it trained 35,000 beneficiaries and conducted 1,100 public meetings.

Over time, the nature of community meetings has evolved, as beneficiaries have become more aware of their entitlements, and a strong state-citizen interface has developed.

Despite the NREGA provisions on social audits, few Indian states have adopted Andhra Pradesh's approach. When audits are conducted, various factors undermine

(continued next page)

BOX 2.3 (continued)

their usefulness. A recent report from Bihar identifies several of these factors. The cross-checking of information is difficult due to low human and technical capacity. Monitoring and information systems do not function effectively, and social auditors must rely on incomplete and unreliable paper records. These audits are also conducted with minimal involvement of beneficiaries, as there is a lack of public awareness about the program and its entitlements. Village meetings are not widely advertised, and most beneficiaries do not know how village projects and work sites are selected. Social audits tend to be stand-alone or short-term exercises conducted by CSOs. Grievance redress processes, which are an integral element of social audits, are also underdeveloped.

Sources: Dutta et al. 2014; Srinivasan and Park 2013.

RCTs cannot capture the variations in SA interventions, an inherent feature of SA implementation. Even the most highly skilled SA practitioners adjust the approaches they take to local contexts. The presentation of an SA intervention to a community must also be adjusted to match the capacity and knowledge of the implementing organization and its staff.[3]

To measure the impact of social accountability accurately, it is important to determine how individual perceptions, decisions, and actions translate into *collective* decisions, actions, and outcomes, something quantitative evaluations fail to explain fully. An SA evaluation needs to pay attention to issues involving trust (toward community members and government) or actions promoting collective action (for example, collective decision making and participation in public actions). In contrast, most quantitative evaluation tools measure the level of change in individual actions and perceptions (for example, household surveys and behavioral games),[4] resulting in a mismatch between levels of analysis.

The use of RCTs can make their limitations more evident. Their short duration can lead to findings that are incomplete or misleading, limiting the ability to measure impact beyond procedural changes and possibly labeling outcomes as "successful" that are neither durable nor sustainable. Focusing on short, time-bounded interventions can obscure changes that are slower to emerge. This short-term focus can also exaggerate the importance of "induced" accountability (interventions by the state or by donors) as opposed to the organic movements or spaces that would appear to be far more promising in terms of results and sustainability.

Even in successful cases, it would be useful to follow up over time, as doing so could potentially reveal the limitations of specific approaches. For instance, the Sierra Leone case study (chapter 7) demonstrates how mistaken the focus on local interventions can be without a strategy for engaging higher-ranking officials, particularly when their cooperation is needed to remove binding constraints. The same study highlights the uncertain sustainability of short-lived, externally funded projects or interventions. In another example, in a Kenyan intervention that trained parents to monitor and evaluate their children's teachers, the researchers found that one year after the end of the intervention, its positive effect on learning outcomes had worn off (Duflo, Dupas, and Kremer 2007).

In some cases, the knowledge that RCTs will be conducted has the effect of making the methodology take precedence over the problem to be addressed, both in design and in implementation of SA interventions.

- In the *design process*, the causal chain for most RCTs in SA appears to start with information, partly because this factor can be isolated most easily. Nevertheless, SA activities are not necessarily started by an information intervention.
- In *implementation*, the need to ensure a large sample size can create pressure to scale up interventions prematurely (where piloting would be preferable), at the same time driving up costs. In addition, implementers may be unable to adjust in real time to early findings, for fear of "contaminating the treatment."[5] RCTs, being highly technical, can make the process alienating for the people who implement the activities and need to understand the outcomes, with possibly damaging results for their work (Hall, Menzies, and Woolcock 2014).

In a welcome development, many SA evaluations have begun to correct for the limitations of standard evaluation tools such as RCTs. The introduction of additional methods and approaches, albeit to varying degrees, is making evaluations richer, more tractable, and more informative. See box 2.4 for an example.

These new mixed-method evaluations, using both qualitative and quantitative data collection instruments, can study complex inputs (not only information) and allow for greater contextual embeddedness. They can register complex impacts on collective action, power imbalances, and the like (King, Rawlings, and Ozler 1999). They can also yield a better

BOX 2.4

**Using Mixed Methods to Understand Social Accountability Better:
The T4D Initiative**

At present, the evidence of successful interventions does not illustrate adequately why they succeeded, how contextual elements contributed to their success, or whether poor communities were truly empowered.

A project at Harvard University's Kennedy School of Government (Transparency for Development or T4D) is examining these issues using an innovative mixed-method evaluation approach. The project is working with two capable, locally embedded CSOs in Tanzania and Indonesia to assess whether carefully designed transparency and accountability interventions can improve health outcomes and, if so, under what conditions. In a first phase, using both quantitative and qualitative methods (RCTs, direct observation, focus groups, interviews, and ethnographic data), the study is investigating not only the results of the intervention on the quality of service delivery and individual health outcomes, but also the reasons why the interventions trigger—or fail to trigger—improvements in health care as well as changes in power dynamics and community relations.

A second phase, dependent on the outcomes of the first, will then be designed. It will trace the intervention as demonstrated through the quantitative data. If the intervention is successful, then a scale-up may be possible, with similar but simplified interventions designed and implemented in other locations. If the intervention's success is deemed more dependent on context, however, then the second phase will focus on context and the effect that the intervention has on in the quality of services in this particular context. If there is no effect on health outcomes, then the study will try to determine why the intervention failed and propose a new, improved intervention that will be evaluated with an RCT.

The T4D initiative suggests that it is wise to think like an evaluator when building a theory of change for an SA intervention and like a practitioner when working in a context that calls for adaptation. This translates into (a) clearly defining expected impact, (b) articulating the steps needed to open the black box—understanding the points between action and ultimate impact, (c) building the role of context more explicitly into evaluation and learning, and (d) recognizing that there is no linear theory of change given the messy reality familiar to practitioners.

Sources: Panel notes from Courtney Tolmie, Senior Program Director, Results for Development Institute presented at Global Partnership for Accountability Global Partners Forum, May 2014, and Results for Development website (http://t4dproject.org/).

understanding of change paths, producing clearer insights into the road-blocks as well as the dynamics of positive change achieved through particular mechanisms (Pandey, Goyal, and Sundararaman 2009). Finally, mixed-method evaluations offer deeper insights into the nature of interactions among various actors (Gertler, Patrinos, and Rubio-Codina 2007). All of these advantages suggest how activities should be designed and tweaked for different contexts or at different moments in time. Annex C provides an overview of alternatives or complements to quasi-experimental program evaluation that are now being promoted in the field.

The increasing use of mixed-method evaluations is a welcome development, provided that their use is as rigorous as that of RCTs, which is not always the case. In fact, there are few rigorous comparative mixed-method studies, because they are less prioritized, more time intensive, complex, and subject to intense debates on the advantages of various qualitative methods.

Unfortunately, carrying out mixed-method evaluations can be problematic: nonexperimental methods are usually not applied with the rigor and care expected of RCTs.[6] Often they are not integrated consistently into the strategy to achieve the evaluation's objectives. In many cases, qualitative methods such as focus groups and in-depth interviews are introduced only when a need arises to explain findings that are counterintuitive or contradict the guiding hypotheses. Efforts to collect qualitative data on a large scale are not always followed by commensurate use and analysis of these data. Too often the findings of any one method are not used strategically to leverage another method.

Most mixed-method evaluations allude to contexts, but without professional standards for demonstrating contextual understanding. These allusions can be highly inconsistent in their relevance and rigor. Although many project materials contain or refer to substantial background information, the wealth of information and knowledge in these background reports is largely lost for public discussion since the qualitative part of these studies is rarely published.

Some Overall Findings

Although the evidence lacks consistency, a few points are worth highlighting. As the rest of the report shows, identifying clear preconditions for SA to work is not possible to date, in light of the complexity of the interactions between contextual factors and SA and the diversity and complex trajectories of SA approaches. But some overall findings can frame the analysis of SA.

SA entails risks and trade-offs. When and how to support SA processes need to be assessed with this in mind, especially when the support is externally funded. SA processes do not automatically lead to positive outcomes. Numerous studies show the risks of instrumentalization or perversion of SA processes, leading to elite capture, tokenistic participation, apathy or disappointment, and even disengagement and retribution (see chapter 1; Mansuri and Rao 2013).

The trade-offs are difficult to assess, but they should always entail a cost-benefit analysis of the engagement from the citizen's perspective. There are many examples of SA accountability processes leading to exit or self-provision, not to stronger accountability. The availability of exit options acts as a particularly strong deterrent to collective action, compared to the risk and transaction costs of exacting accountability. In Andrabi, Das, and Khwaja (2009), parents in Pakistan moved their children from public to private schools after a report card intervention, rather than investing in any kind of collective action or interacting with public providers or state representatives. From the users' perspective, SA mechanisms can be overwhelming:

> Today you ask us why we don't get teachers to come. The NGO [nongovernmental organization] says that we should file an RTI [right to information], meet the district officer, hold up traffic, and force the teachers to come. We have to do this for the schools, for the electricity, for the doctors, for the roads, for the garbage, and for anything at all. You tell me—when should I work in my fields? (interview transcripts from Andrabi, Das, and Khwaja 2009, quoted in Amelina and Bishwakarma 2013)

The opportunity costs that accountability exacts may be prohibitively high, especially for the poor. In circumstances where there is a strong likelihood of reprisals, engaging in accountability efforts is unlikely.

The costs and benefits of state engagement should be weighed. Two elements are worth highlighting here: the presence of unearned revenues and competition. First, "unearned" revenues seem to have a negative impact on the accountability of governments to their citizens. Governments that do not obtain revenues through taxation might be less inclined to give account, because the fundamental relationship between citizens and the state that taxation entails is absent. The resource curse—the wealth generated from natural resources—undermines the accountability of the state to its citizens (Barma et al. 2012; Collier 2009). Aid flows can also shift the accountability away from citizens and toward international donors. Second, governments are more likely to be responsive to the concerns of their citizens when there is competition in the form of political rivals, independent and diversified media, decentralization, or elite competition (Besley and Burgess 2002; Hobolt and Klemmensen 2008). Although by no means a consistently reliable factor for predicting SA effectiveness, the lack of competition is often correlated with poor or no outcomes.

SA is more likely to be effective where it builds on existing "organic" pressures for change and accountability, even where this represents only a "second-best" approach. Discrete, donor-dependent SA interventions may bring about localized changes, but may not be sustainable. Evidence finds that embedding SA interventions and principles in institutions, country systems, and all stages of the policy cycle works better (Gaventa 2008). Building on what already exists is a more effective approach, which means, among other things, (a) actively seeking out and supporting, or at least not undermining, existing pressures for improved accountability and development outcomes, however incremental they may be; (b) supporting the most authoritative and credible forms of civil-political society in the context, which tends toward the more "downwardly accountable" sources of popular agency and often extends beyond professional NGOs to trade unions, political parties, social movements, or grassroots associations; and, more fundamentally, (c) understanding the context-specific "social contract" and supporting SA accordingly, at least through a policy of "doing no harm," especially as the basis for SA claims. Where the contract is strong around a particular set of goods or services, donors might strengthen SA claims; where it is weak, the donors' role is probably somewhat more limited and incremental. This message, more broadly, underpins calls to move from operationalizing SA as a project or discrete intervention and more as part of a process of social and political institutionalization (O'Meally 2013). This is a far cry from applying SA tools across the board through external support and hoping that it will change complex power relations.

Fox's recent review of the evidence indeed points to the difference between tactical and strategic SA approaches (Fox 2014). Although some interventions have proven successful in a short time frame (see box 2.5), there are limits to exclusively localized, information-led demand-side interventions (also known as tactical approaches). In contrast, strategic approaches to SA, which combine information access with enabling

BOX 2.5

Impact of Social Accountability on Health Outcomes in Uganda

In an interesting experiment relating to community-based monitoring of health services in Uganda, Björkman and Svensson (2009), relying on the three levers (information, interface, and civic mobilization), document a significant impact on health outcomes.

The intervention made use of a hybrid methodology with elements of a citizen report card and a community scorecard. The intervention comprised three steps.

Information. Based on the findings from a household survey and surveys with health care providers, each treatment facility and its community was provided with a unique citizen report card with baseline information on the delivery of health services relative to that of other providers and government standards. This allowed the facility and the community to correct information asymmetry with "true" (not perceived) data on services and to support citizens' agency by providing information on rights and entitlements. The information thus compiled both citizen and state information.

Civic mobilization. Local NGOs facilitated village and staff meetings, where members of the community discussed the findings. In separate meetings with health care workers, the facilitators compared the information furnished by health care providers with the findings from the household survey. Community members were encouraged to develop a plan to identify key problems and the steps that providers should take to improve services and to suggest ways the community could monitor progress.

Interface. A joint interface meeting with members of the community and health care workers followed. The outcome was a shared action plan, or contract, outlining what the community and health care workers agreed needed to be done, how, when, and by whom. This community contract also identified means to enable the community to monitor compliance with the agreement and set deadlines.

The project was carried out in 50 communities in nine districts comprising approximately 55,000 households. The intervention was carried out within a short time frame (12 months). A subsequent study documents significant increases in the use of health services and improved health outcomes—reduced child mortality and increased child weight—as well as increased engagement of the community in monitoring health care providers and greater responsiveness by health care workers. The authors acknowledge that long-term effects remain unknown.

Björkman and Svensson (2010) also document another important finding relating to a particular contextual characteristic. In this case, social heterogeneity, and specifically, ethnic fractionalization influenced collective action. In heterogeneous communities, the intervention resulted in a smaller increase in the quantity of primary health care provision.

environments for collective action, can scale up and coordinate with government reforms to encourage actual public sector responsiveness to voice.

Guidance to practitioners on the complex relationships between SA and context is one element that can support stronger choices on whether and how to engage. The following chapters put the existing evidence in a new light, focusing on the contextual drivers of SA to promote a clearer understanding of SA and its outcomes. Chapter 3 considers how broad political and social contextual conditions affect SA design and outcomes. Chapter 4 presents a framework for better understanding the contextual factors for SA effectiveness by aggregating intervention-based factors with broad sociopolitical elements.

Box 2.6 summarizes the key takeaways from this chapter.

BOX 2.6

Key Takeaways: The Evidence on Social Accountability

- While the evidence on SA is growing, the data on various interventions in different contexts are fragmented, and this puzzling body of evidence invites partisan interpretations. Consequently, simply asking, Does SA work or not? is tempting, but not helpful without sufficiently addressing evidence on the multidimensionality of SA interactions, the encompassing role of context, and the difficulty in trying to assess the impact of the more complex potential outcomes of SA processes.

- Indeed, the range of potential outcomes is wide: from benefits to the *state* (better governance), in *state-society relationships* (increased legitimacy), or in *society* (improved provision of public goods) and including both *instrumental* (improved provision of public goods) and *institutional* (state-building) benefits (see table B2.6.1).

- Perspectives on whether SA "works" or not are determined in part by the value attributed to its outcomes, including its intrinsic value. Impact evaluations have been commissioned principally in connection with SA's more measurable impacts on service delivery.

- Biases in methodological choices and implementation of SA impact evaluations can stem from how decisions are made with regard to three challenges: (1) defining the nature of the SA outcome to be evaluated, (2) isolating attribution within complex processes involving multiple actors and strategies, and (3) determining the time

(continued next page)

BOX 2.6 *(continued)*

horizon covered. The preferred choice of experimental and quasi-experimental methods, especially RCTs, can have distinct advantages in specific cases, but they shed little light on change mechanisms or trajectories that can often be critical in understanding the success or failure of SA mechanisms.

- Specifically, the existing evidence offers three lessons: (a) to understand why interventions have the impacts they do, context matters, (b) the range of impacts needs to be enlarged, and impacts must be traced systematically, and (c) closer attention needs to be paid to the mechanisms through which SA initiatives are expected to have an impact.
- SA entails risks and trade-offs. The costs and benefits from the perspectives of both citizens and the state need to be included in the design and evaluations of SA interventions. Designs and evaluations need to take into account deterrent factors such as "unearned" revenues or competition and exit options.

Table B2.6.1 Expanded Impact of Social Accountability

	States ⟷	State-society relationships ⟷	Social actors
Instrumental ↑ ↓ Institutional	• Reduced corruption • Responsive public officials • Better policy design • Good governance	• Institutional channels for interaction • Trust • Legitimacy • State building • Democratic deepening	• Improved provision of public goods • Empowered citizens • Social cohesion • Inclusive social norms

Notes

1. This chapter draws on Joshi's background paper for this report (Joshi 2014) and, for the section on methodology, Amelina's background paper for this report (Amelina and Bishwakarma 2013).
2. O'Neill, Foresti, and Hudson (2007). Narayan (2002) identifies accountability as one of four key elements in empowerment for institutional reform. The other three are access to information, inclusion, and local organizational capacity.

O'Neill, Foresti, and Hudson (2007) draw on various studies that treat citizen empowerment as a prerequisite for demanding accountability.

3. This is a major difference with the use of RCTs in the medical field, where, in most cases, the problem of intervention variation does not arise.

4. Household-level surveys measure changes in attitudes of an individual or household, and collective manifestations of these measures are inferred from these individual statements and assessments. Behavioral games can assist with direct observation of collective dynamics, but these observations are made in highly stylized formats. The ability to model the rich social context in which social decision making rests has not been demonstrated. In their current form, behavioral games may lead to simplistic scenarios and misleading conclusions.

5. Findings from Justice for the Poor program in Sierra Leone and interviews with CSO practitioners in TA Learn conference, March 2014.

6. These statements draw on Amelina and Bishwakarma (2013), which reviewed select SA impact evaluations and followed up by interviewing some of the authors.

References

Agarwal, S., R. Heltberg, and M. Diachok. 2009. "Scaling-up Social Accountability in World Bank Operations." World Bank, Washington, DC.

Aiyar, Y., and M. Walton. 2014. "Rights, Accountability, and Citizenship: Examining India's Emerging Welfare State." Accountability Initiative Working Paper, New Delhi, October.

Amelina, M., and R. Bishwakarma. 2013. "How Can We Measure Social Accountability Better? Stocktaking and Issues Paper." Background paper prepared for this book, World Bank, Social Development Department, Washington, DC.

Andrabi, T., J. Das, and A. I. Khwaja. 2009. "Report Cards: The Impact of Providing School and Child Test-Scores on Educational Markets." Unpublished mss., Harvard University, Department of Economics, Cambridge, MA. http://www.hks.harvard.edu/fs/akhwaja/papers/RC_08Oct09Full.pdf.

Banerjee, A. V., R. Banerji, E. Duflo, R. Glennerster, and S. Khemani. 2010. "Pitfalls of Participatory Programs: Evidence from a Randomized Evaluation in Education in India." *American Economic Journal: Economic Policy* 2 (1): 1–30.

Barma, N. H., K. Kaiser, T. M. Le, and L. Viñuela. 2012. *Rents to Riches? The Political Economy of Natural Resource–Led Development*. Washington, DC: World Bank.

Besley, T., and R. Burgess. 2002. "The Political Economy of Government Responsiveness: Theory and Evidence from India." *Quarterly Journal of Economics* 117 (4): 1415–51. http://qje.oxfordjournals.org/content/117/4/1415.full.pdf.

Björkman, M., and J. Svensson. 2009. "Power to the People: Evidence from a Randomized Field Experiment of a Community-Based Monitoring Project in Uganda." *American Economic Review* 124 (2): 735–69.

———. 2010. "When Is Community-Based Monitoring Effective? Evidence from a Randomized Experiment in Primary Health in Uganda." *Journal of the European Economic Association* 8 (2–3): 571–81.

Boeckmann, S. 2012. "Social Accountability in Fragile States: A Review of the Literature." Unpublished mss., World Bank, Social Accountability and Demand for Good Governance Group, Washington, DC.

Boulding, C., and B. Wampler. 2010. "Voice, Votes, and Resources: Evaluating the Effect of Participatory Democracy on Well-Being." *World Development* 38 (1): 125–35.

Brinkerhoff, D. W., A. Wetterberg, and S. Dunn. 2012. "Service Delivery and Legitimacy in Fragile and Conflict-Affected States: Evidence from Water Services in Iraq." *Public Management Review* 14 (2): 273–93.

Caseley, J. 2003. "Blocked Drains and Open Minds: Multiple Accountability Relationships and Improved Service Delivery Performance in an Indian City." IDS Working Paper 21, University of Sussex, Institute of Development Studies, Brighton, U.K.

Clark, D., J. Fox, and K. Treakle, eds. 2003. *Demanding Accountability: Civil Society Claims and the World Bank Inspection Panel.* Lanham, MD: Rowman and Littlefield.

Collier, P. 2009. *The Political Economy of Fragile States and Implications for European Development Policy.* Oxford, U.K.: Oxford University Press.

de Renzio, P., M. Andrews, and Z. Mills. 2011. "Does Donor Support to Public Financial Management Reforms in Developing Countries Work? An Analytical Study of Quantitative Cross-Country Evidence." ODI Working Paper 329, Overseas Development Institute, London.

Duflo, E., P. Dupas, and M. Kremer. 2007. "Peer Effects, Pupil-Teacher Ratios, and Teacher Incentives: Evidence from a Randomized Evaluation in Kenya." Massachusetts Institute of Technology, Poverty Action Lab, Cambridge, MA.

Duflo, E., R. Hanna, and S. Ryan. 2008. *Incentives Work: Getting Teachers to Come to School.* Cambridge, MA: Abdul Latif Jameel Professor of Poverty Alleviation and Development.

———. 2012. "Incentives Work: Getting Teachers to Come to School." *American Economic Review* 102 (4): 1241–78.

Dutta, P., R. Murgai, M. Ravallion, and D. van de Walle. 2014. *Right to Work? Assessing India's Employment Guarantee Scheme in Bihar.* Equity and Development Series. Washington, DC: World Bank.

Fox, J. 2014. "Social Accountability: What Does the Evidence Really Say?" Global Partnership for Social Accountability Working Paper 1, World Bank, Washington, DC, July.

Gauthier, B. 2006. "PETS-QSDS in Sub-Saharan Africa: A Stocktaking Study." HEC Montreal, Montreal; World Bank, Washington, DC.

Gaventa, J. 2008. "Building Responsive States: Citizen Action and National Policy Change." IDS Research Summary, University of Sussex, Institute of Development Studies, Brighton, U.K. http://www.ids.ac.uk/files/InFocus5.pdf.

Gaventa, J., and G. Barrett. 2010. "So What Difference Does It Make? Mapping the Outcomes of Citizen Engagement." IDS Working Paper 347, University of Sussex, Institute of Development Studies, Brighton, U.K. http://www.gsdrc .org/go/display&type=Document&id=3981&source=rss.

Gaventa, J., and R. McGee. 2013. "The Impact of Transparency and Accountability Initiatives." *Development Policy Review* 31 (11): s3–s28.

Gertler, P., H. Patrinos, and M. Rubio-Codina. 2007. "Empowering Parents to Improve Education: Evidence from Rural Mexico." Impact Evaluation 4, World Bank, Washington, DC. http://www-wds.worldbank.org/servlet /WDSContentServer/WDSP/IB/2008/05/21/000158349_20080521103145 /Rendered/PDF/wps3935.pdf.

Goldfrank, B. 2006. "Lessons from Latin American Experiences in Participatory Budgeting." Presentation at the Latin American Studies Association meeting, San Juan, Puerto Rico, March.

Gonçalves, S. 2009. *Power to the People: The Effects of Participatory Budgeting on Municipal Expenditures and Infant Mortality in Brazil.* London: London School of Economics.

———. 2013. "The Effects of Participatory Budgeting on Municipal Expenditures and Infant Mortality in Brazil." *World Development* 53 (4): 94–110.

Goodwin, L., and V. Maru. 2014. "What Do We Know about Legal Empowerment? Mapping the Evidence." Working paper, Namati, Washington, DC.

Guijt, I., ed. 2007. "Negotiated Learning: Collaborative Monitoring for Forest Resource Management." Resources for the Future, Washington, DC.

Hall, M., with N. Menzies and M. Woolcock. 2014. "From HIPPOs to 'Best Fit' in Justice Reform: Experimentalism in Sierra Leone." In *The International Rule of Law Movement: A Crisis of Legitimacy and the Way Forward.* Cambridge, MA: Harvard University Press.

Hobolt, S. B., and R. Klemmensen. 2008. "Government Responsiveness and Political Competition in Comparative Perspective." *Comparative Political Studies* 41 (3): 309–37. http://personal.lse.ac.uk/HOBOLT/Publications/CPS _eprint_final.pdf.

Hubbard, P. 2007. "Putting the Power of Transparency in Context: Information's Role in Reducing Corruption in Uganda's Education Sector." Working Paper 136, Center for Global Development, Washington, DC. http://www.cgdev.org /content/publications/detail/15050/.

Ibrahim, S., and S. Alkire. 2007. "Agency and Empowerment: A Proposal for Internationally Comparable Indicators." OPHI Working Paper ophiwp005,

University of Oxford, Oxford Poverty and Human Development Initiative, Oxford, U.K.

International Budget Partnership. 2010. *From Analysis to Impact: South Africa, Civil Society Uses Budget Analysis and Advocacy to Improve the Lives of Poor Children.* Partnership Initiative Case Study. Washington, DC: International Budget Partnership.

Joshi, A. 2014. "On Social Accountability, an Issues Paper." Background paper for this book, Institute of Development Studies, London.

Joshi, A., and P. Houtzager. 2012. "Widgets or Watchdogs? Conceptual Explorations in Social Accountability." *Public Management Review, Special Issue: The Politics and Governance of Public Services in Developing Countries* 14 (2): 145–62.

J-PAL. 2012. "Routes to Reduced Corruption." Policy Briefcase, Abdul Latif Jameel Poverty Action Lab, Cambridge MA.

King, E., L. Rawlings, and B. Ozler. 1999. "Nicaragua's School Autonomy Reform: Fact or Fiction?" Impact Evaluation of Education Reforms Working Paper 19, World Bank, Washington, DC.

Lodenstein, E., M. Dieleman, B. Gerretsen, and J. E. Broerse. 2013. "A Realist Synthesis of the Effect of Social Accountability Interventions on Health Service Providers' and Policy Makers' Responsiveness." *Systematic Reviews* 2 (1): 98.

Lynch, U., S. McGrellis, M. Dutschke, M. Anderson, P. Arnsberger, and G. Macdonald. 2013. "What Is the Evidence That the Establishment or Use of Community Accountability Mechanisms and Processes Improves Inclusive Service Delivery by Governments, Donors, and NGOs to Communities?" University of London, Institute of Education, Social Science Research Unit, EPPI Centre, London.

Mansuri, G., and V. Rao. 2013. *Localizing Development: Does Participation Work?* Policy Research Report. Washington, DC: World Bank.

McGee, R., and J. Gaventa. 2010. "Review of Impact and Effectiveness of Transparency and Accountability Initiatives." Synthesis Report prepared for the Transparency and Accountability Initiative Workshop, Institute of Development Studies, Brighton, U.K., October 14–15. http://www.ids.ac.uk/files/dmfile /IETASynthesisReportMcGeeGaventaFinal28Oct2010.pdf.

———. 2011. "Shifting Power? Assessing the Impact of Transparency and Accountability Initiatives." IDS Working Paper 383, University of Sussex, Institute of Development Studies, Brighton, U.K. http://www.ids.ac.uk/files /dmfile/Wp383.pdf.

Molina, E., A. Pacheco, L. Gasparini, G. Cruces, and A. Rius. 2013. "Community Monitoring Interventions to Curb Corruption and Increase Access to Quality in Service Delivery in Low- and Middle-income Countries: A Systematic Review." Campbell Collaboration, Oslo.

Narayan, D. 2002. *Empowerment and Poverty Reduction: A Sourcebook.* Washington, DC: World Bank.

Nguyen, T., and G. Lassibille. 2008. "Improving Management in Education: Evidence from a Randomized Experiment in Madagascar." MIT Working Paper, Massachusetts Institute of Technology, Cambridge, MA.

Olken, B. A. 2007. "Monitoring Corruption: Evidence from a Field Experiement in Indonesia." *Journal of Political Economy* 115 (2): 200–49.

———. 2009. "Corruption Perceptions vs. Corruption Reality." *Journal of Public Economics* 93 (7–8): 50–64.

O'Meally, S. 2013. "Mapping Context for Social Accountability: A Resource Paper." Background for this book, World Bank, Social Development Department, Washington, DC.

O'Neil, T., M. Foresti, and A. Hudson. 2007. *Evaluation of Citizens' V&A: Review of the Literature and Donor Approaches*. London: Department for International Development.

Pandey, P., S. Goyal, and V. Sundararaman. 2009. "Community Participation in Public Schools: Impact of Information Campaigns in Three Indian States." *Education Economics* 17 (3): 355–75.

Paul, S. 2002. *Holding the State to Account: Citizen Monitoring in Action*. Bangalore: Books for Change.

Pradhan, M., D. Suryadarma, A. Beatty, M. Wong, A. Gaduh, and R. P. Artha. 2011. "Improving Educational Quality through Enhancing Community Participation: Results from a Randomised Field Experiment in Indonesia." Policy Research Working Paper 5795, World Bank, Human Development Sector Department, East Asia and Pacific Region, Washington, DC.

Rainbow Insight. 2009. "Evaluating the EITI's Impact on the Transaprency of Natural Resource Revenues." Rainbow Insight, Geneva. http://eiti.org/files /Rainbow%20Insight%20Report.pdf.

Ravindra, A. 2004. *An Assessment of the Impact of Bangalore Citizen Report Cards on the Performance of Public Agencies*. Washington, DC: World Bank.

Rayan, D. 2002. *Empowerment and Poverty Reduction: A Sourcebook*. Washington, DC: World Bank, June.

Reinikka, R., and J. Svensson. 2005. "Fighting Corruption to Improve Schooling: Evidence from a Newspaper Campaign in Uganda." *Journal of the European Economic Association* 3 (2–3): 259–67.

Rocha Menocal, A., and B. Sharma. 2008. *Joint Evaluation of Citizens' Voice and Accountability: Synthesis Report*. London: Department for International Development. http://www.odi.org.uk/sites/odi.org.uk/files/odi-assets/publications -opinion-files/3425.pdf.

Rosser, A., and A. Joshi. 2012. "From User Fees to Fee Free: The Politics of Realising Universal Free Basic Education in Indonesia." *Journal of Development Studies* 49 (2): 175–89.

Schneider, A., and B. Goldfrank. 2002. *Budgets and Ballots in Brazil: Participatory Budgeting from the City to State*. IDS Working Paper 149, University of Sussex, Institute of Development Studies, Brighton, U.K.

Singh, R., and V. Vutukuru. 2010. *Enhancing Accountability in Public Service Delivery through Social Audits: A Case Study of Andhra Pradesh.* New Delhi: Center for Public Research.

Srinivasan, S., and S. Park. 2013. "Conducting Social Audits to Monitor Social Service Delivery: A Guidance Note." Draft Paper, World Bank, Human Development Chief Economist Office, Washington, DC, October.

Sundet, G. 2008. *Following the Money: Do Public Expenditure Tracking Surveys Matter?* Bergen: Anti-Corruption Resource Centre.

Touchton, M., and B. Wampler. 2013. "Improving Social Well-Being through New Democratic Institutions." *Comparative Political Studies [Sage Journal],* December 27. doi: 10.1177/0010414013512601.

Westhorp, G., W. Walker, N. Overbeeke, P. Rogers, G. Brice, and D. Ball. 2013. *Community Accountability, Empowerment, and Education Outcomes in Low- and Middle-Income Countries: A Realist Review.* Systematic Review. London: University of London, Institute of Education, Social Science Research Unit, EPPI Centre.

Woolcock, M. 2009. "Towards a Plurality of Methods in Project Evaluation: A Contextualised Approach to Understanding Impact Trajectories and Efficacy." BWPI Working Paper 7309, Brooks World Poverty Institute, University of Manchester, Manchester, U.K.

World Bank. 2008. *Brazil: Toward a More Inclusive and Effective Participatory Budget in Porto Alegre.* Vol. 1: *Main Report.* Washington, DC: World Bank Group.

———. 2011. *World Development Report 2011: Conflict, Security, and Development.* New York: Oxford University Press.

Zamboni, Y. 2007. "Participatory Budgeting and Local Governance: An Evidence-Based Evaluation of Participatory Budgeting in Brazil." Working Paper, University of Bristol, Bristol, U.K.

CHAPTER 3

Social Accountability and a Country's Social and Political Characteristics

This chapter reviews the evidence pertaining to the broad contextual elements that bear on the form and effectiveness of social accountability (SA).[1] The evidence is structured along the two institutional spheres of political and civil society and their interactions (state-society and intra-society). These spheres are distinguished for clarity of analysis, but they are not exclusive of each other (chapters 5 and 6 delve more deeply into the interactions between these spheres). Three additional factors cut across these spheres and need special attention: cultural norms, global factors, and the political settlement that, in any state context, can determine key characteristics of political society as well as the nature of state-society relations. These relationships are presented in figure 3.1.

Three major findings emerge from reviewing the broad contextual determinants of SA effectiveness.

First, political and power relations are at the forefront of understanding and operationalizing SA. The findings point to the critical importance of power and political relationships in shaping SA processes and outcomes, challenging the tendency to promote SA as a "technical" process that operates in and through formal institutional frameworks. The evidence suggests that civil society (CS) is not immune to power relations: CS actors may have incentives to maintain, as well as challenge, accountability failures; and civil society organizations (CSOs) may find very little room to maneuver given the broader politics of patronage and exclusion (Citizenship DRC 2011; Evans 2010; Gurza Lavalle, Houtzager, and Acharya 2005).

Second, links and networks have to be built between pro-accountability state and society actors.[2] Much attention has been focused on

Figure 3.1 Main "Macro" Contextual Factors for Social Accountability Effectiveness

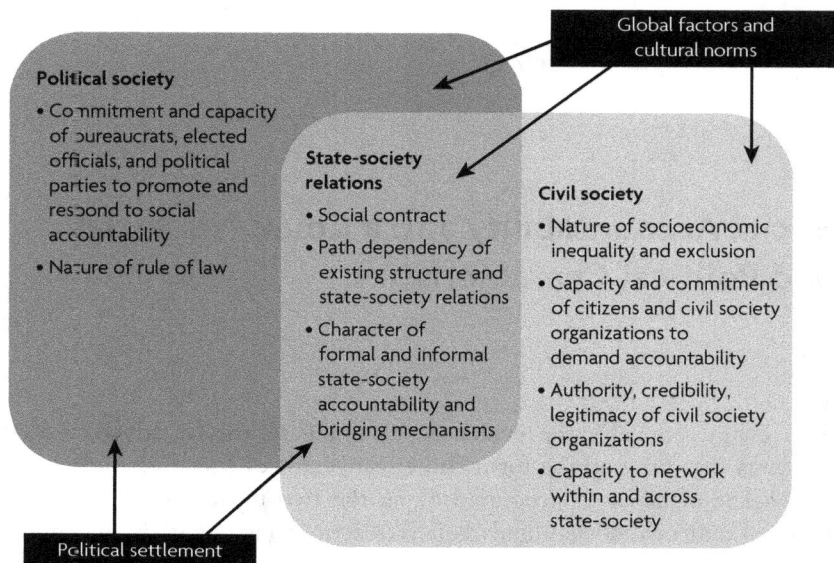

individual actors from the "state" or "citizenry," such as CS strengthening. However, what seem to be particularly important are the relations and interactions between the different actors and the incentives that flow from these relations. The findings urge us to go beyond the supply-demand, principal-agent, and state-citizen dichotomies and instead to understand the more progressive and regressive coalitions that cut across state and citizenry, which are rarely homogeneous entities. In Booth's view, "Governance challenges are not fundamentally about one set of people getting another set of people to behave better. They are about both sets of people finding ways of being able to act collectively in their own best interests" (Booth 2012a). On the one hand, he cautions against supply-side, principal-agent approaches that tend to assume that there is political commitment to reform and that the problem is mainly about compliance and information asymmetry down the chain of command and, on the other, against the demand-side, principal-agent logic, which treats citizens, voters, or service users as (homogeneous) "principals," seeking to get compliance from politicians and civil servants (Booth 2012b).

Third, a sharper focus is needed on the dynamics of inequality and exclusion. Poverty, inequality, and exclusionary dynamics shape the extent to which many citizens can engage effectively in or benefit from SA claims. This implies the need to put inequality-mitigating measures at the center of all SA thinking and implementation, rather than addressing these issues in a piecemeal or ad hoc manner or assuming that by doing an SA intervention these needs are automatically addressed. Furthermore, it may also be useful to focus not only on inclusion in processes, but also on outcomes, which would entail giving more attention to services that are naturally nonrivals.[3]

Actors and Dynamics in Political Society: Important Factors in Explaining the Form and Effectiveness of SA

Political society is broadly understood as the arena within which people perceive and encounter the state on an everyday basis and that creates and maintains different patterns of political rule. It is the "place where public demands get tackled by specific political institutions" (Hyden and Court 2003, 18).

It is constituted by a loose community of recognized elected politicians, political parties, local political brokers, councilors, and public servants, and it forms a set of institutions, actors, and cultural norms that provide the links between the government and the public.

What we currently know suggests that the nature of the state—the actors and dynamics of the political society that govern and interact with state institutions—are as important as, if not more important than, civil society in explaining the form and effectiveness of SA. Some key issues are evident.

First, the commitment of key actors, both bureaucrats and elected officials, is critical not only to promote SA, but also to respond to SA demands. This commitment includes the commitment to "answer" accountability demands as well as the commitment and willingness to stimulate such demand by pushing for accountability reforms and even stimulating social actors to mobilize to make demands on government (Houtzager and Joshi 2008). In this regard, influential elected officials play a critical role, because they are more susceptible to popular pressure and in a position to shape the behavior of public officials and service providers through sanctions and other forms of supply-led accountability (Bukenya, Hickey, and King 2012). This is significant and points to the need to think about ways of linking social accountability interventions with forms of political accountability, particularly through making links to supply-led enforcement mechanisms and involving elected officials in the design of demand-led initiatives. Conversely, some circumstances might lower the need to engage on accountability, among them the importance of "unearned revenues" (for example, natural resources or international aid; see the section on global factors).

It is therefore important for SA practitioners to understand the level and drivers of political will within a given context and to act accordingly. This also entails understanding the terms of the existing political settlement (see box 3.1) and the incentives that this places before the elites to act in favor of certain interests over others—that is, the interests of those groups that

---

BOX 3.1

Political Settlement and Social Accountability

Political settlement can be defined as a combination of institutions and a distribution of power between organizations (for example, political parties, military, and bureaucracy) that is reproducible over time. Once a particular political settlement emerges, the relative power of different organizations is relatively stable and evolves along predictable paths (Khan 2010).

Social accountability approaches operate within a specific political settlement. The developmental character of the settlement is important—that is, the extent to which its legitimacy and stability are based on furthering broad-based development, along with some degree of redistribution and social development. It is closely related to the level of elite predation. As Devarajan, Khemani, and Walton (2011) note,

If politicians, and especially leaders, do not have the incentives to deliver on development, putting extra pressure on bureaucratic state agencies is likely to have limited, or local, effects. When the political leadership has some commitment to development, civil society may have a role to play in how internal state mechanisms work.

Relatedly, the extent to which the settlement is "inclusive" may shape the constraints and opportunities for SA. Settlements manifest themselves in "the structure of property rights and entitlements, which gives some social actors more distributional advantages than others, and in the regulatory structure of the state" (Di John and Putzel 2009). As such, the way in which entitlements are distributed and certain groups are included or excluded in a given context will shape SA dynamics.

(continued next page)

BOX 3.1 *(continued)*

A second dimension of the settlement that is potentially relevant to SA is its capacity to manage the social and political changes underpinning development and thus the demands that SA might place on it. This relates to organizational and technical capacity, but also to political capacity. Political capacity refers to the state's ability to maintain enough stability for society to undergo change (Khan 2010, 52) and to maintain synergistic and legitimate relations with different social actors (vom Hau 2012). Where the settlement is weak or fragile, SA—if at all appropriate—may take a more modest, incremental form that links state formation with civic engagement, often at the local level. Political instability and transitions present opportunities to demand accountability.

Finally, the ideas, values, and ideologies of the ruling elite can be influential in shaping elite thinking and action on accountability issues. As noted, settlements tend to be bound together by a set of norms and by ideas of what are, or are not, legitimate forms of governance. A growing body of literature notes how elite ideas about public service and development—as well as norms and narratives of legitimacy and accountability—can shape their actions and receptiveness to SA claims (Harris, Kooy, and Jones 2011; Reis and Moore 2005).

are required to sustain a particular political settlement. The need within ruling coalitions to maintain certain types of relationships both horizontally (with other elite factions) and vertically (with organized social groupings) in order to preserve stability and survival can create strong incentives and room for maneuver to respond or not to given demands, and these may vary by sectors or over time (Bukenya, Hickey, and King 2012).

Second, capacity is seen as important for SA outcomes in a variety of ways, with the capacity to forge and maintain relations with different social actors emerging as key. The effectiveness of SA partially depends on the organizational, technical, and political capacity of the state to respond to demands. The presence of functioning state institutions is often, but not always, a key condition for accountability reforms (Mansuri and Rao 2013). But the developmental capacity of the state needs to be defined not only in terms of its organizational competence (for example, the levels of human, financial, and technical resources) but also, and perhaps more important, in terms of its capacity to forge and maintain synergistic relations with different social actors (vom Hau 2012).

Evidence does not suggest, however, that there is no role whatsoever for SA in low-capacity environments. SA might just take on a more modest form of citizenship formation, trust building, state formation, or local associational development (Gaventa and Barrett 2010). State capacity can be a valuable outcome of SA processes: capacity, especially relational capacity, is built through practice.

Third, the categorization of countries as more or less democratic, with the assumption that SA will be more effective in more democratic settings, is challenged by the evidence. This finding is also linked to the definition used to label countries as "democratic" (see Fox 2007), and transitions to accountability are distinct from transitions to democracy. Moving away from superficial criteria to focus on broader forms of state-society relations within which accountability resides (that is, the citizen-state interface in our analytical framework) and the types of political institutions that mediate the relationship between broad democratic procedures, such as elections and public policy processes, is more helpful in this case (Bukenya, Hickey, and King 2012).

Nevertheless, more democratic systems tend to have a wider range of accountability mechanisms and intra-state checks and balances that may be triggered by SA (box 3.2). They also offer the opportunity to gain more traction around accountability issues through elections (McGee and Gaventa 2011). The presence of certain legal accountability mechanisms and the extent to which they are legitimate and enforceable in a given context will shape the form and prospects of different types of SA. For example, legitimate constitutional provisions can provide a basis for making and justifying SA claims or SA can play a key role in triggering existing accountability mechanisms within the state. As McGee and Gaventa (2011) note, "In a regime lacking the essential freedoms of association, voice, or media, citizen-led TAIs [transparency and accountability initiatives] do not have the same prospects for success as in societies where these conditions exist." Highly democratic contexts tend to permit the widest range of SA approaches to emerge.

The literature suggests that the broad level of democratization only tells part of the story and that positive outcomes of civic engagement are not necessarily linked linearly to the level of democratization in a given setting (Gaventa and Barrett 2010). While the presence of formal democratic institutions and frameworks is important in many contexts, in others it is the informal institutions and the underlying political settlement that explains what happens and why (Crook and Booth 2011). Different forms

BOX 3.2

Does Social Accountability Support or Hinder Political Accountability?

SA complements political accountability (the responsiveness of government policies to the preferences of the electorate) in two ways. First, through the logic of elections and political competition, it creates incentives for elected officials in certain contexts (especially "new" democracies) to explore mechanisms for engaging with citizens outside election cycles as part of "top-down good governance drives." Second, as documented in Peruzzotti and Smulovitz (2002), social accountability movements or campaigns across Latin America demanding justice and the rule of law managed to put sufficient pressure on key politicians to change their incentive structure: doing justice, instead of covering up wrongdoing in exchange for favors, became the better strategy for advancing their political careers.

SA mechanisms can also displace structures for political accountability. By creating user committees or parallel structures to local-level councils with the intention of better engaging citizen voice in holding service providers accountable, SA may, in fact, undermine the authority of elected local leaders who were neither consulted nor invited to join these new groups and potentially displace other forms of accountability that could be considered more democratic, legitimate, and effective (Brett 2003; Cooke and Kothari 2001; Hickey and Mohan 2008). Moreover, they may have the unintended effect of strengthening existing power structures, thereby reinforcing inequality for the very reasons that democratic decentralization (Crook and Sverrisson 2001; Manor 2004) and induced participatory movements (Mansuri and Rao 2013) have been blamed for reinforcing inequalities. In such cases, the more articulate, better-educated elites within the wider local community often become the representatives of citizen voice for SA mechanisms, voicing demands not for public goods but for special interests. This dilemma does not arise when local elites work with decentralized administrations to obtain better services or greater social inclusion for their community (Yilmaz, Beris, and Serrano-Berthet 2008). When this is *not* the case, however, there may be only the illusion of deepening democracy and political accountability or simply no real change attributable to SA mechanisms (Banerjee et al. 2008).

of accountability, sometimes around a social contract, might form within semi-authoritarian environments (Stasavage 2005; Tsai 2007). Direct and participatory forms of democracy may be less relevant in explaining why SA processes achieve their objectives than other variables such as the role of political representation and political parties (Brautigam 2004). This aspect is discussed further in chapter 5.

Influence of Civil Society

> Civil society is commonly understood as the arena outside of the family, the state, and the market where people associate to advance common interests—where citizens become aware of and may raise issues to get the attention of public authorities. The term "civil society" refers to both organized and unorganized citizens acting independently from government, political parties, and for-profit organizations in order to transform society and governance. Civil society includes religious and professional organizations, labor unions, grassroots organizations, and nongovernmental organizations (NGOs), but also reaches beyond these groups to include the participation of citizens outside of formal organizations (Ackerman 2004, 2005).

In analyzing the role of CS in supporting SA, two common pitfalls must be avoided. First is an overly simplistic view that civil society is an autonomous arena that is free from the logic of how power and politics operate and that it will automatically challenge existing accountability relations. The willingness of CS to challenge existing accountability relations is shaped by a variety of factors, including its incentives, interests, past experiences with SA, and relationship with powerful actors. The literature suggests that civil society is neither homogeneous in its willingness to challenge the accountability status quo and be a force for change nor a panacea for challenging entrenched accountability problems. In some cases, strengthening CSOs has undermined more legitimate forms of accountability or bolstered existing power structures (Banks and Hulme 2012; Booth 2012b).[4] As Whitehead (2002, 77) notes, "Those with abundant social capital and the densest associative life can also use it to defend their privileges and to marginalize the less well-endowed majority."

A second pitfall is a focus on CSOs' technical and organizational capacities, as opposed to their political capabilities and ability to mobilize citizens and build alliances across society and state-society boundaries.

The former, including their capacity to manage and use information for different constituencies, does matter, but probably less than their political capabilities (box 3.3).

What emerges as a fundamental characteristic that explains the success or failure of SA demands is the extent to which CSOs are capable of exerting influence over the often-contested and politicized decision making. This capacity is determined by three interrelated elements.

- *The capacity of civil society organizations to mobilize citizens and build alliances across society.* This is closely related to the degree to which CS is fragmented or unified around an SA goal, and it highlights the key role of broad-based alliances across classes and social categories.
- *The capacity of civil society to build and link up with networks and ally with pro-reform actors within the state.* This capacity is perhaps the most critical variable in explaining the success of SA. A key issue is the nature of the political capability of CS, which includes political literacy and civic mobilization, networking, coalition building, and negotiation

---

BOX 3.3

Capacity, Willingness, and Political Maneuvering: Nijera Kori in Bangladesh

Nijera Kori, a Bangladeshi NGO, focuses on civic mobilization for rural and landless citizens. It has achieved the following:

- An increase in wages wherever Nijera Kori groups have engaged in successful collective bargaining
- A reduction in bribes paid to health officials
- An increase in more regular teacher attendance wherever its members have become school committee members.

Nijera Kori has succeeded because of two important elements. It was equipped to engage the state in sustained bargaining and simultaneously to mobilize and represent marginalized groups. It also influenced politics, educating its members about their constitutional and voting rights and encouraging them to approach their elected representatives and government officials.

Sources: Kabeer 2003, 2005.

skills in the interaction with actors from the political society. Therefore, assessing the strength of CS alone might be less useful than identifying and assessing the nature of the relationships and networks across state and society and supporting their strengthening in more progressive directions (Unsworth and Moore 2010). The capacities of CSOs to be effective in a politicized and relational realm have less to do with their autonomy than with the relationships and networks they are able to forge with actors from within this realm but also within political society (Evans 2010; Gurza Lavalle, Houtzager, and Acharya 2005). These capacities can be built up over time through successive rounds of bargaining with the state (Houtzager and Joshi 2008, 2012).

- *The authority, credibility, and legitimacy of CSOs.* SA initiatives have tended to be more successful when the lead CSOs are perceived as credible and legitimate by both the citizenry and state actors who are being mobilized. In addition, CSOs that are able to draw on popular support and be accountable to their own constituents, as opposed to being upwardly accountable to donors, seem to be more effective in achieving SA goals. This type of CS is not limited to professional NGOs—it includes other sources of popular agency, including trade unions, social movements, and religious organizations (Banks and Hulme 2012; Hickey and Bracking 2005).

The sustainable financial capacity of CSOs is very relevant to this third point. Sustainable financial capacity is a key factor contributing to and enabling SA interventions: there are interesting examples of legislation to support this. For example, in Albania, the government and CSOs concluded an agreement to facilitate resource mobilization for CSOs, and the government enacted legislation to encourage philanthropy and financial contributions to CSOs.[5] The issue of financial independence is complex: there are many examples of donor- or government-funded CSOs considered as legitimate and independent, but some of the case studies in chapter 7 provide examples of negative perceptions of donor-funded NGOs.

The legal and regulatory frameworks providing for rights such as freedom of expression, of association, and of information and their degree of implementation will have an impact on what is feasible for individuals or groups engaged in SA. Increasingly, the ecosystem for SA is part of the World Bank Group policy dialogue, and its development policy lending (DPL) supports fundamental changes in a country's accountability systems (see box 3.4).

BOX 3.4

Supporting the Ecosystem for Social Accountability with DPL Operations

In several cases, World Bank–supported development policy lending has been instrumental in supporting the ecosystem for stronger social accountability.[a] World Bank–financed DPLs have supported the enactment of right to information and freedom of access to information legislation and, in some cases, its implementation regulations (for example, Latvia, 2000; Karnataka State, 2001; India, 2004; Ghana, 2009; and Tunisia, 2011). DPLs have also supported budget transparency. Some prior actions have involved the publication and active dissemination of budgets (for example, the 2002 Oil Fund Budget in Azerbaijan and the 2003 Budget Law in Chad). Others have supported the publication of budget data (for example, the monthly online posting of disaggregated central government expenditures and subnational accounts in Ecuador and the online publication of updated month-end accounts of local bodies in rural Orissa, India), in particular, in connection with extractive industries (for example, online reports on the use of mining revenues in the Central African Republic and the management of oil resources in the Democratic Republic of Congo). Some prior actions have gone a step further, not only encouraging the regular publication of budgets, but also actively disseminating information on budgetary allocations for specific service delivery units (for example, a public information campaign to disseminate data on budgetary allocations in Guinea's fiscal 2001 Budget Law for schools and primary health care centers in Conakry and the administrative region of Kindia).

The Tunisia DPL series illustrates the use of such an instrument to support a transition government. The DPL promotes improved transparency and accountability and greater public participation in policy making. In 2011, the interim government introduced reforms aimed at improving accountability in public service delivery—for example, through participatory monitoring of public service delivery by third parties. This reform was supported simultaneously by two others: the Law of Associations was revised to remove any room for discretion in registration procedures, and a Decree Law was adopted, giving the public the right to access information, including economic and social data, held by public bodies. Efforts to strengthen accountability in social services were reinforced by measures on the supply side in 2012, through accreditation agencies for health and higher education. The DPL supports the adoption of

(continued next page)

> **BOX 3.4** *(continued)*
>
> a decree to institutionalize the mechanisms for participatory evaluation of public service performance. The decree includes four reforms:
>
> - The introduction of participatory audits as part of the mandate of the National Controllers Body for Public Services (CGSP) to be overseen by a joint government–civil society coordinating committee
> - The adoption of international standards for participatory monitoring
> - The stipulation that all evaluations be published to reinforce access to information and accountability
> - Clear emphasis on neutrality, objectivity, and transparency of the CGSP's mission. Institutionalizing participatory evaluation of performance will help to strengthen the mechanisms for holding service delivery providers accountable.
>
> In most cases, the adoption of the law or policy constituted an important step forward. The implementation of such laws or policies also needs to be actively supported and sustained to make these frameworks effective.
>
> *Sources:* DPL database, Budget Transparency Initiative, Tunisia DPL program documents.
> a. Development policy lending is one of the instruments that the World Bank uses (often in collaboration with other development organizations) to support a country's reform program. Prior actions are a set of policy and institutional actions deemed critical to achieving the objectives of a World Bank–supported program that are mutually agreed by the World Bank and the client.

Relatedly, the role of a free, pluralistic media in supporting SA cannot be stressed enough. Many SA approaches rely on the media to disseminate and support their demands. The media have a crucial role to play in processes of accountability and citizen engagement. Its independence from government authorities and from commercial pressures that can bias content and limit its reach is a prerequisite if the media are to play such a role (Odugbemi and Lee 2011; World Bank 2003). In many contexts, the media do not enjoy such independence and are unable to perform a direct watchdog function on government. Yet their role remains important in enabling civic mobilization and in providing a public sphere that can itself become an interface between citizens and the state. Meaningful participation by citizens requires informed participants. In this regard, the criticality of information becomes all the more imperative, since imperfections of information create agency problems for citizens (Hirschman 1970). Box 3.5 discusses opportunities and challenges for the media in facilitating SA.

BOX 3.5

Opportunities and Challenges for Media in Facilitating Social Accountability

Media have several potential roles to play in facilitating SA.

Media as a strategic intermediary. News media, including both traditional forms (print, broadcast) and new (bloggers, social media, and citizen-journalists) can be strategic intermediaries for enabling inclusive citizen engagement. Broadcast and print media in particular reach even the remotest communities (including fragile and conflict-effected states and lower-income countries) at rates far greater than Internet penetration. The media can thus serve as a public platform for amplifying citizen voice in diverse communities (including, particularly, the poor and marginalized) and enabling broad public participation, discussion, and debate on issues that citizens themselves identify as salient to their livelihoods.

Media as platform and barometer (for public opinion). Media can also serve as a barometer for gauging public opinion, stress-testing decisions, and, in this way, helping to close feedback loops to government and service providers by focusing attention on issues of concern to the public that require action. In some lower-income countries and middle-income countries, media can further enable mass public consumption of data, raising public awareness, promoting a fuller understanding of specific accountability issues, and, ultimately, fostering data-driven decision making at all levels.

Media as a primary user of government data and the transmission of data. Media are a crucial user and reuser of government data, including demystifying government information for broad public access and understanding of key issues and enabling the public to voice their priorities and perspectives and become more active agents of their own development. As more central and local governments around the world open up their budget data and implement access to information legislation—for instance, as part of the Open Government Partnership—the media's role in facilitating the *demand* by citizens to use open data is key for greater transparency leading to greater accountability.

New media as empowering previously excluded and weaker sections of society. New technologies and broader access to information are shifting the distribution of power (see chapter 4). The role of social media (such as Facebook, Twitter) in social movements in pursuit of accountability (for instance, during the Arab Spring) has attracted growing attention (Gerbaudo 2012; Howard et al. 2011; Khondker 2011). In particular,

(continued next page)

BOX 3.5 (continued)

digital media combined with the growth in numbers of mobile phone users have significantly lowered the transaction costs of informing and in some cases mobilizing disparate groups of individuals to engage in collective action.

However, challenges to media accountability remain. All types of media struggle to enforce their rules on ethics and control the quality of information. The absence of media accountability systems may worsen the environment for social accountability by spreading misinformation. Media can stifle citizen "voice" that is challenging a dominant discourse promoted by the state and can fuel conflict (for example, the role of Radio Mille Collines in the genocide in Rwanda), even when its ostensible aim is to communicate information on issues of economic development, such as health and education services.

Overregulation of the media, however, can be equally detrimental to SA initiatives, as a controlled media can weaken state accountability.

The relationship between the media and good governance is particularly fragile in transitional democracies, where the roles, expectations, and norms that shape the primary relationship between the government and citizens are still disputed among the actors involved in communicating public issues (Voltmer 2013). The tension between the need for an open media and the push to have media subservient to particular values or institutions of state power is central to the "conservative dilemma" and heightened by the growth of the Internet and social media (Shirky 2011).

Influence of Intra-Society Relations

Intra-society relations can be understood as the field of power relationships that shape social interactions and popular agency within society. They are particularly relevant in understanding some of the barriers that prevent people from participating effectively in, and deriving benefits from, SA, as levels of inequality and social exclusion have been found to play an important role in shaping SA outcomes.

Two key subdimensions of intra-society relations are citizens' individual capacities and the nature of socioeconomic inequality and exclusion. Better-off citizens generally—although not always—tend to benefit more from SA processes, and socially excluded groups can be marginalized in such activities. The capacity of citizens to engage in SA initiatives and to hold public officials to account is closely shaped and differentiated by power relations involving inequality and exclusion along multiple lines (for example, education, class, ethnicity, and caste). It also depends on the density and nature of the existing social networks.[6]

Citizenship-based activities are strongly circumscribed by the level of agency that different individuals are able to exert within particular contexts (Hickey 2010; Mansuri and Rao 2004, 2013). The ability of individual citizens to engage in SA are notably influenced by their income, education, and, more broadly, their political capabilities. A wide body of evidence illustrates that many SA and broader participatory initiatives have struggled to benefit the poor and, in particular, the poorest (Bukenya, Hickey, and King 2012). Poorer individuals tend to lack the time and technical skills needed to engage; they may have limited political awareness and literacy—for example, limited awareness of certain entitlements or limited recognition as citizens; they may lack networking and negotiation skills; and they may be dependent on personal relationships for access to critical goods and services. Writing on the social embeddedness of agency, Cleaver (2004) identifies several obstacles, including social status, confidence, time, and a lack of able-bodiedness.

This is closely related to the willingness of citizens to pursue SA goals and challenge the state. The drivers of such willingness seem to be related to the previous experiences of citizens with state-citizen bargaining; their perception of the significance of the accountability issue in question; their calculations of risk and incentives that potentially jeopardize their means of survival by challenging existing relationships, particularly when they are dependent on patron-client relationships (box 3.6); and the prevailing culture of legitimacy and accountability that may or may not encourage challenging the status quo. While it is useful to separate capacity and willingness for analytical purposes, the literature suggests that the success of SA often depends on citizens having a high degree of both.

The impact of inequality on SA is, however, arguably ambiguous. In countries like Brazil, India, and South Africa, it is the perception of inequalities that has stimulated aggrieved citizens to call on the state to do something. Some studies, though, note that the degree of fractionalization along religious, ethnic, and class lines, among others, can negatively affect the capacity of citizens to undertake collective action (Bukenya, Hickey, and King 2012). Therefore, what might be of key importance is the popular perception of the fairness and legitimacy of inequality levels along with perceptions of whether it is the state's responsibility to rectify them (World Bank 2012).

> ## BOX 3.6
>
> **Inequality and Exclusion: Village Education Committees in Bihar, India**
>
> Village-level education committees have been established in parts of India with goals that include improving accountability and education services. An evaluation points to the challenge of fostering participation and accountability in the context of social inequalities and exclusion. Corbridge et al. (2005, 149) argue that attempts to set up village education committees have benefited the wealthier and more capable groups:
>
> > To expect Musahar [lower-caste] children—boys as well as girls—to go to school in Bihar, or, still more optimistically, to expect their parents to take part in village education committees, is to miss the very obvious point that these families lack even the most basic assets: land, of course, but also a sense of self-worth and the prospect of secure and properly paid employment.

State-Society Relations: A Determinant and a Goal of SA

In an overarching sense, the capacity and commitment to deliver accountable forms of governance are located within the character of state-society relations. Efforts to promote social accountability are an attempt to institutionalize more democratic and developmental relationships between state and society and are closely shaped by the existing character of these relations. What matters for SA are the forms of the social contract, the history of state-citizen relations in state formation and service provision, the character of formal and informal state-society accountability and bridging mechanisms, and the depth and character of networks between state and society actors.

Social Contract

To make accountability claims, "There must be an ... assumption about responsibilities of the state, as well as the ... entitlements of citizens" (Newell and Wheeler 2006). This can be conceptualized as the presence and character of a social contract around specific public goods, which can be strengthened over time through successive rounds of state-society bargaining (Joshi and Houtzager 2012). Different forms of social contract will emerge in different contexts, depending in part on the balance and interaction between democratic and more clientelist forms of politics. Elections can provide a window of opportunity for politicizing certain demands and beginning to forge new public agreements around them (de Waal 1996).

The broad notion of social contract can be broken down further by examining the agreements or settlements that exist around different sectors (Skocpol 1992). This is critical, as what is expected by citizens and what states are prepared to commit to delivering vary according to the particular goods and services under discussion, to their level of popular and political importance, and the history of state-society bargaining around them (Houtzager and Joshi 2008).

Assessing the possibilities for locating social accountability interventions within existing social contracts and deepening them as a result could therefore start from an analysis of how the rights of citizens to different resources and public goods (for example, education, land, health, and social security) have been differentially distributed to different individuals and groups over time and on what basis. Recent calls to "work with the grain" of governance in developing countries (Booth 2012b) suggest that it might be wise for external actors to promote social accountability initiatives where a degree of commitment already exists rather than seek to create new contracts. Box 3.7 offers some brief examples.

However, the notion of social contracts derives from a particular history of state formation in the West (Hickey 2011). In some contexts, state-society relations are largely informal and driven by the logic of patronage. The dominant theory of change at play here suggests that the social world consists of autonomous, well-informed, and active citizens who are capable of making demands on public officials who, in turn, are capable and, potentially, incentivized to respond accordingly. This theory of change is glaringly at odds with the realities on the ground in many countries (Booth 2005, 2012b).

History of State-Citizen Relations in State Formation and Service Provision

SA initiatives tend to be more effective in countries with a strong history of civic engagement. A history of CS activism can support the creation of "a repertoire of activism, replete with skills, networks, and tactics on which these later campaigns could build" (McGee and Gaventa 2010; also see Goodin and Tilly 2006; Joshi and Houtzager 2012; Shankland 2010). Moreover, the extent to which the experience of citizen engagement has

---

BOX 3.7

Three Examples of Social Contracts and the Nature of the Citizen-State Interface for Social Accountability

In Malawi, citizen scorecard initiatives were found to be more effective in localities where social contracts were strong; that is, where there was widespread agreement with regard to the state's role in service delivery. In these localities, the process was able to nurture "collaborative spaces" that brought communities, service providers, local authorities, and others together to solve service delivery problems collectively, with each type of actor contributing to improvements according to its endowments.

n Brazil, a participatory budgeting initiative in Porto Alegre was successful in part because transparent budgets and citizen participation formed part of the social contract between the Workers Party and civil society. This contract had been negotiated before the Workers Party came to power.

n Uganda, it has been argued that the state-citizen contract around education is strong, with households valuing education for its critical role in poverty reduction and development. This attitude contributed to citizen mobilization around a newspaper campaign aimed at fighting corruption to improve schooling.

Sources: Goldfrank 2007; Reinikka and Svensson 2011; Wild and Harris 2012, 22.

---

been positive or negative shapes the willingness of citizens to engage in current SA initiatives, particularly because engaging in SA may divert the resources of actors from other activities.

Character of Formal and Informal State-Society Accountability and Bridging Mechanisms

Formal and informal state-society accountability and bridging mechanisms cover multiple mechanisms ranging from the media and legal redress mechanisms to participatory spaces and customary institutions. The extent to which such mechanisms are authoritative, legitimate, and effective has been found to shape the prospects for SA effectiveness. Equally, in spite of the relatively limited evidence base, it seems that informal accountability institutions—and their interaction with formal mechanisms—are important in shaping SA outcomes.[7] In many developing-country contexts, informal rules are prevalent and "often involve patrimonial structures of exchange, which rely on different logics of accountability and appeal to different narratives of legitimacy" compared to the more "democratic," formal SA models (Harris, Kooy, and Jones 2011). Also, in contexts where formal accountability mechanisms are weak, SA activities may play a role in improving services by, for example, leveraging informal networks or through symbolic acts or protest (Unsworth and Moore 2010).

Depth and Character of Networks between State and Society Actors

A key variable in explaining the effectiveness of SA interventions is the existence of pro-reform state-society networks. Such networks do not, however, form overnight—they form over time through interaction and rounds of bargaining, and they can be reshaped, co-opted, or changed by numerous internal and external drivers (Fox 2007; Sorensen and Torfing 2005).

Importance of Cultural Norms

Culture is concerned with identity, aspiration, symbolic exchange, coordination, and structures and practices that serve relational ends, such as ethnicity, ritual, heritage, norms, meanings, and beliefs (Rao and Walton 2004).

As culture informs relationality—that is, the relationships among individuals within groups, among groups, and between ideas and perspectives—the cultural context can profoundly influence the nature of relations within civil society, political society, and state-society relations that this chapter outlines as the macro context for SA.

The *World Development Report 2015: Mind and Culture* (World Bank 2015) explores three ideas that have a bearing on SA:

- Bounds on rationality, which limit the ability of individuals to process information and lead them to rely on rules of thumb
- Social interdependence, which leads people to care about others and respect the social norms of their communities
- Culture, which provides mental models that influence what individuals pay attention to, perceive, and (mis)understand.

Social interdependencies and cultural processes (such as kinship or other traditional networks) can have a positive influence on the coordination of collective action or drive moral systems that give citizens incentives to be moral agents of SA, but they also depend on the social configuration of local communities. Tsai's work on accountability of village-level officials in China shows that informal mechanisms for accountability worked well when these officials belonged to embedding and encompassing social organizations such as temple groups (Tsai 2007). In such cases, fear for their reputations made them act in the interests of their constituents; social groups lacking this characteristic, such as church groups or lineage groups that did not include the entire village, did not induce accountability. In fact, the ways in which power and agency work within communities may be underlined by the very same cultural processes that nurture the patronage systems driving social exclusion, limiting the voice of certain social groups, and causing "relational deprivation" (Sen 2001).

When the state of Ceará in Brazil recruited a new cadre of grassroots workers—documented in Tendler's seminal account (Tendler 1997)—the importance of their work was impressed on them in human and moral terms. The results were high morale and an esprit de corps among the recruits, who demonstrated a commitment to their work that made the citizen-state engagement successful.

Accountability is understood differently depending on the prevailing norms. In many societies, the distinction between public and private spheres of conduct is often blurry and subjects both spheres to a moral code that may draw on the pervasive moral economy or norms within tribal structures. At times, demands for accountability "from below" may penalize the breach of patron-client relations rooted in authoritarian elite, religious, or spiritual codes of conduct, cultural traditions, and customs rooted in moral traditions.

Cultural values can further inform the organizational norms that influence how state agencies respond to citizens. In two case studies, both focusing on dam construction in China's Sichuan Province, Mertha (2008) shows how an appeal to cultural values and norms can be more effective than protests. In Pubugou, citizens staged protests against the groundbreaking of a dam, demanding compensation and more input in decision making. The government characterized the protests as a threat to social stability, suppressed them, and went ahead with building the dam. In Dujiangyan, in contrast, activists framed the building of a dam as an issue of environmental protection and cultural preservation, enlisting the support of bureaucratic agencies also interested in cultural and environmental preservation. This framing was instrumental in their success.

Importance of Global Factors

Global factors relate to the way in which global actors and processes can support or undermine accountability for development and SA.

Donor accountability and donor-state relations, especially in highly aid-dependent countries, can be important in a variety of ways: (a) aid conditions may create or limit space for national deliberation and accountability over appropriate policies and measures; (b) donor agencies, when taking too much responsibility for service provision, may undermine the emergence of a state-citizen contract; (c) aid flows may provide (dis)incentives for political elites to be more responsive to local citizens and to engage in tax bargaining; and (d) direct aid flows to CS could undermine citizens' independence, effectiveness, and downward accountability (Banks and Hulme 2012; Booth 2012b; O'Neill, Foresti, and Hudson 2007).

The accountability of "international" power holders beyond the state is increasingly pertinent. Multinational corporations or international NGOs have both been found to shape domestic accountability, especially when the state is unwilling or unable to regulate their activities; their impact can be positive or negative (Bebbington, Hickey, and Mitlin 2008; Garvey and Newell 2004). There are various examples of multinational corporations that have violated poor communities' rights, leading to forms of SA that target the corporations rather than just the state.

More broadly, international economic and political processes are understood to shape domestic accountability. They include, but are not limited to, (a) the level of a country's global economic integration, as more extreme forms of globalization can undermine accountability by limiting the state's capacity to debate and determine social and economic policy democratically (Rodrik 2011; Scott 2012); (b) international trade and financial flows (such as trade in illicit goods or money laundering), which can shape the incentives of political and economic elites to pursue anti-development practices; (c) international human rights norms, which can pressure certain states to open spaces for greater accountability; (d) international initiatives such as the Extractive Industries Transparency Initiative (see box 3.8)

BOX 3.8

EITI and Engagement with Civil Society

The Extractive Industries Transparency Initiative (EITI) is a global initiative in which signatory companies and compliant countries publish payments and revenues in the extractive industries, with civil society playing the role of third-party monitor. There are currently 29 EITI-compliant countries and 16 countries awaiting admission. Representatives of civil society, government, and industry have formed a Multi-Stakeholder Working Group (MSG) and collectively manage the process of complying with the requirements for EITI candidacy through a dedicated EITI national secretariat.

EITI primarily facilitates transparency with respect to extractives revenues, yet a new standard requires that EITI reports also include more detailed payment information to show how extractives payments reach the subnational level through subnational government transfers and to report companies' social contributions.

Since October 2011, a multidonor trust fund managed by the World Bank has provided direct support to CSOs in the form of country-level grants to implement civil society–led activities that can (a) increase the participation of CSOs in the MSG (ownership and contribution), (b) broaden the range of CSOs that participate in the EITI, and (c) increase the use of EITI information for greater accountability.

The program has demonstrated the ability of participating local CSOs to advocate and influence the national dialogue on the governance of extractive industries. Participants have been able to identify and prioritize key issues to advance transparency and accountability in the extractive industries at the local and national levels. For instance, through such engagements, participants have learned how to assess the amount of local revenues that should be collected and to identify the groups or agencies that should report these revenues.

Although capacity gaps are often cited as a weakness among CSOs in EITI-implementing countries, when CSOs in the targeted countries receive sufficient financial resources and technical assistance, they have been able to conduct effective advocacy campaigns that advance EITI implementation. The program encourages CSOs that are MSG members to reach out to community-based CSOs (for example, in Kazakhstan, Mozambique, Niger, and Tanzania). The objective is to train the greatest number of community representatives possible, who will then share the information within their extended networks. Some projects have a communication component that is targeting

(continued next page)

BOX 3.8 *(continued)*

a wider sector of the population through the media—in radio broadcasts in Niger and television programs in Mozambique. In Tanzania, a regional workshop led to support for an organized CSO platform to sustain citizen advocacy.

Although there is greater transparency with regard to revenues, transparency has not necessarily translated into increased accountability. It is therefore important to step up citizen engagement in order to strengthen linkages between transparency and accountability. As a starting point, information should be made more widely accessible (beyond websites and EITI reports).

For CSOs to become watchdogs in resource-rich countries, three conditions must be met: a conducive environment, sector expertise, and tools to monitor and disseminate information effectively. Unfortunately, these conditions are rarely met in low-income countries. When EITI facilitates an enabling country context for the governance of extractive industries, it needs to be complemented by better awareness of citizen groups on technical issues of the sector as well as mechanisms for citizens to provide information that improves the monitoring of extractives and leads to greater accountability.

or the Open Government Partnership (see Unsworth and Moore 2010; World Bank 2011); and (e) transnational global citizen movements (Keck and Sikkink 1998).

Conclusion

This chapter has reviewed the evidence on the two institutional spheres of civil and political society and their interactions as well as the issues around global factors and cultural norms. These are essential elements to be considered in understanding the drivers of SA effectiveness. What is missing is an overarching framework with which to assess contextual elements of SA both in general (country-level analysis) and with respect to specific issues and problems (absenteeism in primary health). That framework is the subject of chapter 4. Box 3.9 summarizes the key takeaways of this chapter.

BOX 3.9

Key Takeaways: Social Accountability and a Country's Social and Political Characteristics

SA is shaped by the two institutional spheres of political and civil society and their interactions (state-society and intra-society). Three additional factors cut across these spheres and require special attention: cultural norms, global factors, and the prevailing political settlement (see figure B3.9.1).

Three major findings emerge from a review of the broad contextual determinants of SA effectiveness. First, political and power relations are at the forefront of understanding and operationalizing SA. Second, links and networks have to be built between pro-accountability state and civil society actors. Third, closer attention should be given to the dynamics of inequality and exclusion.

The following are the important messages of the chapter:

- Actors and the dynamics of political society might be the most important factors in explaining the form and effectiveness of SA in a given context.

Figure B3.9.1 Main "Macro" Contextual Factors for Social Accountability Effectiveness

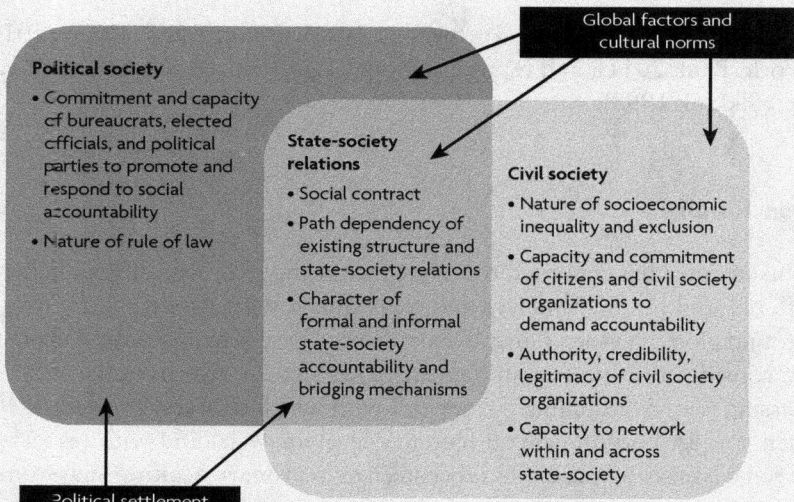

Global factors and cultural norms

Political society
- Commitment and capacity of bureaucrats, elected officials, and political parties to promote and respond to social accountability
- Nature of rule of law

State-society relations
- Social contract
- Path dependency of existing structure and state-society relations
- Character of formal and informal state-society accountability and bridging mechanisms

Civil society
- Nature of socioeconomic inequality and exclusion
- Capacity and commitment of citizens and civil society organizations to demand accountability
- Authority, credibility, legitimacy of civil society organizations
- Capacity to network within and across state-society

Political settlement

(continued next page)

BOX 3.9 *(continued)*

- The role of civil society in promoting SA is fundamental, but the prevalent, overly simplistic view that civil society is autonomous and somehow immune to the influence of power and politics is naïve. CSOs and the media need to be viewed as politically embedded institutions. It is not their technical capacities alone that influence SA.
- The history of state-society relations and the nature of the existing social contract mediate the effectiveness of SA. One goal of SA mechanisms could be to change perceptions of the responsibilities of the state and the entitlements of citizens, which are fundamental to any social contract.
- Distinct from the notions of political society, civil society or state-society relations are *cultural* factors that can profoundly influence the relationships among individuals within groups, among groups, and between ideas and perspectives.
- The role of external actors (especially donor agencies) and external processes (for example, trade) or institutions (for example, EITI) can influence SA processes, with both positive and negative consequences.

Notes

1. This chapter draws heavily on O'Meally (2013) and Bukenya, Hickey, and King (2012), which are background papers for this report.
2. Networks can be broadly understood as links between interdependent actors who interact to produce outcomes. Networks have been found to fulfill six main functions: (1) filtering (managing information and deciding what information deserves attention), (2) amplifying (taking complex ideas and combining them in a simple, broad-based one), (3) investing (providing members with the resources needed to carry out their activities), (4) convening (bringing together different individuals and groups), (5) community building (promoting and sustaining shared values and ideas across the network), and (6) facilitating (enabling network members to carry out their activities more effectively and efficiently. See, for example, Portes and Yeo (2000).
3. Many thanks to Anuradha Joshi for this insight.
4. According to Devarajan, Khemani, and Walton (2011), "In political economy environments characterized by high degrees of clientelism and rent seeking, an unqualified faith in civil society as a force for good is more likely to be misplaced. The evidence base on the organization of civil society suggests that historic institution of poverty and inequality, or of ethnic identity, can inhibit collective action in the broader public interest."

5. Thanks to Jeff Thindwa for this point.
6. Thanks to Jonathan Fox for this observation.
7. A more formal institutional perspective views accountability as enshrined in the formal institutions of state sovereignty; a more informal perspective emphasizes whether institutions are actually legitimized by and accountable to the social and political foundations of political and economic elites and society.

References

Ackerman, J. 2004. "Social Accountability for the Public Sector: A Conceptual Discussion." Draft mss., World Bank, Washington, DC.

———. 2005. "Social Accountability in the Public Sector: A Conceptual Discussion." Social Development Paper, Participation and Civic Engagement 82. World Bank, Washington, DC.

Banerjee, A. V., R. Banerji, E. Duflo, R. Glennerster, and S. Khemani. 2008. "Pitfalls of Participatory Programs: Evidence from Randomized Experiments in Education in India." Poverty Action Lab Paper, Massachusetts Institute of Technology, Cambridge, MA.

Banks, N., and D. Hulme. 2012. "The Role of NGOs and Civil Society in Development and Poverty Reduction." University of Manchester, Brooks World Poverty Institute, Manchester, U.K.

Bebbington, A. J., S. Hickey, and D. C. Mitlin. 2008. Can NGOs Make a Difference? The Challenge of Development Alternatives. London: Zed Books.

Booth, D. 2005. Missing Links in the Politics of Development: Learning from the PRSP Experiment. London: Overseas Development Institute.

———. 2012a. "Development as a Collective Action Problem: Addressing the Real Challenges of African Governance; Synthesis Report." Africa Power and Politics Programme, London. http://www.institutions-africa.org/page/appp+synthesis.

———. 2012b. "Working with the Grain and Swimming against the Tide: Barriers to Uptake of Research on Governance and Public Services in Low-Income Africa." Public Management Review 14 (2): 168–80.

Brautigam, D. 2004. "The People's Budget? Politics, Participation, and Pro-Poor Policy." Development Policy Review 22 (6): 653–68.

Brett, E. A. 2003. "Participation and Accountability in Development Management." Journal of Development Studies 40 (2): 1–29.

Bukenya, B., S. Hickey, and S. King. 2012. "Understanding the Role of Context in Shaping Social Accountability Interventions: Toward an Evidence-Based Approach." Social Accountability and Demand for Good Governance Team Report, World Bank, Washington, DC. http://web.worldbank.org/WBSITE

/EXTERNAL/TOPICS/EXTSOCIALDEVELOPMENT/0,,contentMDK:21211
265~pagePK:210058~piPK:210062~theSitePK:244363,00.html.

Citizenship DRC. 2011. "Blurring the Boundaries: Citizen Action across States
and Societies; a Summary of Findings from a Decade of Collaborative
Research on Citizen Engagement." Citizenship DRC, Brighton, U.K. http://
www.drc-citizenship.org/system/assets/1052734700/original/1052734700
-cdrc.2011-blurring.pdf.

Cleaver, F. 2004. "The Social Embeddedness of Agency and Decision-Making." In
*Participation: From Tyranny to Transformation? Exploring New Approaches
to Participation in Development*, edited by S. Hickey and G. Mohan, 271–77.
London: Zed Books.

Cooke, B., and U. Kothari, eds. 2001. *Participation: The New Tyranny?* London:
Zed Books.

Corbridge, S., G. Williams, M. Srivastava, and R. Veron. 2005. *Seeing the State:
Governance and Governmentality in India*. Cambridge, U.K.: Cambridge
University Press.

Crook, R., and D. Booth. 2011. "Working with the Grain? Rethinking
African Governance." *IDS Bulletin* 42 (2): 97–101. http://www.ids.ac.uk/go
/idspublication/working-with-the-grain-rethinking-african-governance.

Crook, R. C., and A. S. Sverrisson. 2001. "Decentralization and Poverty Alleviation
in Developing Countries: A Comparative Analysis, or Is West Bengal Unique?"
IDS Working Paper 130, University of Sussex, Institute of Development Studies,
Brighton, U.K.

Devarajan, S., S. Khemani, and W. Walton. 2011. "Civil Society, Public Action, and
Accountability in Africa." Policy Research Working Paper 5733, World Bank,
Washington, DC.

De Waal, A. 1996. "Social Contract and Deterring Famine: First Thoughts."
Disasters 20 (3): 194–205.

Di John, J., and J. Putzel. 2009. "Political Settlements." Issues Paper, University
of Birmingham, Governance and Social Development Resource Centre,
Birmingham, U.K. http://www.gsdrc.org/docs/open/EIRS7.pdf.

Evans, P. 2010. "The Challenge of 21st Century Development: Building Capability-
Enhancing States." United Nations Development Programme, New York.

Fox, J. 2007. *Accountability Politics: Power and Voice in Rural Mexico*. Oxford,
U.K.: Oxford University Press.

Garvey, N., and P. Newell. 2004. "Corporate Accountability to the Poor: Assessing
the Effectiveness of Community-Based Strategies." IDS Working Paper 227,
University of Sussex, Institute of Development Studies, Brighton, U.K. http://
www.drc-citizenship.org/system/assets/1052734410/original/1052734410
-garvey_etal.2004-corporate.pdf?1289390069.

Gaventa, J., and G. Barrett. 2010. "So What Difference Does It Make? Mapping
the Outcomes of Citizen Engagement." IDS Working Paper 347, University of

Sussex, Institute of Development Studies, Brighton, U.K. http://www.gsdrc.org /go/display&type=Document&id=3981&source=rss.

Gerbaudo, P. 2012. *Tweets and the Streets: Social Media and Contemporary Activism*. London: Pluto Press.

Goldfrank, B. 2007. "Lessons from Latin America's Experience with Participatory Budgeting." In *Participatory Budgeting*, edited by A. Shah. Washington, DC: World Bank.

Goodin, R., and C. Tilly, eds. 2006. *The Oxford Handbook of Contextual Political Analysis*. Oxford: Oxford University Press.

Gurza Lavalle, A., P. P. Houtzager, and A. K. Acharya. 2005. "Beyond Comparative Anecdotalism: How Civil and Political Organizations Shape Participation in São Paulo, Brazil." *World Development* 33 (6): 951–61.

Harris, D., M. Kooy, and L. Jones. 2011. "Analyzing the Governance and Political Economy of Water and Sanitation Service Delivery." Working Paper 334, Overseas Development Institute, London.

Hickey, S. 2010. "The Government of Chronic Poverty: From Exclusion to Citizenship?" *Journal of Development Studies* 46 (7): 1139–55.

———. 2011. "The Politics of Social Protection: What Do We Get from a 'Social Contract' Approach?" *Canadian Journal of Development Studies* 32 (4): 425–38.

Hickey, S., and S. Bracking. 2005. "Exploring the Politics of Poverty Reduction: From Representation to a Politics of Justice?" *World Development* 33 (6): 851–65.

Hickey, S., and G. Mohan. 2008. "The Politics of Establishing Pro-Poor Accountability: What Can Poverty Reduction Strategies Achieve?" *Review of International Political Economy* 15 (2): 234–58.

Hirschman, A. O. 1970. *Exit, Voice, and Loyalty: Responses to Decline in Firms, Organizations, and States*. Cambridge, MA: Harvard University Press.

Houtzager, P., and A. Joshi. 2008. "Introduction: Contours of a Research Project and Early Findings." *IDS Bulletin* 38 (6): 1–9.

———. 2012. "Widgets or Watchdogs? Conceptual Exploration in Social Accountability." *Public Management Review* 14 (2): 145–62.

Howard, P., et al. 2011. "Opening Closed Regimes: What Was the Role of Social Media during the Arab Spring." Working Paper 2011.1, Project on Information Technology and Political Islam, University of Washington, Seattle. http://pitpi .org/wp-content/uploads/2013/02/2011_Howard-Duffy-Freelon-Hussain -Mari-Mazaid_pITPI.pdf.

Hyden, G., and J. Court. 2003. "Political Society and Governance in 16 Developing Countries." World Governance Survey Discussion Paper 5, Overseas Development Institute, London, July. http://www.odi.org.uk/sites/odi.org.uk/files/odi-assets /publications-opinion-files/4100.pdf.

Joshi, A., and P. Houtzager. 2012. "Widgets or Watchdogs? Conceptual Explorations in Social Accountability." *Public Management Review, Special*

Issue: The Politics and Governance of Public Services in Developing Countries 14 (2): 145–62.

Kabeer, N. 2003. "Making Rights Work for the Poor: Nijera Kori and the Construction of 'Collective Capabilities' in Rural Bangladesh." IDS Working Paper 200, University of Sussex, Institute of Development Studies, Brighton, U.K.

———. 2005. "Growing Citizenship from the Grassroots: Nijera Kori and Social Mobilization in Bangladesh." In *Inclusive Citizenship: Meanings and Expressions*, edited by N. Kabeer. London: Zed Books.

Keck, M. E., and K. Sikkink. 1998. *Activists beyond Borders: Advocacy Networks in International Politics*. Ithaca, NY: Cornell University Press.

Khan, M. H. 2010. "Political Settlements and the Governance of Growth-Enhancing Institutions." Unpublished mss., July. http://eprints.soas.ac.uk/9968/1/Political _Settlements_internet.pdf.

Khondker, H. 2011. "Role of the New Media in the Arab Spring." *Globalizations* 8 (5): 675–79.

Manor, J. 2004. "Democratisation with Inclusion: Political Reforms and Peoples Empowerment at the Grassroots." *Journal of Human Development* 5 (1): 5–29.

Mansuri, G., and V. Rao. 2004. "Community-Based and -Driven Development: A Critical Review." *World Bank Research Observer* 19 (1): 1–39.

———. 2013. *Localizing Development: Does Participation Work?* Policy Research Report. Washington, DC: World Bank.

McGee, R., and J. Gaventa. 2010. "Review of Impact and Effectiveness of Transparency and Accountability Initiatives." Synthesis Report prepared for the Transparency and Accountability Initiative Workshop, University of Sussex, Institute of Development Studies, Brighton, U.K., October 14–15. http://www.ids.ac.uk/files/dmfile/IETASynthesisReportMcGeeGaventaFinal 28Oct2010.pdf.

———. 2011. "Shifting Power? Assessing the Impact of Transparency and Accountability Initiatives." IDS Working Paper 383, University of Sussex, Institute of Development Studies, Brighton, U.K., http://www.ids.ac.uk/files /dmfile/Wp383.pdf.

Mertha, A. 2008. *China's Water Warriors: Citizen Action and Policy Change*. Ithaca, NY: Cornell University Press.

Newell, P., and J. Wheeler. 2006. "Rights, Resources, and the Politics of Accountability: An Introduction." In *Rights, Resources, and the Politics of Accountability*, edited by P. Newell and J. Wheeler. London: Zed Books.

Odugbemi, S., and T. Lee, eds. 2011. *Accountability through Public Opinion: From Inertia to Public Action*. Washington, DC: World Bank.

O'Meally, S. 2013. "Mapping Context for Social Accountability: A Resource Paper." Background for this book, World Bank, Social Development Department, Washington, DC.

O'Neill, T., M. Foresti, and A. Hudson. 2007. *Evaluation of Citizens' V&A: Review of the Literature and Donor Approaches.* London: Department for International Development.

Peruzzotti, E., and C. Smulovitz. 2002. "Held to Account: Experiences of Social Accountability in Latin America." *Journal of Human Development* 3 (2): 209–30.

Portes, R., and S. Yeo. 2000. "'Think-Net': The CEPR Model of a Research Network." Centre for Economic Policy Research paper prepared for the workshop on Local to Global Connectivity for Voices of the Poor, World Bank, Washington, DC, December 11–13. http://www.cepr.org/aboutcepr/cepr/cepr_think.pdf.

Rao, V., and M. Walton, eds. 2004. *Culture and Public Action.* Stanford, CA: Stanford University Press.

Reinikka, R., and J. Svensson. 2011. "The Power of Information in Public Services: Evidence from Education in Uganda." *Journal of Public Economics* 95 (7–8): 956–66.

Reis, E., and M. Moore, eds. 2005. *Elite Perceptions of Poverty and Inequality.* London: Zed Books.

Rodrik, D. 2011. *Has Globalization Gone Too Far?* Washington, DC: Institute for International Economics.

Scott, J. C. 2012. "Squeezing the State: Tariff Revenue, State Capacity, and the WTO's Doha Round." BWPI Working Paper 169, Brooks World Poverty Institute, Manchester, U.K. http://www.bwpi.manchester.ac.uk/resources/Working-Papers/wp_16912.html.

Sen, A. 2001. *Development as Freedom.* New York: Knopf.

Shankland, A. 2010. "The Indigenous People's Movement, 'Forest Citizenship,' and Struggles over Health Service in Acre, Brazil." In *Mobilizing for Democracy: Citizen Action and the Politics of Public Participation*, edited by V. S. P. Coelho and B. V. Lieres. London: Zed Books.

Shirky, C. 2011. "The Political Power of Social Media." *Foreign Affairs* 90 (1): 28–41.

Skocpol, T. 1992. *Protecting Soldiers and Mothers: The Political Origins of Social Policy in the United States.* Cambridge, MA: Harvard University Press.

Sorensen, E., and J. Torfing. 2005. "The Democratic Anchorage of Governance Networks." *Scandinavian Political Studies* 28 (3): 195–218.

Stasavage, D. 2005. "The Role of Democracy in Uganda's Move to Universal Primary Education." *Journal of Modern African Studies* 43 (1): 53–73.

Tendler, J. 1997. *Good Governance in the Tropics.* Baltimore, MD: Johns Hopkins University Press.

Tsai, L. L. 2007. *Accountability without Democracy: Solidarity Groups and Public Goods Provision in Rural China.* New York: Cambridge University Press.

Unsworth, S., and M. Moore. 2010. *An Upside Down View of Governance.* Brighton, U.K.: Institute of Development Studies.

Voltmer, K. 2013. *The Media in Transitional Democracies: Contemporary Political Communication.* Cambridge, MA: Polity.

vom Hau, M. 2012. "State Capacity and Inclusive Development: New Challenges and Directions." ESID Working Paper 2, Effective States and Inclusive Development Research Centre, Manchester, U.K. http://www.dfid.gov.uk/r4d /Output/189981/Default.aspx.

Whitehead, L. 2002. *Democratisation: Theory and Experience.* Oxford, U.K.: Oxford University Press.

Wild, L., and D. Harris. 2012. "The Political Economy of Community Scorecards in Malawi." Overseas Development Institute, London. http://www.odi.org.uk /sites/odi.org.uk/files/odi-assets/publications-opinion-files/7543.pdf.

World Bank. 2003. "Enabling Environments for Civic Engagement in PRSP Countries." Social Development Note 82, World Bank, Washington, DC.

————. 2011. *World Development Report 2011: Conflict, Security, and Development.* New York: Oxford University Press.

————. 2012. *Societal Dynamics and Fragility: Engaging Societies in Responding to Fragile Situations.* Washington, DC: World Bank.

————. 2015. *World Development Report 2015: Mind and Culture.* New York: Oxford University Press.

Yilmaz, S., Y. Beris, and R. Serrano-Berthet. 2008. "Local Government Discretion and Accountability: A Diagnostic Framework for Local Government." World Bank, Social Development Department, Washington, DC.

Contextual Drivers of Social Accountability: An Analytical Framework

Chapter 4 proposes a framework for operationalizing social accountability (SA). Building on the fact that SA outcomes result from an iterative engagement between a broad sociopolitical context and elements of the intervention (Bukenya, Hickey, and King 2012), it enriches the analysis of chapter 3 by incorporating intervention-based factors into an analytical framework for "opening the black box" of contextual factors for SA effectiveness. This framework builds on a careful remapping of the available evidence along SA's five constitutive elements and identifies various "drivers" of contextual effectiveness, which can guide practitioners in designing, implementing, monitoring, and evaluating SA to take into account a broad range of contextual factors.

These drivers of contextual effectiveness encompass a broad range of contextual factors—for example, social, political, and intervention-based factors, including elements of information and communication technology (ICT). They can assume different permutations to influence the five constitutive elements of SA and thereby the specific change paths leading to SA outcomes.

As noted in chapter 1, the overall framework emphasizes (a) the dynamic interplay of the five key elements—citizen action, state action, information, interface, and civic mobilization; (b) the complexity of each of these five elements and their interrelations; and (c) the multiple contextual factors (clustered in drivers) that mediate relationships among actors.

The framework (and the guiding tables presented at the end of the chapter) is intended to help practitioners to analyze the context for SA, including constraints and opportunities, both at a country level (World Bank's systematic country diagnosis) and for particular cases (a specific issue or problem in a particular sector).[1] On the general level, the framework's five interconnected elements offer a convenient framing for mapping archetypal contexts (see chapters 5 and 6). For a particular intervention, the framework and its set of drivers can be used to analyze contextual opportunities and constraints iteratively and to identify change paths that will make it possible to advance accountability demands (see chapter 7).

This framework and the guiding tables can support the design and implementation of SA in the following ways:

- By supporting the understanding of critical aspects of context and assessing each element's drivers and potential contributing factors; the framework can help users to identify various entry points for accountability work and assess their feasibility
- By supporting the development and revision of a reasonable theory of change
- By supporting an iterative diagnosis as well as strong monitoring and evaluation of SA interventions
- By ensuring proper documentation of cases, with the right level of detail; the framework should prompt intensified efforts to document contextual factors that to date have been overlooked in design and evaluation. Such documentation can yield a fuller theory of iterative change and support monitoring and evaluation.

The chapter is structured as follows. The first section describes the method followed in building this framework and, in particular, in identifying the drivers. The second provides an overview of these drivers. The third focuses on the potential that new ICTs have for supporting SA, since an overview of contextual factors that mediate SA effectiveness would not be complete without looking at the potential brought about by new ICTs (these are also reflected in the guiding tables). The fourth section offers a set of guiding tables that constitute the first steps of a toolkit to assess, adjust, monitor, and evaluate contextual drivers of SA effectiveness mapped along each of SA's constitutive elements.

From Causal Chains to Drivers to the Analytical Framework

Capturing the full complexity of SA entailed referring to multiple SA models and schools of thought. The framework and the guiding tables were built iteratively based on the conceptual and empirical literature in various disciplines, with feedback from practitioners and academics. Specifically, we started with—and built on—the principal-agent model, which assumes that service delivery will improve when citizens demand accountability and begin to participate (in decision making, agenda setting, and government activity monitoring). In addition, the behavior change model draws on studies of collective action, which emphasize the incentives that SA activities can give citizens, citizen groups, and government officials to do things differently. Finally, our thinking drew on the relevant political science literature and institutional economics literature to capture how SA processes and results depend on contextual power relations, interactions among different stakeholders, and the institutional frameworks that mediate an intervention and its impacts.

We used both the growing body of evidence on SA impact (see appendix B) and practical cases to refine the framework. While drawing on the existing knowledge, the team explored the framework's empirical application with teams working on SA projects in several countries (see chapter 7). In this way, it was progressively refined.

In approaching the problem of when, how, and why various SA processes lead to various outcomes, we began with causal chains. As Pawson (2003) explains, the objective of causal chain analysis is to create

> a sort of "highway code" to program building, alerting policy makers to the problems that they might expect to confront. … [It provides a framework to facilitate the] process of thinking through the tortuous pathways along which a successful program [could] travel … What it produces is: "remember A," "beware of B," "take care of C," "D can result in both E and F," and "if you try G, make sure that H is in place."

We used a causal chain approach to retrofit existing impact evaluations (see appendix D for an illustration) to identify the following:

- Generic steps along SA trajectories
- Potential bottlenecks encountered in designing and monitoring SA approaches
- Risks to various activities at each step along a change path
- Critical context-specific or sector-specific factors throughout the chain

Although our work on causal chains never aimed to prescribe a generic process for SA design and evaluation, we hoped to map at least some of the links between SA's constitutive elements. Nevertheless, unlike the linear, unidirectional, stepwise moves that causal chains imply, SA is typically circular and iterative: each incremental change reconfigures the contextual conditions for the next. Accordingly, even the causal link most tested by quasi-experimental impact evaluations—from information to individual citizen action—proved difficult to capture in generic terms. For example, the causal chain in Lieberman, Posner, and Tsai (2013) compellingly accounts for this link in a particular intervention. Yet this causal chain cannot be generalized. Appendix D explains how we used existing evidence and a causal chain approach to build the proposed dynamic framework for assessing contextual factors in SA.

The approach helped us to identify a set of factors that will have an impact on the effectiveness of SA, and these factors were then clustered into a set of drivers (for instance, elements around type of information, novelty, or consistency of the information were clustered under "framing" of information) and mapped to each of the five constitutive elements of our framework.

In light of the state of the evidence, and perhaps by design, it is not possible to propose generic steps leading to SA outcomes; the five constitutive elements of SA respond to variable drivers that can take different shapes to influence specific change paths. Making explicit the assumptions underlying a projected path to citizen or state action on a given issue, with reference to the particular SA levers employed— such as information, interface, or civic mobilization—allows for better tracking of an intervention's impact trajectory. This flexibility allows for course correction, as envisioned by the problem-driven iterative adaptation approach.[2]

The Analytical Framework

This section begins by briefly introducing the contextual drivers of SA effectiveness, mapped to the five constitutive elements (see figure 4.1).

The guiding tables presented later in this chapter document the following:

- A set of assumptions and influencing factors pertaining to each of the five constitutive elements for SA, clustered into the drivers (for instance, for citizen action: awareness of the issue, salience of the issue, intrinsic motivation, efficacy)

Figure 4.1 The Analytical Framework and Its Contextual Drivers

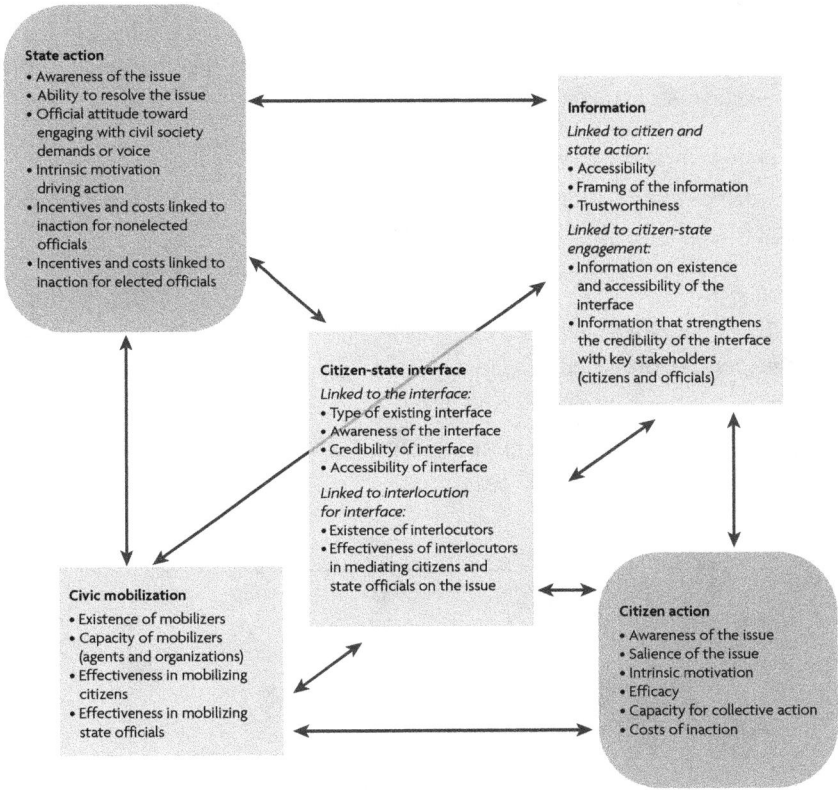

State action
- Awareness of the issue
- Ability to resolve the issue
- Official attitude toward engaging with civil society demands or voice
- Intrinsic motivation driving action
- Incentives and costs linked to inaction for nonelected officials
- Incentives and costs linked to inaction for elected officials

Information
Linked to citizen and state action:
- Accessibility
- Framing of the information
- Trustworthiness

Linked to citizen-state engagement:
- Information on existence and accessibility of the interface
- Information that strengthens the credibility of the interface with key stakeholders (citizens and officials)

Citizen-state interface
Linked to the interface:
- Type of existing interface
- Awareness of the interface
- Credibility of interface
- Accessibility of interface

Linked to interlocution for interface:
- Existence of interlocutors
- Effectiveness of interlocutors in mediating citizens and state officials on the issue

Civic mobilization
- Existence of mobilizers
- Capacity of mobilizers (agents and organizations)
- Effectiveness in mobilizing citizens
- Effectiveness in mobilizing state officials

Citizen action
- Awareness of the issue
- Salience of the issue
- Intrinsic motivation
- Efficacy
- Capacity for collective action
- Costs of inaction

• Indicative questions that can guide practitioners in questioning their assumptions vis-à-vis a specific intervention
• Potential enabling factors, which build on the review of the evidence, including elements described in chapter 3, but also some sector-specific elements as well as elements linked to each lever (information, interface, and civic mobilization)
• A categorization of these factors between actor-based and structural factors for state action and citizen action and short-term and long-term horizons for the three levers, as characterizing factors in this way helps to give a sense of the time horizon or level of challenge in dealing with some of these contextual factors

- Some examples of inconsistency in the findings (counterfactuals), which underline the need to question consistently the theory of change for specific approaches
- Examples of intervention strategies to facilitate SA mapped to the three levers

Drivers of Citizen Action and State Action

What drives state action and citizen action? Figure 4.2 presents a way to visualize the relation of these drivers to one another.

Citizen Action

The drivers of citizen action include salience of the issue to citizens, efficacy or the perception of citizen agency to bring about change, the capacity

Figure 4.2 Assessing Drivers of State and Citizen Action

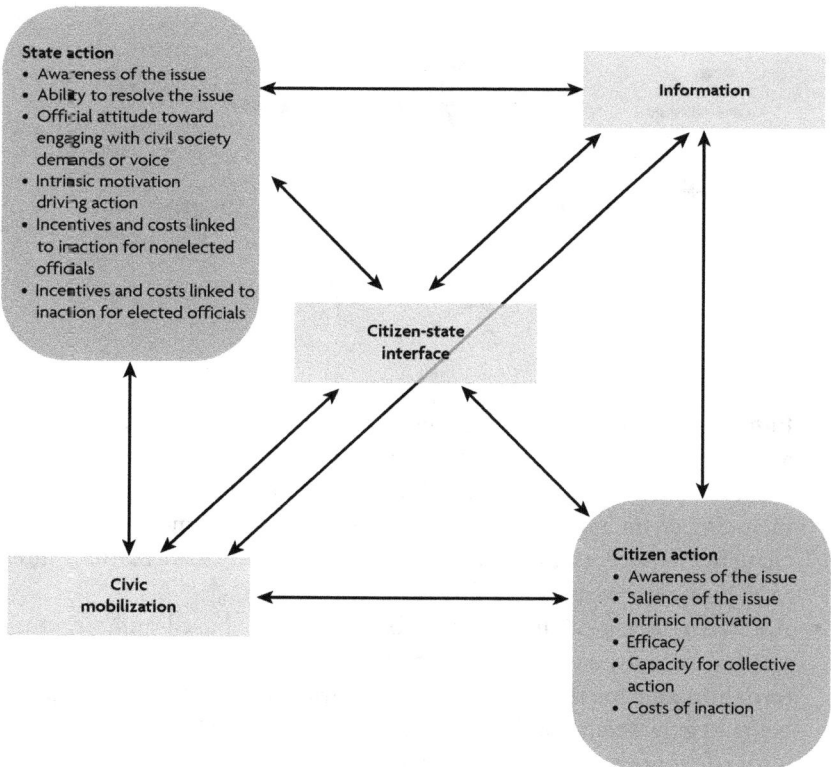

State action
- Awareness of the issue
- Ability to resolve the issue
- Official attitude toward engaging with civil society demands or voice
- Intrinsic motivation driving action
- Incentives and costs linked to inaction for nonelected officials
- Incentives and costs linked to inaction for elected officials

Information

Citizen-state interface

Civic mobilization

Citizen action
- Awareness of the issue
- Salience of the issue
- Intrinsic motivation
- Efficacy
- Capacity for collective action
- Costs of inaction

challenges that stem from the broader sociopolitical context, as well as a deeper understanding of the costs or incentives for citizen (in)action on the issue that determine whether citizens choose to act or not. The contextual factors that contribute to citizen action may be either actor centric (for example, linked to individual literacy or intrinsic motivation) or structural in nature (for example, drawing on the past legacy of citizen-state engagement, the level of social exclusion, or patron-client political settlements that increase the costs for very poor citizens to act on an issue).

State Action

State action can depend on a variety of factors ranging from a very basic awareness on the part of state officials of the issue and how to act to broader issues of state capacity and the structure of incentives or costs that influence whether officials will act, even if there is awareness of the need to act. State action also depends on the attitude of the state (more broadly) and of officials (more specifically) toward engaging with civil society demands or citizen voice on the issue that requires a state response.

Drivers of Information, Interface, and Civic Mobilization

Figure 4.3 visualizes the relationships between information, interface, and civic mobilization as the drivers of state and citizen action.

Information

The way that information is created, collected, and disseminated is key to understanding its credibility or impact on whether citizen action or state action follows based on the information alone (figure 4.3). Accessibility of the information, its framing (supporting salience of the issue for citizens or the state, presenting it in a novel way, or providing consistent messages to trigger action), and the level of trust that citizens or the state have in the information and its medium are essential drivers for citizen and state action. In some cases, information can be made available by public officials; in others, it might be collected by social groups through monitoring exercises to lay a foundation for making claims and demanding accountability. Information can be used by groups or media to mobilize citizens or state actors or by both mobilizers and interlocutors to popularize the citizen-state interface.

Interface

Two related factors are critical to interface: the nature of the interface itself (credibility, representation, awareness, accessibility) and the existence and

Figure 4.3 Assessing and Supporting Drivers of Information, Interface, and Civic Mobilization

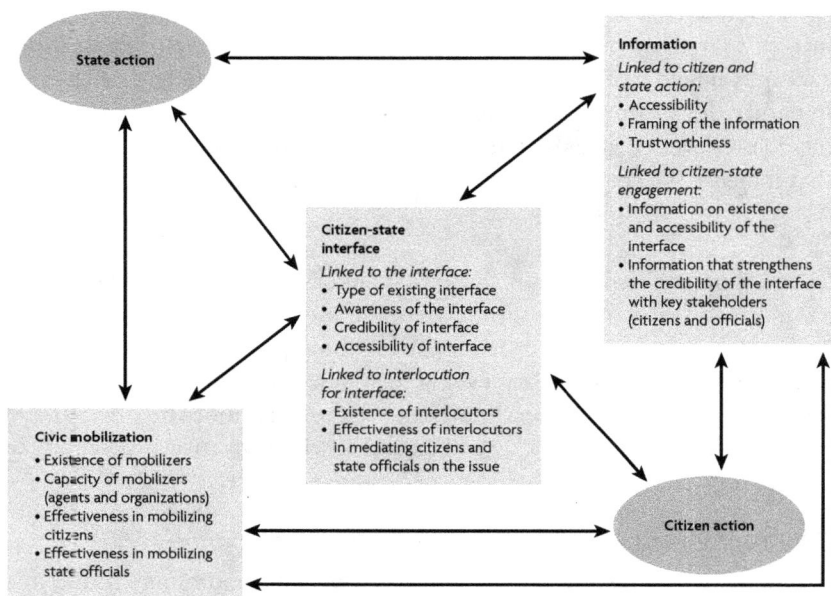

quality of interlocutors that mediate the interaction. Drawing on Tembo (2012), interlocutors are the organizations or individuals with the necessary characteristics to address a collective action problem for citizens or a situation of state inaction so that appropriate solutions for a citizen-state interface can be found. Interlocutors are skilled at building the "mutually reinforcing cross-sectoral coalitions between state and society, grounded in mutually perceived shared interests," underpinning the idea that the state and civil society are not homogeneous entities (Fox 2004).

In any context, public decision making can take place in three types of spaces (closed spaces, invited spaces, and claimed spaces), and the type of space determines the nature of the interface (Gaventa 2006). By definition, closed spaces are limited to a small group of policy elite and closed to broader publics. Invited spaces are those in which people are "invited to participate by various kinds of authorities, be they government, supranational agencies, or nongovernmental organizations" (Cornwall 2002, quoted in Gaventa 2006). Claimed spaces are largely "organic." They are created by mobilized citizens who share a set of common concerns or a common identity. Many social accountability initiatives that emerge organically in specific contexts seem to involve creating claimed spaces for public deliberation about accountability failures—for example, social audits, which arose through civil society–led public hearings about the implementation of public programs (Pande 2013; see also box 2.4).

Civic Mobilization

Finally, civic mobilization is important to SA because it can provide citizens with both organizational and leadership capacity to come together as individuals and take collective action.[3] Civic mobilization occurs not just within society, but also within the state, as public officials face the challenge of responding to demands. When considering civic mobilization, we focus on the existence, capacity, and effectiveness of agents and organizations to mobilize both state and citizen actors to engage in SA. The role of civil society organizations (CSOs) in fostering SA is often a critical part of civic mobilization. The ability of CSOs to engage in public debate and in systems of social accountability differs significantly across contexts. The World Bank's ARVIN tool facilitates a comprehensive assessment of (a) legal and regulatory, (b) political and governmental, (c) sociocultural, and (d) economic factors that constitute the enabling environment for CSOs. The ARVIN acronym synthesizes five critical dimensions that are enabling elements for CSOs and broader civic engagement: (a) association, (b) resources, (c) voice, (d) information, and (e) negotiation.[4]

In light of the fundamental changes in the field of SA brought about by the ICT "revolution," the next section documents these changes in connection with each of the constitutive elements of SA. The guiding tables include elements regarding the potential for using ICTs for SA, as relevant.

SA in a Connected World: Leveraging ICTs

ICTs are transforming how citizens and states generate, use, and share information, how they coordinate for civic mobilization, and how they interact with government and public institutions through the digital citizen-state interface. Table 4.1 summarizes the opportunities that ICTs offer along SA's five constitutive elements as well as their possible risks.

The rapid spread of the Internet and the worldwide increase in the penetration of mobile telephony are revolutionizing how information is generated, disseminated, and used. Traditionally, governments dominated

Table 4.1 ICTs for Social Accountability: Opportunities and Risks

Constitutive element	Opportunities		Risks
	State action	Citizen action	
Information	• Accessibility: (a) reduction of time and cost to disclose and distribute information, (b) reduction of time and cost for data and information entry, management, and storage	• Accessibility and inclusiveness: (a) reduction of time, cost, and distance to gain access to information and (b) reduction of information asymmetries • Independent generation of information (thus bypassing government controls) • Faster and easier "translation" of information: complex data and information made easier for ordinary citizens to understand (for example, visualization) • Better-informed citizens	• Digital divide • Mismatch of information needs between state and citizens • Possible breaches of privacy and sensitive information
Civic mobilization	• Government coordination: easier and faster coordination within government agencies and across different levels of government	• Horizontal coordination: (a) facilitation of virtual communities of like-minded citizens and (b) cyber-coordination for collective action • Collective voice and action: real-time and asynchronous crowd voicing • Civic mobilization of nontraditional actors (for example, youth)	• Digital divide • Participation and representation asymmetries • Weak or no sustainability; short-lived enthusiasm • Diffusion of collective voice and action • Manipulation of voice by interested parties and elites • Diffusion of government responsibilities and accountability

(continued next page)

Table 4.1 ICTs for Social Accountability: Opportunities and Risks (*continued*)

Constitutive element	Opportunities		Risks
	State action	Citizen action	
Citizen-state interface	• An intrinsic value: democratization of information flows • Accessibility and inclusiveness: (a) reduction of time and cost for instantaneous citizen-state interaction and (b) availability of direct citizen-state interaction channels beyond geographic barriers • Co-planning, co-creation, and co-delivery: (a) improved quality of participation and decision making as citizens are better informed, (b) facilitation of joint decision making, (c) facilitation of participatory monitoring and co-management of public resources, and (d) facilitation of timely and appropriate government response to citizens	• Same as for state action	• Digital divide • Participation and representation asymmetries • Fear of participation due to privacy, Internet security, and surveillance issues • Proliferation of engagement platforms • Poor or lack of sustainability; short-lived enthusiasm • Lack of timely responsiveness due to capacity or willingness • Limited or differing quality and effect of participation in comparison to face-to-face participation • Mismatch of interest areas for collaboration between citizens and state

Sources: U.K. Cabinet Office 2014; Cullen and Sommer 2011; Gigler, Bailur, and Anand 2014; Linders, Wilson, and Bertot 2013; Osimo 2008; Siegle 2014; World Bank 2014.

the creation and distribution of content (Hanna 2009). New technologies have broken this monopoly, enabling third parties to bypass traditional media and the state in the production of information. The instant and ubiquitous connectivity provided by mobile phones and Internet access allows citizens and public service users to access and produce information and share it with their fellow citizens and their governments at low cost and in real time (ITU 2014).[5] This "democratization" of information flows and channels for transmitting them enlarges the notion of participation and allows citizens to become partners with government (Linders 2012; Linders, Wilson, and Bertot 2013), thereby encouraging citizens to participate in public affairs (Rodríguez Bolívar, Muñoz, and López Hernández 2013).

In facilitating and enhancing SA, ICTs can be a game changer for two main reasons: their accessibility and potential for inclusiveness.

- *Accessibility: speed, space, and cost.* Beyond penetration, new technologies reduce temporal and spatial constraints (Amelina 2011). Electronic communications are unique insofar as they are instantaneous and asynchronous (Hanna 2012; World Bank 2014). They are also unrestrained by geographic locations or borders. These features can potentially reduce the costs of generating, storing, using, and sharing information as well as interaction. In such cases, a reduction in costs encompasses affordability, transaction costs, and the cost of investments in acquiring technology and access (Hanna 2009, 2012). They also reduce transaction costs, in terms of time, energy, and logistical costs borne by citizens to engage with governments and vice versa.
- *Inclusiveness.* New technologies offer opportunities for greater inclusiveness in two ways. They can enhance inclusiveness and participation at the global level, connecting different segments of the world and various stakeholders virtually, creating an immediate "crowd effect," not only for information sharing and coordination, but also for co-planning, co-creation, and co-delivery. More important, the accessibility of new technologies offers tremendous opportunity for including vulnerable groups, the poor, and traditionally excluded individuals and groups in development processes.

Yet ICTs are not a silver bullet for SA. They work best when they are embedded in SA institutions, processes, or systems and not stand-alone solutions. ICTs are a supplementary channel for information, participation, and collaboration, not a replacement. The design and implementation of ICTs also need to be user centric—that is, they need to give users more control, more choices, or more flexibility.

The risks of further excluding the most vulnerable because of a "digital divide" must be taken into account. The digital divide in its most simplistic form is understood as the "haves" and "have-nots" of technology (Wattal et al. 2011). In a development context, however, the divide is not so simple, since it is not merely a technological gap, but also a social and a political problem (Miller 2011; Millington and Carter 2013; van Dijk 2005). In addition to physical access to technology and telecommunication services, the digital divide also encompasses skills, including basic and technological literacy, as well as motivation and use (van Dijk 2005). All of these factors are influenced by the socioeconomic and cultural contexts, such as gender, age, class, race, income, geographic location (urban-rural), and household composition, among others, of individuals and groups (Miller 2011; Millington and Carter 2013). A hybrid approach is one way to mitigate this. The so-called traditional ICTs, such as community radios and televisions, are powerful tools that can supplement the benefits of new technologies while increasing access.

The effectiveness of ICT-enabled approaches to SA depends on the environment: the existence of information technology (IT) infrastructure, supportive laws and regulations, and "infomediaries."

- *IT infrastructure.* IT connectivity is one of the foundations for transformations and innovations to take full advantage of the benefits of ICTs.
- *Laws and regulations for protecting, handling, and sharing data as well as Internet protection and security.* Personal and sensitive data and information must be protected, in part to protect privacy and in part to limit government abuse of power over citizens and the private sector (telecommunication service and content providers). Some states do not have such laws, and some have used legal clauses relating to a "state of emergency" or "national security" to limit or close down telecommunication services (for instance, during the Arab Spring). Many states do not have privacy laws, or their privacy laws and regulations have waiver clauses, creating the risk of backlash for social activists, civic hackers, and users more generally who, in some contexts, are dependent on a subjective interpretation of the state.

- *Infomediaries*. Infomediaries are groups and individuals who "translate" data and information, making it understandable and usable for a general public with neither the time nor skills to take full advantage of the growing amount of data and information available. Infomediaries help the public to use information and adapt it to the needs of society at-large or of a particular interest group. Oftentimes this role is played by CSOs, including nongovernmental organizations (NGOs), professional associations, unions, media and journalists, academia, research institutions, and civic hackers (Hanna 2012). In addition to translating information, infomediaries sometimes take on the roles of organizers, advocates, monitors, and mobilizers, intermediating citizen-state interactions (Hanna 2012).

How effective are ICTs for SA? The evidence is anecdotal and mixed. One specific challenge is the difficulty in isolating the impact of ICTs. Nevertheless, some recent studies are capturing the innovative uses of technology to support and expand SA mechanisms (see box 4.1) Many examples show that there has been more success in amplifying citizen voices than in effectively "closing the loop."

BOX 4.1

Effectiveness of ICT-Enabled Social Accountability Interventions: Examples from Brazil, Pakistan, and the Democratic Republic of Congo

In the state of Rio Grande do Sul, Brazil, Internet voting (i-voting)[a] and mobile solutions are used to collect and crowdsource citizen voices in the process of state-level participatory budgeting, complementing traditional face-to-face meetings. In attempting to reach more citizens and, in particular, citizens who have not participated in participatory budgeting processes before, a wiki-survey was conducted using the Internet and a mobile telephone application. Participants answered a series of questions with two-answer options given for each question. To overcome the digital divide, the project team conducted a three-part outreach campaign. Vans equipped with Internet

(continued next page)

BOX 4.1   *(continued)*

access and manned by trained personnel were deployed across the state to reach the least privileged sectors of society. Citizens were encouraged to participate in the survey through a Facebook application developed specifically for the exercise. In the poorest regions of the state, complementary face-to-face meetings took place, so that policy proposals could be explained in greater detail and participants could complete the survey in these meetings.

During the referendum on state-level spending priorities in 2012, more than 22,000 people participated through i-voting. For the most part, those who participated in the traditional face-to-face meetings participated regardless of the introduction of i-voting. Nevertheless, i-voting led to increased participation among segments of the population who had not been previously engaged. These new participants—as online-only users— were, however, likely to be more socioeconomically privileged.

In Pakistan's Punjab Province, widespread public perception of endemic corruption in public administration and service delivery, an increasingly vibrant media, and the high penetration of mobile telephones (80 percent of the poorest quintile households in Punjab have mobile phones) provided an environment conducive to the use of ICTs to engage government service users and elicit their direct feedback for improving governance and addressing issues in service delivery. This process, known as the Punjab model, comprises three basic stages: (1) when a citizen uses the government's administrative services, a government official records the user's mobile telephone number and the details of the transaction and then transmits the information to the Punjab Information Technology Board; (2) personalized short messaging services (SMS) texts are sent following an automated call to alert the citizen, asking questions about the quality of services they received, including experience of corruption. During this process, agents at a third-party call center follow up with a subset of citizens in an attempt to overcome problems related to low levels of literacy; (3) the feedback data—via SMS or call center—are aggregated and analyzed to benchmark services across the province. Then district-level reports, the district scorecards, are sent by the Chief Secretary Office to each district officer for regular discussions on results, and actions needed to improve services are taken when deemed appropriate.

Since 2012, 4.8 million citizens have been contacted in an effort to monitor services of the police, urban development, land revenue, emergency response, and health and

(continued next page)

BOX 4.1 *(continued)*

food departments. Some 0.7 million citizens have provided feedback. Nearly 4,000 corrective actions have been taken on the basis of the feedback. In June 2011, the commissioner of Bahawalpur took disciplinary action against nine government officials on the basis of feedback. A substantial majority say they are happy just to be contacted and heard. The early-stage qualitative evaluation of the Punjab model indicates that one of its most powerful features is its capacity to generate real-time data on service provision through a direct communication channel with citizens for the first time.

The government of the Democratic Republic of Congo launched the ICT for Governance (ICT4Gov) program in the province of South Kivu in 2009 with the aim of strengthening decentralization by empowering citizens through participatory budgeting. For outreach and civic mobilization, a hybrid of non-ICT and ICT approaches was employed—a combination of face-to-face meetings and mobile SMS. SMS messages were sent directly to households to announce the community meetings, and citizens could also vote via SMS to indicate their priorities with regard to budget allocations. They could also send their feedback on the program via SMS.

South Kivu epitomizes the challenges of a low-capacity, fragile environment. Despite these challenges, this initiative was deemed successful. As a result of this participatory decision-making process, local governments developed budget allocations more aligned with citizens' needs. Increasingly, citizens saw the benefits of this process, especially women, who participated in the community meetings to express their concerns and opinions for the first time. This effort built trust in local government since citizens were able to see the links between their participation in decision making and actual budgetary allocations, and participating municipalities recorded increases in tax collection (up to 20 times more than previously recorded). Local governments also started to receive budget transfers from the central government, which was unprecedented.

Sources: Bhatti, Kusek, and Verheijen 2015; Caleen and Hasanain 2011; Peixoto forthcoming; World Bank 2013; World Bank Institute 2012.

a. "i-voting" is a subset of electronic voting (e-voting), which includes all forms of voting that use electronic means to count or cast votes. For the purpose of this report, i-voting refers to voting conducted remotely via the Internet, using nondedicated devices for voting, including laptops and smartphones. i-voting is different from so-called e-petitions and e-surveys, as i-voting produces a binding decision on the selection of candidate(s) and the implementation of public policies. See Peixoto (forthcoming).

Guiding Tables

Table 4.2 Unpacking State Action as a Constitutive Element of Social Accountability

State action	Indicative question	Potential contributing contextual factors	
		Actor based	**Structural**
Awareness of the issue	• Do state officials' know the reasons why this issue exists? • Do officials get regular or updated information on this issue? • Are officials (especially, if elected) aware of the saliency of the issue for citizens?	• *Level of understanding of the broader dynamics or causes of the issue among key officials*	• **Cultural or political norms** that influence openness in sharing and disseminating information on the issue • **Level of incentives, especially for elected officials, to be responsive to citizens' salient issues** (assuming this level is higher in particular types of democracies; see Harding and Stasavage 2014)
Ability to resolve the issue	• Do officials targeted by the intervention have responsibility or the authority needed for addressing the particular request or issue? • Do officials know what action to take to address the issue? • Do officials have a plan or strategy in place to address the issue?	• **Capacity levels of concerned officials** (an aspect of state capacity to act on the issue) + Counterfactual: Might spur official action if officials are not directly responsible for the poor state of services—that is, could become allies (state fragmentation as entry point) • **Level of resources** officials need access to in order to resolve the issue (an aspect of state capacity to act on the issue)	• **Nature of delegated authority to act effectively on the issue** • **Level of collaboration needed from different parts of the state or support from across official hierarchy**

(continued next page)

Table 4.2 Unpacking State Action as a Constitutive Element of Social Accountability (continued)

State action	Indicative question	Potential contributing contextual factors	
		Actor based	Structural
Official attitude toward engaging with civil society demands or voice	• Do officials have reservations regarding civil society motivations to act on this issue? • Do officials perceive individuals or organization(s) capable of mobilizing resources for popular support on this issue?	• *Level of trust officials have in the demand or the organization mobilizing citizen action* + Counterfactual: Credibility of the organization may be secondary if demand is widespread • *Benefits of citizen buy-in are recognized (such as social harmony, stability, or higher taxes)*	• **Nature of existing political settlement** • **Nature of compact** • **Embeddedness of key local officials within society in that area**
Intrinsic motivation driving action	• Do officials feel a moral responsibility to address this issue?	• **Intrinsic motivation or belief** in addressing the issue (sense of duty, altruistic motives, embeddedness, or strong ties with constituency)	• **Influence of social and cultural norms** (Tsai 2007)
Incentives and costs linked to (in)action (nonelected officials)	• Do nonelected officials (bureaucrats and providers) perceive any costs (or benefits) to them if they do not act on this issue? • Do they perceive any rewards if they do act or are seen to act on this issue?	• **Level of incentives** for individual official bureaucrats and providers to act on the issue, including elements around social harmony and stability; prospects of higher revenues for point of service • **Existence or not of informal sanction and fear of shaming and ostracism for inaction** on the issue	• *Nature of compact (formal or informal): fear of official sanction or prospect of official reward based on (in)action on the issue (for example, promotion linked to objective criteria around citizen satisfaction or service delivery targets)* • **Sector characteristics that influence bureaucrat or provider incentives:** level of competition and exit options, level of information asymmetry and visibility of outputs, level of discretion and transaction intensity

(continued next page)

Table 4.2 Unpacking State Action as a Constitutive Element of Social Accountability (continued)

State action	Indicative question	Potential contributing contextual factors	
		Actor based	**Structural**
Incentives and costs linked to (in) action (elected officials)	• Do elected officials perceive any costs (or benefits) to them if they (politicians) do not act on this issue? • Do elected officials perceive any rewards if they do or are seen to act on this issue?	• *Level of personal incentives for politicians or other elected officials to act on the issue* • **Existence or not of informal sanction** (fear of shaming and ostracism of elected officials for inaction on the issue) • **Elite capture of political positions** (particularly relevant if the issue needs the targeting of socially excluded groups)	• **Political competition** (level of competition, program based, salience and visibility of issue, timing of elections) + Counterfactual: Level of political competition is low (for example, single-party system) but level of fragmentation is high (for example, among elites), creating political incentives to support citizen demands, or single-party emphasizes a developmental state • **Nature of existing political settlement** (for example, significant use of coercion, threat of powerful excluded elite, fragile legitimacy of institutions, high dependence on donors)
Incentives and costs linked to strength of horizontal accountability institutions or the media	• Are horizontal accountability institutions (for example, judiciary, legislative, and other oversight authorities) active in holding officials accountable for this issue? • Do officials perceive that the media may support mobilization around this issue?	• *Perception of level of effectiveness and independence of concerned horizontal accountability institutions by officials*	• **Nature of political settlement** (for example, level of empowerment of state, horizontal accountability institutions, judiciary, audit agencies, legislative oversight) • **Role of media:** assuming that the existence of a free and fair media is associated with increased government responsiveness (Besley and Burgess 2002)

Note: Factors in italics are more easily changeable through an intervention.

a. The term "officials" is used hereafter to denote the subgroup of bureaucratic officials, frontline providers, or elected officials responsible or with a stake in the identified issue. If different levels within the state are relevant, the table may need to be applied separately for each level of official.

Table 4.3 Unpacking Citizen Action as a Constitutive Element of Social Accountability

Citizen action	Indicative question	Potential contributing contextual factors	
		Actor based	Structural
Awareness of the issue	• Are citizens (or groups of citizens) aware of this issue as something needing attention? • Do citizens perceive the issue as either a state responsibility or caused by state inaction?	• *Level of understanding of the broader dynamics or causes of the issue (may be linked to individual literacy, education levels)*	• **Cultural or social norms** that influence openness in sharing or disseminating information on the issue • **Exit options** (for example, alternate providers)
Salience of the issue	• Is this issue of fundamental importance to citizens? • Is this issue relevant to an identifiable targeted group or does it concern all citizens?	• **Importance of consequences for the citizen resulting from issue (in absolute or relative terms)**—for example, issues related to land eviction can be more salient than issues related to preventive health for rural farmer communities	• **Nature of influence of cultural or social norms on how the issue is framed** • **Exit options** (for example, alternate providers) • **Level of social inclusion or cohesion contributing to the salience of the issue** • **Existence of supportive legislation** that makes addressing the issue an entitlement or rights issue (Joshi 2013)
Intrinsic motivation	• Do citizens feel a moral responsibility to address this issue? • Does the issue conflict with citizens' moral values or other moral obligations (that is, religious or cultural conflicts)?	• **Level of intrinsic motivation among citizens to address the issue**	• **Influence of social and cultural norms** (can go both ways: enabling or disabling) (Tsai 2007) • **Culture of poverty arguments that influence individual or collective agency on the issue** • **Capacity to aspire** (Appadurai 2004)

(continued next page)

Table 4.3 Unpacking Citizen Action as a Constitutive Element of Social Accountability *(continued)*

Citizen action	Indicative question	Potential contributing contextual factors	
		Actor based	**Structural**
Efficacy (perception of citizen agency to bring change)	• Do citizens believe they (individually or collectively, as relevant) have the ability to make a difference on this issue? • Do citizens believe their actions will likely have an impact?	• *Capability-linked (for example, minimum level of education needed or skills required for proposed citizen action) or level of political efficacy (Pollock 1983)* + Counterfactual: A low external political efficacy ("state will not respond to my demands") combined with high internal political efficacy ("I'm aware of my entitlement that the state must provide") may actually spark action	• **Political structures** (patron–client systems, level of political competition) or historically constituted expectations of the state from citizens • **Level of social inclusion or cohesion** contributing to collective citizen action on the issue • **Rights-based legislation** that enables citizen action on the issue (Maru 2010) • **Level of institutionalization of citizen participation in the governance of services** (Cornwall and Coelho 2004, 2007; Fung and Wright 2003; Gaventa 2006; Manor 2004) • **Types of identity and "differentiated citizenships"** (Holston 2008)
Capacity of individuals for collective action	• Do citizens expect fellow citizens to join them in addressing this issue? • Does strong, broad-based, recognized leadership among citizens exist to engage on this issue? (If no, can collective action on the issue be created without such leadership?)	• **Level of participation that the issue generates in the community** (also linked to salience of the issue) + Counterfactual: A high level of perceived participation on the issue could also deter action ("free-rider" issue) + Counterfactual: Aggregated individual responses without the need to form collective groups or organizations, due to ICT enablers (for example, Ghana radio experience; Selormey 2013)	• **Nature of past citizen–state engagement** (including path dependency of existing structures or patterns of state-society engagement) • **Level of inclusiveness of social organizations** • **Freedom of association or availability of public spaces and ease of congregation** (infrastructure, legislation, culture)

(continued next page)

Table 4.3 Unpacking Citizen Action as a Constitutive Element of Social Accountability *(continued)*

Citizen action	Indicative question	Potential contributing contextual factors	
		Actor based	Structural
Capacity for collective action (of groups or organizations)	• Do CSOs or community-based organizations (CBOs) currently have a strategy or plan in place to address the issue and adequate capacity to follow through? • Do CSOs or CBOs have the necessary capacity to launch or set an agenda on the issue? • Do citizens (as CSOs or CBOs) have strong leadership?	• *Level of capabilities within the organization (whether financial, human, technical, or political)* • *Existence or not of engagement campaign or strategy within the organization on the issue (including organic participation on the issue)* • *Organizations' networks (formal or informal),* including political (bridging) networks	• **Nature of past citizen-state engagement** • **Level of inclusiveness of social organizations** (including through memberships or representation) • **Extent to which organization is based on traditional structure** (Narayan 1999)
Costs of (in)action	• From the perspective of citizens (whether as individuals or in groups, as relevant), are the expected benefits (material and nonmaterial) from their participation likely to be higher than the costs of participation? • Are citizens afraid to act on this issue?	• *Level of ease to participate for individual or collective actors and level of targeted benefits* • *Opportunity costs of participation* + Counterfactual: Fear may actually spark action (Eyerman 2005; Flam and King 2005)	• **Political structures** (patron–client systems, level of political competition) that may enable or disable formation of social capital and level of citizen agency • **Level of social inclusion or cohesion** (in close-knit communities, concerns about social harmony resulting from citizen action on the issue)

Note: Factors in italics are more easily changeable through an intervention.

Table 4.4 Unpacking Information as a Constitutive Element of Social Accountability

Information	Indicative question	Potential contributing contextual factors		Intervention strategy[a]
		Short term	Longer term	
Information linked to citizen action				
Accessibility	• Is the information on the issue accessible to the citizens? • Is the information provided on the issue easy to understand for the citizens?	• **Socioeconomic status, literacy, or other relevant individual capabilities** (including ownership or access to mobile phones, Internet, if relevant) • **Level of connectivity** (ICT-based such as cell phones, Internet) • **Level of familiarity with specific sector or issue** + Counterfactual: Depending on the individual, "fuzziness" of information provided might actually incentivize to take further action (for example, by asking for clarifications, denouncing unclear information)	• **Freedom of information and independence of media** • **Elite capture restricting or biasing information** (patron–client relations) or social exclusion of targeted citizens (Olken 2007) • **Availability of public spaces and ease of congregation** (infrastructure, legislation, culture) • **Targeted-area geography:** existence of remote areas difficult to access	• Simplify information and adapt communication to target group (language, media), specific attention to vulnerable or excluded groups • Explore effectiveness of intermediation (but mediation of information by intermediaries might also potentially distort its reception) • Explore ICT role in making information more accessible

(continued next page)

Table 4.4 Unpacking Information as a Constitutive Element of Social Accountability *(continued)*

Information	Indicative question	Potential contributing contextual factors		Intervention strategy[a]
		Short term	Longer term	
Salience to drive citizen action	• Is the information on the issue significant enough for the citizens to care? • Does the information demonstrate causality between state (in)action and outcomes?	• **Level of citizen interest in the issue as framed by the information** (Banerjee et al. 2008; Duflo, Dupas, and Kremer 2012)		• Strategically frame information on the issue (including emphasizing rights and entitlements and giving legitimacy to action, emphasizing future relevance of the issue, or focusing on comparative data rather than focusing solely on performance gaps) • Frame information on tangible observables (rather than on intangible outputs) • Disseminate information on government performance through legitimate (third-party) and inclusive forums or individuals (Keefer and Khemani 2005)
Trustworthiness	• Are citizens likely to trust the source of information or the setting through which information on the issue is given?	• **Individual and collective (dis)trust of information source** (whether stemming from perception of government, CSO, facilitators, or external donor-driven agenda) + Counterfactual: Existence of highly biased information may motivate citizens to produce their own information (case dependent on type of information and its purpose)	• **Mistrust in source of information linked to existing social dynamics** • **Existence of legitimate (and inclusive) forums (such as parent-teacher associations and health committees)** • **Independence and freedom of media**	• Relay information through existing legitimate (and inclusive) forums (such as parent-teacher associations and health committees) or trusted intermediaries (such as Twaweza)

(continued next page)

Table 4.4 Unpacking Information as a Constitutive Element of Social Accountability (*continued*)

Information	Indicative question	Potential contributing contextual factors		Intervention strategy[a]
		Short term	**Longer term**	

Consistency or novelty	• Are citizens likely to find the information consistent with what they already know or learn through other channels on the issue?
	
	• Will the information corroborate existing knowledge on the issue?
		• **Level of information consistency and frequency** (Keefer and Khemani 2011; Pandey, Goyal, and Sundararaman 2009)
		  + Counterfactual: Inconsistent information may actually trigger citizen awareness or action if the issue is salient or polemical (Reinikka and Svensson 2004)
		  + Counterfactual: Level of polarization on the information drives salience of the issue
		
		• **Level of novelty in the information** ("old" information does not trigger action or reaction; Lieberman, Posner, and Tsai 2013)
			• **Historical or cultural legacies counter to information on the issue** (cognitive dissonance)	• Foster aggressive media campaign or individual outreach
				• Promote repeated messages (Pandey, Goyal, and Sundararaman 2009) or use various channels or multistep individualized outreach or framing
				• Frame the issue or the information on the issue as new

Information linked to state action				
Salience to drive state action	• Do officials agree with the information and the framing of this information on the issue? • Do officials find the level of existing information sufficient to act on the issue?	• **Capability of officials to comprehend and analyze the information** • **Level of usefulness of information to officials** + Counterfactual: Officials who disagree with the information as presented may be incentivized to act to present more complete information		• Frame information on the issue strategically for state officials (including an emphasis on incentives for officials, where possible) rather than as a media campaign that focuses only on gaps in service-provider performance • Disseminate information, designed by the intervention, through legitimate (third-party) and inclusive forums or individuals on government performance (Keefer and Khemani 2005)

(continued next page)

Table 4.4 Unpacking Information as a Constitutive Element of Social Accountability *(continued)*

Information	Indicative question	Potential contributing contextual factors		Intervention strategy[a]
		Short term	**Longer term**	
Trustworthiness	• Do officials trust the information on the issue?	• **Level of trust that officials have on the source of information or the methodology used to collect it** (sampling, representativeness)		• Build capacity of citizens to communicate with government using existing interface or through intermediation • Build capacity of civil society actors or groups to generate rigorous data
Information linked to citizen-state engagement				
Information on existence and accessibility of the interface	• Is there information for citizens or for officials about the citizen-state interface platform(s) on the issue? • Is there information for citizens or for officials on how to access the interface platform(s) on the issue?	• **Literacy and other relevant individual capabilities** (including ownership or access to mobile phones, Internet, and others, if relevant)	• **Elite capture restricting or biasing information** (patron–client relations)	• Conduct a communication campaign and wide dissemination of information about the interface • Mitigate the effect of social dynamics • Use multiple interface locations and channels • Engage an information campaign to make interface space known and build its credibility
Information that strengthens the credibility of interface with key stakeholders (citizens and officials)	• Do citizens or officials trust the interface channels or mechanisms?	• **Individual or collective (dis)trust of information channels** (whether stemming from perception of government, CSO, or facilitators)	• **Mistrust in channel of information linked to existing social dynamics**	• Use mobilizers and interlocutors to take information on the interface to targeted groups and mitigate the effect of social perceptions on the interface • Conduct a communication campaign

a. The intervention strategy or measures mentioned are illustrative and need to be tailored to the particular context. Longer-term contributing factors are less likely to be addressed by an intervention without having focused adequately on contributing contextual factors that can potentially be addressed in the short term.

Table 4.5 Unpacking Mobilization as a Constitutive Element of Social Accountability

Civic mobilization	Indicative question	Potential contributing contextual factors		Intervention strategy[a]
		Short term	Longer term	
Existence of mobilizers	• Do groups or media exist that can mobilize citizens and state officials on the issue?	• **Availability of mobilizers on the issue within the local context**—CSOs or CBOs, media, or within state (for example, legislators or government bodies) • **Existence of external nongovernmental agencies (including donors) that promote citizen action and state action on the issue**	• **High level of media penetration and pluralist media within the local context**, assuming that the reach of media can be a powerful mobilizer (Tembo 2012)	• Use existing CSOs or associations and networks to mobilize citizens (including traditional institutions) and state officials • Promote use of local media • Harness the potential of external nongovernment agencies supportive of citizen-state engagement to address the issue
Capacity of mobilizers (agents, organizations)	• Do the individuals, groups, or organizations mobilizing citizens and state officials on the issue have a strategy or plan of engagement? • Do mobilizers have adequate capacity to follow through on their plan of engagement? • Do mobilizers (whether as groups or organizations) have strong leadership, if needed to be effective?	• **Level of awareness of mobilizers on social accountability mechanisms or on the issue** • **Level of capabilities (financial, human, technical, and political) supporting mobilization** (whether individuals, groups, or organization) • **Existence or not of engagement strategy** within the organization, group, or individuals mobilizing citizens and state officials		• Build capacity and create awareness on social accountability processes to assist CSOs, CBOs, and the media or other groups that mobilize citizens and state officials on the issue • Build capacity of the mobilizing group or organization to manage its own financial and human resources, if needed for the mobilization to succeed • Build an engagement strategy (where previously absent) for groups or organizations mobilizing citizens and state officials on the issue

(continued next page)

141

Table 4.5 Unpacking Mobilization as a Constitutive Element of Social Accountability *(continued)*

Civic mobilization	Indicative question	Potential contributing contextual factors		Intervention strategy[a]
		Short term	**Longer term**	
Effectiveness and legitimacy in mobilizing citizens	• Do mobilizers have networks or credibility with citizens?	• **Organizations' social networks** (formal or informal) • **Level of inclusiveness of social organizations engaged in mobilization** (including through memberships or representation)	• **Freedom of association or CSO law that fosters pluralism and independence of CSOs** • Clout, membership base, prior positioning, and track record of relevant CSOs	• Promote the importance of building social networks for the groups or organizations engaged in mobilization of citizens • Draw attention to the importance of gender disparities and social exclusion (where necessary) for mobilizing groups or organizations engaging citizens on the issue
Effectiveness and legitimacy in mobilizing state officials	• Do mobilizers have networks or credibility with state officials?	• **Mobilizing organizations' networks** (formal or informal), including political (bridging) networks		• Promote the importance of groups or organizations engaged in mobilization and building of networks and coalitions with the state to support the issue (for example, among legislators, nonelected policy makers, and bureaucrats)

a. The intervention strategy or measures mentioned are illustrative and need to be tailored to the particular context. Longer-term contributing factors are less likely to be addressed by an intervention without having focused adequately on contributing contextual factors that can potentially be addressed in the short term.

Table 4.6 Unpacking Citizen-State Interface as a Constitutive Element of Social Accountability

Citizen-state interface	Indicative question	Potential contributing contextual factors		Intervention strategy[a]
		Short term	**Longer term**	
Interface platform				
Type of existing interface platform(s)	• Is there an existing channel or mechanism for citizens and officials to engage on the issue? • Is the existing interface space on the issue closed, invited, or claimed in relation to citizens?	• **Nature of interface "space" on the issue—claimed, invited, or closed** (Cornwall 2002; Gaventa 2004)	• **Degree of institutionalization of particular interface on the issue** (can go both ways)	• Create or strengthen an existing weak interface between citizens and state officials on the issue • Promote institutionalization of the citizen-state engagement "space" (trajectory from closed to invited to claimed space) to improve its sustainability (need to be aware of trade-offs of institutionalization)
Awareness of the interface platform(s)	• Are citizens or officials adequately aware of the citizen-state interface platform(s) on the issue?	• **Capability related** (for example, education, literacy) • **Exposure to information on the existing interface platform(s)**		• Conduct an active media and targeted information campaign on the interface platform(s) • Build awareness of the interface space through mobilization (table 4.5) or through interlocution
Credibility of interface platform(s)	• Is the existing channel or mechanism to engage on the issue trusted by citizens and officials? • Do citizens and officials share a common expectation of the interface to address the issue?	• **Level of trust in the interface** (for citizens and officials) • **Nature of citizen role in the interface**—primarily consultative or binding on decisions of officials	• **Scale and quality of institutional structures to enable the interface platform on the issue**	• Use interlocutors to build trust (or address fears) of citizens and officials in the interface

(continued next page)

Table 4.6 Unpacking Citizen-State Interface as a Constitutive Element of Social Accountability *(continued)*

Citizen-state interface	Indicative question	Potential contributing contextual factors		Intervention strategy[a]
		Short term	Longer term	
Accessibility of interface platform(s)	• Is the existing channel or mechanism to engage on the issue readily accessible to both citizens and officials? • What is the method to identify or select participants (among citizens and officials)?	• **Adaptability of the interface to minimize costs for participants** (citizens or state officials)—linked to "incentives and costs for (in) action" for citizen action and state action • **Level of ICT penetration** (cell phones, Internet, radio) • **Level of self-selection in the participatory arrangements of the interface** (which can exclude individual or minority groups)—for example, CSO-mediated selection processes or nature of randomized or stratified methods (mini-publics)	• **Challenges of geographic remoteness or population density in the target area**	• Promote adaptability of interface channels to targeted users or choice of time, length, and location to maximize the number of participants • Promote the provision for anonymous feedback for protection • Include specific strategies for inclusiveness (using interlocutors or targeted media)
Interlocution that strengthens interface				
Existence of interlocutors	• Do interlocutors exist who can engage citizens (individuals or groups) and state officials for the interface on this issue?	• **Availability of CSOs or CBOs** that can perform the role of interlocutors within the local context on the issue • **Role of media** in facilitating an interface on the issue	• **Existence of CSOs or CBOs (including traditional networks) within local society that can perform the role of interlocutors** (Tsai 2007)	• Strengthen local associations as interlocutors between citizens and the state • Promote use of media (if acceptable to state officials) • Engage in creating CSOs or CBOs that may perform the role of interlocutors on the issue in the longer term

(continued next page)

Table 4.6 Unpacking Citizen-State Interface as a Constitutive Element of Social Accountability *(continued)*

Citizen-state interface	Indicative question	Potential contributing contextual factors		Intervention strategy[a]
		Short term	Longer term	
Effectiveness of interlocutors in mediating citizens and state officials on the issue	• Do interlocutors have adequate capacity to engage citizen and state officials effectively on the issue? • Do interlocutors have sufficient networks or credibility with citizens and state officials to mobilize their participation in the interface space? • Do interlocutors (as individuals, groups, or organizations) have strong leadership, if needed to be effective?	• **Level of awareness of interlocutors on social accountability mechanisms or on the issue** • **Level of influence of interlocutors in bringing citizen engagement in the interface space** (including social inclusiveness of interlocution or leadership skills of interlocutors, where important) • **Level of influence of interlocutors in mobilizing state officials or their participation in the interface space**		• Identify and build as interlocutors (as much as possible) individuals or groups that are already embedded within the local social context • Promote interlocutors who ensure social inclusion or have existing networks within government or legislature (building capacity wherever needed) • Explore the creation of local-level social accountability committees (comprising citizens and state officials), facilitated by the interlocutor, that raise their influence on both groups

a. The intervention strategy or measures mentioned are illustrative and need to be tailored to the particular context. Longer-term contributing factors are less likely to be addressed by an intervention without having focused adequately on contributing contextual factors that can potentially be addressed in the short term.

Conclusion

The drivers of SA effectiveness take into account a broad range of contextual factors (social, political, and intervention-based factors, including ICT elements). They can assume different permutations to influence specific change paths leading to SA outcomes.

The guiding tables form the first steps for a toolkit to assess, adjust, monitor, and evaluate contextual drivers of SA effectiveness. Box 4.2 presents the key takeaways from this chapter.

In chapters 5, 6, and 7, we apply this framework in two ways: to map country archetypes and to assess specific cases. Chapters 5 and 6 apply the analytical framework to discuss two archetypes of challenging contexts: countries where the space for citizen engagement is formally constrained and fragile and conflict-affected situations (FCSs). The chapters highlight what we know about SA potential and outcomes in such contexts. Chapter 7 illustrates how to use the framework for designing and implementing SA to address a specific issue or problem. It provides examples from SA engagements in Sierra Leone, Pakistan, the Republic of Yemen, and the Kyrgyz Republic.

BOX 4.2

Key Takeaways: An Analytical Framework on Contextual Drivers of Social Accountability

The analytical framework presented here builds on a careful remapping of the available evidence along SA's five constitutive elements. This mapping helped us to identify a set of factors that will have an impact on the effectiveness of SA, which were then clustered into a set of drivers (for instance, elements around type of information, novelty, or consistency of the information were clustered under "framing" of information) and mapped to each of the five constitutive elements of our framework (see figure B4.2.1).

(continued next page)

BOX 4.2 (continued)

Figure B4.2.1 The Analytical Framework and Its Contextual Drivers

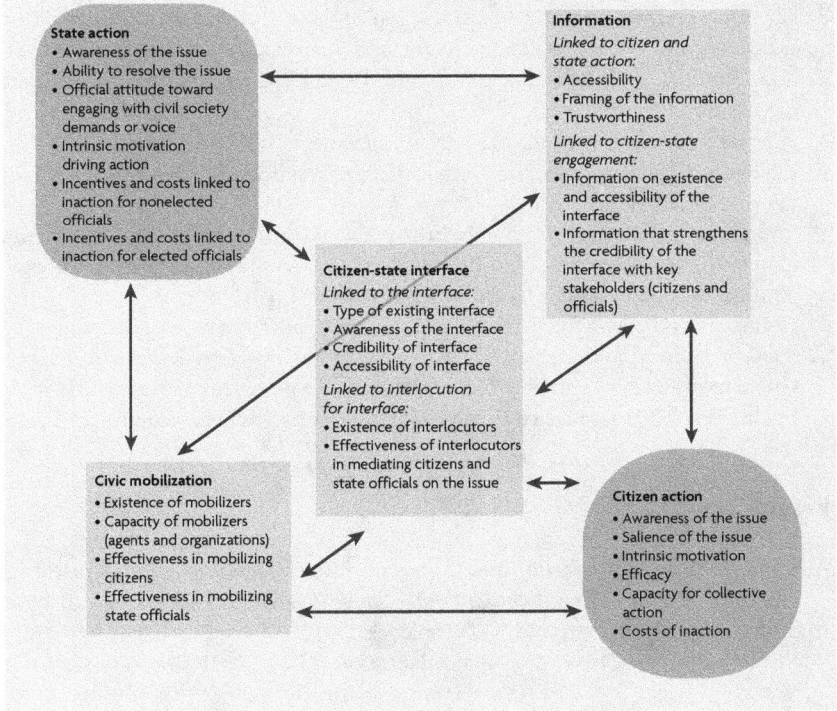

State action
- Awareness of the issue
- Ability to resolve the issue
- Official attitude toward engaging with civil society demands or voice
- Intrinsic motivation driving action
- Incentives and costs linked to inaction for nonelected officials
- Incentives and costs linked to inaction for elected officials

Information
Linked to citizen and state action:
- Accessibility
- Framing of the information
- Trustworthiness

Linked to citizen-state engagement:
- Information on existence and accessibility of the interface
- Information that strengthens the credibility of the interface with key stakeholders (citizens and officials)

Citizen-state interface
Linked to the interface:
- Type of existing interface
- Awareness of the interface
- Credibility of interface
- Accessibility of interface

Linked to interlocution for interface:
- Existence of interlocutors
- Effectiveness of interlocutors in mediating citizens and state officials on the issue

Civic mobilization
- Existence of mobilizers
- Capacity of mobilizers (agents and organizations)
- Effectiveness in mobilizing citizens
- Effectiveness in mobilizing state officials

Citizen action
- Awareness of the issue
- Salience of the issue
- Intrinsic motivation
- Efficacy
- Capacity for collective action
- Costs of inaction

Notes

1. The team is working on adapting this framework to fit specific accountability profiles of key services to support teams better.
2. The problem-driven iterative adaptation approach is based on four core principles. It focuses on solving locally nominated and defined problems in performance (as opposed to transplanting preconceived and packaged best-practice solutions). It seeks to create an authorizing environment for decision making that encourages positive deviance and experimentation (as opposed to designing projects and programs and then requiring agents to implement them exactly as designed). It embeds this experimentation in tight feedback loops that

facilitate rapid experiential learning (as opposed to long lag times in learning from ex post evaluation). It actively engages broad sets of agents to ensure that reforms are viable, legitimate, relevant, and supportable, as opposed to a narrow set of external experts promoting the top-down diffusion of innovation (Andrews, Pritchett, and Woolcock 2012).

3. There is currently considerable discussion on how and when individual action translates into collective action (Bauhr and Grimes 2014; Lieberman, Posner, and Tsai 2013; Persson, Rothstein, and Teorell 2013), but this is a separate discussion.

4. A good introduction to the ARVIN framework is in World Bank (2003). To look at its application, see, for instance, Beck, Mendel, and Thindwa (2007) for the case of Mongolia.

5. The global penetration of mobile broadband is expected to reach 32 percent, almost double the penetration rate of 2011. In developing countries, the penetration of mobile cellular is expected to reach 90 percent by the end of 2014. Connectivity through fixed broadband also continues to grow, and the number of fixed-broadband subscriptions in developing countries overtook that in developed countries in 2013. The number of Internet users is expected to reach almost 3 billion by the end of 2014, and two-thirds of Internet users live in developing countries.

References

Amelina, M. 2011. *Information and Communication Technologies for Demand for Good Governance: Enabling the Power Shift.* Washington, DC: World Bank.

Andrews, M., L. Pritchett, and M. Woolcock. 2012. "Escaping Capability Traps through Problem-Driven Iterative Adaptation (PDIA)." HKS Faculty Research Working Paper RWP12-036, Harvard Kennedy School, Cambridge, MA, August.

Appadurai, A. 2004. "The Capacity to Aspire: Culture and the Terms of Recognition." In *Culture and Public Action*, edited by V. Rao and M. Walton, 59–84. Stanford, CA: Stanford University Press.

Banerjee, A. V., R. Banerji, E. Duflo, R. Glennerster, and S. Khemani. 2008. "Pitfalls of Participatory Programs: Evidence from Randomized Experiments in Education in India." Poverty Action Lab Paper, Massachusetts Institute of Technology, Cambridge, MA.

Bauhr, M., and M. Grimes. 2014. "Indignation or Resignation: The Implications of Transparency for Societal Accountability." *Governance* 27 (2): 291–320. DOI: 10.1111/gove.12033.

Beck, L., T. Mendel, and J. Thindwa. 2007. *The Enabling Environment for Social Accountability in Mongolia.* Washington, DC: World Bank, Social Development Department, Sustainable Development Network.

Besley, T., and R. Burgess. 2002. "The Political Economy of Government Responsiveness: Theory and Evidence from India." *Quarterly Journal of Economics* 117 (4): 1415–51. http://qje.oxfordjournals.org/content/117/4/1415 .full.pdf.

Bhatti, Z. K., J. Z. Kusek, and T. Verheijen. 2015. *Logged On: Smart Government Solutions from South Asia*. Washington, DC: World Bank. https:// openknowledge.worldbank.org/bitstream/handle/10986/20487/9781464803123 .pdf?sequence=1.

Bukenya, B., S. Hickey, and S. King. 2012. "Understanding the Role of Context in Shaping Social Accountability Interventions: Toward an Evidence-Based Approach." Social Accountability and Demand for Good Governance Team Report, World Bank, Washington, DC. http://web.worldbank.org/WBSITE /EXTERNAL/TOPICS/EXTSOCIALDEVELOPMENT/0,,contentMDK: 21211265~pagePK:210058~piPK:210062~theSitePK:244363,00.html.

Caleen, M., and A. Hasanain. 2011. "The Punjab Model of Proactive Governance: Empowering Citizens through Information Communication Technology." University of California, San Diego; Lahore University of Management Sciences, Lahore, Pakistan.

Cornwall, A. 2002. "Making Spaces, Changing Places: Situating Participation in Development." IDS Working Paper 170, University of Sussex, Institute of Development Studies, Brighton, U.K.

Cornwall, A., and V. S. Coelho. 2004. "New Democratic Spaces?" *IDS Bulletin* 35 (2): 1–10.

———, eds. 2007. "Spaces for Change? The Politics of Citizen Participation in New Democratic Arenas." In *Spaces for Change? The Politics of Citizen Participation in New Democratic Arenas*, edited by A. Cornwall and V. S. P. Coelho. London: Zed Books.

Cullen, R., and L. Sommer. 2011. "Participatory Democracy and the Value of Online Community Networks: An Exploration of Online and Offline Communities Engaged in Civil Society and Political Activity." *Government Information Quarterly* 28 (2): 148–54.

Duflo, E., P. Dupas, and M. Kremer. 2012. "School Governance, Teacher Incentives, and Pupil-Teacher Ratios: Experimental Evidence from Kenyan Primary Schools." NBER Working Paper 17939, National Bureau for Economic Research, Cambridge, MA.

Eyerman, R. 2005. "How Social Movements Move: Emotions and Social Movements." In *Emotions and Social Movements*, edited by H. Flam and D. King, 41–56. London: Routledge.

Flam, H., and D. King, eds. 2005. *Emotions and Social Movements*. London: Routledge.

Fox, J. 2004. "Empowerment and Institutional Change: Mapping 'Virtuous Circles' of State-Society Interaction." In *Power, Rights, and Poverty: Concepts and Connections,* edited by R. Alsop. Washington, DC: World Bank; London: Department for International Development.

Fung, A., and E. O. Wright, eds. 2003. *Deepening Democracy: Institutional Innovations in Empowered Participatory Governance.* London: Verso.

Gaventa, J. 2004. "Towards Participatory Local Governance: Assessing the Transformative Possibilities." In *Participation: From Tyranny to Transformation,* edited by S. Hickey and G. Mohan, 25–41. London: Zed Books.

———. 2006. "Finding the Spaces for Change: A Power Analysis." *IDS Bulletin* 37 (6): 23–33.

Gigler, B.-S., S. Bailur, and N. Anand. 2014. *The Loch Ness Model: Can ICTs Bridge the "Accountability Gap"?* Washington, DC: World Bank.

Hanna, N. K. 2009. *e-Transformation: Enabling New Development Strategies.* New York: Springer.

———. 2012. "Open Development: ICT for Governance in Africa." World Bank, Africa Public Sector Governance and ICT Unit, Washington, DC.

Harding, R., and D. Stasavage. 2014. "What Democracy Does (and Doesn't) Do for Basic Services: School Fees, School Quality, and African Elections." *Journal of Politics* 76 (1, January): 229–45.

Holston, J. 2008. *Insurgent Citizenship: Disjunctions of Democracy and Modernity in Brazil.* Princeton, NJ: Princeton University Press.

ITU (International Telecommunication Union). 2014. *The World in 2014: ICT Facts and Figures.* Geneva: ITU, April. http://www.itu.int/en/ITU-D/Statistics /Documents/facts/ICTFactsFigures2014-e.pdf.

Joshi, A. 2013. "The Impact of Social Accountability Initiatives on Improving the Delivery of Public Services: A Systematic Review of Four Intervention Types: Protocol." Unpublished mss., University of Sussex, Institute of Development Studies, Brighton, U.K.

Keefer, P., and S. Khemani. 2005. "Democracy, Public Expenditures, and the Poor." *World Bank Research Observer* 20 (1): 1–28.

———. 2011. "Mass Media and Public Services: The Effects of Radio Access on Public Education in Benin." Policy Research Working Paper 5559, World Bank, Washington, DC.

Lieberman, E., D. N. Posner, and L. Tsai. 2013. "Does Information Lead to More Active Citizenship? Evidence from an Education Intervention in Rural Kenya." Political Science Department Research Paper 2013-2, Massachusetts Institute of Technology, Cambridge, MA.

Linders, D. 2012. "From E-Government to We-Government: Defining a Typology for Citizen Coproduction in the Age of Social Media." *Government Information Quarterly* 29 (4): 446–54.

Linders, D., S. C. Wilson, and J. C. Bertot. 2013. "Open Government as a Vehicle for Government Transformation." In *Public Sector Transformation through*

E-Government: Experiences from Europe and North America, edited by W. Weerakkody and C. G. Reddick, 9–24. New York: Routledge.

Manor, J. 2004. "Democratisation with Inclusion: Political Reforms and People's Empowerment at the Grassroots." *Journal of Human Development* 5 (1): 5–29.

Maru, V. 2010. "Allies Unknown: Social Accountability and Legal Empowerment." *Health and Human Rights in Practice* 12 (1): 83–93.

Miller, V. 2011. *Understanding Digital Culture.* London: Sage.

Millington, P., and L. Carter. 2013. "Rational Choice Theory: Using the Fundamentals of Human Behavior to Tackle the Digital Divide." In *Public Sector Transformation through E-Government: Experiences from Europe and North America,* edited by V. Weerakkody and C. G. Reddick, 140–51. New York: Routledge.

Narayan, D. 1999. "Bonds and Bridges: Social Capital and Poverty." Policy Research Working Paper 2167, World Bank, Washington, DC.

Olken, B. A. 2007. "Monitoring Corruption: Evidence from a Field Experiment in Indonesia." *Journal of Political Economy* 115 (2): 200–49.

Osimo, D. 2008. *Web 2.0 in Government: Why and How?* Luxembourg: European Commission.

Pande, S. 2013. "The Right to Know, the Right to Live: Grassroots Struggle for Information and Work in India." PhD thesis, University of Sussex, Brighton, U.K.

Pandey, P., S. Goyal, and V. Sundararaman. 2009. "Community Participation in Public Schools: The Impact of Public Information Campaign in Three Indian States." *Education Economics* 17 (3): 355–75.

Pawson, R. 2003. "Nothing as Practical as a Good Theory." *Evaluation* 9 (4): 471–90.

Peixoto, T. Forthcoming. "Effects of the Internet on Participation: A Study of a Public Policy Referendum in Brazil." Policy Research Working Paper, World Bank, Washington, DC.

Persson, A., B. Rothstein, and J. Teorell. 2013. "Why Anti-Corruption Reforms Fail: Systematic Corruption as a Collective Action Problem." *Governance* 23 (3): 449–71.

Pollock, P. H. III. 1983. "The Participatory Consequences of Internal and External Political Efficacy: A Research Note." *Western Political Quarterly* 36 (3): 400–09.

Reinikka, R., and J. Svensson. 2004. "The Power of Information: Evidence from a Newspaper Campaign to Reduce Capture." Policy Research Working Paper 3239, World Bank, Washington, DC.

Rodríguez Bolívar, M., L. Muñoz, and A. M. López Hernández. 2013. "Profiling E-Participation Research in Europe and North America: A Bibliometric Analysis." In *Public Sector Transformation through e-Government: Experiences from Europe and North America*, edited by V. Weerakkody and C. G. Reddick, 120–39. New York: Routledge.

Selormey, E. 2013. "Citizen Voice and Bureaucratic Responsiveness: FM Radio Phone-Ins and the Delivery of Municipal and Local Government Services in Accra, Ghana." PhD thesis, University of Sussex, Institute of Development Studies, Brighton, U.K.

Siegle, J. 2014. "ICT and Accountability in Areas of Limited Statehood." In *Bits and Atoms*, edited by S. Livingston and G. Walter-Drop, 61–75. Oxford: Oxford University Press.

Tembo, F. 2012. "Citizen Voice and State Accountability: Towards Theories of Change That Embrace Contextual Dynamics." Working Paper 343, Overseas Development Institute, London.

Tsai, L. L. 2007. "Solidary Groups, Informal Accountability, and Local Public Goods Provision in Rural China." *American Political Science Review* 101 (2): 555–72.

U.K. Cabinet Office. 2014. "Government Digital Inclusion Strategy." U.K. Cabinet Office, London. https://www.gov.uk/government/publications/government-digital -inclusion-strategy/government-digital-inclusion-strategy.

van Dijk, J. A. 2005. *The Deepening Divide: Inequality and the Information Society*. London: Sage.

Watta, S., Y. Hong, M. Mandviwalla, and A. Jain. 2011. "Technology Diffusion in the Society: Analyzing Digital Divide in the Context of Social Class." Proceedings of the 44th Hawaii International Conference on System Sciences, Kauai, January 4–7. http://www.computer.org/csdl/proceedings/hicss/2011/4282/00/03-01-03 -abs.html.

World Bank. 2003. "Enabling Environments for Civic Engagement in PRSP Countries." Social Development Note 82, World Bank, Washington, DC, March.

———. 2013. "Social Accountability Case Examples: Information and Communication Technologies (ICTs)—South Asia Region: Pakistan, the Punjab Model of Proactive Governance: Empowering Citizens through ICT." World Bank, Washington, DC. https://saeguide.worldbank.org/sites/worldbank.org .saeguide/files/documents/ICT%20SAR%20Pakistan.pdf.

———. 2014. "Strategic Framework for Mainstreaming Citizen Engagement in World Bank Group Operations (Draft)." Draft from the Decision Meeting on July 8, World Bank Group, Washington, DC.

World Bank Institute. 2012. "Information and Communication Technology for Governance (ICT4Gov) Program: Case Study Contributing to the 'Study on Strengthening Inclusive Stakeholder Ownership through Capacity Development.'" World Bank Institute, Washington, DC.

Social Accountability in Countries Where Space for Citizen-State Engagement Is Formally Constrained

Chapters 5 and 6 explore the use of SA in challenging contexts. The rationale for doing so stems from a pragmatic assessment: SA approaches are pursued in most countries, yet some countries are particularly challenging, because they lack the capacity or willingness to support or engage in SA. It also comes from the hypothesis that countries with lower capacity or willingness to engage in SA stand to benefit most from such approaches, and therefore we need to build the knowledge base on these specific contexts.

Chapter 5 analyzes experiences in designing and implementing SA in countries where the space for citizen-state engagement is formerly constrained and explores the opportunities, specific constraints, and risks associated with such approaches. While this chapter looks at how social accountability can unfold in contexts with weak state-society relations, it does not include "fragile" states (the focus of chapter 6), but instead focuses on states that have some level of administrative capacity for responsiveness.

Chapter 6 analyzes experiences in designing and implementing SA in FCSs, starting from the acknowledgment that lack of accountability is a key element of fragility and exploring whether and how SA can support stronger accountability and stronger state-society relationships.

There is a major caveat to exploring archetypes: no two FCSs are similar, and no two countries where the space for citizen-state engagement is formally constrained are alike. In the previous chapters, we have explored the complexity of factors that matter for SA and the diversity of its drivers.

This does not sit well with the use of archetypes for what are, ultimately, a very diverse group of countries and contexts.

We nonetheless focus on some common characteristics of challenging contexts that are important for SA and highlight some findings on the opportunities, constraints, and risks associated with SA. The particularities of each context always need to be taken into account when looking at these findings, however.

Designing and implementing social accountability (SA) in countries where space for citizen-state engagement is formally constrained entails specific constraints and risks. In such contexts, state action and its responsiveness to any social accountability processes must take place without links to electoral accountability and with weak institutions of accountability, and a legal and regulatory framework that constrains some basic freedoms (association, information). This chapter examines how these countries' common social and political features constrain citizen and state action for SA following the categories presented in chapter 3. Using the analytical framework, it then considers how constraints on information, the interface between civil society and governments, and civic mobilization might be overcome to spur citizen action and state action. Finally, it considers some of the strategies that have been adopted to open up space for greater accountability.

Common Social and Political Features That Constrain Citizen and State Action for SA

Countries where space for citizen-state engagement is formally constrained differ markedly. Nevertheless, they share several characteristics that distinguish them from other contexts in relation to social accountability approaches (see figure 5.1).

What Are the Characteristics of Political Society and the Constraints to State Action and Responsiveness?

In countries where space for citizen-state engagement is formally constrained, accountability to an electorate is not a constraint on states—at least at the center. In such countries (monarchies, single-party states, or military governments), political and other freedoms, as well as pluralism, are absent or strictly curtailed. The electoral accountability that constitutes the backbone of vertical accountability in representative democracies either

Figure 5.1 Summarizing an Archetypal Institutional Landscape in Countries Where Space for Citizen-State Engagement Is Formally Constrained

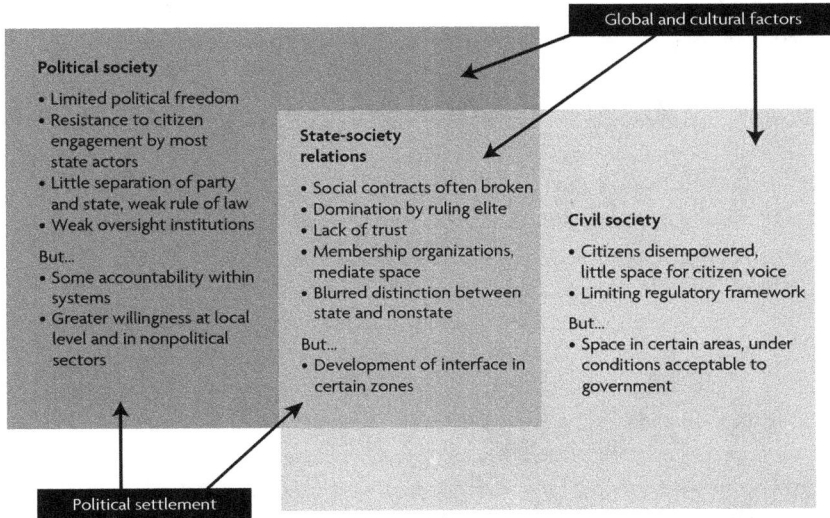

Global and cultural factors

Political society

- Limited political freedom
- Resistance to citizen engagement by most state actors
- Little separation of party and state, weak rule of law
- Weak oversight institutions

But...
- Some accountability within systems
- Greater willingness at local level and in nonpolitical sectors

State-society relations

- Social contracts often broken
- Domination by ruling elite
- Lack of trust
- Membership organizations, mediate space
- Blurred distinction between state and nonstate

But...
- Development of interface in certain zones

Civil society

- Citizens disempowered, little space for citizen voice
- Limiting regulatory framework

But...
- Space in certain areas, under conditions acceptable to government

Political settlement

does not exist or does not function effectively, even though, in some cases, local elections are actively contested.

Allocating resources to supporters of the state or to actors who are necessary to maintain it is the main co-optation strategy. Systems of patronage, cronyism, or high levels of military spending are common (Gandhi and Przeworski 2007; Lust-Okar 2007; Svolik 2008). As a result, the most powerful groups in society may resist attempts to promote transparency. Co-optation is usually used in combination with other strategies, such as repression and building of legitimacy for the state (Tullock 1987; Wintrobe 1998).

In countries with a strong development agenda, where the ruling elite fosters developmental strategies to improve the lives of citizens or to deliver services to at least some parts of society as a way to build legitimacy, social accountability can be part of the development agenda. Understanding incentives, at both national and local levels, and the scope and content of developmental strategies is key to understanding how spaces for social accountability may emerge (see box 5.1).

Systems of accountability are incomplete but do exist. A majority of countries where space for citizen-state engagement is formally constrained

BOX 5.1

Political Society Takes Many Forms and Poses Different Challenges for Social Accountability

A key characteristic of countries where space for citizen-state engagement is formally constrained could determine the state's willingness to respond to citizens' demands. This characteristic is the type of ruling organization (Charron and Lapuente 2011). Some states operate through a small coalition with a strong hold over the polity and society, while others—for example, China, Ethiopia, and the former Soviet Union—rule through one-party systems. Still others have many of the trappings of democratic institutions, such as legislatures and multiparty systems. Even with this last type of state, there are many variations across and within countries over time. For example, General Musharraf of Pakistan allowed a vibrant elected legislature to operate independently for six years of his nine-year rule. In the legislature, the opposition parties debated politically controversial issues (see Aslam 2010). By contrast, Sheikh Al Maktoum of Dubai limited himself to devising a consultative assembly of several thousand dignitaries selected by a handpicked electorate (Wallis 2006). These different configurations of political society present different challenges—and opportunities—with regard to social accountability (for example, see Charron and Lapuente 2011).

operate with representative institutions in some form, and in many cases there is a potential to promote spaces for accountability. Many such countries have seemingly representative institutions such as legislatures that may offer some form of opportunity for the preferences of citizens to be represented and the state apparatus to show responsiveness (Charron and Lapuente 2011; Global Integrity 2013; Magloni 2006; Malesky, Schuler, and Tran 2012; Nathan 2003; Oi 1992; Rosberg 1995, cited in Meng, Pan, and Yang 2014). In single-party systems, a structure of accountability often exists within the party. At times, political competition within the party creates incentives for national and local officials to demonstrate their popularity with citizens and keep their ranking on the party list or satisfy senior officials.

Formal institutions of accountability are, for the most part, weak and controlled. Formal institutions of accountability such as anti-corruption institutions, ombudsmen, human rights commissions, and regulatory agencies may be established, but a formal system of oversight tends to be incomplete (Global Integrity 2013). Close ties between business and the ruling elite mean that powers of enforcement can be easily circumvented.

The space for accountability appears to be even smaller in such countries that are rich in natural resources. These systems have far fewer incentives to create independent institutions of accountability that may trigger sanctions. Compared to economies where "the rulers must rely on bankers to loan them money, peasants to produce food, and scientists to do research" (Gandhi and Przeworski 2007), states that have "unearned" resources at their disposal are less inclined to establish institutions that ensure accountability (see chapter 2).

What Are the Characteristics of Civil Society and the Constraints to Citizen Action?

State control over civil society and its development is pervasive. The agency and space for civil society are strictly controlled. Because basic freedoms are overtly or subtly curtailed, legal and regulatory frameworks for citizen voice (such as freedom of expression, freedom of association, the right to information, and freedom of the press) are, for the most part, absent. In some states, structures and systems may exist to silence voice that criticizes the state. Civil society is formally truncated by means of laws and institutions that make it difficult for organizations outside the control of the state or the elite to emerge. The freedom to associate may be tolerated, but only to enable governments to broker conflicts in an organized fashion (Schmitter 1975) or to perform other functions (Gandhi 2014). In general, however, civil society must adhere to a predefined set of rules and be perceived to be focused on issues tolerated by the state, since the state possesses the power to legitimize or delegitimize its existence.

This dynamic encourages the civil society to self-censor even in the absence of a restrictive legal and regulatory framework. Civil society actors such as militant labor unions or political parties representing ethnic or religious groups know that they could be banned or their members harmed (for example, journalists, persons investigating illegal logging).[1] The selective enforcement of laws also encourages self-censorship. As a consequence, in order to continue to operate and remain relevant, civil society tries to strike a balance where it can play some role in representing citizens' views and promoting accountability.

Assessing the autonomy of civil society or understanding how its distance from state control affects social accountability approaches and outcomes is far from straightforward. While some civil society organizations (CSOs) are co-opted by the government, others may try to survive in a restrictive environment. Whichever the case, they may operate in the same way. For example, state-owned media do not function independently, but self-censorship may also limit the independence of privately owned media outlets. As a result, citizens and sometimes the international community tend to distrust civil society, even when CSOs have not been co-opted by the state. The reputation and links of individual organizations must therefore be thoroughly studied.

Responding to this pressure, nonstate actors often choose a nonconfrontational, constructive path. They pursue development objectives or deliver services and refrain from playing any advocacy role. Citizens may be more inclined to be associated with such organizations because the risks are lower.

Having earned a degree of trust by delivering services, some organizations may shift their efforts to promoting accountability, either by changing their mandate or "wearing two hats." Many domestic nongovernmental organizations (NGOs) move from humanitarian assistance to service delivery and, sometimes, to social accountability. They may perform some of these roles at the same time (Plummer and Dolk 2013).

Governments may nevertheless open up space for citizen engagement. Governments might encourage citizens to participate in less-threatening (that is, nonpolitical) associations as a substitute for their political aspirations. CSOs might participate in formal political institutions such as parties and legislatures. When they do, they can force governments to make nonpolitical policy concessions. If channeled correctly, this participation can provide a safety valve for citizens and civil society groups to vent their discontent and receive benefits (Gandhi 2014).

In many one-party states, associations must be registered with the government and "hosted" by a government agency or ministry. Official sponsorship clarifies which institution of government is responsible for monitoring them. Regulation in this form typically provides a platform for coordination. It also enables the state to deny some organizations formal recognition. The registration process can also be used to halt activities that challenge the status quo and reward others that further the interests of the state.

Civil society may actually help states with low capacity in a variety of ways. First, NGOs may provide various kinds of useful information to the government. The government may need technical advice on how to formulate policy. In Vietnam, for example, NGOs produced studies and held hearings to assist policy makers in crafting more effective domestic violence laws (Wischermann 2011).

Second, they may help the state to address deficiencies in service delivery. The Muslim Brotherhood in the Arab Republic of Egypt, for example, was allowed to operate as a community-based service organization (rather than a political party) under the Mubarak government because it provided valuable health and education services to poor neighborhoods and did not engage in open political opposition.

Government may even encourage the proliferation of associations in order to fragment civil society. For decades, leaders in the Middle East supported the formation of nonstate associations (Cavatorta and Elananza 2010) and encouraged the flow of external aid to civic organizations (Bianchi 1989).

These divisions within society make citizen action even harder. Collective efforts to bring about accountability of the state necessitate bringing together individuals with similar goals. Studies have shown that governments tend to hold onto power by reinforcing ethnic, regional, and religious differences—for example, through the unequal distribution of resources—to reduce claims on the center (Andersen 2008; Gaventa and Barrett 2010).

The capacity of CSOs is weak. Control over the way civil society forms and overlaps with the state tends to produce a relatively weak civil society that is neither politically savvy nor well networked. Civil society is not able to build capacities owing to overt and covert repression by the state.

With little experience and opportunity, CSOs often lack the technical capacity to pursue SA activities. CSOs often have little knowledge of government policies, standards, targets, budgets, and expenditures, and the knowledge of what the state should be accountable for. Moreover, if citizens perceive a civic association as having little knowledge, capacity, or credibility with regard to an issue, they will not trust it to monitor officials or facilitate activities aimed at enhancing accountability.

Another related challenge is an antagonistic relationship with the government. Because of the legacy of poor relations between the states and CSOs, CSOs that are not co-opted by the state usually come to be seen as repos_tories of dissent, a challenge to state authority, and a constraint on the ability of the state to perform its functions. In a contentious environment, civil society does not have practical experience approaching government. Few seek meetings with government officials for fear that doing so might harm their credibility and mission. CSOs lack not only the incentives to engage with the government, but also the capacity or the networks needed for such engagement.

Restrictions and repression also result in the fragmentation of civil society to the extent that there is distrust within civil society itself. This fragmentation implies that there is a lack of cooperation within civil society, so that relationships among organizations are strained and cautious.

The range of organizations in these countries is wide. For example, in Ethiopia, CSOs ranged from the mass organizations that played an important role in the peace process to user groups focused on services such as water, to more independent NGOs that attempted, albeit tentatively, to hold the state to account for human rights, poverty reduction, and due process in the promulgation of laws. This spectrum was difficult for both government and civil society actors to navigate.

In addition to formal civil society, a rich associational life can and has played an important role in promoting social accountability and improving the enabling environment for it.

Faith-based organizations and other forms of traditional organizations, for example, continue to flourish. Citizens mobilize along "traditional" cleavages, such as religion or kinship, to achieve short-term collective objectives, including demanding accountability on the part of officials. Tsai (2007), for example, discusses the importance of village temple associations not only in maintaining local Buddhist sites of worship, but also in holding accountable local officials who are embedded in such groups. This may not always be the case, however. In addition, traditional cleavages may not always be inclusive of all groups in the community.[2]

Similarly, local associations continue to flourish at the local level to pursue local development needs or to address specific grievances, much the same as in democracies.[3] Similar to the community-based organizations found in more open environments, community-based groups such as water user associations or school support committees are frequently established or strengthened to help to improve service delivery. Citizens often form groups to defend local interests when these are under threat. In China and Vietnam, local environmental groups formed to protect livelihoods and the environment on which they depend (Mertha 2008; O'Rourke 2002).

The local water user group in the Thai Long Dam example given in chapter 3 illustrates how farmers, with external help, can organize to defend their interests (Tsai 2007).

With increased urbanization and commercialization, professional and business associations are also emerging. These can play roles in exacting accountability from the state on behalf of citizens. In Jordan, for example, in the absence of political parties (banned prior to 1989), professional associations brought together a wide range of professionals who imparted knowledge and established democratic procedures for internal decision making. Their professional expertise and the fact that they were long considered "the only institutions with truly democratic electoral procedures" provided them with public legitimacy, which at times allowed them to mobilize large numbers of citizens (Larziliere 2012). Similarly, lawyers in Pakistan played a critical role in challenging the Musharraf government's treatment of the high court and its vocal chief justice, Iftikhar Chaudhry. By pressing for Chaudhry's reinstatement, the Lawyers' Movement demonstrated its support for a strong judiciary, independent of executive interference (for example, see Aslam 2010).

What Are the Characteristics of State-Society Relations?

The relationships between the state and society are characterized by an imbalance of power between the state and citizens.

Typically, state structures and the ruling elite dominate society and everyday life, and state–civil society relations are characterized by distrust. Citizens are fearful, reticent, or wary of interactions with government. Governments discourage citizens from voicing their opinions, and officials are not disposed to hear them. Distrust and fear are reinforced through everyday patterns of behavior, but also at flashpoints—moments of crisis when officials' behavior reinforces existing power structures.

State actors may be reluctant to engage with independent intermediaries or interlocutors. Governments are wary of CSOs they cannot control. State actors (of the executive) are more comfortable engaging with citizens (and mass organizations) than with more independent NGOs that may have the interlocution skills to support the SA process. Furthermore, facilitation does not build on a vast cadre of skilled resource people able to mobilize citizens, liaise with the right officials, and manage a dialogue. This resistance and gap in skills are complicated by a history of intermediaries that are quasi-state (village chiefs), carrying and filtering messages from citizen groups, especially at the grassroots.

The types of interfaces vary, are ad hoc, and can be altered or removed by the state at any time. Most countries where space for citizen-state engagement is formally constrained operate without a constitution or any other legal framework that defines the relationship between the state and citizens. For example, when the military held power in Pakistan, civil society often relied on the judiciary to act as an interface with the state and to negotiate various aspects of the relationship between the state and citizens. At multiple times, however, the military blocked this interface without due process (Aslam 2010). In more authoritarian systems, the interface is highly structured, formal, and inflexible. In others, the interface may be tokenistic, or, in isolated instances, it may have developed effectively for specific ends. States may also shift between these three types of interface.

At the local level, especially in countries that have endured long conflict, there is a strong motivation to ensure social stability and therefore favor consensus over accountability. Where officials or service providers are part of a community, there may be an overriding desire to ensure social stability, even where the social contract has been broken. Yet groups that comprise both the elite and others often build consensus, not accountability.

Overcoming Constraints to Information, Interface, and Civic Mobilization

This section provides an overview of the constraints on the three "levers" of SA: information, interface, and civic mobilization.

Overcoming Constraints to Information

Secrecy is fundamental. Secrecy and an asymmetry of information fundamentally help countries to maintain the status quo where the space for citizen engagement is formally constrained. By controlling the flow of information, governments can limit challenges to their power structures. Legislation making libel a criminal offense can be used to silence critics, and governments often routinely censor or distort the information that is available to the public. When information is available, it is at the aggregate level and therefore of no use to citizens demanding accountability. In systems that use co-optation and allocate resources to selected groups or individuals, information about public finances, assets, and resources is severely curtailed. In countries rich in natural resources, maintaining secrecy about ownership and revenues is paramount.

In most countries where the space for citizen engagement is formally constrained, the media are not independent, either because they are owned by the state, controlled by groups connected to the ruling elite, or heavily regulated. This lack of media freedom can severely limit the dissemination and absorption of information and subsequent action. Increasingly, controls are being extended to the Internet and electronic media, with crackdowns evident at political flashpoints (for example, see King, Pan, and Roberts 2013).

Yet some useful information is available to civil society. The state might have a need for feedback from its citizens, especially if there is little risk that it can have a destabilizing effect. To improve services or avoid large-scale unrest, it is in the interests of some states to overcome informational gaps by seeking citizen or beneficiary feedback. Officials may also seek information about the performance or behavior of local officials to be certain that its policies are being carried out. Finally, the state may want information about nonstate actors to regulate or control them or to elicit assistance with service delivery and development initiatives (for example, see O'Rourke 2004). In such cases, information on policy and regulatory frameworks, including the standards of service that should be provided by frontline workers, is often available and can be instrumental to localized social accountability processes.

The lack of an enabling framework, such as access to information legislation, can be overcome by operating with lower-level regulations. While many countries where space for citizen-state engagement is formally constrained will enforce restrictions, not all have a legislative framework in place, especially in connection with information. SA activities that focus on open information or budget transparency may be possible by working within policy and other regulatory frameworks.

When information is in the public domain but is not easily accessible or is not being used, there is an opportunity for civil society to explore access and use with relatively low risk. Civil society organizations need to have a good understanding of any information "comfort zones." Accessing information and building citizen awareness of information require reflection on what information (policies, standards, budgets, outcomes) at what level (project, local, sector, national) is restricted and when (around elections). In many cases, however, inadequate CSO capacity limits the use of such information (see box 5.2).

Local Government Disclosure of Development Projects and Budgets in Cambodia

Limited capacity may prevent CSOs from making use of information that has been disclosed. Since 2009, a website launched by the National Committee for Sub-National Democratic Development (NCDD), a national committee responsible for the decentralization reform in Cambodia, has provided information on the funds that every commune spends on community projects every year. It goes so far as to disclose full details of contracts and costs related to about US$14 million in annual spending at the lowest level of government. It even names contractors debarred for failure to comply with procedures. This remarkable example of disclosure is unusual in a country with no law guaranteeing access to information, strict media controls, and a poor record with regard to disclosure. Yet since its inception, civil society has never made use of this information. In 2013, nonstate actors began coordinating with the NCDD to post budgets and performance information in public locations and build awareness in communities.

Supporting Civil Society to Generate and Verify Information. Civil society organizations can help citizens by simplifying, disseminating, and building awareness on how to use information. Civic groups can provide various kinds of information to citizens so that they are aware of the standards of services to which they are entitled and whether official means exist to have their grievances addressed. They can also monitor the performance of public officials and inform citizens of instances of negligence or corruption. More generally, they may monitor certain issues and alert not only the public, but also government officials to potential problems. Each of these strategies contributes to the process that makes it possible for public officials to be held accountable. Each of the strategies is discussed in turn.

In countries where the space for citizen engagement is formally constrained and where information is limited and unreliable, state actors can play a role in verifying information. In the Lao People's Democratic Republic, in community-driven development activities, social audit meetings are used to disclose information about projects to communities and provide a forum for verification, public scrutiny, and feedback. Issues such as the underpayment of casual laborers have come to light in these meetings. In Myanmar, where there is a history of forced labor, the International Labour Organization (ILO) relies on community-based facilitators in townships to monitor labor practices. In this instance, the ILO, an international organization that enjoys the trust of both government and civil society, plays a key third-party monitoring role that a CSO may not be able to play. Such results are not necessarily common. Other countries where the space for citizen engagement is formally constrained offer examples of the capture of third-party monitoring activities by state actors.

Citizens and CSOs can frequently provide other nonstate actors and state authorities with information about certain issues. For example, information on basic services and environmental protection seems to fit within the "go area."

Information on health, education, and water supply has been used to exact accountability in countries where the space for citizen engagement is formally constrained, just as it has in less constrained environments. In Ethiopia, the fiscal transparency component of the Protection of Basic Services project allowed for new flows of information on local budgets and on the performance of health, education, water, and agricultural extension programs. The same is true in Cambodia, Morocco, and the Russian Federation, for instance.

Environmental protection, including regulation of pollutants, is another area where information is more readily available and action can be taken based on it (see, for instance, O'Rourke 2002).

Information generated by civil society is often viewed with skepticism and may even be dismissed; it needs to stand up to scrutiny, which requires skills that might not be available. Many efforts on the part of civil society to generate information entail collecting and compiling citizens' perceptions. While these are indicative and useful in measuring performance and satisfaction, the information falls on more receptive ears when accompanied by evidence. An investigation into corruption in connection with the supply of water in rural Ethiopia was well received by the Anti-Corruption Commission and the Ministry of Water Resources because it used mixed methods, obtaining feedback from communities and then measuring the depth and quality of local borehole drilling with the use of closed-circuit television equipment (Calow, MacDonald, and Cross 2012, cited in Plummer 2012).

The role and limits of media and social media

When the media are subject to strict regulation or censorship, partnerships aimed at facilitating the flow of information to promote social accountability might not be an option. Even where space exists, the potential for fostering accountability might be limited. When the state controls media content, the public may not receive information that is unbiased or that challenges public officials. Even when free of state control, newspaper and television outlets may be driven by the same profit motives that influence reporting in more open settings. As a result, information may be incomplete or biased, diverting attention away from important issues. In Vietnam, for example, rather than report on the systemic failings of the health care system as uncovered by public surveys, newspapers focused on cases of petty corruption or other sensational stories.[4] Furthermore, some local associations have been able to establish cooperative relations with local officials and convince them to make reforms because they were under the radar and did not attract the attention of the media (Spires 2011).

The advent of social media such as Twitter and Facebook may enable both associations and individuals to bring about social accountability more easily by spreading information, but exposure alone is no guarantee that change or sanctions will result.

Social media enable citizens to share information and air grievances, opening the way to find others who are like-minded and to make demands on the strength of their numbers. In China, parents of children who died in the 2008 Sichuan earthquake led the calls for an investigation into inferior construction of schools by posting information and complaints online.

Social media also make it possible to report and share incidents of wrongdoing by public officials. Social media can also mobilize public action and shame officials into correcting their behavior. During the 2008 elections in Zimbabwe, citizens documented instances of electoral fraud by using mobile phones to send photographs of wrongdoing in polling stations to newspapers and the opposition party (Hellström 2008). Similar uses of social media exposed fraud in the 2007 Nigerian elections and in the 2011 Russian elections, where young activists revealed instances of fraud on YouTube.

Nevertheless, there are limitations to using social media for SA. Many governments nowadays permit the free use of social media as long as the content poses no threat. As shown in a 2013 study, in China, for example, citizens are increasingly allowed to post online complaints about government officials and policies, but the government routinely censors posts that call for collective action (King, Pan, and Roberts 2013).

Just as individuals have increasingly taken advantage of the power of social media, so have governments (Morozov 2011). Governments not only have the potential to censor social media, but also to distort its content and use it to post pro-government propaganda.

The role of international partners

Many countries where the space for citizen engagement is formally constrained and that rely on external financing are responding to the disclosure requirements of donors. Both the Australian Agency for International Development and the World Bank have overhauled their policies relating to access to information. Both require a greater degree of public disclosure on the part of themselves and the recipients of their aid. Their environmental and social safeguard policies also require some forms of social accountability.[5] These policies have been an entry point for social accountability in Central Asia and North Africa. Donor requirements such as these have triggered changes in the degree of transparency even in the most constrained settings.

Information is also generated by global actors, even though its impact on a given country may be limited. Working across borders, global watchdog organizations generate and disseminate information on issues of global concern. The publication of data on oil, mining, and gas revenues in Kazakhstan and the Republic of Congo exposed the misappropriation of revenues and led to demands for more transparency in order to hold regimes accountable and pressure private companies and affiliated European and American banks (Global Witness 2004). While some international NGOs collect and publish information aimed at an international audience, information flows are still controlled in individual countries. The impacts of releasing damaging information on land grabbing and forest concessions, for instance, will be minimal when it cannot be used.

Addressing the Constraints of the State-Civil Society Interface

Understanding the historical and political context of the interface between the state and civil society is critical. The space and nature of the interface will change according to the focus area. Awareness and credibility of and accessibility to the interface platform will differ widely for citizens demanding accountability according to sector—for example, education as opposed to land management.

"Gray zones" may enable alternative rules for engagement. In contexts where lines of accountability are unclear, gray zones may emerge in which CSOs may launch SA activity. In 2007, for example, an international NGO used the gray zone to track public spending on human immunodeficiency virus (HIV) and acquired immunodeficiency syndrome (AIDS) in Ethiopia, the first budgetary analysis led by civil society. Such initiatives have to be conducted discreetly and opportunities assessed carefully, however, because failure can adversely affect civil society as a whole.

Existing structures that confound lines of accountability and filter voice may need attention. It is not uncommon for states that have reached a peace settlement under authoritarian or quasi-authoritarian rule to develop interfaces through multistakeholder committees or groups (for example, school support committees, village health groups) that combine users, service providers, and government representatives, blurring the lines of accountability. Conflicts of interest are built into policy through guidelines on membership and the composition of committees and can remain unresolved for decades. In other contexts, there is a plethora of citizen-officials who control a vaguely defined state-society interface. Creating structures and processes with accountability loops is critical to strengthening the process.

When relations between a state and its citizens are in flux, SA might be introduced. The Arab Spring led some governments of the Middle East to reconsider relations with their citizens. Several of them are building new institutions to bolster their legitimacy or seeking technical assistance to foster participation and consultation and introduce mechanisms that will allow them to explain their actions to citizens (see box 5.3). In the Republic of Yemen, a National Dialogue was conducted in which stakeholders negotiated the basic principles that will guide the drafting of the country's new constitution and serve as the foundation for a social contract (see chapter 7).

What is impossible at the national level may be possible at the local level. It is not uncommon for village and local state agencies to test engagement with citizens or users in "bottom-up" planning processes. Finding ways of working with and transforming existing engagement structures and shifting toward accountability loops will be more sustainable and have greater impact than one-off discrete activities.

Joint capacity-building events for state and civil society provide an interface, at least for the lifetime of a project. In the context of a project, joint learning is a strategy frequently used to bring state and nonstate

BOX 5.3

**Supporting Morocco's Governance Reform Program:
A New Focus on Open, Citizen-Centered Governance**

In 2011, the government of Morocco launched a two-prong governance reform program focusing on the modernization of public financial management and open governance with the aim of improving the allocative and operational efficiency of scarce public resources and giving citizens a greater voice in the development process. This program, partly financed through the World Bank's transparency and accountability development policy loan series, supports the concretization of governance principles and rights introduced in the constitution in response to citizen demand. It aims to maximize the window of opportunity for transformational reforms that the 2011 constitution presented.

The 2011 constitution introduced new rights relating to public engagement, including the right of citizens to petition public bodies, present legislative motions to parliament, and obtain access to information about the public sector. These rights are now being enacted in laws. To date, the World Bank has supported the design and consultation process on a law ensuring access to information, an organic law on public petitions and legislative motions, as well as a draft policy on public consultations and an e-consultation platform. These laws now need to be adopted and matched by clear and simple procedures to ensure that they are effectively implemented.

Meanwhile, citizen demands for participation remain strong, as shown by the results of a recent (April 2014) World Bank Nano-Survey assessing citizen perceptions of access to information and public engagement. This Internet-based survey garnered 15,000 responses, 71 percent of them calling for greater access to public sector information and 26 percent indicating a willingness to pay for it. Likewise, the majority of respondents (58 percent) wanted to be more engaged, even as often as once a week.

The survey sheds light on expectations regarding new rights introduced by the constitution. It highlights the disparities in public awareness, as well as the impediments to free access to information and active engagement.

Source: Morocco World Bank Governance Team.

officials together. In most countries where the space for citizen engagement is formally constrained, efforts to build trust between state officials and NGOs—for instance, by means of community scorecards—are achieved by using joint capacity-building events to agree on subsequent processes.

Evidence shows that nonconfrontational interfaces can be more effective. With little space to conduct SA activities, CSOs in many countries focus their efforts around a call for "constructive engagement." This engagement can also take the form of hybrid approaches or partnerships where SA tools might be used to identify accountability failures, but joint state-nonstate approaches are developed to effect change (Plummer and Dolk 2013).

In the absence of a formal interface, in many cases, citizens rely on direct relationships with government institutions to exact accountability from the government. Most often citizens need to recruit state actors (for example, officials, agencies, or institutions) to punish or reward other state actors on their behalf.[6]

Overcoming Constraints to Civic Mobilization and Association

In countries where the space for citizen engagement is formally constrained, citizens need support in mobilizing to demand accountability from the government. Independent NGOs are normally vital to the mobilization of citizens and community-based organizations. NGOs, with the skills and funding to mobilize, build understanding of the problem and facilitate the interface with the state.

In some such countries, these organizations are weak and lack credibility and capacity. SA interventions can build the capacity of these organizations, improving their understanding of a particular issue, the communities where they work, and the conditions in question, along with organizational know-how. Aside from technical skills, it is also important to train CSOs on how to engage the government, especially because relations with the government have historically been confrontational in countries where the space for citizen engagement is formally constrained.

Is technology changing the game? Information and communication technology (ICTs) can also play a role in mediating the individual-to-collective relationship (Joshi 2014). ICTs are now offering new possibilities for individuals to engage in public action, because they reduce transaction costs and the potential for reprisal. They also present opportunities to engage or disengage swiftly with collective action, depending on priorities.

When available, ICTs can support mobilization through cyber-coordination. ICTs can help to spread logistical information—for example, on the location of a protest and expected number of protestors. ICTs, especially social media, played a key role in the Arab Spring. When individuals know that others are likely to participate, they become more willing to do so as well. There is less fear of retribution by the state and greater optimism about the likelihood of success (Kuran 1991). Given the risk of clashes with security forces, the April 6th movement in Egypt launched a "Stay at Home" campaign to minimize confrontations (Ezbawy 2012).

Nevertheless, the "digital divide" needs to be taken into consideration. In many countries, limited access to the Internet or the unavailability of mobile telephone networks restricts access to ICTs to the elite and urban populations. State authorities can also exert control over access. In Ethiopia in 2007, after postelection violence, the state reasserted its control by blocking text messages. Still, there are promising examples of ICTs being used to promote social accountability (see box 5.4).

BOX 5.4

Using ICTs to Promote Social Accountability in Russia:
Progress and Challenges

ICTs for SA interventions have been evolving rapidly in recent years in Russia. At first, the government established a Department for the Formation of an "Open Government System" and launched an Open Data Initiative. In parallel, the general public increasingly began to demand SA projects. However, the initial impetus around open government has slowed and changed direction in the past two years. Instead of pursuing ambitious openness projects, the Russian government has supported the introduction of platforms that facilitate direct interaction between government officials and citizens, provide e-services, and closely control users' behavior on the platform.

These initiatives focus on the creation of direct channels of communication between citizens and government, offering citizens opportunities to provide feedback and lodge complaints directly, without having to depend on intermediaries. Some of these initiatives—in particular, platforms that encourage citizens to report municipal problems—have attracted a considerable number of users and proven effective in responding to complaints.

Despite their strengths, because these initiatives are designed without citizen inputs, they also have their limitations. While there is an active civil society in Russia, its participation in ICT for SA endeavors remains limited. Because of a centralized governance

(continued next page)

BOX 5.4 *(continued)*

system with limited experience in engaging with social intermediaries, ICT for SA initiatives are often driven by supply-side interests and introduced in a top-down manner,
without the involvement of civil society or other interested stakeholders. These platforms are therefore designed mainly to comply with legislative requirements on access
to information. As a result, information does not necessarily respond to actual citizen
needs and demands, and the platforms remain underused. Furthermore, these platforms
provide limited avenues for citizens to shape or influence the channels of communication. Consequently, the potential of these mechanisms is not fully realized, and it is not
clear whether citizens are satisfied with the responses they receive from authorities.
Source: World Bank 2014a.

Operational Implications: Finding the Right State Partner, at a Cost

A review of SA activities in countries where the space for citizen engagement is formally constrained suggests that the accountability loop, which
either sanctions the state or induces it to be responsive, occurs through
(a) an appeal to personal or professional integrity, (b) an appeal to the government's interest in improving service delivery and efficiency, (c) an effort
to link up across state and society to achieve social accountability goals, or
(d) government-endorsed, donor-financed initiatives.

Appealing to Personal or Professional Integrity

As discussed in chapter 3, social norms matter. Appealing to an official's
professional reputation or personal integrity can sometimes effect change.
At times, social norms may override political constraints. Service providers
and government officials can be responsive if they are driven by professional
norms or their standing in a community. This presents an opportunity to
effect low-level immediate change, however limited. This phenomenon
has been observed in East Asian societies, for example, where the fear of
diminished status in society can compel service providers and officials to
take community feedback personally and respond to the degree possible,
within their mandate. Community monitoring of health centers can succeed in bringing about improvements in the performance of health care
workers, in terms of attitude, cleanliness, and absenteeism—for example,

even without publishing the results of an inspection—because the workers wish to avoid shame. In such a situation, the threat of shame is as effective as the shame itself.[7]

"Naming and shaming" strategies are not always effective. They are more likely to succeed at the local level, where fear of community ostracism is often strongest. Most often, citizens need to appeal to high-level officials or state agencies to punish or reward other officials or agencies on their behalf. The scope and effectiveness of such strategies are therefore limited.

Appealing to Government Interests in Improving Service Delivery and Efficiency

Governments often appreciate the potential that social accountability approaches have to improve services, particularly when they see these approaches as a way to prevent unrest and political protest. Government agencies in Belarus, China, Moldova, Russia, Vietnam, and others have shown particular interest in satisfaction surveys, complaint resolution methods, and other feedback mechanisms (see box 5.5).

BOX 5.5

Social Accountability in Belarus Municipal Services:
A Citizen Involvement Centered around Grievance Redress Mechanisms

Several SA mechanisms exist in the housing, water, and district heating sectors to communicate proactively with citizens and hear their grievances. In accordance with the national law on citizen appeals, authorities are obliged to respond to citizen requests and complaints within a specific time frame. Accordingly, they have created several channels for interacting with citizens, including office hours for local officials, hotlines, mail, and e-mail addresses for written requests. These mechanisms are advertised in public places and widely used by the population.

Nevertheless, citizens indicate that, although grievance redress mechanisms (GRMs) seem responsive, there are two weaknesses: the quality of the government's responses to complaints and a lack of transparency regarding the content of citizen requests. Government grievance redress processes are a "black box." Specifically, complaints and

(continued next page)

BOX 5.5 *(continued)*

the government's responses are not made public, and there are no transparent quality control mechanisms. This lack of information is a missed opportunity that makes
it difficult to conduct a systematic assessment of the quality of government services,
identify strengths and weaknesses in the operation of multiservice utilities, reward good
performers, help poor performers, and generally improve the provision of services.

CSOs are only marginally involved in the utilities sector. Government authorities
are typically reluctant to work with CSOs and often do not appreciate their potential
value. At the same time, citizens do not view CSOs as reform champions and expect the
authorities to take the lead in managing the sector. As a result, the involvement of CSOs
in government policies and activities has been limited.

Source: World Bank 2013.

Governments may use decentralization and social accountability
approaches to extend their reach. The social accountability component of
the Burkina Faso Local Governance Support project is less about providing
resources than it is about creating space for these activities. After a split
within the ruling party in 2013, the government was intent on establishing
a greater presence in rural communes and ensuring that commune governments improved service delivery. As part of the project, NGOs were given
the task of mobilizing citizens, local government stakeholders, and sector
associations (water user associations) in each region of the country in a
project prioritization process with the commune council. The government
saw an opportunity to make commune councils accountable to it and to
build political support by improving services.

State incentives can be aligned with citizens' needs by building on
accountability within systems. In countries where the space for citizen
engagement is formally constrained, accountability within government
agencies can be strong and, if aligned with the widely shared interests of
citizens, can be harnessed to produce positive outcomes (such as increasing universal access to public services of adequate quality in countries like
China or Singapore). The desire to have lower echelons of government
carry out central government directives can be used to promote accountability measures to achieve these same ends. For example, citizen and
community monitoring can be used to inform the central government

about whether its lower echelons are complying with directives—for example, in connection with the allocation of budgets for schools and health clinics.

Partnering with Other Elements of the Accountability Framework: An Entry Point for Change

A first step that civil society actors can take to exact accountability from the state is to establish links with other parts of the state's accountability framework. Citizens and civil society organizations can appeal to those public officials or institutions that have the power either to sanction other officials or agencies or to change a policy or regulatory framework. This is possible due to reporting and accountability relationships within the state and relationships with other actors (such as donors) that put external pressure on different parts of a government. Parliamentarians may be instrumental in achieving government accountability by using the tools at their disposal (for instance, question and answer periods with government ministries).

In order to identify workable links between social accountability and one or more parts of the formal system of accountability, it is necessary to understand fully the lines of accountability, both implicit and explicit. These lines may vary significantly. For instance, militaries generally govern by coalition, and their accountabilities are dominated by lines within the military closely linked to an executive; these lines tend to be explicit. In countries where a sole leader dominates the state, lines of accountability are less predictable and play out over long periods; patron-client ties and personal loyalties are key. In states dominated by a single party, lines of accountability within the party are often highly structured. It is therefore more difficult in constrained SA environments to sketch out a generic accountability framework linking actors, especially where electoral, judicial, and oversight institutions are undefined or changing. Working this out is a useful first step.

Aligning with a part of government (or "piggybacking" on an accountability pathway) is often possible in states with a diversity of voices. While some countries where the space for citizen engagement is constrained are homogeneous, others operate as "governments of parts." Because of this, reforms or actions may be taken at different levels in a partial way. Evidence suggests that states can and do align themselves with civil society because of divergent roles and mandates—and sometimes competition and divergent goals between ministries or agencies (Fox 2007).

As noted in chapter 1, individual champions matter, too. For example, progressive officials in the Egyptian Ministry of Education used community scorecards to assess the success of money transferred to schools for school improvement plans.

Institutional fragmentation can open space for SA. Diversity of views within a ruling party may serve as entry points for civil society. Diversity of views can create opportunities for local organizations to identify allies within a government and push for greater accountability.

Decentralization alters power structures and moves budgets from higher to lower levels of government, creating entry points for SA. The decentralization literature describes the contradictory implications of decentralization reforms on accountability. There are, however, examples of decentralization opening the door to SA approaches:

- *Champions of decentralization generally support some form of localized needs-based decision making consistent with the goals of social accountability.* In Cambodia, the NCDD envisaged downward accountability as a part of reform and ultimately saw the benefit of a joint "social accountability framework," which provided space for CSOs to engage in and for government to improve access to information, open local budgets, and citizen monitoring (see box 5.6).
- *The split between national and local can also create opportunities for civil society action and partnerships.* In some cases, local governments are far enough removed from the center to act independently and form partnerships with other nonstate actors that can help them to accomplish local goals. National actors can also authorize processes that promote local accountability, as has been done in some cases in China (Plummer and Taylor 2004).

The most obvious entry points from which to align civil society action for accountability with state institutions are the formal oversight institutions of government, which often have a mandate that is aligned with social accountability objectives. Even states with restrictions on information and freedom of association may have institutions that provide for checks and balances. These include anti-corruption and human rights commissions, ombudsmen, and national audit agencies. CSOs can strategically use oversight institutions to bring about the accountability they want, provided these institutions have some degree of autonomy, credibility, and a mandate to act. Several years after it was established, Ethiopia's Anti-Corruption Commission proposed a strategy to combat corruption and

BOX 5.6

Cambodia: Partnering with Local Government for Improved Local Services

In Cambodia, World Bank support for citizen engagement was launched with a block grant to the country's 1,800 communes. The communes were required to conduct annual participatory planning to ensure that decisions responded to local needs. Although there is agreement that the grant was pro-poor, an analysis in 2011 found that citizen engagement in the planning process was often tokenistic and that the grievance redress mechanism was little used and lacked credibility. An opportunity to enhance citizen engagement in local development arose when the national committee responsible for local governance and local development harmonized and aligned donor projects with a national program. As a result, space opened for a new integrated platform for voice and accountability in local development.

Building on the results and lessons learned in a three-year pilot program, a landmark agreement between civil society and the government on a social accountability framework was gradually reached. Although it took years to put in place, it helped to confirm the space for subnational social accountability in Cambodia and areas where civil society and the government could cooperate and have the greatest impact. It also led to an agreement on the principles of engagement. Chief among these were "partnering" and "constructive engagement." Although this approach was required by the government, the rules of the game were driven by civil society.

The final policy comprises three substantive strategies: (1) improved local information and transparency, (2) open budgets, and (3) citizen monitoring of local administration and basic services. The framework defines complementary roles for both government (elected officials and service providers) and local civil society to meet objectives and makes facilitation a priority (figure B5.6.1). The need for action on the part of the government as well as civil society is explicitly recognized, and the framework calls for joint action, with the government responsible for generating data and civil society responsible for disseminating information. While the government produces budgets, civil society provides training in budget literacy. NGOs are assigned responsibility for citizen monitoring (scorecard processes), and commune councils are responsible for ensuring that action plans are approved and executed. The focus of the social accountability framework is multisectoral: local governments, health centers, and schools. Implementation is scheduled to begin in late 2014.

(continued next page)

BOX 5.6   (continued)

Figure B5.6.1 Joint Action in Social Accountability: Who Does What in the Social Accountability Framework in Cambodia?

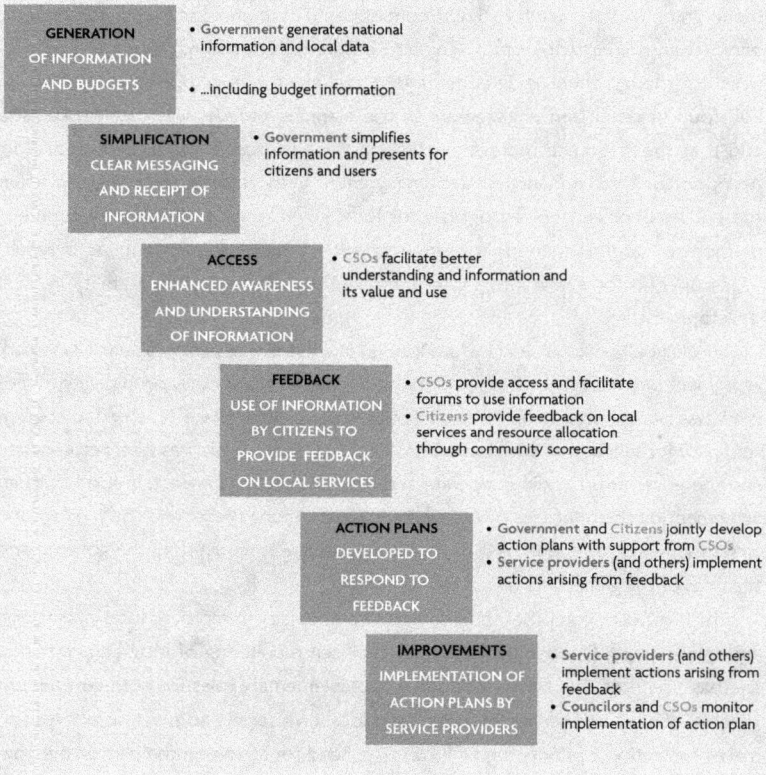

GENERATION OF INFORMATION AND BUDGETS
- Government generates national information and local data
- ...including budget information

SIMPLIFICATION CLEAR MESSAGING AND RECEIPT OF INFORMATION
- Government simplifies information and presents for citizens and users

ACCESS ENHANCED AWARENESS AND UNDERSTANDING OF INFORMATION
- CSOs facilitate better understanding and information and its value and use

FEEDBACK USE OF INFORMATION BY CITIZENS TO PROVIDE FEEDBACK ON LOCAL SERVICES
- CSOs provide access and facilitate forums to use information
- Citizens provide feedback on local services and resource allocation through community scorecard

ACTION PLANS DEVELOPED TO RESPOND TO FEEDBACK
- Government and Citizens jointly develop action plans with support from CSOs
- Service providers (and others) implement actions arising from feedback

IMPROVEMENTS IMPLEMENTATION OF ACTION PLANS BY SERVICE PROVIDERS
- Service providers (and others) implement actions arising from feedback
- Councilors and CSOs monitor implementation of action plan

enhance the integrity of line ministries. Transparency International and other organizations lent assistance, and the Anti-Corruption Commission worked with them in documenting potential corruption in a broad range of sectors (Plummer 2012).

In countries with an independent judiciary, accountability goals might be best achieved in the courts. During Mubarak's rule in Egypt (Moustafa 2007), human rights groups enlisted the courts in their fight for accountability and greater political freedoms. In such cases, justices appear to be motivated by the desire to generate legitimacy and to safeguard or expand their institutional powers and prestige (Helmke 2005; Helmke and Rosenbluth 2009). Aware of their dependence on other government entities to enforce their decisions, the courts act strategically in choosing cases to hear and in ruling on their outcomes (Staton 2010; see box 5.7).

BOX 5.7

Egypt's Judiciary: An Ally for Civil Society in Demanding Human Rights

The Center for Human Rights Legal Aid (CHRLA) became one of the most dynamic human rights organization in Egypt under the Mubarak government. Founded in 1994, the organization's mission was to provide free legal representation to citizens who had suffered abuses at the hands of public officials. In the 1990s, the CHRLA's team of trained lawyers and staff took advantage of a newly empowered Supreme Constitutional Court (SCC) not only to take up the cases of thousands of Egyptians, but also to challenge repressive legislation systematically. By filing cases with a court whose justices were sympathetic to their cause and intent on asserting judicial authority, the organization was able to hold responsible officials accountable in at least some cases. Other civic associations, such as the Land Center for Human Rights and the Human Rights Center for the Assistance of Prisoners, took note of CHRLA's success and adopted a similar strategy in the courts. As the director of the Center for Human Rights Legal Aid, Gasser 'Abd al-Raziq, observed at the time, "In Egypt, where you have a relatively independent judiciary, the only way to promote reform is to have legal battles all the time. It's the only way that we can act as a force for change."

While political in nature, the legal challenges initiated by human rights organizations in Egypt nevertheless achieved a measure of success. Increasingly, the SCC sided with litigants challenging the government, granting some redress to individuals who had suffered abuse at the hands of the government. At the same time, the explicitly political nature of CHRLA's claims, combined with the SCC's rulings, led the government to strengthen its resolve. Although the Supreme Constitutional Court—strategically—did not challenge the right of the government to try citizens in military courts, the government passed legislation to assert greater control over CSOs and the courts, so that, by the mid-2000s, civic activism in the area of human rights and judicial independence had become a thing of the past.

There is more tolerance for SA in some sectors than in others. State actors may be willing to champion citizens' interests in certain policy areas such as consumer regulation or social sectors. Forming links with the administrative system of accountability in the social sectors is a tried and tested area of SA in countries where the space for citizen engagement is formally constrained. Citizen monitoring by means of community scorecards and citizen report cards can provide useful feedback on the performance of local service providers. When these are "linked in," they not only rely on changes in "integrity-based performance" to improve the services provided, but also can leverage sanctions. It is therefore important to understand the systems of inspection or local administrative oversight (for example, school inspectors or health quality assessment systems). CSOs often lack this understanding. Knowing how to establish effective links with administrative accountability systems for local-level action should be given greater priority.

The sectors that finance the regime, such as natural resources, are generally out of bounds. For instance, civil society activism is rarely tolerated in areas such as monitoring of illegal logging.

There are still challenges to overcome. After identifying a strategy for partnering with the state, the first challenge is to determine whether officials who have an incentive to stand with citizens also have enough power and resources vis-à-vis other state agents to do so. Even if the goals of an institution are aligned with citizens' demands and individuals within that organization can be identified, these pro-accountability champions may be changed and more pliable successors appointed. Many organizations and officials do not want any association with challenging claims or do not have adequate resources to take on powerful adversaries.

Citizens and civic associations must actively work to "form structures that correspond to the state's institutions and can therefore better respond to their challenges" (Aiyede 2003). The existence of institutional fragmentation and state officials with interests complementary to those of citizens does not guarantee social accountability. Local associations and communities have to cultivate potential partners among government officials to address their demands for change, be they national (to conduct policy experiments, obtain information about outcomes in different localities, and keep tabs on local government officials and service providers) or local (to bring about localized change).

Action entails trade-offs, too. Cooperation with the state in such contexts often results in the placement of constraints on civic action. In exchange for access, civil society groups have increasingly focused on issues such as women's empowerment or projects aimed at enhancing the technical capacity of state institutions, rather than on campaigns challenging the government's monopoly of politics (Bush 2013). If achieving the desired outcomes requires cooperation with public officials, civic associations agree to channel their grievances through certain state institutions and forgo more contentious claims or actions. Doing so may result in "safe negotiations with the state," precluding the development of a strong, homegrown domestic movement (Hughes 2007).

Civil society organizations may choose to adopt a "constructive engagement" approach because it is the only space they can get or out of fear of reprisal. Civil society action with regard to social accountability more often takes the form of constructive engagement rather than confrontation, in terms of both the focus of the engagement and the approach—the way they manage activities. CSOs may consistently steer away from confrontational topics in the proposals they submit for donor financing and explicitly endorse principles such as "constructive engagement" and "partnership." This involves working together to find solutions, having fairly high levels of consensus, and finding agreeable ways to remove nonperforming officials.

There are benefits and trade-offs to civil society pursuing this route. When civil society organizations take a nonconfrontational stance, not only do they ensure their safety but they also develop capacity and knowledge of mechanisms on easier tracks: it is far easier to monitor health and education services and see results for their efforts than to investigate natural resource management. The skills they develop may then be directed at other sectors. They can also earn trust and goodwill that will enable them to take on more contentious issues later. Doing so naturally entails trade-offs.

Leveraging Government-Enforced Donor-Financed Initiatives

International actors often create space for action, but there are drawbacks. Partnerships with international actors can be effective, provided that they understand and support the domestic agenda. Some countries where the space for citizen engagement is formally constrained are off-limits for international organizations, and cooperation between domestic and international organizations can be problematic, if it exists at all. In others, however, international actors have introduced effective social accountability activities (Durac 2013; Wu 2003). In Kenya in the early 1990s, local NGOs successfully advocated against a legal amendment that would have tightened controls on the operations of NGOs. International NGOs lent them assistance by drawing attention to the issue and putting pressure on Arap Moi's government (Ndegwa 1994).

International donors can play a catalytic role in triggering and financing SA. Whether SA is triggered through safeguards, governance, or efforts aimed at improving service delivery, donors can play a useful role. For example, the World Bank has incorporated citizen participation and feedback components into many of the projects it has funded. Familiarity with these mechanisms encourages CSOs to incorporate them in other settings. In this regard, donor-funded projects represent safe zones. One of the primary constraints to social accountability is inadequate financing, and this constraint is made worse in states where support to civil society requires government approval. Wherever this is the case, programs go unfunded or projects stall, especially when donors are concerned about jeopardizing their relations with the government. When successfully negotiated, however, as in the case of third-party monitoring of irrigation projects in Uzbekistan, donor financing can have a significant impact (based on Van Wicklin 2014; see box 5.8).

International NGOs are becoming increasingly familiar with social accountability, comparing experiences and sharing skills and resources. They are also adapting their work to different contexts. Many international

---

BOX 5.8

Ethiopia Introduces Financial Transparency and Social Accountability in Local Basic Services

The Protection of Basic Services (PBS) project was launched in 2006 after postelection violence halted donor financing to the government of Ethiopia. Now in its second phase, the PBS aims to protect and expand the delivery of basic services by subnational governments, while promoting transparency and local accountability in service delivery, a condition of the multidonor response. A key component of this project ensures new standards of open government and of fiscal transparency and accountability (FTA), while a second more recent component (Ethiopia Social Accountability Program, ESAP) aims to strengthen CSOs, enabling them to become social accountability implementation partners (SAIPs), and to facilitate an interface between citizens and government in connection with core basic services.

Financial transparency. Although it was challenging to get FTA off the ground, after completion of a first phase, a baseline survey confirmed that a consensus existed

(continued next page)

BOX 5.8 *(continued)*

within the Ethiopian government. Activities focused on public dissemination of budgets and expenditures, the development and testing of financial and accountability tools, and the establishment of a role for the media. In a second phase, the project has further promoted transparency by means of customized tools to suit regional and local conditions; institutionalized them in the government system; engaged in demand-side efforts to build awareness, demystify budget and expenditure, provide service delivery information, and foster budget literacy, among others; and obtained citizen feedback from users and citizens to improve the processes. By 2009, more than 90 percent of *woredas* (districts) had posted budget and spending information in *woreda* and *kebele* (village) offices and public marketplaces. What was not possible nationally became possible locally. The scale is notable: more than 2,000 local governments were displaying budgets and performance information, and 50,000 Ethiopians were trained in budget literacy.

Social accountability. The overall objective of the ESAP is to strengthen the capacity of both citizen groups and the government to work together, with CSOs facilitating the dissemination of information and mobilizing citizens to participate in interface meetings with service providers and local councils. By the end of March 2014, the ESAP was being implemented by 49 primary CSOs as SAIPs in 223 *woredas* in all regions of Ethiopia and directly reaching more than 71,000 citizens with information on their entitlements and responsibilities to plan and monitor basic services. The application of SA tools took off slowly. The majority of CSOs-SAIPs have focused on implementing community scorecards in which citizens provide information on the challenges they encounter in getting connected to basic public services in the areas of education, health, water and sanitation, agriculture, and rural roads. The process has gained momentum, and 36 percent of all *woredas* covered by the ESAP have conducted *woreda*-level interface meetings and produced joint service improvement action plans. Service improvement action plans, currently at different stages of implementation across ESAP areas, represent a new compact, assigning responsibilities to the *woredas* and to citizens.

Grievance redress mechanism. Based on the recommendations of a study conducted in 2011, GRM was included as a subcomponent of the PBS project. Thanks to the project support, the Ethiopian Institute of Ombudsman (EIO) is expanding its branch offices at the regional level. Grievance-handling officers have received training and

(continued next page)

BOX 5.8 *(continued)*

are expected to foster accountability at the regional, *woreda*, and *kebele* levels of government. All regions now have regional public grievance-handling offices. In most regions, these offices have a presence at the zone, *woreda*, and *kebele* levels and are empowered by proclamations and regulations that enable them to operate in a structured and rule-based manner. The EIO case-handling manual, developed in-house by the EIO, is disseminated for use. Strong political will and the basic institutional setup for GRM in the regions, coupled with an ongoing media campaign to enhance citizens' understanding of the GRM system, is reflected in the number of cases presented to the EIO branch and *woreda* public grievance-handling offices: in Ethiopian fiscal 2005 (2012/13) and 2006 (2013/14), 2,892 and 2,706 appeals and grievances were received by the EIO, and 44 and 41 percent of them, respectively, were investigated; the remaining appeals were found to be either outside the mandate of the EIO or without merit; in one *woreda* (Debre Markos Zuria of Amhara) for fiscal 2013/2014, 1,836 appeals and grievance cases were received, and 1,707 of them were investigated and addressed.

Lessons from the PBS experience. Some important lessons have emerged from the implementation of project components relating to transparency and accountability. External financing and leverage by international donors played a significant role, but the government was particularly receptive to a "good governance" agenda of civil service reform as a way to legitimize its control. Linking the FTA initiative to the broader budgetary support offered as part of the PBS project ensured that the initiative received the attention it deserved from both the government and donors. This commitment from the highest levels of the ruling party and the government helped to ensure political support at all levels of government. Nevertheless, the initial design of the ESAP component underestimated the time and effort required to make citizens and government officials understand the very concept of social accountability and to mobilize citizens in regions where they had been powerless and fearful. The PBS project experience in Ethiopia highlights the scope of FTA-ESAP linkages that can further strengthen the provision of basic services. Finally, the ESAP component, in particular, relied on CSOs to play an important role as facilitators. It is unlikely that an initiative centered on CSOs would have been possible in the Ethiopia context if it had not been funded by donors intent on having these organizations as SAIPs. The longer-term sustainability of CSOs acting as SAIPs without such financial commitment remains equally unlikely.

Sources: World Bank 2014b; PBS project documents.

NGOs are developing the internal resources (capacity and funding) to extend support globally. They are also stimulating action with local civil society partners or building social accountability skills and networks. Partnerships with local actors are an essential ingredient, and strategic adaptations are needed to make engagements effective.

In settings where social accountability is a challenging goal, the role of international NGOs is not always straightforward. If they have been allowed to operate at all or continue operating after a regime is toppled, international NGOs working in countries where the space for citizen engagement is formally constrained confront numerous obstacles. While their role is often critical, building capacity and supporting local nonstate activity is not as straightforward as the traditional activities of providing services. Laws regulating NGOs in the late 2000s posed a threat to international NGOs supporting social accountability. In Ethiopia in 2008, for example, the PBS initiative (box 5.8) suffered a setback when the government passed a law barring NGOs from conducting certain activities. The law would have halted the work of international NGOs that were helping national partner organizations to develop capacity to promote accountability. Because more than US$1 billion in assistance was contingent on this component, a waiver was granted to allow the NGOs funded under the initiative to continue working. Ethiopia has since introduced SA concepts in local governments throughout the country. Whether CSO-supported activities can be sustained after the project has been completed remains to be seen. More generally, there is concern over the potential impact of a 2009 regulatory framework that defines permissible CSO activities.

Conclusion

On the whole, the evidence from countries where the space for citizen engagement is formally constrained indicates that social accountability activity may be possible, but its scope and mechanisms are constrained:

- Social accountability activities can have an impact in the (limited) domains in which they operate. The gains are partial and may be restricted to the scope of a project.
- Paradoxically, to date these domains have been (locally) pro-poor and pro-environment. Given that the space for social accountability in these environments is limited and that SA activity is often more easily directed at basic services (for example, water, health, and education),

the evidence suggests that SA can be introduced in projects and sectors that explicitly target the poor and the environment.

- Doing so is not easy, however, and any efforts to advance social accountability must overcome stiff resistance and imbalances that underline the importance of citizen empowerment and independent voice. There is a risk of further strengthening existing power structures.

- Trajectories are difficult to predict. Lower-level action could either displace key debates or lead to greater accountability and more efficient states. Do local-level sector-based partnerships lead to relationships that advance social accountability in the long term or in other policy spheres? Can solving local problems be scaled up to the national level?

Box 5.9 offers the key take-aways from this chapter.

BOX 5.9

Key Takeaways: Social Accountability in Countries Where Space for Citizen-State Engagement Is Formally Constrained

Designing and implementing SA in countries where the space for citizen engagement is formally constrained faces specific constraints and risks. Although these countries are far from similar, they share some attributes that distinguish them from other contexts in relation to social accountability approaches. Figure B5.9.1 summarizes these attributes.

What are the possibilities for overcoming the constraints to information, interface, and civic mobilization?

- Secrecy and asymmetry of information are fundamental attributes of these environments, which is compounded by the fact that the media are often state controlled, state owned, or heavily regulated. Nevertheless, CSOs and citizens may provide useful information or a forum for verification, public scrutiny, and feedback to the government that opens spaces for citizen-state interface.

- Understanding the historical and political context of the interface between the state and civil society is particularly critical. The space and nature of the interface may differ greatly depending on the sector or between national and local level. Evidence suggests that the channels of state-society interface that are effective are most often nonconfrontational.

(continued next page)

BOX 5.9 *(continued)*

Figure B5.9.1 Summarizing an Archetypal Institutional Landscape in Constrained Environments

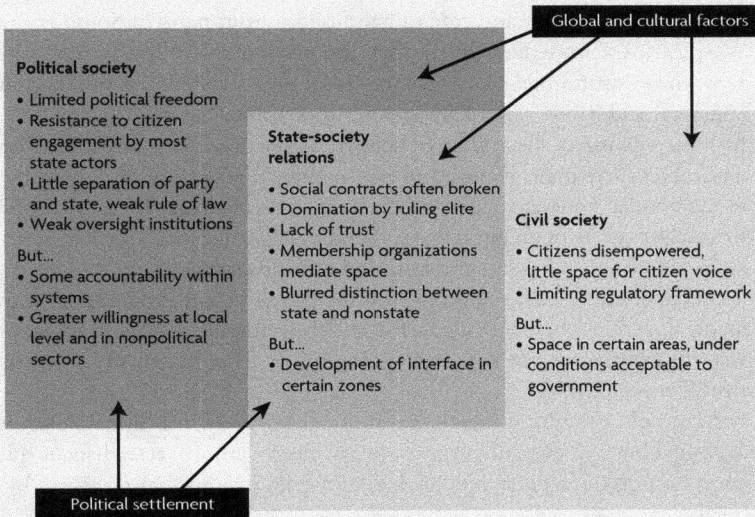

Global and cultural factors

Political society
- Limited political freedom
- Resistance to citizen engagement by most state actors
- Little separation of party and state, weak rule of law
- Weak oversight institutions

But...
- Some accountability within systems
- Greater willingness at local level and in nonpolitical sectors

State-society relations
- Social contracts often broken
- Domination by ruling elite
- Lack of trust
- Membership organizations mediate space
- Blurred distinction between state and nonstate

But...
- Development of interface in certain zones

Civil society
- Citizens disempowered, little space for citizen voice
- Limiting regulatory framework

But...
- Space in certain areas, under conditions acceptable to government

Political settlement

- Government may regulate CSOs strictly, but government may also support particular associations that mobilize citizens to help the state to address deficiencies in service delivery. ICTs can play a role within such contexts to create spaces that help to aggregate individual "voice" into collective citizen action, for instance, by supporting mobilization through cyber-coordination.

Based on the evidence, several entry points and approaches enable state actors or institutions to be responsive to citizen feedback. The accountability loop, which either sanctions or brings about responsiveness of the state, occurs through five approaches: (1) appealing to personal or professional integrity (which may have limited effect), (2) appealing to a government's instrumental interests in delivering services more efficiently, (3) linking SA mechanisms to make the state's own ("horizontal") accountability framework more effective, (4) identifying opportunities linked to institutional fragmentation, or (5) working within the boundaries of government-endorsed, donor-financed initiatives.

On the whole, the evidence in these polities shows that SA activity may be possible, but that its scope and mechanisms are constrained, with its impact often limited to the domains in which donors operate. Gains are partial and often project based. Moreover, efforts to promote SA run the risk of entrenching existing power structures.

Notes

1. For example, see Niazi (1986, 1992, 1994) about how the media were encouraged and almost forced to self-censor in Pakistan during Ayub's regime in 1956–66 and Zia's regime in 1977–88.
2. Baur and Kyed (2007) on Zimbabwe; see also Mapedza (2007). The experience of rural councils and traditional authorities in parts of South Asia and West Africa shows that, unless they are accountable "downward" to citizens, these institutions may be simply local manifestations of state authority (Agrawal and Ribot 1999; Larson and Ribot 2004).
3. In some situations the collective action has livelihood implications, such as natural resource management and environmental protection. Analytical work in Cambodia finds that, despite the risk, citizens were driven to mobilize themselves (without an intermediary) and to challenge local officials over livelihood issues, such as land grabbing and forest degradation.
4. See Vian et al. (2012). A United Nations Development Programme study of media coverage of corruption in the health sector showed that most reports were of health care workers demanding bribes from patients (31 percent of stories reported).
5. For example, the World Bank's Operational Manual Operational Policy (OP) 4.12-Involuntary Resettlement requires disclosure of resettlement plans, consultation, third-party monitoring, and grievance redress measures by the borrower.
6. See Gandhi (2014) for examples of how a direct relationship of individuals with government officials allowed citizens to interface with the state.
7. As shown in Olken (2007, 2009), the threat of audit is as effective as the audit itself.

References

Agrawal, A., and J. Ribot. 1999. "Accountability in Decentralization: A Framework with South Asian and West African Cases." *Journal of Developing Areas* 33 (Summer): 473–502.

Aiyede, E. R. 2003. "The Dynamics of Civil Society and the Democratization Process in Nigeria." *Canadian Journal of African Studies* 37 (1): 1–27.

Andersen, L. 2008. "Fragile States on the International Agenda." In *Fragile Situations Background Report; Part I: Background Papers,* edited by L. Engberg-Pedersen, L. Andersen, F. Stepputat, and D. Jung, 7–20. Copenhagen: Danish Institute for International Studies.

Aslam, G. 2010. "Dictatorship as a Bargaining Process: The Case of Pakistan." PhD thesis, George Mason University, Fairfax, VA.

Bianchi, R. 1989. *Unruly Corporatism: Associational Life in Twentieth-Century Egypt.* New York: Oxford University Press.

Buur, L., and H. M. Kyed. 2007. "Traditional Authority in Mozambique: The Legible Space between State and Community." In *State Recognition and Democratization in Sub-Saharan Africa: A New Dawn for Traditional Authorities?* edited by L. Buur and H. M. Kyed, 105–30. New York: Palgrave Macmillan.

Bush, S. 2013. "Confront or Conform? Rethinking U.S. Democracy Assistance." Policy Brief, Project on Middle East Democracy, Washington, DC.

Calow, R., A. MacDonald, and P. Cross. 2012. "Rural Water Supply Corruption in Ethiopia." In *Diagnosing Corruption in Ethiopia: Perceptions, Realities, and the Way Forward for Key Sectors*, edited by J. Plummer, 121–80. Washington, DC: World Bank.

Cavatorta, F., and A. Elananza. 2010. "Show Me the Money! Opposition, Western Funding, and Civil Society in Jordan and Lebanon." In *Contentious Politics in the Middle East: Political Opposition under Authoritarianism*, edited by H. Albrecht, 75–93. Gainesville, FL: University Press of Florida.

Charron, N., and V. Lapuente. 2011. "Which Dictators Produce Quality of Government?" *Studies in Comparative International Development* 46 (4): 397–423.

Durac, V. 2013. "Entrenching Authoritarianism or Promoting Reform? Civil Society in Contemporary Yemen." In *Civil Society Activism under Authoritarian Rule: A Comparative Perspective*, edited by F. Cavatorta, 135–57. London: Routledge.

Ezbawy, Y. A. 2012. "The Role of the Youth's New Protest Movements in the January 25th Revolution." *IDS Bulletin* 43 (1): 26–36.

Fox, J. 2007. *Accountability Politics: Power and Voice in Rural Mexico.* Oxford: Oxford University Press.

Gandhi, J. 2014. "Literature Review: Social Accountability Mechanisms and Their Impact in Closed Polities." Background paper for this report, World Bank, Washington, DC.

Gandhi, J., and A. Przeworski. 2007. "Authoritarian Institutions and the Survival of Autocrats." *Comparative Political Studies* 40 (11): 1279–31.

Gaventa, J., and G. Barrett. 2010. "So What Difference Does It Make? Mapping the Outcomes of Citizen Engagement." IDS Working Paper 347, University of Sussex, Institute of Development Studies, Brighton, U.K. http://www.gsdrc.org/go/display&type=Document&id=3981&source=rss.

Global Integrity. 2013. *Global Integrity Report: 2013.* Washington, DC: Global Integrity.

Global Witness. 2004. "Time for Transparency." Global Witness, London.

Hellström, J. 2008. "Mobile Democracy: Challenges and Way Forward." In *Big Brother and Empowered Sisters: The Role of New Communication*

Technologies in Democratic Processes, 53–68. Proceedings of a conference at Uppsala Universitet, Uppsala, Sweden, April 16–17.

Helmke, G. 2005. *Courts under Constraints: Judges, Generals, and Presidents in Argentina*. New York: Cambridge University Press.

Helmke, G., and F. Rosenbluth. 2009. "Regimes and the Rule of Law: Judicial Independence in Comparative Perspective." *Annual Review of Political Science* 12 (June): 345–66.

Hughes, C. 2007. "Transnational Networks, International Organizations, and Political Participation in Cambodia: Human Rights, Labour Rights, and Common Rights." *Democratization* 14 (5): 834–52.

Joshi, A. 2014. "On Social Accountability: An Issue Paper." Background paper prepared for this book, World Bank, Social Development Department, Washington, DC.

King, G., J. Pan, and M. Roberts. 2013. "How Censorship in China Allows Government Criticism but Silences Collective Expression." *American Political Science Review* 107 (2, May): 1–18.

Kuran, T. 1991. "Now Out of Never: The Element of Surprise in the East European Revolution of 1989." *World Politics* 44 (1): 7–48.

Larson, A., and J. Ribot. 2004. "Democratic Decentralization through a Natural Resource Lens: An Introduction." *European Journal of Development Research* 16 (1): 1–25.

Larzilière, P. 2012. "Political Commitment under an Authoritarian Regime: Professional Associations and the Islamist Movement as Alternative Arenas in Jordan." *International Journal of Conflict and Violence* 6 (1): 11–25.

Lust-Okar, E. 2007. "The Management of Opposition: Formal Structures of Contestation and Informal Political Manipulation in Egypt, Jordan, and Morocco." In *Debating Arab Authoritarianism. Dynamics, and Durability in Nondemocratic Regimes*, edited by O. Schlumberger, 39–58. Stanford, CA: Stanford University Press.

Magloni. B. 2006. *Voting for Autocracy: Hegemonic Party Survival and Its Demise in Mexico*. Cambridge, U.K.: Cambridge University Press.

Malesky, E., P. Schuler, and A. Tran. 2012. "The Adverse Effects of Sunshine: A Field Experiment on Legislative Transparency in an Authoritarian Assembly." *American Political Science Review* 106 (4): 762–86.

Mapecza, E. 2007. "Traditional Authority: Accountability and Governance in Zimbabwe." In *State Recognition and Democratization in Sub-Saharan Africa? A New Dawn for Traditional Authorities?* edited by L. Buur and H. M. Kyed, 183–208. New York: Palgrave Macmillan.

Meng, T., J. Pan, and P. Yang. 2014. "Conditional Receptivity to Citizen Participation: Evidence from a Survey Experiment in China." *Comparative Political Studies* (December 16): 1–35.

Mertha, A. 2008. *China's Water Warriors: Citizen Action and Policy Change.* Ithaca, NY: Cornell University Press.

Morozov, E. 2011. "Technology's Role in Revolution Internet Freedom and Political Oppression." *Futurist* 45 (4): 18–21.

Moustafa, T. 2007. *The Struggle for Constitutional Power: Law, Politics, and Economic Development in Egypt.* New York: Cambridge University Press.

Nathan, A. 2003. "Authoritarian Resilience." *Journal of Democracy* 14 (1): 6–17.

Ndegwa, S. 1994. "Civil Society and Political Change in Africa: The Case of Non-Governmental Organizations in Kenya." *IJCS* 35 (1-2): 19–36.

Niazi, Z. 1986. "Press in Chains." Karachi Press Club, Karachi.

———.1992. "The Press under Siege." Karachi Press Club, Karachi.

———. 1994. "The Web of Censorship." Karachi Press Club, Karachi.

Oi, J. 1992. "Fiscal Reform and the Economic Foundations of Local State Corporatism in China." *World Politics* 45 (1): 99–126.

Olken, B. A. 2007. "Monitoring Corruption: Evidence from a Field Experiement in Indonesia." *Journal of Political Economy* 115 (2): 200–49.

———. 2009. "Corruption Perceptions vs. Corruption Reality." *Journal of Public Economics* 93 (7-8): 50–64.

O'Rourke, D. 2002. "Community-Driven Regulation: Toward an Improved Model of Environmental Regulation in Vietnam." In *Livable Cities? Urban Struggles for Livelihood and Sustainability*, edited by P. Evans. Berkeley, CA: University of California Press.

———. 2004. *Community-Driven Regulation: Balancing Development and the Environment in Vietnam.* Cambridge, MA: MIT Press.

Plummer, J., ed. 2012. *Diagnosing Corruption in Ethiopia: Perceptions, Realities, and the Way Forward for Key Sectors.* Washington, DC: World Bank.

Plummer, J., and A. Dolk. 2013. "Beneficiary and Third-Party Monitoring of District Services: Enhancing the Performance of One Window Service Offices through Monitoring and Awareness Building." Demand for Good Governance (DFGG) Learning Note 3, World Bank and The Asia Foundation, Washington, DC.

Plummer, J., and J. Taylor. 2004. *Community Participation in China: Issues and Process for Capacity Building.* London: Earthscan.

Rosberg, J. 1995. "Roads to the Rule of Law: The Emergence of an Independent Judiciary in Contemporary Egypt." PhD thesis, Massachusetts Institute of Technology, Cambridge, MA.

Schmitter, P. 1975. *Corporatism and Public Policy in Authoritarian Portugal.* London: Sage Publications.

Spires, A. 2011. "Contingent Symbiosis and Civil Society in an Authoritarian State: Understanding the Survival of China's Grassroots NGOs." *American Journal of Sociology* 117 (1): 1–45.

Staton, J. 2010. *Judicial Power and Strategic Communication in Mexico*. New York: Cambridge University Press.

Svolik, M. 2008. "Authoritarian Reversals and Democratic Consolidation." *American Political Science Review* 102 (2): 153–68.

Tsai, L. L. 2007. "Solidary Groups, Informal Accountability, and Local Public Goods Provision in Rural China." *American Political Science Review* 101 (2): 555–72.

Tullock, G. 1987. *Autocracy*. Dordrecht, Netherlands: Kluwer.

Van Wicklin, W. 2014. "Interviews with Staff Working in Countries Where SA Is Formally Constrained." Background paper for this book, World Bank, Washington, DC.

Vian, T., D. Brinkerhoff, F. Feeley, M. Salomon, and N. Thi Kieu Vien. 2012. "Confronting Corruption in the Health Sector in Vietnam: Patterns and Prospects." *Public Administration and Development* 32 (1): 49–63.

Wallis, J. J. 2006. "The Concept of Systematic Corruption in American History." In *Corruption and Reform: Lessons from America's Economic History*, edited by E. L. Glaeser and C. Goldin, 23–62. Chicago: University of Chicago Press.

Wintrobe, R. 1998. *The Political Economy of Dictatorship*. Vol. 6. Cambridge, U.K.: Cambridge University Press.

Wischermann, J. 2011. "Governance and Civil Society Action in Vietnam: Changing the Rules from Within; Potential and Limits." *Asian Politics and Policy* 3 (3): 383–411.

World Bank. 2013. "Social Accountability in Municipal Services Social Accountability Review: Housing and Utilities Services in Belarus." World Bank, Washington, DC.

———. 2014a. "Information and Communication Technologies for Social Accountability in Russian Region." World Bank, Washington, DC, July.

———. 2014b. "Listening to Citizens: Learning from Projects in Africa ESW." World Bank, Washington, DC.

Wu, F. 2003. "Environmental GONGO Autonomy: Unintended Consequences of State Strategies in China." *Good Society* 12 (1): 35–45.

Social Accountability in Fragile and Conflict-Affected Situations

The questions of whether and how social accountability (SA) activities can promote greater accountability and stronger state-society relationships in fragile and conflict-affected situations (FCSs) need to be explored further. The first section discusses the relevance of SA in FCSs. The second focuses on the characteristics common to FCSs that have a bearing on SA. The third considers how the constraints to association, information, and the interfaces between civil society and governments might be overcome. A final section discusses the operational implications for task teams.

In selecting examples of FCSs, we used a broad definition drawn from the FCS list in the country assistance strategy and interim strategy note baseline study conducted by the Center for Conflict, Security, and Development in 2013.[1] The list of FCSs in the baseline study was compiled based on the following criteria: (a) inclusion at least once in the World Bank FCS list during fiscal 2004–12, (b) presence of an episode of violence during fiscal 2008–12, (c) presence of more than 50,000 internally displaced persons during fiscal 2010–12, and (d) a portfolio of more than five active projects. As this list covers countries up to fiscal 2012, we added the World Bank's fiscal 2013 and 2014 FCS lists to it as well as recommendations of fragile countries from experts. We triangulated the final FCS list with the United Nations Development Programme's *Users Guide on Measuring Fragility* (UNDP 2009) and the Organisation for Economic Co-operation and Development's *Fragile States: Resource Flows and Trends* (OECD 2013).

Relevance of SA in FCS

There is a consensus among practitioners and scholars that a lack of accountability on the part of the state is one of the main characteristics of FCSs. The *World Development Report* (WDR) *2011*, for example, argues that countries experience fragility and violence when "states or institutions lack the capacity, accountability, or legitimacy" to deal with the external stressors that include insecurity, injustice, and a lack of economic opportunity (World Bank 2011).[2] The WDR suggests that, for countries to make successful transitions out of endemic fragility and cyclical violence, they require legitimate institutions that can provide basic services, including security, justice, and economic opportunity.

The primary strategy for addressing fragility has therefore focused on strengthening the capacity of state institutions to deliver services. By doing so, it is expected that states will gain legitimacy. This is referred to as the "capacity-deficit paradigm."

It has recently been recognized that not only the effectiveness of state institutions but also other dynamics in societies contribute to fragility. For example, the World Bank (2012) has identified dysfunctional relationships between citizens and the state and across groups of citizens as fundamental drivers of fragility.[3]

This literature also suggests that state legitimacy needs to be understood in a broader context of state-society relationships (for example, see Elgin-Cossart, Jones, and Esberg 2012). In this context, the ability of a state to provide services is only one factor affecting its legitimacy. Although availability of services may be necessary to build legitimacy, it is by no means sufficient (Hilhorst, Christoplos, and Van der Harr 2010). Other drivers of legitimacy derive from a broader understanding of the social contract between state and citizens, including the state's ability to build inclusive political settlements and mediate relations across various groups (for example, Brinkerhoff, Wetterberg, and Dunn 2012). This is especially true in FCS contexts.

The relevance of social accountability in FCSs derives from the expectations that it has a potential to mediate these societal dynamics and to have a positive impact on state legitimacy. The following two sections detail these expectations.

Expectations for State Legitimacy and State-Society Relationship

Social accountability activities can build up or reinforce the social contract between state and citizens. Any accountability relationship requires some identification of who is accountable to whom, for what, and how it is to be monitored. As citizens demand accountability from the government and government provides citizens with spaces to make these demands, this reinforces a relationship in which the state is answerable to citizens for its actions and citizens can sanction it for not fulfilling its obligations.

Social accountability activities can also help to build legitimacy of the state within this broader context of social contract. Political legitimacy refers to whether people who make decisions at the national, state, or local level are seen as legitimately representing the interests of citizens.[4] In addition to elections, legitimacy can also be derived from negotiations and consultations between government and citizens. SA approaches can encourage dialogue and engagement between the state and society at various levels. Some scholars have even suggested that social accountability can help to strengthen an understanding of citizenship (for example, Pearce 2007).

Social accountability can also help to promote political inclusion, thereby reducing perceptions of injustice and strengthening state legitimacy. In the absence of political inclusion and opportunities to participate in the political process, citizens deem the state unjust (Colletta and Cullen 2000). This perception of injustice is also linked to a lack of accountability and is especially pronounced when the issue relates to the distribution of resources across various groups (see Greenberg and Folger 1983; Lind and Tyler 1988; Tyler and Bies 1990; Tyler et al. 1997). In such cases, different groups may lose faith in the state's ability to mediate among groups. By encouraging the dissemination of information and providing avenues of engagement with the state, SA activities can help to dispel perceptions of injustice and build state legitimacy.

Social accountability helps to create a culture of engagement between state and citizens. Efforts to disseminate information, a key ingredient in SA approaches, aim to disclose details relating to a government's actions, enabling citizens to scrutinize the government. SA activities also provide interfaces between citizens and governments, where citizens can provide feedback and query state officials about their performance and state officials can account for themselves. Ultimately, when citizens have a role to play in decision making, when they can voice their concerns, when information is available to them, and when they can evaluate and criticize government actions and performance, they will have trust in the state. These are key steps toward constructive relations between the state and citizens.

Expectations for Intra-Society Relationships

Fragile and conflict-affected situations are marked by a breakdown in trust and social cohesion, which can inflame tensions and perpetuate violence. Relationships within society must be restored before social and institutional relationships can be reestablished and trust restored. Strengthened state-society relations through social accountability can also encourage citizens to exercise their citizenship rights, something that conflict has prevented (Gaventa and Barrett 2010; King, Samii, and Snilstveit 2010; World Bank 2005).

Almost all SA activities entail increased face-to-face interaction among community members to build trust and ultimately enable them to coordinate collective action better. It is generally agreed that personal interaction can build trust within a community.[5] Mutual trust is a prerequisite for cooperation. It helps to surmount obstacles to collective action.[6] Conversely, SA activities that make collective action possible engender a sense of community and enable greater collective action in the future.

The most important mechanism through which social accountability activities can contribute to better intra-society relations is, perhaps, improving the capacity of individuals who participate in these collective activities. Participation in collective activities to demand accountability from the government can build competencies and skills that are necessary for organizing collective action. These include the ability to manage organizations and communicate effectively (Brady 1999; Putnam 1993). Participants also develop more sophisticated understanding of issues as well as of the system in which they are situated (Bennett 1975; Jennings and Niemi 1981).

Through participation and the process of engagement in social accountability activities, citizens may also learn the norms of inclusion.[7] Through this engagement, citizens learn to develop a broader perspective, recognize and respect diverse and opposing opinions, and develop a capacity for cooperation and reciprocity—a process that scholars have called "social identification" (Paxton 2007; Putnam 1993; Warren 2001). These effects of participation in collective projects can be enduring: they are "an inheritance people take along with them in their life cycle" (Hooghe 2003) and that they can apply to other domains of public life.

How Are These Expectations Met in Practice?

The links between SA approaches and positive outcomes for state-society and intra-society relationships can be articulated theoretically, when certain assumptions hold. In practice, however, these assumptions might be even more difficult to hold in FCSs. For instance, low institutional capacity and poor legitimacy of the state, which might be improved through SA, create specific challenges to any form of citizen-state engagement.

Evidence of the impact of SA on state-society relations or intra-society relations is thin. One reason for this paucity of evidence relates to the difficulty in measuring the long-term impact of SA activities on institutions (see chapter 2). The evidence that does exist on the impact of social accountability on state-society and intra-society relations is presented in the following paragraphs.

While few in number, some empirical studies document the positive impact that social accountability activities have had on various aspects of the state-society relationship. Different indicators can be used to measure state legitimacy and accountability. Most often, "input-oriented" indicators of legitimacy (Oosterom 2009), such as participation of greater numbers of citizens in the governance process, greater capacity and willingness of citizens to ask questions of governments, and increased civic and political knowledge, are used for this purpose. These results show that SA activities can lead to increased capacity on the part of both the state and citizens to solve problems collaboratively, for example, in connection with service delivery. See box 6.1 for a discussion of the impact on state-society relations of a local civic engagement program in Iraq and box 6.2 for other examples.

BOX 6.1

A Fragile Political Settlement, Legitimacy, and Local Civic Engagement in Iraq

In the context of a fragile political settlement in Iraq, several civic engagement activities took incremental steps to build the perceived legitimacy of local government bodies. For example, a local governance program provided assistance to build the technical skills and capacity of local councils to win the trust of citizens and give them legitimacy. Following the initial cessation of hostilities in the country, the program supported the creation of these councils and helped them to interact with citizens in

(continued next page)

BOX 6.1   *(continued)*

meaningful ways. While the councils were designed initially to interface with the U.S. military, their role expanded. They conducted assessments of service needs, participated in joint planning exercises with local government departments, voiced citizens' concerns, and sought to hold officials accountable.

One evaluation of the program found that capacity building succeeded in several ways. The program gave the councils legitimacy in the eyes of its constituents. Participatory processes helped to ensure that membership on the councils was representative and minimized the risk of elite capture. The formation of the councils led to increased trust among citizens. The evaluation, however, cautioned that these gains could be lost wherever conflict continued, the legacy of government oppression remained strong, and the central government opposed decentralization.

Sources: Boeckmann 2012; Brinkerhoff and Mayfield 2005.

BOX 6.2

Select Examples of Impact on State-Society and Intra-Society Relations

Impact on state-society relations. McGee and Kroesschell (2013) synthesize findings from Bangladesh, Mozambique, and Nepal and argue that externally created spaces for accountability served as "schools for citizenship." Cima (2013) suggests that public audits in Nepal created the space and the skills that citizens needed to engage with the government. Faehndrich and Nhantumbo (2012) measure the impact of the governance activities of the Governance, Water, and Sanitation Program in Mozambique and find that they contributed to increased trust between citizens and government officials. Cornwall, Cordeiro, and Delgado (2006) describe how the municipal health council in one Brazilian city is gradually transforming a "culture of clientelist into a culture of accountability."

Oosterom (2009) finds that in Mozambique, inclusion of citizens in budget committees to monitor the performance of government officials resulted in a better understanding on the part of local government officials and citizens of their shared needs and

(continued next page)

constraints and therefore led to more constructive engagement. Similarly, Young (2003) notes that in Central Asia, community groups and government officials participated in joint project reviews (through Mercy Corps programming), which helped to increase trust between communities and the government. Similarly, community participation in monitoring the implementation of a water project in Koryantok, Uzbekistan, mitigated the resentment that citizens had of the local government through a better understanding on the part of government of the resource constraints facing the community (Young 2003).

Impact on intra-society relations. Fearon, Humphreys, and Weinstein (2011) find that in Liberia, activities that engaged citizens intensively in development planning led to greater social cohesion measured in terms of the ability to coordinate collective action. Coleman and López (2010) find that a similar program in Colombia had the same results. Beath et al. (2010) also find that engagement activities had positive, albeit weak, effects on interpersonal trust in Afghanistan. In Tajikistan, when citizens were brought together in water user associations, cohesion increased among groups (World Bank 2005). Saferworld (2008) notes that interaction among government officials, community members, and refugees led to improved relations when each group had a better understanding of the views and concerns of the others. A World Bank study of 13 community-driven development programs in conflict-affected states finds that the cohesion that resulted from cooperation in community-driven development programs spilled over into broader social life after citizens had worked together for four or five years (World Bank 2005).

There is some evidence to suggest that interventions that encourage citizens to engage with one another to achieve a common goal tend to improve social relations. Some studies have found that such activities can enhance mutual trust and cooperation among citizens and enable them to coordinate collective action. However, these studies consider the impact of several types of interventions that promote interaction among citizens, not all of which have greater social accountability as their goal. The dynamics between individuals may change when demanding accountability becomes one of the primary aims of these activities.

Common Social and Political Features of FCSs and Constraints on Citizen Action and State Action

FCSs differ from each other perhaps more than any other category of states, and one needs to acknowledge the caveats and limitations of any approach that attempts to use an FCS "archetype." Nevertheless, FCSs share some features in common that can be analyzed in relation to SA. In this section, we apply the framework described in chapters 3 and 4 to analyze the general characteristics of (a) state-society relations, (b) political society and the associated constraints on state action, and (c) citizen action and its constraints on citizen-state engagement. The third section discusses the constraints and opportunities related to the three levers of information, interface, and civic mobilization.

What Are the Characteristics of State-Society Relations?

The social contract in FCSs is in flux. In FCSs, there is often no shared understanding about the nature of a social contract; what is right and legitimate and how rights should be understood and defined are difficult questions, with no consistent answers in situations where institutions have been undermined or destroyed. There may be lingering unaddressed grievances. The absence of a common understanding of a social contract may lie at the heart of conflict and fragility. Without a clear framework for engagement and some clarity on the compact between the state and citizens within which engagement takes place, there is the risk that SA engagement will not yield the desired outcomes.

Moreover, whatever understanding exists on a social contract is expected to vary over time, as it is constantly being redefined in-depth until the state consolidates power (Lund 2006). This situation is manifested either in negotiation (see the discussion of the National Dialogue in the case study of the Republic of Yemen in chapter 7) or through conflict. For example, the political settlement in Kenya shifted as a result of the postelection violence. The revised constitution moved toward greater devolution, diffusing the power base that had existed previously. This not only requires adaptation, but also can provide opportunities.

In some cases, there is no longer a social contract, but instead a pervasive sense that the state has failed its citizens. Citizens might not necessarily reject the state, however, or refuse to make an attempt to reestablish a relationship with it. In fact, they may continue to aspire to a social contract with a state that would meet its obligations to guarantee security and public goods. These aspirations, however, are not linked to the existing state structure.

The notion of social contract often differs across groups. State-society relations and the social contract in FCSs often mean different things to different groups. Discord, conflicts, and disputes over resources and the role of the state in mediating these are at the basis of fragility and conflict in most, if not all, FCSs. As a consequence, different groups have had different relationships with the state, and their conception and expectations of it will depend on how they perceive these historical relations (for example, see Collier 2000; Stewart and Fitzgerald 2000). Groups also perceive state legitimacy in different ways (Brinkerhoff, Wetterberg, and Dunn 2012). While large groups of citizens may consider the state to be illegitimate and predatory, others may believe that it represents their interests. Some groups have close ties with government institutions and easy access to decision makers, while others define their relationship with the government in terms of remoteness, a lack of ties, and opposition.

State-society relationships of this nature present risks to SA in three ways. First, within this situation, all efforts geared toward strengthening state legitimacy and state capacity will be controversial and sensitive. SA may reignite conflicts in such circumstances. If the process and impact of SA are perceived to be excluding a group, this can create or revive tensions within groups or between certain groups and the state that may have caused the conflict in the first place. SA interventions need to be sensitive to opposing values, interests, and perceptions.

Second, since in many FCSs the state is in the process of consolidating power, there is a risk that an intervention supporting certain actors and institutional reforms may unwittingly favor one group over another. It may also lead to an overly powerful state and close off the space for citizen engagement.

Third, the government may be fearful of opening up the space for negotiation and dialogue. The government may fear that opening up the space may incentivize citizens to lodge contentious action toward the state. In FCSs where political settlements are fragile, such confrontation can be perceived as a risk for the very foundations of the state.

The Characteristics of Political Society and the Constraints on State Action

Political society in FCSs is often divided and has low capacity. Political society is often polarized, so that reaching agreements among stakeholders is a daunting task. In FCSs, political society comprises factions and stake-holders that led the country to violence and fragility. As a result, mutual distrust prevails among stakeholders when they enter the political arena, usually through some sort of political settlement. These groups gener-ally lack a common understanding of the problems facing the country. Perceptions of injustice and unfair treatment persist among groups.

Moreover, political actors are weak and incapable of fulfilling their roles. Sometimes, patronage networks, particularly at the local level, have supplanted politicians, creating asymmetries of power.

The state is only one actor among many. In FCSs, the state often does not have full or exclusive authority over its territory and is competing with other groups for legitimacy.[8] State administrative structures are absent from some areas or face competing sources of authority in society. Such condi-tions create a challenging context for SA, as they make identification of state responsibilities unclear and state action tentative. Moreover, the absence of complete state authority creates a high level of insecurity, as various groups compete for territorial authority, making any operations and implementa-tion of interventions within these areas almost impossible. In addition, these areas are most often devoid of capable civil society organizations (CSOs) that could mediate and support SA approaches. As a result of lack of capacity and security, the range of SA approaches tends to be more limited (for instance, third-party monitoring is more challenging without capable local CSOs).

The Characteristics of Civil Society and the Constraints on Citizen Action

Conflict and fragility limit the capacity of citizens to take part in collec-tive action. Conflict and fragility can have a detrimental impact on the agency of individuals, which in turn affects their ability to participate in collective action. As discussed in chapter 3, citizenship-based activities are severely circumscribed by the level of agency that different individuals are able to exert in particular contexts. Poverty and the lack of basic services in FCSs can seriously erode agency. The effects of poverty will necessarily differ among citizens. Those who feel its effects more acutely will doubtless be unable or reluctant to take part in collective action. Furthermore, in FCSs, the understanding of citizenship may have been shaped by violence and conflict. Fear, insecurity, repression, displacement, and violence may result in feelings of powerlessness, marginalization, and humiliation. These feelings can undermine the basic requirements for citizen participation—a sense of civic agency, aspiration, the will and capacity to interact, and the experience and skills to use voice—and have long-lasting consequences for the way people behave once the crisis has ended. Nevertheless, as discussed in the section on civic mobilization, violence and conflict can also encourage some citizens to become engaged and to mobilize.

When it exists, the space for participation does not guarantee that participation will be meaningful. At the same time, there is the risk that existing inequalities and exclusion will be perpetuated. Exclusion and marginalization, whether real or perceived, play an important role in FCSs, either fomenting conflict or resulting from it.[9] In many FCSs, patterns of exclusion are deliberate, based on historical legacies and embedded in organizations. In many cases, as in the Republic of Yemen, citizens have internalized their own status as "marginalized." In a focus group on local governance, a woman in Burundi expressed this sentiment as follows (see box 6.3 for more details):

> These questions you are asking—on the development of the budget, tax collection, prioritizing the communal development plan—these questions and issues are for "them." "They" are the ones to make decisions and tell us. It is not my place to discuss these issues and make decisions.

BOX 6.3

The Tyranny of Participation and the Internalization of Exclusion

In Burundi, a long tradition of the "tyranny of participation" appears to have cultural roots, particularly in relation to the country's rural population (Gaynor 2011, 2013). Even where officials attempted to work closely with citizens, in the Commune of Rutegama, for example, self-exclusion, poverty (manifested in low levels of education), and a widely held view that the state was not genuinely interested in a candid dialogue kept the attempt from being meaningful. This sentiment was expressed most strongly on the subjects of politics and the central government, while participants acknowledged greater interaction with and confidence in communal administration officials. A Kirundi proverb reflects this cultural norm: *Nta muntu vitumira mu rubanza*, meaning, "Everyone knows exactly who is invited and who is not invited to any given forum." Therefore, institutional constraints do not represent the only obstacle to greater social accountability in Burundi. Cultural norms that limit the opportunities for citizens to participate in civic affairs also play a role. This reality is compounded by a lack of trust, the product of cycles of violence dating back to the 1960s.

In such circumstances, there are formidable challenges in undoing the causes of exclusion or in combating them. Consequently, when opportunities to participate are created, they can be captured by some groups, while others remain spectators.

In contexts of fragility, promoting meaningful participation is particularly difficult owing to asymmetries of power and insecurity. When there is a culture of fear, insecurity, social exclusion, and asymmetries of power either within a community or between citizens and government officials, citizens often fear involvement in SA activities. If they do become involved, their participation might be only perfunctory.

The state has low capacity to deliver, respond, and sanction. FCSs are characterized by weak administrative capacity. Destruction and displacement in conflict or postconflict situations can seriously undermine the capacity of the state to rule over its territory, let alone deliver services. A weak and dysfunctional administration will have inadequate capacity to respond to citizens' demands.

It is unlikely that either enforcement or sanctions can be effective. In systems with weak state structures, competing mechanisms for governance and rule of law often translate into a constantly negotiated space for the imposition of sanctions. The relational space for enforcement and answerability is a moving target and will be interpreted and acted on differently in each social accountability relationship. It is therefore unlikely that sanctions can be enforced amid instability. Furthermore, conventional mechanisms to promote accountability through formal political channels often fail in FCSs because these channels are too weak to serve an enforcing or sanctioning role (U4 2011).

Conflict and fragility damage the collective, limiting its ability to take unified action. Fragile states ruled by authoritarian governments often suppress collaborative social relations that might threaten the state's domination (Brinkerhoff and Mayfield 2005). These governments sometimes deliberately encourage discord among their citizens, reinforcing ethnic, regional, and religious differences to weaken their opponents, for example, through the unequal distribution of resources. When citizens contend with each other for some small share of political power, power concentrated at the center often goes uncontested (Lust-Okar 2005). These regimes usually respond to efforts aimed at promoting participation with repression and even violence (Andersen 2008; Gaventa and Barrett 2010).

Conflict and the insecurity it engenders disrupt social relations, undermining any attempt to organize collective action. After the fall of the

Khmer Rouge in Cambodia, relations among villages were characterized as "every household is an island" (Ovesen, Trankell, and Ojendal 1996). In the province of Khyber Pakhtunkhwa (KP) in Pakistan (see the case study in chapter 7), violence restricted the public space where political and social life could be expressed (Mumtaz 2010). The *hujra*, where communities had debated social and political issues for centuries, ceased to exist (Ghani 2011). Out of fear, citizens avoided public places. Fear discouraged people from expressing their opinions openly (Mustafa and Brown 2010). As a teacher in a village in Swat stated, "The custom of late-night meetings in *hujras* is finished. People have limited their dealings with each other."

This breakdown of ties and lack of interaction often result in deep mistrust of others, a self-reinforcing phenomenon. This distrust is a serious constraint on collective action. People are reluctant to engage with one another when social ties are broken (Oosterom 2009). Pearce (2007) notes that, while "violence does not make participation impossible," it has "the effects of sealing space, freezing social relationships, and homogenizing populations, thereby limiting participation." After protracted violence in Aceh and KP, Pakistan, neighbors were reluctant to speak with each other, fearing that they could be informants for the opposition group (see World Bank 2012; the Pakistan case study in chapter 7). A similar phenomenon is reported in northern Mali after the 2013 revolt: "Even neighbors no longer trusted people they had known for decades. Communities were shattered" (van Wicklin 2014).

In addition, when social networks exist, they are usually "bonding" rather than "bridging" networks and may cause violence in the society. If strong social relationships are concentrated within specific sections of society (where these sections are defined by space, ethnicity, religion, or other identity markers) without connections across these sections (that is, bonding relationships), the society may become even more segmented. Bonding relationships may not only create constraints for collective action, but also have an "illiberal effect" on the society overall in the form of violence across groups (Leonard 2004). There are numerous examples of such incidents. A strong exclusionary social capital among Hutus was instrumental in the Rwanda genocide (Colletta and Cullen 2000). In Liberia, following the conflict, bonding ties within communities had increased, with stronger ability to survive amid hostility and conflict and to build institutions from the bottom, yet bridging ties were lacking (Sawyers 2004).

Nongovernmental organizations (NGOs) have low capacity and legitimacy in FCSs. When state capacity is low or nonexistent, NGOs are supported by donors or external parties and often used to deliver humanitarian assistance or provide emergency services. When funding for civil society comes from outside sources—for example, through donor support—civil society is seen as accountable to these sources rather than to the people (for example, in Afghanistan and Pakistan). This is even more the case in FCSs due to concerns about security, trust, and intra-society relationships.

With a history of antagonistic relations, CSOs in FCSs can become stuck in a confrontational stance vis-à-vis the state. In addition to the lack of incentive to engage with the government, CSOs may also lack both the capacity for such engagement and the networks through which this engagement can take place. State authorities can be equally distrustful of CSOs, as the state perceives them as challenging its authority and constraining its ability to perform its functions. This antagonistic relationship creates challenges for SA.

However, the role of local associations that remain strong in some FCSs is crucial. An abundant literature documents how local organizations and community-based organizations are particularly strong in some fragile contexts by necessity. Gaventa and Barrett (2010) recognize "the role which local associations and other citizen activities can play [in FCSs] in the strengthening of cultures of citizenship, which in turn can contribute to building responsive states."

Traditional and customary institutions can serve as alternatives to CSOs and can potentially be used to anchor SA activities. Hagmann (2007) and Eubank (2010) point to the important role of clan elders in parts of Somalia and maintain that in the absence of a central state and significant international assistance, efforts by Somali clan elders to broker peace and build institutions were instrumental in resolving conflict, maintaining security, and providing basic services. This was also the case in Somaliland (see Aslam 2014).

However, the reliance on traditional institutions has its limitations. First, in some cases, these institutions may lack legitimacy, and they may also fail to be fully representative of society (see the case study of the Republic of Yemen). In such circumstances, relying on traditional institutions to anchor SA activities must be done cautiously. Second, reliance on traditional institutions may also perpetuate existing patterns of exclusion and reinforce a strong in-group identity, while harming bridging ties. Third, reliance on traditional institutions may lead to widespread distrust of initiatives aimed at strengthening the role of the state, as seen in Somaliland and KP, Pakistan (chapter 7).

Overcoming Constraints to Information, Interface, and Civic Mobilization in FCSs

This section highlights the challenges entailed in disseminating information, constructing and strengthening interface, and supporting civic mobilization in FCSs. It also offers recommendations with regard to operations to mitigate these challenges.

Information

In FCSs, the flow of accurate and unbiased information is essential for rebuilding trust between citizens and the state and for supporting efforts to restore peace. Information about public policies, budgets, administrative processes, and other matters is also necessary for officials to be held accountable.

Accurate and unbiased information is not readily accessible. Of greatest concern are the physical barriers to the flow of information. The infrastructure needed to disseminate information is often lacking in fragile contexts. In Liberia, for example, much of the landline telecommunication infrastructure was stolen during the war (Reeve 2011). Even when infrastructure is present, access may be limited to urban centers or to the most affluent citizens or regions of the country. Moreover, repeated interruptions resulting from the rudimentary nature of infrastructure in FCS contexts may severely limit access.

Most often, the state is the only entity with the necessary infrastructure to produce and disseminate information in these fragile contexts. When this is the case, information flows only vertically and tends to be biased and hierarchical. Even when private media outlets exist, the government may control them, and when there is no overt control, intimidation and violence may force journalists to censor themselves.

Insecurity puts obstacles in the way of producing and disseminating information. There is a scarcity of information flows into and out of areas of a country where there is violence and insecurity.

In postconflict settings, information about public life is usually colored by the history of violence and can be framed maliciously. Information generally reflects the worldviews of those who gather and disseminate it. In a postconflict setting, it can also reflect a particular, often skewed, interpretation or understanding of the history of the conflict. For example, "Many journalists … still have a 'war mentality,' which they cannot easily abandon. Within this context the 'war frame' prevails in their reporting and can hardly be replaced by balanced and reconciliatory stories" (IFP 2012). In such circumstances, citizens are unable to see beyond the confines of their own identity groups or to appreciate different perspectives.

This phenomenon raises issues of trust, where citizens are wary of information sources that do not conform to their views of history. Competing pieces of information cause confusion and can potentially reinforce the divisions that led to conflict in the first place.

When information is inaccessible, rumors abound. In the absence of formal, trustworthy sources of information, citizens rely instead on their networks of friends, family, and local leaders for information about the outside world. Information from these alternate sources might be based less on fact or be deliberately biased, reinforcing their worldviews and sharpening divisions in society.

SA interventions need to support information flows in sensitive and transparent ways. "People need time to understand and trust what you are doing. What information, how to disseminate it, and to whom: these are major questions in an FCS context" (IFP 2012). Transparency is essential if citizens are to have an understanding of how decisions are reached (in particular, funding or targeting decisions) and to avoid fueling conflict. But this transparency needs to be managed carefully to avoid misperceptions of elite capture or favoritism toward particular individuals or groups. Due to specific constraints to access linked to low literacy, local languages, and poor infrastructure, multipronged strategies need to be put in place to support communication flows. According to a staff member working on a Sri Lanka housing reconstruction project, "There were ethnic tensions among people, yet the project was 'ethnic-blind.' To avoid increasing these tensions we made the process of selection of beneficiaries transparent by disseminating information and providing a grievance redress mechanism" (van Wicklin 2014).

Information must be disseminated as widely as possible to all groups in society. To do so, knowing the different media on which citizens rely for information is essential, as is disseminating information in different formats to reach different audiences. Following are some specific steps that can be taken in SA interventions to support equal access to unbiased, reliable information.

First, support and encourage government to become a trustworthy source of accurate information, able to heed and address the concerns of the public, build public trust, and ensure public support for reconstruction (Von Kaltenborn-Stachau 2008). Doing so is important generally, but insufficient information from government officials can become a serious source of wider grievance.

Second, support the institutions of civil society that advocate for an independent media. There are various examples of such institutions in countries around the world, such as press clubs and local chapters of organizations that call for the protection of journalists.

Third, strengthen the professionalism of journalists and media organizations and ensure that they are able to report with sensitivity. In FCSs, journalists are often untrained and unskilled. Often, there are no schools of journalism, and the only training that reporters receive is on the job. Sensitivity training is essential in fragile contexts, especially when biased reporting could stem from a lack of understanding or sympathy and an inability to understand events from different perspectives. It is, however, crucial that this kind of support be provided uniformly throughout the country.

Finally, identify opportunities to harness information and communication technology and other modern information technologies. However, be mindful of the risk of further widening the "digital divide." It is accordingly necessary to devote resources to support hybrid strategies to avoid excluding the most vulnerable groups.

Interface

As described in the first section, since the social contract is in flux, the basis for creating an interface is unclear. In fragile contexts, citizens often do not know what the roles and responsibilities of the central or local government are, how the state can make a difference in their daily lives, or how government should respond to their needs and concerns (McGee and Kroesschell 2013).

There is often a lack of interfaces at the local level to allow constructive citizen engagement (McGee and Kroesschell 2013). In some cases, an SA intervention may have to start with building an interface (see the case of Sierra Leone in chapter 7).

Even when an interface exists, its credibility can be questionable, and it might not be uniformly deemed legitimate across all groups. It is important to learn whether existing interfaces are uniformly credible among all groups in society. They may, in fact, be systematically biased in favor of certain groups and inaccessible to some. When some groups are unable to engage with the state at the same level, the sense of injustice will persist. This sense of injustice may have been a source of violence and conflict in the first place. It is especially important in the case of FCSs for interfaces to be accessible to all groups (McGee and Kroesschell 2013).

The local level is a strong entry point for creating an effective interface for several reasons. First, the local level is the most immediate point of contact between citizens and the state as well as others in positions of authority. It is where citizens learn what the state can and cannot do. Second, the local level is often the entry point for service delivery and conflict resolution. The issues that citizens face on a daily basis are by and large local in nature. For these reasons, government legitimacy ultimately takes shape or unravels at the local level.

Civic Mobilization

Civic mobilization in FCSs is a daunting task. Effective mobilizers need to be able to forge shared agendas in a deeply divided society, develop social bonds cutting across identity groups that may have been at the base of conflict, and create and reinforce citizenship identity when the "state" is a remote concept for most citizens.

Identifying a mobilizer who is able to transcend identity lines is especially complicated yet crucial. Since many FCSs are ethnically fragmented, individuals tend to stick to community, ethnic, and other identity groups. At the same time, if a mobilizer is not able to focus on common bonds that can hold the community together, tensions within societies can reignite.

In conflict situations, mobilizers are targeted specifically because of their ability to encourage or generate collective action. The rationale behind this targeting presumably is that mobilizers can persuade other people to raise voice against violence; eliminating these voices removes resistance to the violence. In KP, Pakistan, the militant group Tehrik-e-Taliban Pakistan targeted *maliks* and *khans* (traditional local leaders) extensively (Khan 2013). Public places were also targeted with an explicit goal to restrict public life (Mustafa and Brown 2010). Consequently, not only is there a dearth of effective mobilizers in the community, but there is also reluctance among citizens to show their capacity as mobilizers for fear of being targeted. A focus group participant (see chapter 7) expressed this as follows: "No single individual can show himself as a leader because leaders were targeted more in the past."

Research suggests, however, that the experience of conflict can also result in political and social empowerment, enabling some community members to act as effective mobilizers.[10] In Sierra Leone, violence failed to demoralize or deter certain citizens. Instead it spurred them to be mobilizers themselves and made them community activists.[11] Similarly, actively taking part in conflict "emboldens women to take political action not only during the conflict but also subsequently" (Kaufman and Williams 2010).[12] These findings are consistent with studies in psychology showing that shocks including violence can permanently alter a person's outlook on life or appreciation of the importance of social networks, leading him or her to participate in public life (Tedeschi and Calhoun 2004).

This phenomenon was seen in the Republic of Yemen (chapter 7). The "change movement," as citizens called the Arab Uprising in the Republic of Yemen, has inspired the younger generation to participate in public life. Referred to as "community activists," these young people identify themselves primarily as citizens rather than as members of a tribe. They seem to have a willingness to become engaged in the public sphere. They have a good understanding of the state's obligation to be accountable to Yemenis. They have been able to find common cause with others they see as fellow citizens. Since Yemenis view the 2011 movement favorably and deem its goals to be just, these young community activists are also perceived as legitimate by others.

In order to support civic mobilization in fragile and postconflict settings, it is essential to analyze social networks carefully to identify those with the potential to mobilize others. Where such mobilizers do not seem to exist, a strategy can be to identify actors who could potentially act as mobilizers and support their technical capacity.

Civil society organizations, tribal institutions, and the media can often mobilize citizens. As noted earlier, the constraints facing these organizations in FCSs should be examined carefully before engaging them in a mobilizing role. The case studies in chapter 7 discuss how these institutions can and have assumed this role, what are their constraints, and what SA can do to support them.

Implications for Support

Based on the sections above as well as on interviews with World Bank staff (Van Wicklin 2014), this section examines the operational implications of these findings for task teams engaged in SA interventions.

Assessing the Trade-Offs between the Potential Gains and Risks

In FCSs, SA is deemed a priority because, in the absence of a social contract, there is the risk of recurrent violence, and the consequences can be tragic for individuals and households.

212 OPENING THE BLACK BOX

Addressing issues of trust, legitimacy, and justice through SA sometimes takes precedence over issues of service delivery in FCSs, as state building becomes a more difficult undertaking unless there is some notion of a social contract to provide the basis for state-society interaction. Building a state that is not deemed legitimate, is not trusted, or is perceived to be unjust can prove to be highly counterproductive. SA holds potential to address grievances and open a link to formal processes and institutions. It thus can mitigate the factors that can make people move further away from the state and push them to a point of violence.

The stakes are indeed high, but so are the risks: the characteristics of FCSs that warrant an urgent response in the form of an SA intervention also make it more risky. In the words of a World Bank staff person, FCSs are "social and governance minefields." While risks of SA exist in all contexts, they can have more serious consequences in FCSs.

In some contexts, the minimum requirement to engage in SA may be lacking. If conflict is particularly intense and there is no end in sight, supporting SA is probably premature. The basic structures of local governance, for example, need to be in place for citizens to be able to engage with them. There should be some notion of a social contract or at the least the possibility of negotiating one. Basic infrastructure is also necessary to disseminate information.

In general, whether to engage in SA or not should be decided on a case-by-case basis, and the following risks should be weighed.

First, there is a risk that SA can create expectations on the part of citizens that the state is unable or unwilling to respond to, putting the legitimacy of the state at further risk. Expectations that cannot be met may arise not only in connection with SA activities, but also through the actions of the state, particularly if it touts transparency and accountability but fails to deliver on its commitments. Frustration and grievances can only mount in such a situation (McGee and Kroesschell 2013), and these need to be addressed. SA, especially when it is part of a political transition, may become a destructive force if expectations outpace institutional change (as shown in the Middle East after the Arab Spring).

Second, there is a risk for SA to lead to elite capture, exacerbating existing power asymmetries and aggravating perceptions of injustice among certain groups. Elite capture and its consequences can inadvertently close the space for citizen engagement rather than open it. Elites may also mediate the relationship of the state with citizens, preventing citizens from engaging directly with state structures. This is a significant risk in FCSs, where it is already difficult to include the poor and marginalized in SA activities.

Third, participants in SA activities face personal risk. This risk can manifest itself after donor support ends and before the impact of the activities supported can be felt or if the activities fail to produce an impact. Citizens, individually and collectively, as well as organizations that had a role in SA activities may be perceived as "enemies" by the government or sometimes by their fellow citizens.

Finally, the greatest risk in fragile situations is without a doubt the potential of SA to reignite old tensions, plunging the country back into fragility and conflict:

- *An SA intervention can create "losers" in communities.* As noted, SA may result in a redistribution of social and political power, even within a community. For example, when marginalized groups are brought into a participatory forum, tensions can result. In a situation where differences between groups are a source of friction, even small tensions may be disruptive.
- *Some SA activities may be confrontational.* For instance, when teachers themselves are members of the community, scorecards that point to a problem of pervasive absenteeism among teachers may create unease.

Box 6.4 presents some strategies to mitigate risks associated with implementing SA in FCSs.

Investing in Understanding the Context in the Design Phase and throughout Implementation and Adjusting Accordingly

As one World Bank employee stated in an interview, "Context matters more in FCSs than in other situations," as it evolves rapidly. The process of building legitimacy in FCSs is a continuous one, where citizens' experience of government and their engagement with it in connection with service delivery, security, political participation, and accountability yield greater legitimacy when their experience is positive and their engagement active and yield less legitimacy otherwise. The relationship between citizens and the state, therefore, is neither static nor linear, but instead a dynamic interaction subject to repeated renegotiation based on empirics, expectations, and perceptions (Brinkerhoff, Wetterberg, and Dunn 2012).

Significant attention and resources are necessary to gain an understanding of the specific context, including, but not limited to, the causes of conflict and the motives for perpetuating it, how the situation is evolving, the influence of officials in positions of authority and the status of any political settlement, the nature of the existing social contract and how it varies

BOX 6.4

Some Strategies to Mitigate Risks Associated with Implementing Social Accountability in Fragile and Conflict-Affected Situations

State engagement

- Ensure that there is a focus on the supply side as well as the demand side, so that the state's capacity to respond to and manage the mounting aspirations of its citizens, not just for greater accountability on the part of the government, but also for a larger role in public life, is strengthened.
- Continue to engage with the state to ensure that it delivers on its promises.

Elite capture

- Bring elites on board as allies in the empowerment of the poor.
- Even out the distribution of power among citizens by strengthening the capacity of the marginalized (McGee and Kroesschell 2013)—for example, in Kenya, SA played a crucial role in breaking down vertical relationships and preventing elite capture by supporting horizontal relationships among local governors and among citizens to engage with governors.

Social cohesion

- Be mindful of differences.
- Focus on collaboration rather than confrontation.

Source: Interviews with World Bank staff.

across groups, and how access to services, information, and the structures of government varies from group to group. The first principle is to "do no harm," which means understanding where things could go wrong and how the program design can be altered should this happen.

SA approaches need to be adapted and often readjusted to fit a complex context. FCSs change rapidly, and it is unrealistic to assume that circumstances will remain unchanged over the life of a project. Accordingly, it is necessary to design projects so that they can be adjusted to suit and respond to dynamic circumstances. At the same time, it is important to assess changes resulting from any political settlement, a shift in power relations, and other contextual elements over the course of project implementation and to make changes to its design and work plans accordingly (see box 6.5 for an example).

Repeated adjustments might be at odds with the customary design and implementation of World Bank projects. Many of the organization's employees working in FCSs noted as much. In many cases, projects in FCSs are "emergency" projects, which need to be launched quickly, leaving little time for a thorough analysis of context. World Bank operations also lack the flexibility needed to adjust rapidly to changes in the environment or community dynamics, for instance, by shifting among activities and redirecting financing.

"Working with the Grain"

SA approaches in general, but perhaps even more so in FCSs, need to build on existing structures and local priorities and norms (see, for example,

---

BOX 6.5

How Contextual Analysis Affected the Design of the South Sudan Local Governance and Service Delivery Project

Despite constraints and the low capacity in existing local government structures, the South Sudan Local Governance Service Delivery project chose to work through local governments to engage with communities and enhance the legitimacy of the state in the eyes of its citizens.

Before the launch of the project, an exhaustive diagnostic study was conducted to uncover the causes, drivers, and nature of conflict. This analysis led to a broad understanding of issues, measures to mitigate conflict, and the various manifestations of conflict. Pathways of causes and effects were mapped and used to inform the project concept. Periodic monitoring was built into the project.

Close attention was given to measures to (a) prevent elite capture, (b) provide communication on a continuing basis and create multiple channels for disseminating information, and (c) proactively manage potential sources of conflict by building conflict management techniques into project activities. A considerable amount of hand holding, training, supervision, and monitoring was necessary.

Diligence has paid off, and there is a better understanding on the part of the government and citizens of community development processes.

Source: Interviews with World Bank task team staff.

Crook and Booth 2011). SA approaches based on organic structures and initiated by local stakeholders themselves tend to be the most successful and judged by Bank staff to be the most legitimate.

Inducing rapid change may be counterproductive. In order to induce change in behaviors (for example, discourage exclusionary behavior), it is necessary to work through the social norms that sanction a particular mode of behavior, not against them. Doing so does not mean abandoning some minimum of standards or expectations, but instead calibrating them so that they are not artificial or unrealistic. Otherwise, there might be misconception that what is sought is only token participation or representation, and this faulty understanding can result in mistrust and weaken the intervention. To anchor SA activities fully in a particular context, a flexible approach is essential.

Working with and through customary institutions means incorporating them into SA activities. A failure to do so can make SA interventions a competing and even superfluous mechanism. Competition with customary institutions can lead to discord and distrust of SA in the community. Grievance redress mechanisms sometimes compete with the conflict resolution and grievance redress mechanisms that customary institutions use, resulting in tensions. Another challenge that arises when SA approaches are not rooted in local institutions relates to the tension between different accountabilities. For instance, local authorities' concern for upward accountability and the state's responsiveness to local authorities instead of to citizens weaken the SA attempts.

Many World Bank employees working in FCS contexts suggested that SA can and should be anchored locally and, wherever feasible, build on existing government and traditional institutions.

Engaging with Local Facilitators

Understanding the local context and ensuring that the SA approaches are rooted in the social norms of the community point to the importance of facilitators. Local knowledge consists of factual knowledge, skills, and capabilities. It is culturally situated and best understood as a social product. Therefore, it is difficult for an outsider to comprehend (Antweiler 1998). Facilitators who belong to the community can help donors to understand this local knowledge and to adapt their technical knowledge to the context. In addition to the local knowledge they bring to the project, local facilitators also provide the opportunity to build local capacity.

The risks associated with local facilitation must be taken into account and managed. Local facilitators may be unable to put aside personal bias, the product of their interpretation or understanding of history, or their perspective on the causes and drivers of conflict. Wherever tensions among groups are dangerously high, a facilitator's affiliation with one group may make communication with another difficult if not impossible.

Identifying a Window of Opportunity

While working in unstable environments is challenging and sometimes risky, by their very nature, FCSs present windows of opportunity. While a social contract is being renegotiated or under negotiation, this time of "flux" can provide an opportunity for the "champions of reform." Together, these two elements—flux and champions of reform—make SA engagement possible. For example, in the Republic of Yemen, the National Dialogue, which aims to redefine the social contract, has provided an opportunity to promote citizen engagement and encourage citizens to exercise their rights and demand accountability from the government at several levels.

In every interview, World Bank employees stressed the importance of "seizing the moment" when it presents itself and supporting reformers. Examples include decentralization reforms in Kenya and partnering with a champion of reform in the Niger Delta.

Starting Small, Proceeding Gradually and Iteratively, and Staying the Course

In order to implement SA effectively, government must endorse the agenda. Ensuring the government's support is therefore essential. Educating all stakeholders about SA processes and the expected outcomes and promoting trust are equally important. In many cases, SA entails a redistribution of power, and the uncertain result of this reapportioning of power may make a government reluctant to cooperate. Highlighting the advantages for the government by choosing the terminology carefully and using the right language to describe the participation of citizens for improved accountability is crucial, as is choosing appropriate entry points.

Once implemented, SA requires a change in attitudes and behavior, and change takes time. In order to promote accountability and give citizens incentives to demand accountability from their government, habits and social structures have to change (Cima 2013). These habits and social structures are shaped in part by the legacies of previous engagement between collective and state actors (Joshi and Houtzager 2012). Citizens may be unfamiliar with the concept of a relationship of accountability with their government. They may never before have had an opportunity to voice their opinions or their demands. At the same time, it may never have occurred to government officials that they are answerable to the country's citizens. It takes time and continuous engagement before either citizens or government officials trust and acknowledge their respective roles in SA.

In light of these complexities, SA in fragile contexts requires an iterative approach with incremental shifts as its impact gradually becomes apparent. Every result within the key SA processes builds on the previous one, and every change creates a stronger enabling environment for the next SA intervention. Achieving one critical step makes the achievement of that goal more possible than before, even if one particular intervention does not come full circle. It also allows institutional learning where each intervention is able to take advantage of what was learned in the design and implementation of earlier interventions. This assumes even more importance when considering that context changes rapidly in FCSs.

Expectations of what can be achieved in FCSs in a given time period should be realistic. Achieving ambitious institutional goals in a short period of time is as unlikely as it is unrealistic, a frustration expressed by many World Bank staff members in interviews. Evaluations of SA interventions should also take this reality into account. There is a need therefore to identify intermediate outcomes, set modest goals, and think about what SA mechanisms can realistically achieve.

Emphasizing Collaboration Rather Than Confrontation

Despite their limitations, collaborative strategies appear to be more effective than confrontational strategies. First, confrontational strategies may create discord among stakeholders. Second, citizens may be reluctant to take a confrontational stance and more willing to take part in a collaborative action. Finally, collaborative strategies may simply be more productive. For example, in some cases the government officials accountable to the community might actually need the support of the community to make improvements in service delivery. In such cases, providing venues through SA that encourage mutual cooperation will benefit all concerned. Collaborative strategies are the mode of engagement most documented in SA literature and the preferred approach of Bank practitioners working in FCSs.

Conclusions

Social accountability processes may, at times, be controversial and sensitive, because they often entail a reconfiguration of social and political power. As fragile states try to reestablish their relations with society, the international community, understandably, is often wary of initiatives that can be perceived as challenges to government ownership. Even so, processes that in reality are captured by the elite and not owned wholly by citizens are often characterized, inaccurately, as ownership. Donors and practitioners need to be aware of the difference between government ownership and country ownership, where country ownership is a process invested across all sections of society and geographic areas (Dom and Gordon 2011).

These processes are also time-consuming because people need sufficient time to develop political capabilities. Staying the course and allowing these processes to unfold, while still managing them, is essential. Doing so, however, is sometimes at odds with the nature of donor engagements.

Donors also need to be careful that primary lines of accountability are drawn between the state and society, rather than between citizens and development partners. Otherwise, the relationship between the state and society can, in fact, atrophy when a connection between the government and citizens is removed. As McGee and Kroesschell (2013) argue, however, even if the externally created spaces for accountability cannot last indefinitely, they can serve as "schools for citizenship" while in existence.

External support to fragile states may lessen the government's dependence on tax revenues, threatening to remove the most fundamental connection between the state and society. Referring to Somaliland, Eubank (2010) notes that the lack of outside support provided a compelling reason to accept compromise and co-option of opposition groups.

Donors must be careful in managing relationships with NGOs, which have become increasingly instrumental in the implementation of SA. Overreliance on CSOs weakens the state-society contract by further distancing the state from its citizens (Hickey and Mohan 2005). Patron-client relationships between CSOs and development agencies and between CSOs and communities tend to negate the objectives of participatory development by disempowering the "lower partner" (Fowler 2002; Hickey 2002).

Box 6.6 presents the key takeaways from this chapter.

BOX 6.6

Key Takeaways: Social Accountability in Fragile and Conflict-Affected Situations

Lack of accountability is one of the main characteristics of FCSs. Although the evidence on the impact of SA in FCSs is thin, there are indications that such citizen-engaged accountability initiatives could be effective provided they overcome significant constraints.

FCSs probably differ more than any other category of states, and one needs to acknowledge the caveats and limitations of an approach around an FCS "archetype." Yet FCSs share some similarities regarding the "macro" contextual factors influencing SA effectiveness:

- *Weak state-society relations.* The social contract in FCSs tends to be in flux, and both the expected role of the state and the responsibilities of citizens may differ across social groups, making SA approaches particularly controversial and sensitive in such contexts.
- *Divided political society and the constraints to state action.* Political society in FCSs is often divided, and the state has low capacity to deliver, respond, and sanction. State action engaging with SA mechanisms in FCSs can be curtailed, as the state often does not have full or exclusive authority over its territory and is competing with other groups for legitimacy to exercise state powers.
- *Intra-society conflicts and the constraints to citizen action.* Conflict and fragility divide civil society in two ways: (a) it hampers an individual's capacity to participate in collective action, and (b) it damages the collective, thereby affecting its ability to coordinate collective action when individual agency may exist. Space for participation, when it exists, risks reproducing existing inequalities and exclusions. Further, when social networks exist, they usually strengthen bonds within tribal or ethnic social groups rather than bridging existing tensions between such groups in society.
- *Importance of local engagement.* CSOs and NGOs may often have low capacity and legitimacy, but the role of local associations and, in some cases, of traditional or customary institutions is especially important in FCS contexts as channels for information and civic mobilization.

What are the constraints to information, interface, and civic mobilization in FCSs? In FCSs, the flow of accurate and neutral information essential for rebuilding trust between

(continued next page)

BOX 6.6 (continued)

citizens and the state is particularly hard to access. (Re)building the information ecosystem and emphasizing inclusive information flows (to reach all groups within society) are a pressing agenda that SA interventions may enable.

The basis for creating an interface is unclear, with the social contract in flux or its credibility not uniformly accepted across groups. SA interventions, however, may help to create local-level citizen interfaces at which constructive citizen engagement can occur, providing an entry point for service delivery, conflict resolution, and other issues facing people on a daily basis.

Civic mobilization in FCSs can be a more daunting task than in other contexts, with the need to identify a mobilizer able to transcend identity lines being of paramount importance. CSOs, tribal organizations, and media institutions often serve such a role as mobilizers for SA interventions, but in FCS contexts it is essential to analyze social networks carefully to identify legitimate mobilizers above and beyond their technical capacities to mobilize citizens.

What are the implications for support to SA interventions?

- It is important to assess the trade-offs between the importance of citizen engagement to improve services or trust in the state and the high risks of SA interventions failing given "macro" contextual constraints.
- SA approaches in FCSs need to be adapted and adjusted constantly to the complex and fluid local environment, perhaps more so than in any other context.
- SA "levers" of information, interface, and civic mobilization may be more sustainable in FCSs "working with the grain" of existing imperfect institutional structures.
- Engaging with local-level facilitators is paramount.
- SA approaches may use a more opportunistic approach of responding to a "window of opportunity" within FCS contexts.
- SA interventions may need to be small, proceeding gradually and iteratively, given the instability within political society, civil society, and consequently state-society relations.

Notes

1. The following countries or economies are included: Afghanistan, Angola, Bosnia and Herzegovina, Burundi, Cameroon, the Central African Republic, Chad, Colombia, the Comoros, the Democratic Republic of Congo, the Republic of Congo, Côte d'Ivoire, Djibouti, the Arab Republic of Egypt, El Salvador, Eritrea, Georgia, Guatemala, Guinea, Guinea-Bissau, Haiti, Honduras, Indonesia, Iraq,

Kenya, Kiribati, Kosovo, the Kyrgyz Republic, the Lao People's Democratic Republic, Lebanon, Liberia, Libya, Madagascar, Malawi, Mali, the Marshall Islands, the Federated States of Micronesia, Myanmar, Nigeria, Pakistan, Papua New Guinea, the Philippines, Rwanda, Sierra Leone, the Solomon Islands, Somalia, South Sudan, Sri Lanka, Sudan, the Syrian Arab Republic, Tajikistan, Timor-Leste, Togo, Tunisia, Tuvalu, Uganda, Uzbekistan, West Bank and Gaza, the Republic of Yemen, and Zimbabwe.

2. Scholars have also argued that a lack of accountability lies at the heart of fragility in many situations. For example, Knopf (2013) argues that lack of accountability is the primary source of lingering fragility in South Sudan. Elgin-Cossart, Jones, and Esberg (2012) also note that a lack of accountability has been a leading cause of fragility. In interviews, World Bank practitioners said that a lack of accountability is a key driver of fragility in the Republic of Yemen, for example.

3. Other studies have also identified state-society and intra-society relationships. Poor intra-society relations constitute an important underlying cause of fragility (Kaplan 2014).

4. Functional legitimacy and political legitimacy do not always go hand in hand. For example, a local government may be deemed politically legitimate if it came to power through a generally accepted electoral process and if citizens believe that it treats them justly. The same government may not have any functional legitimacy if it fails to deliver social services, ensure security, or resolve conflicts.

5. For example, Almond and Verba (1963); Coleman (1990); Ostrom, Gardner, and Walker (1994); Putnam (1993, 1995, 2000); and Van Deth, Montero, and Westholm (2007). These studies generally define voluntary associations as organized groups that are independent of control by the state or any other outside group. Citizens are free to join or leave them, and their objectives are set collectively. Mobilization through SA often occurs via associations that are very similar in structure and objective, especially in terms of the opportunities they provide for their members to interact. It is safe to conclude that the impact of participation in SA associations would be similar.

6. Participants in collective action learn how to detect and deal with uncooperative behavior (Levi 1988), and when they do, trust among the participants and the incentive to cooperate grow.

7. See Thomassen (2006) on the discussion of how public discourse could produce tolerance and "inclusion of the other."

8. There are numerous examples of this phenomenon. Some include violent vigilante groups in the Niger Delta in Southern Nigeria (Gaventa and Barrett 2010; Lund 2006), church groups or local nongovernmental organizations that provide food aid based on political, religious, or ethnic affiliation in Angola and Guinea-Bissau (World Bank 2005); the Nuer and Dinka in South

Sudan (Slaymaker, Christiansen, and Hemming 2005); or elite groups who capture and divert local government resources (Oosterom 2009).

9. There are numerous examples of legacies of exclusion. Brinkerhoff and Mayfield (2005) describe the process of deliberate exclusion and isolation by the Ba'aath Party under Saadam Hussein and the challenges faced by local governance programs in undoing the damage caused by institutionalized exclusion. Colletta and Cullen (2000) give Cambodia and Rwanda as examples of countries facing daunting challenges in citizen participation and state accountability as they deal with complex legacies of exclusion that resulted in deadly violence (Colletta and Cullen 2000).

10. There is a debate among scholars on what types of conflicts are most favorable to political engagement.

11. Citizens who have had direct experience of violence during the recent civil war in Sierra Leone are more supportive of political mobilization and engagement and more inclined to contribute to the public good than others who were insulated from it. Families of the victims of the conflict are more likely to attend community meetings, join social and political groups, register to vote and join school committees, and even maintain roads. Controlling for chief status, prewar community leadership, or socioeconomic status, for example, does not change the results.

12. Other scholars have reported similar results. For example, Blattman (2009) notes that Ugandans abducted by the Lord's Liberation Army are more politically active.

References

Almond, G., and S. Verba, eds. 1963. *The Civic Culture: Political Attitudes and Democracy in Five Nations.* Princeton, NJ: Princeton University Press.

Andersen, L. 2008. "Fragile States on the International Agenda." In *Fragile Situations Background Report; Part I: Background Papers,* edited by L. Engberg-Pedersen, L. Andersen, F. Stepputat, and D. Jung, 7–20. Copenhagen: Danish Institute for International Studies.

Antweiler, C. 1998. "Local Knowledge and Local Knowing: An Anthropological Analysis of Contested Cultural Products in the Context of Development." *Anthropos* 93: 469–94.

Aslam, G. 2014. "Somaliland: Exploring How Social Accountability Contributes to State-Society Relationship." Draft mss., World Bank, Washington, DC.

Beath, A., C. Fotini, R. Enikolopov, and S. A. Kabuli. 2010. "Randomized Impact Evaluation of Phase II of Afghanistan's National Solidarity Programme (NSP): Estimates of Interim Program Impact from First Follow-up Survey." National Solidarity Programme, Afghanistan.

Bennett, J. W. 1975. "Communes and Communitarianism." *Theory and Society* 2 (1): 63–94.

Blattman, C. 2009. "From Violence to Voting: War and Political Participation in Uganda." *American Political Science Review* 103 (2): 231–47.

Boeckmann, S. 2012. "Social Accountability in Fragile States: A Review of the Literature." Unpublished mss., World Bank, Social Accountability and Demand for Good Governance Group, Washington, DC.

Brady, H. E. 1999. "Political Participation." In *Measures of Political Attitudes*, edited by J. P. Robinson, P. R. Shaver, and L. S. Wrightsman, 737–801. San Diego, CA: Academic Press.

Brinkerhoff, D. W., and J. Mayfield. 2005. "Democratic Governance in Iraq? Progress and Peril in Reforming State-Society Relations." *Public Administration and Development* 25 (1) 59–73.

Brinkerhoff, D. W., A. Wetterberg, and S. Dunn. 2012. "Service Delivery and Legitimacy in Fragile and Conflict-Affected States: Evidence from Water Services in Iraq." *Public Management Review* 14 (2): 273–93.

Cima, O. 2013. "Accountability at the Local Level in Fragile Contexts: Nepal Case Study." University of Sussex, Institute of Development Studies, Brighton, U.K.

Coleman, J. S. 1990. "Commentary: Social Institutions and Social Theory." *American Sociological Review* 55 (June): 333–39.

Coleman, E. A., and M.-C. López. 2010. "Reconstructing Cooperation from Civil Conflict: Experimental Evidence from Colombian Development Policy." Unpublished mss., Florida State University, Department of Political Science; Universidad Javeriana, School of Environmental and Rural Studies.

Colletta, N. J., and M. L. Cullen. 2000. *The Nexus between Violent Conflict, Social Capital, and Social Cohesion: Case Studies from Cambodia and Rwanda.* Washington, DC: World Bank.

Collier, P. 2000. *Economic Causes of Civil Conflict and Their Implications for Policy.* Washington, DC: World Bank.

Cornwall, A., S. Cordeiro, and N. G. Delgado. 2006. "Rights to Health and Struggles for Accountability in a Brazilian Municipal Health Council." In *Rights, Resources, and the Politics of Accountability*, edited by P. Newell and J. Wheeler. London: Zed Books.

Crook, R., and D. Booth. 2011. "Working with the Grain? Rethinking African Governance." *IDS Bulletin* 42 (2): 97–101. http://www.ids.ac.uk/go /idspublication/working-with-the-grain-rethinking-african-governance.

Dom, C., and A. Gordon. 2011. *Budget Support in Fragile Situations.* Oxfam Discussion Paper. Oxford: Oxford University.

Elgin-Cossart, M., B. Jones, and J. Esberg, eds. 2012. *Pathways to Change: Baseline Study to Identify Theories of Change on Political Settlements and Confidence Building.* New York: New York University, Center on International Cooperation.

Eubank, N. 2010. "Peace-Building without External Assistance: Lessons from Somaliland." Working Paper 198, Center for Global Development, Washington, DC.

Faehndrich, M., and I. Nhantumbo. 2012. "Advancing Accountability through Conselhos Consultivos in Mozambique: PROGOAS Case Study." IDS Working Paper 2013.420, University of Sussex, Institute of Development Studies, Brighton, U.K.

Fearon, J., M. Humphreys, and J. Weinstein. 2011. "Democratic Institutions and Collective Action Capacity: Results from a Field Experiment in Post-Conflict Liberia." Prepared for the Annual Meetings of the American Political Science Association, Seattle, September.

Fowler, A. 2002. "Civil Society Research Funding from a Global Perspective: A Case for Redressing Bias, Asymmetry, and Bifurcation." *Voluntas: International Journal of Voluntary and Nonprofit Organizations* 13 (3): 287–300.

Gaventa, J., and G. Barrett. 2010. "So What Difference Does It Make? Mapping the Outcomes of Citizen Engagement." IDS Working Paper 347, University of Sussex, Institute of Development Studies, Brighton, U.K. http://www.gsdrc.org /go/display&type=Document&id=3981&source=rss.

Gaynor, N. 2011. "Opportunities for Citizen Participation in Local Governance in Burundi." Research Report, Dublin City University, Dublin.

———. 2013. "The Tyranny of Participation Revisited: International Support to Local Governance in Burundi." *Community Development Journal* 49 (2): 295–310.

Ghani, E., ed. 2011. *The Poor Half Billion in South Asia: Who Is Holding Back Lagging Regions?* Oxford: Oxford University Press.

Greenberg, J., and R. Folger. 1983. *Procedural Justice, Participation, and the Fair Process Effect in Groups and Organizations.* New York: Springer.

Hagmann, T. 2007. "Bringing the Sultan Back in: Elders as Peacemakers in Ethiopia's Somali Region." In *State Recognition and the Democratization of Sub-Saharan Africa: A New Dawn for Traditional Authorities?* edited by L. Burr and H. M. Kyed, 31–51. New York: Macmillan.

Hickey, S. 2002. "Transnational NGDOS and Participatory Forms of Rights-Based Development: Converging with the Local Politics of Citizenship in Cameroon." *Journal of International Development* 14 (6): 841–57.

Hickey, S., and G. Mohan, eds. 2005. *Participation: From Tyranny to Transformation? Exploring New Approaches to Participation in Development.* London: Zed Books.

Hilhorst, D., I. Christoplos, and G. Van Der Harr. 2010. "Reconstruction 'From Below': A New Magic Bullet or Shooting from the Hip?" *Third World Quarterly* 31 (7): 1107–24.

Hooghe, M. 2003. "Participation in Voluntary Associations and Value Indicators: The Effect of Current and Previous Participation Experiences." *Nonprofit and Voluntary Sector Quarterly* 32 (1): 47–69.

IFP (Initiative for Peacebuilding). 2012. "Conflict Prevention." Seminar Report for the Media and SEE: Progress or Regression seminar, Halki, Greece, June 7–10.

Jennings, M. K., and R. G. Niemi. 1981. *Generations and Politics: A Panel Study of Young Adults and Their Parents*. Princeton, NJ: Princeton University Press.

Joshi, A., and P. Houtzager. 2012. "Widgets or Watchdogs? Conceptual Explorations in Social Accountability." *Public Management Review, Special Issue: The Politics and Governance of Public Services in Developing Countries* 14 (2): 145–62.

Kaplan, S. 2014. "Identifying Truly Fragile States." *Washington Quarterly* 37 (1): 49–63.

Kaufman, J. P., and K. P. Williams. 2010. *Women and War: Gender Identity and Activism in Times of Conflict*. Boulder, CO: Kumarian Press.

Khan, N. A. 2013. "Socioeconomic and Political Status of Women in FATA: The Process of Development and Phenomenon of Militancy." *TIGAH: A Journal of Peace and Development* II (December): 1–21.

King, E., C. Samii, and B. Snilstveit. 2010. "Interventions to Promote Social Cohesion in Sub-Saharan Africa." *Journal of Development Effectiveness* 2 (3): 336–70.

Knopf, K. 2013. *Fragility and State-Society Relations in South Sudan*. Research Paper 4. Washington, DC: Africa Center for Strategic Studies.

Leonard, W. 2004. "The Paradox of 'Warlord' Democracy: A Theoretical Investigation." *American Political Science Review* 98 (1): 17–33.

Levi, M. 1988. "Book Review: Individual Interests and Collective Action: Selected Essays. James S. Coleman, Jon Elster, Gudmund Hernes." *Ethics* 99 (1): 177–80.

Lind, E. A., and T. R. Tyler. 1988. *The Social Psychology of Procedural Justice*. New York: Springer.

Lund, C. 2006. "Twilight Institutions: Public Authority and Local Politics in Africa." *Development and Change* 37 (4): 685–705.

Lust-Ckar, E. 2005. *Structuring Conflict in the Arab World*. Cambridge, U.K.: Cambridge University Press.

McGee, R., and C. Kroesschell. 2013. "Local Accountabilities in Fragile Contexts: Experiences from Nepal, Bangladesh, and Mozambique." IDS Working Paper 422, University of Sussex, Institute of Development Studies, Brighton, U.K.

Mumtaz, H. 2010. "Regaining Cultural Space." *The Dawn*, March 21. http://www.dawn.com/wps/wcm/connect/dawn-content-library/dawn/the-newspaper/local/regaining-cultural-space-130.

Mustafa, D., and K. E. Brown. 2010. "The Taliban, Public Space, and Terror in Pakistan." *Eurasian Geography and Economics* 51 (4): 496–512.

OECD (Organisation for Economic Co-operation and Development). 2013. *Fragile States: Resource Flows and Trends.* Paris: OECD Publishing.

Oosterom, M. 2009. "Fragility at the Local Level: Challenges to Building Local State-Citizen Relations in Fragile Seetings." Working Paper, Civic Engagement in Post-Conflict Settings Project. Paper prepared for the Local Governance in Fragile Settings workshop, Hivos, Interchurch Organization for Development Cooperation (ICCO), and Institute of Development Studies, The Hague, Netherlands, November.

Ostrom, E., R. Gardner, and J. Walker. 1994. *Rules, Games, and Common-Pool Resources.* Ann Arbor, MI: University of Michigan Press.

Ovesen, J., I. Trankell, and J. Ojendal. 1996. "When Every Household Is an Island: Social Organisation and Power Structures in Rural Cambodia." Uppsala Research Reports in Cultural Anthropology 15, Uppsala University, Department of Cultural Anthropology, Uppsala, Sweden.

Paxton, P. 2007. "Association Memberships and Generalized Trust: A Multilevel Model across 31 Countries." *Social Forces* 86 (1): 47–76.

Pearce, J. 2007. "Violence, Power, Participation: Building Citizenship in Contexts of Chronic Violence." IDS Working Paper 274, University of Sussex, Institute of Development Studies. Brighton, U.K.

Putnam, R. 1993. *Making Democracy Work: Civic Traditions in Modern Italy.* Princeton, NJ: Princeton University Press.

———. 1995. "Bowling Alone: America's Declining Social Capital." *Journal of Democracy* 6 (1): 65–78.

———. 2000. *Bowling Alone: The Collapse and Revival of American Community.* New York: Simon and Schuster.

Reeve, R. 2011. "Sustaining the Conversation: Media, Information Flows, and Conflict in Liberia." Initiative for Peacebuilding, London.

Saferworld. 2008. "Water and Conflict: Making Water Delivery Conflict-Sensitive in Uganda." Saferworld, London, August.

Sawyers, A. 2004. "Social Capital, Survival Strategies, and Their Implications for Post Conflict Governance in Liberia." Presented at a workshop on Political Theory and Policy Analysis, Indiana University, Bloomington, July 2–6.

Slaymaker, T., K. Christiansen, and I. Hemming. 2005. "Community-Based Approaches and Service Delivery: Issues and Options in Difficult Environments and Partnerships." Unpublished report, Overseas Development Institute, London.

Stewart, F., and V. Fitzgerald. 2000. *The Economic and Social Consequences of Conflict.* Vol. 1. Oxford: Oxford University Press.

Tedeschi, R. G., and L. G. Calhoun. 2004. "Posttraumatic Growth: Conceptual Foundations and Empirical Evidence." *Psychological Inquiry* 15 (1): 1–18.

Thomassen, L. 2006. "The Inclusion of the Other? Habermas and the Paradox of Tolerance." *Political Theory* 34 (4): 439–62.

Tyler, T. R., and R. J. Bies. 1990. "Beyond Formal Procedures: The Interpersonal Context of Procedural Justice." In *Applied Social Psychology and Organizational Settings*, edited by J. S. Carroll, 77–98. Hillsdale, NJ: Erlbaum.

Tyler, T., R. Boeckmann, H. Smith, and Y. Huo. 1997. *Social Justice in a Diverse Society*. Boulder, CO: Westview Press.

U4. 2011. "Social Accountability in Situations of Conflict and Fragility." U4 Brief 19, U4 Anti-Corruption Research Centre, Bergen, Norway.

UNDP (United Nations Development Programme). 2009. *Users Guide on Measuring Fragility*. Oslo: German Development Institute and UNDP, Bureau for Development Policy, Democratic Governance Group.

Van Deth, J. W., J. R. Montero, and A. Westholm, eds. 2007. *Citizenship and Involvement in European Democracies: A Comparative Analysis*. Routledge Research in Comparative Politics. London: Taylor and Francis.

van Wicklin, W. 2014. "Interviews of World Bank Staff Working in FCSs." Background paper for this report, World Bank, Washington, DC.

Von Kaltenborn-Stachau, H. 2008. *The Missing Link: Fostering Positive Citizen-State Relationships in Post-Conflict Environments*. Washington, DC: World Bank, Communication for Governance and Accountability Program (CommGAP), Development Communication Division, External Affairs.

Warren, M. E. 2001. *Democracy and Association*. Princeton, NJ: Princeton University Press.

World Bank. 2005. "Engaging Civil Society Organisations in Conflict-Affected and Fragile States: Three African Country Case Studies." Report 32538-GLB, World Bank, Social Development Department, Washington, DC.

———. 2011. *World Development Report 2011: Conflict, Security, and Development*. New York: Oxford University Press.

———. 2012. *Societal Dynamics and Fragility: Engaging Societies in Responding to Fragile Situations*. Washington, DC: World Bank.

Young, A. 2003. "Ferghana Valley Field Study: Reducing the Potential for Conflict through Community Mobilization." Mercy Corps Central Asia, Portland, OR.

CHAPTER 7

Using the Analytical Framework to Address Specific Issues: Four Examples

To use the framework prospectively to address a particular issue, the following steps are suggested:

1. Identify an issue or problem, which can be traced back or linked to an accountability issue.
2. Map the institutional terrain and assess the opportunities and constraints linked to the heterogeneity of the state and citizens.
3. Assess opportunities and constraints for citizen action and state action.
4. Assess opportunities and constraints for the three levers (information, interface, and civic mobilization) in relation to citizen and state action.
5. Develop a reasonable theory of change for the specific issue.
6. Support iterative diagnosis and monitoring and evaluation of the SA approach chosen.

Relying on four case studies, this chapter follows these steps and shows how the framework described in chapter 4 can be used to assess the context for a specific social accountability (SA) intervention.[1] In one instance, the framework is used retrospectively to map an intervention already completed, which was later the subject of an impact evaluation. The intervention took the form of community participation in local health compacts in Sierra Leone. The other three cases illustrate prospective uses of the framework to assess bottlenecks and opportunities for SA interventions in three countries[2] with the goal of (a) designing and implementing SA mechanisms to support the vision of the new government of the province of Khyber Pakhtunkhwa in Pakistan through an ongoing World Bank–financed governance support project, (b) exploring challenges and opportunities for

SA in the context of local governance reforms in the Republic of Yemen, and (c) introducing and strengthening SA mechanisms for a new phase of a community-driven development project in the Kyrgyz Republic.

The case studies were chosen with two main criteria in mind. First, all four studies occurred in challenging contexts, mostly fragile and conflict-affected situations (FCSs)—that is, contexts less chartered and most interesting for their potential to support broad institutional outcomes through SA approaches. Second, an engagement was either planned or under way in connection with a World Bank–funded operation that could be a staging ground for the case study and would benefit from it. This particular set of case studies is thus not representative of either the range of country contexts for SA or the range of activities that can be supported to foster stronger SA.

Supporting the Free Health Care Initiative in Sierra Leone

This case study begins by describing the country context, the intervention, and the institutional landscape. It then assesses the intervention with regard to the five constitutive elements that make up social accountability interventions.

Country Context

Sierra Leone, a small country with just under 6 million residents, emerged from a devastating civil war in 2002 (Zhou 2009). The country is still considered an FCS, struggling to consolidate peace and improve human development in the wake of the war (World Bank 2013). While Sierra Leone has enjoyed relative peace and stability for the past 12 years and experienced strong economic growth more recently, more than half of the population lives below the poverty line.[3]

Sierra Leone ranks close to the bottom of the United Nations human development index and has some of the worst global health indicators in the world. According to the United Nations International Children's Fund, in 2012, Sierra Leone had the highest mortality rate in the world for children under five years of age, and in May 2014, the World Health Organization reported that Sierra Leone had the world's highest maternal mortality rate. Health service delivery challenges include a set of weak incentives for service providers, with many health care workers not on any payroll and, instead, dependent on contributions from patients and the community for compensation.

In response to formidable challenges, the government of Sierra Leone launched a free health care initiative (FHCI) in 2010, guaranteeing free health services to pregnant and nursing women and to children under five years of age. The government also introduced a range of measures to enable facilities to provide these free services, including higher salaries for health care workers, large-scale drug procurement, and performance-based incentives for staff.

Health reforms are being introduced in the context of the implementation of a decentralization program that began in 2004. The delivery of health services is currently being devolved to a variety of actors at the district and clinic levels. The aims of decentralization include improving service delivery and strengthening relations between citizens and their government.

Despite progress, significant challenges remain. Government clinics have seen a significant increase in the use of maternal and child health services. Civil society organizations (CSOs) have pointed to persistent problems, including the leakage of drugs, the charging of improper fees for health services, and absenteeism among health workers, in part the result of inadequate supervision or monitoring.

Social accountability appealed to the government for both its potential intrinsic and instrumental value. In light of the gaps identified in health service delivery and the intended goals of decentralization, the government identified social accountability as a potentially powerful tool for empowering citizens as monitors and arbiters of improved health services and, in this way, for helping to forge stronger relationships between citizens and the state. The view was that strengthening state institutions by merely providing more services on the supply side was only one way to address challenges in service delivery. Effective health service delivery also called for greater accountability, and patients, who were only too familiar with the shortcomings, could be reliable actors in supporting it.

With technical support from the World Bank Justice for the Poor Program (J4P), the government decided to invest in a pilot program that would engage citizens as participants in health care delivery. Building on an encouraging research study just conducted in Uganda, which showed that community participation in local compacts led to a significant drop in under-five mortality rates (described in box 2.5 in chapter 2), Sierra Leone's government decided to adapt this approach to the country's particular context. A mixed-methods research evaluation strategy was used to assess the intervention, including a random control trial and qualitative research in a subset of locations.

The Intervention

This account offers a general description of the intervention in its final form. In keeping with the principles of "problem-driven iterative adaptation," however, the design evolved considerably over the course of piloting and implementation. Unlike many traditional development projects that are subject to midterm and final reviews and use data collected by external evaluators, this project entailed continuing critical self-reflection, evaluation, and adaptation (for further details on this iterative process, see Hall, Menzies, and Woolcock 2014). In concrete terms, the project began with a design focused on community clinic compacts, which relied on local solutions to provide nonfinancial awards, and then evolved to test the efficacy of paralegals in responding to capacity and sustainability concerns.

The intervention used CSOs to mobilize citizens[4] and state agents (health workers) to create an interface (a series of meetings) animated by information (scorecards, health education, rights, and compacts), thus supporting the three levers of the analytical framework to trigger action. The scorecard compared the maternal and child mortality figures reported by the clinic (and reflected in official government records) with similar information reported by community members. The fact that the figures provided by the community were much higher than the official figures prompted a discussion during the initial community meeting as to why citizens were not using the clinic. CSO facilitators also shared information on both healthy behaviors (for example, increased early referrals to the clinic and decreased defecation in the open) and on citizens' service entitlements and staff obligations (for example, the FHCI). During the meeting, facilitators encouraged community members to consider actions that they could take to address health issues. Health clinic staff attended a separate meeting and conducted the same exercise. Community members and clinic staff then attended an interface meeting where they discussed health challenges and made mutual commitments to one another (recorded in public in a written compact) to improve health care delivery and address the problems identified.[5]

Following the initial meeting, community representatives and nurses at each clinic met with facilitators quarterly to evaluate and score each other's compliance with the compact and to set new commitments. The focus on mutual accountability in the compact—with both citizens and health staff committing to act—intentionally framed the intervention as addressing a collective action problem rather than one where the principals (citizens) sought to exact better performance from their agents (clinic staff).

This framing responded to features of the local context: the power of clinic staff meant that citizens did not see themselves as "principals," citizens were unwilling to act unilaterally for fear of retaliation by staff (denial of service), and the real constraints facing health staff limited their ability to improve service without assistance. The quarterly meetings allowed for an iterative approach to identifying and solving local health service problems, with opportunities to correct course.

The intervention ran for nine months, and results showed improvements in institutional deliveries (approximately a 10 percent increase), a reduction in improper fee charges (approximately a 27 percent reduction), as well as an improvement in some measures of malnutrition. Other improvements reported by communities and nurses included better hygienic conditions in villages, construction of small infrastructure at the clinic (such as latrines and waiting rooms), and improved community-nurse relations.

As the design of the intervention evolved, the team recognized some limitations in it. In particular, nurses and community members were often unable to resolve issues that involved greater power imbalances or accountability gaps "up the chain of command" within government. For example, when nurses were erroneously dropped from the payroll (and responded by charging improper fees), nurses and communities could often do little to address this larger institutional breakdown.

To resolve these issues, the government and J4P piloted work engaging community-based paralegals in addressing local grievances regarding health service delivery. The hypothesis was that paralegals could represent the interests of nurses and community members in tackling more challenging issues involving vertical accountability. Paralegals were present in 40 percent of Sierra Leone's chiefdoms, representing an established group of mobilizers and representatives with the knowledge to navigate the authority of the government and of chiefs. The structure of paralegals in Sierra Leone, with more experienced supervising paralegals above community-based workers and then a small group of lawyers above community workers, provides both quality control and "teeth" in dealing with more intractable problems and graver power imbalances. For example, in some clinics where nurses lacked basic medical equipment such as a refrigerator for storing vaccines and beds for admissions, paralegals proved effective in pressuring Ministry of Health and Sanitation officials at the district level to provide them. In the Port Loko District in the north of Sierra Leone, one clinic had been awaiting delivery of a bed for more than a year because the district health management team had no incentive to transport it from the district medical stores. The paralegals ultimately intervened in the case and persuaded the team to deliver the bed. Nonetheless, the work of the paralegals had limitations, and their degree of success depended on their level of training, their experience, and the nature of the cases in which they intervened. They had limited success in cases involving the systemic bureaucratic red tape that transcends the district level.

Mapping the Institutional Landscape Influencing the Intervention

While there are various theories about the causes of Sierra Leone's violent conflict, it is generally agreed that key contributors included accountability failures and citizens' perception that government was not delivering essential services or responding to their needs (Zhou 2009). Social relations were fractured during the war, as alliances among armed groups continually shifted during the course of the conflict. An important part of the postconflict agenda, therefore, has been promoting social cohesion and strengthening structured citizen engagement with the state around development needs and related grievances.

Like many countries, particularly FCSs, Sierra Leone is politically and socially heterogeneous. It also has some particularities, three of them the focus of this study: incomplete decentralization, low state capacity, and the role of chiefs.

Even after 10 years of decentralization reforms, devolution remains incomplete. Tensions remain between central government ministry actors, local government actors, and chiefs, who have state-related functions (including some powers of local taxation). Incomplete devolution affects the health sector significantly, particularly where the accountability chains are becoming more complex because of this incomplete devolution process. Responsibility for hiring health workers and procuring drugs, for example, continues to rest—in practice—with the central Ministry of Health and Sanitation, even though by law these responsibilities are supposed to be devolved to district governments. In practice, supervisory responsibilities lie with district governments, which lack the power to reward or sanction staff meaningfully.

In this landscape, nongovernmental organizations (NGOs) play a powerful role, often compensating for the government's low capacity to provide services. Many nurses operate clinics even though they are not on the government payroll. Others operate clinics lacking basic drugs or supplies to treat patients, and they must resort to their own "drug sourcing and distribution channels" to meet needs. The work of NGOs has been inadequately coordinated, undermining state legitimacy and capability when NGOs construct and supply their own clinics, distribute health products, and conduct their own health educational programs. In these ways, NGOs have become significant power brokers at the local level, and, where they have been enlisted to "monitor" government health care providers, relationships have often been adversarial (Amnesty International 2001).

Chiefs and mammy queens[6] hold authority in many communities, with responsibility for matters relating to security, dispute resolution, land use, and taxation. Community members in most rural areas are typically neither engaged nor well connected with government actors. Citizen-state relations reflect a legacy of mistrust from the years of civil war. Even where citizens are aware of the activities (or misdeeds) of local service providers, lack of trust or fear of retaliation may prevent them from challenging that behavior. Instead, chiefs and other local actors have greater influence over service delivery and associated policies. For instance, a 2011 public services perception survey found that chiefs received the most complaints relating to services (47 percent), with only 6 percent of complaints going to district medical officers and 7 percent going to local councilors, the two local actors directly responsible for the delivery and quality of health care services (IRCBP Evaluations Unit 2012).

The following sections assess the drivers of the elements that comprise SA and analyze their implication for the intervention's design.

Assessing the Drivers of State and Citizen Action

There are many potential challenges to state and citizen action with regard to the failings in Sierra Leone's health care system. Many of these failings are the result of the country's history of violence and inadequate government capacity to provide high-quality essential services.

State Action

At the macro level, the state's willingness to promote social accountability in health delivery is largely dependent on external actors and, at times, on political motives. Politics play a powerful role in the health sector, with the FHCI and other government-inspired initiatives often driven by electoral campaign platforms targeting voters with simplistic messages, but without developed policies to support them. Donors and NGOs also play powerful roles. Donors influence government policy based on their own institutional priorities and on "evidence" of what works in other countries (community compacts, performance-based financing, health insurance). For their part,

NGOs, including Amnesty International, have played a critical role in "naming and shaming" the Ministry of Health and Sanitation, forcing it to be more accountable.

The agencies responsible for delivering health services are keenly aware of the ministry's failings. The Ministry of Health and Sanitation and the Ministry of Local Government's Decentralization Secretariat are the key central government entities with responsibility for setting policies and implementing programs for health. Launched in March 2010 with donor assistance, the FHCI was a response to the financial barriers to maternal and under-five health care and the disturbingly high mortality rates for these groups. In the years since implementation of the FHCI, NGOs and donors have helped to elucidate the challenges encountered, including accountability gaps that have led to inappropriate fees being charged and unsanctioned nurse absenteeism. The government has responded to this pressure from civil society, but at times its response has been perceived to be politically motivated. For example, many citizens characterized the government's establishment of community-level accountability committees to monitor health service delivery as a campaign tactic. The committee members received generous training stipends and cellular telephones to report misconduct—what some members of civil society perceived as "election-time gifts" for powerful constituents and a largely symbolic gesture toward promoting accountability.

The central government actors have not always been fully aware of more nuanced sources of problems, however. With insufficient funding or staff capacity to monitor local service delivery closely, the government has at times been unaware of the policy gaps confronting health care users. For example, there is uncertainty about whether fuel for ambulances or patient registration cards should be provided free of charge under the FHCI. This uncertainty is particularly evident when the government has run out of these supplies and nurses or citizens must purchase replacements.

Further, central government actors lack the background knowledge of what remedies would be most appropriate for communities. For example, on learning that improper fees were being charged under the FHCI, the central government instituted two programs to promote accountability. One was an NGO-led "monitoring program" entailing spot checks of clinics in which citizens were asked to report the fees they had been charged. The other organized local committees and asked citizens to report to committee representatives the fees they were charged, and the representatives relayed the information using a call center in the capital. In both instances, community members were reluctant to file complaints, even when they paid for services that they knew should be free of charge. Nurses also felt alienated by these measures. The adversarial nature of these attempted remedies did not conform to local-level realities, including fears of retaliation after holding a nurse to account as well as sympathy for nurses who confronted genuine constraints (Hall 2012).

Local state actors—and nurses in particular—have a much keener sense of local realities and problems, as well as what remedies would be most appropriate. These agents often face obstacles in meeting the challenges contributing to poor health outcomes, however. For example, nurses often could not meaningfully respond to the problems of poor attendance at the clinic or had inadequate knowledge about preventive health measures in villages. These nurses needed community-level action to facilitate their efforts. Many of them could make only limited improvements on their own, without the intervention of more senior state authorities. If a nurse was not on payroll or was assigned to a clinic in disrepair or if there was confusion about the policies relating to FHCI, only a senior government official could remedy these problems, and health workers needed an advocate to represent them.

Nurses also often had little incentive to act or to improve their behavior. With limited monitoring, the costs of failing to comply with government policy were low, and the potential for rent capture was high. Given their control over drugs, treatment, and other key health resources, nurses are significant power brokers in their communities. From this position of power, they are capable of co-opting even the accountability committees that are supposed to oversee their work. Some clinic staff adopt a "divide and serve" approach, providing attentive care to the more influential members of the community (who may have some authority to question nonperformance or to offer resources in return for services) and providing too little care to less powerful members of the catchment.

The intervention responded to the lack of national and local government capacity by first focusing on changes that were potentially attainable at the local level. This intervention consisted of compacts specifying mutual commitments by frontline service providers and citizens. The commitments and assessments were made in open community meetings in order to "bind" state actors through the sanction of public shaming should they fail to comply. The use of paralegals responded to the concern that nurses and community members would "hit a ceiling" with regard to local improvements. Paralegals were identified as potentially powerful agents who could prompt state action, from both frontline service staff and state representatives farther up the delivery chain. In this way, paralegals were seen as useful by both community members and clinic staff, potentially preserving fragile bonds of trust.

Table 7.1 summarizes the key bottlenecks and opportunities that were identified as well as strategies for addressing them in the program's design.

Table 7.1 Key Bottlenecks or Opportunities for State Action and Strategies for Addressing Them: Implications for the Intervention Design in Sierra Leone

Bottleneck or opportunity	Strategy
• *Lack of knowledge of the local context.* Central government is aware of basic problems but lacks deep knowledge of the local context and scope.	• Share local-level knowledge through feedback loops (nongovernmental organization and other reporting) to allow for iterative development of responsive policy
• *Unclear policy.* Policy from the Ministry of Health and Sanitation is unclear.	• Provide feedback "up the chain" to central government actors, so that they can clarify identified policy gaps and provide reasonable responses
• *Lack of accountability.* Central government is willing to hold local service providers (nurses) accountable for charging improper fees and absenteeism—for example, to the extent that it can mobilize donor resources and attract favorable publicity—but it lacks both the capacity to monitor rigorously and a deep understanding of underlying problems.	• Take advantage of the window of opportunity provided by the Ministry of Health and Sanitation's willingness to work on accountability gaps to engage in a social accountability intervention • Conduct enforcement and monitoring at the local level because central government has low incentives and capacity to engage in these activities
• *Willingness of district and local actors to engage.* District and local actors are less willing to engage in accountability dialogue, creating room for opportunism on the part of nurses and room for complicity by district-level authorities.	• Include district-level actors more meaningfully in the intervention
• *Lack of incentives.* Local service providers have greater awareness of problems but lack incentives to deal with those they are responsible for and the ability to influence citizen behavior and vertical accountability structures.	• Focus on local-level problems that actors can solve with their own resources • Emphasize mutual accountability with citizens, whereby citizens assist nurses and take more responsibility for their health • Conduct a pilot intervention to engage agents to represent nurse or community grievances that are more complex or involve more senior government actors
• *Low cost of noncompliance.* Local service providers perceive a low cost for noncompliance with government policy.	• Emphasize public commitments to bind their actions through soft law, norms, and public shaming

Citizen Action

Early field research and a national citizen perception survey conducted before the start of the program demonstrated that the majority of citizens were aware of the broad categories of recipients eligible for free health care, yet "gray zones" remained (see IRCBP 2012). In particular, the specific entitlements provided under the FHCI were often unclear, and the gray space led to opportunism on the part of clinic staff. As one step, the intervention aimed to clarify government policy in order to help citizens to become more aware of their rights and facilitate open discussions between users and staff to outline more clearly the charging of improper fees.

Similarly, citizens were generally aware of health challenges in their communities, including the harsh realities of maternal and under-five mortality; however, they experienced mortality as a deeply personal event, without realizing the aggregate toll that maternal and under-five mortality took on the overall population. The community scorecards aggregated deaths in each catchment village around a clinic and compared these figures with clinic-reported mortality figures. This exercise demonstrated that the problem was more severe than nurses had realized, based on their experience in the clinics, and prompted a discussion about why citizens were not seeking professional care.

Despite a general awareness of health problems, citizens were either reluctant or unable to address them. On their own, they were reluctant to take any action to improve the general welfare of their communities, because they feared retaliation from nurses. Nurses are powerful actors in villages: they control access to key resources like drugs, possess the ability to skew their services and provide the "illusion" of good performance, and are capable of co-opting their own "monitors."

Further, citizens confronted constraints on collective action, fearing that others might not invest equally in improvements. For this reason, a mutual accountability approach was emphasized, with intermediation by outside facilitators to help to enforce commitments. Citizens readily embraced this approach, internalizing and localizing commitments by enacting bylaws, appointing inspectors, and introducing other (often punitive) measures to ensure compliance at the village level. Furthermore, the paralegal intervention considered whether paralegals (as lay persons trained in the basics of law) could help to increase citizens' efficacy in addressing concerns.

In the design, the team assumed the salience of the problem of high mortality and poor health. The assumption was that the scale of the health statistics would make health matters a serious concern and that people would naturally want to act together to make improvements. In hindsight, while health issues certainly affected the majority of households in Sierra Leone, other factors were at play as well. Citizens generally had a low sense of control over health outcomes, adopting a fatalistic outlook toward adverse events. There were higher-priority items for citizen organization (such as concerns related to land or farming), and there were substitutes for formal health services, in the form of "drug peddlers" and traditional healers. In some instances, choosing one of these substitutes may have been rational given the overall low quality of health service provision in government health clinics. In practice, the implementing NGOs had first to educate citizens on basic disease pathways, on how illness is linked to poverty, and how citizens could bring about meaningful change.

Certain citizens also saw major trade-offs in engaging in time-intensive day-long meetings, as well as the activities proposed in these meetings. Farming matters often took priority, and many participants expressed concerns about the opportunity costs associated with particanipating in the meetings. The initial perception—perhaps colored by the past decade of mostly unsuccessful donor interventions—was that their activities would not lead to much meaningful change. These concerns were allayed by providing small transportation reimbursements (what community members often called "sitting fees") to defray the costs. Over time, the thought was that citizens would value the meetings and their consequences more highly, making such reimbursements less needed to prompt involvement. The reimbursements entailed their own set of challenges, however, including the "capture" of rents by more powerful members of villages. Further, many villages chose to distribute the rents by alternating who would attend meetings, with significant implications for the continuity of discussions in meetings where the compacts were concluded.

Initially, involvement was superficial. In many instances, community members did not meet their commitments fully until after the second joint meeting. In the first two meetings, while nurses reported often dramatic improvements with regard to their attendance and fees charged, community members lagged behind, often receiving low scores for their efforts. See table 7.2 for a summary of the challenges or opportunities for citizen action and strategies for addressing them.

Table 7.2 Bottlenecks or Opportunities for Citizen Action and Strategies for Addressing Them: Implications for the Intervention Design in Sierra Leone

Bottleneck or opportunity	Strategy
• *Unclear policy.* Citizens were generally aware of free health care entitlements and health care challenges, but they were unclear about the details, and this lack of clarity created opportunism for nurses.	• Have facilitators educate citizens on the health policy and their entitlements
• *Limited capability.* Community members had limited capability to respond effectively to the challenges identified.	• Have facilitators suggest concrete solutions to local-level problems such as early referrals and construction of local pit latrines • Find local methods of addressing challenges to collective action (such as bylaws or inspectors backed up by chiefs), as they are an important lower layer for accountability
• *Fear of retaliation.* Citizens were afraid that clinic staff would retaliate if they complained.	• Emphasize mutual and collective accountability to bind individuals to behavior • Collectivize complaints to lower the risk of retaliation
• *Lack of understanding of community impact.* Health challenges were often understood based on individual experience, but not in the aggregate.	• Use scorecards to present aggregate information on health problems
• *Low priority given to health matters.* While health matters affected many community members, they were given lower priority than other matters: community members had no sense of control over health outcomes (fate), had higher priorities (land), and had exit options (seeking care from traditional healers or drug peddlers rather than from nurses).	• Educate on salience of the problem, availability of reasonable solutions, and the risks of using alternative healers
• *Low motivation to participate.* Intrinsic motivation was low owing to community development fatigue (too many projects to invest in) as well as the opportunity costs of farming and other livelihood activities.	• Emphasize and demonstrate over time the payoffs to involvement (for example, publicize the increased use of maternal and under-five health services) • Offer transportation stipend to offset costs

Assessing and Supporting Drivers of Information, Interface, and Mobilization

This section turns to the three drivers of state action and citizen action.

Information

The interventions targeted information to citizens, clinic staff (frontline state actors), and national-level officials. Key information took the form of scorecards illustrating comparative mortality statistics, compacts recording commitments, and fact sheets clarifying citizen rights under the FHCI and providing information about sound health behaviors. The experience illustrated the importance of not only the content and the processes of sharing information, but also the processes of producing it. Through the use of community scorecards that aggregated statistics on mortality, both community members and nurses came to understand the true scope of the problem. Discussing the scorecards in a public forum created a shared sense of the problem. The local sourcing of these data from community members and clinic staff made the information more credible to recipients, who often distrust government data. Because they were produced and ratified locally and publicly, the compacts facilitated the clarity—and enforceability—of health policy. The process of producing the fact sheets emphasized to Ministry of Health and Sanitation staff the risk of confusion and the scope for opportunism, as it became apparent that a range of matters needed to be clarified, such as opening hours and variations in services between different health clinics. The information that NGO facilitators shared about health behaviors came from international sources that were considered reliable.

The use of external facilitators helped to promote trust in the information, because both nurses and community members considered facilitators to be "neutral" actors, who were unbiased and trustworthy in presenting information. The facilitators generally communicated in the local language, giving them the ability to connect with stakeholders while maintaining their neutrality. This appears to have given greater credibility to the interface meetings.

Citizen-State Interface

Meaningful engagement between citizens and state actors at all levels (local, district, and national) was poor at the start of the intervention. Citizens typically had the closest relations (both productive and fraught) with nurses, who were embedded in the community, and more attenuated interactions with government actors at higher levels (see IRCBP 2012).

Earlier attempts to improve relations, which relied to a large extent on "peer monitoring" of health workers by either citizens or NGOs, resulted in tensions. Such monitoring exacerbated adversarial relations with nurses.

Instead, framing the compact in terms of mutual accountability aimed not to point a finger at "bad actors," but rather to bind the community and clinic staff together in a joint effort to support local development.

The intervention endeavored to build constructive relations between community members and nurses and to increase their understanding of—and sympathy for—the challenges confronting the other party. Facilitators reinforced this message in all of the joint meetings, allaying tensions when they arose in the discussions.

No platform existed for the type of constructive citizen-state engagement envisioned. In general, neither nurses (who are often already overburdened) nor community members had the capacity or expertise to create such an interface. This limitation extended to community-level accountability committees tasked with monitoring health service delivery. External support was therefore necessary to create a platform for engagement, and NGOs played this critical role. NGOs visited each catchment village, invited representatives, facilitated meetings, recorded the commitments in compacts, and disseminated copies of the compacts to relevant local actors. The transportation stipends that the NGOs provided made the interface more accessible.

The quality of engagement differed considerably from clinic to clinic, depending on the skills of the NGO facilitators and local-level power dynamics. In general, the compact interface excluded chiefs and district officials, an omission that may have limited its usefulness. Greater inclusion might have improved the overall results of the intervention but would have run the risk of inviting local elite capture. Despite attempts by external facilitators to steer the discussion delicately, in some instances the meetings were captured by elites whose interests were not aligned with those of the broader community.

The involvement of NGOs as the "hosts" of the platform for engagement raised questions about sustainability, because they were funded specifically to play this role. The subsequent use of paralegals was, in part, a response to this concern about sustainability, as paralegals were widely represented in Sierra Leone and already engaged in responding to community grievances.

Civic Mobilization

Mobilization around the compact was exogenous to the parties involved. The intervention did not rely on any preexisting group of individuals within the community to create the interface. NGOs mobilized citizens and nurses to participate and may have played a role in enforcing participation and compliance. At the start of the intervention, local mobilizers were largely nonexistent. Many clinics had been underperforming or had even been shuttered for months without any corrective action at the local level. In certain instances, chiefs or other local elites had tried unsuccessfully to lobby district health authorities for change. Nonetheless, across the board, most communities were unable to mobilize on their own, just as state officials were unable to work together. This gap may be one of the legacies of war and broken social networks.

Several community members reported a widespread reluctance to complain in order to try to effect change. Perhaps, having experienced poor service delivery for so long, citizens were not inclined to identify or use existing grievance channels. A recent national public services perception survey suggested that these dynamics are improving slightly, with citizens now more willing to complain about service delivery but still largely unaware of how best to do so (see IRCBP 2012).

Notably, the survey results differed widely from one community to the next and across the country's various regions and cultural divides. One community that recorded significant gains in the compact process benefited from its history of social cohesion, the result of a collective development project undertaken years before the start of the civil war. Older men recalled a wealthy tailor who, more than 20 years before, had encouraged men to work together to improve the community's access to markets and distribution channels. Under his leadership, young men from neighboring villages had come together for the first time to construct a road. The men developed ties during the course of the year-long project and began hosting social activities across the villages. Inter-village marriages resulted, and a deep level of social cohesion developed that survived the war. This community, which performed comparatively well in the intervention, reported that the intervention had rekindled their resolve to work together on a development project. In the wake of the intervention, a new mobilizer class appears to have emerged in the community, and meetings have continued even after the intervention ended. Table 7.3 summarizes the bottlenecks and opportunities for the levers of information, interface, and civic mobilization and strategies for addressing them.

Conclusion and Next Steps

While the use of social accountability mechanisms showed some gains in improving health service delivery, the experience calls for reflection.

Table 7.3 Bottlenecks or Opportunities for Information, Interface, and Civic Mobilization and Strategies for Addressing Them: Implications for the Intervention Design in Sierra Leone

Bottleneck or opportunity	Strategy
Information gaps. There was ample room for discretion for local government actors (nurses) to fill in gaps in policy information with interpretations favorable to them.	• Encourage nurses and citizens to discuss policy gaps publicly and to agree mutually on solutions
Lack of awareness of community impact. Citizens were largely unaware of aggregate health experiences.	• Use scorecards to present collective experience of the community (they are credible and consist of locally sourced information) and to create a shared understanding of the gravity of the problem
Lack of trust. There was a lack of trust at the local level among citizens and between citizens and nurses.	• Use external actors who have credibility to broker difficult conversations and compromises
Adversarial citizen-state engagement. Past attempts at citizen-state engagement were too adversarial and alienated both nurses and citizens; citizens had real fears of retaliation in complaining about nurses; citizens lacked a "culture of complaining."	• Frame obligations as mutual commitments and concerns as collective community complaints, detached from individuals
Lack of local mobilizers. Local mobilizers were largely nonexistent.	• Mobilize externally through international nongovernmental organizations, but be mindful of the risk of weakening sustainability

The original aim of the intervention was to boost the level of local health services, absent improvement in the broader health system. The focus on mutual accountability between service providers and users proved successful in a context marked by distrust and limited state capacity. Nevertheless, because health care workers have the potential to evade or shape attempts by "normal" users to improve accountability, the experience suggests that only limited gains can be achieved unless mutual incentives for improved service can be built vertically (between frontline service providers and their supervisors) and horizontally (with local authorities such as chiefs and councilors). Building incentives in this way might also increase the chances that improved accountability will become embedded and survive without continued external support.

Operationally, the next steps are to use the findings to inform improved citizen involvement in an ongoing health performance–based financing project and to continue to assess the willingness and ability of paralegals to effect systemic change.

Building Citizens' Trust in the Government through SA: The Governance Support Project in Pakistan's Khyber Pakhtunkhwa Province

This case study is based on a World Bank–financed project aimed at strengthening governance in the Pakistan's Khyber Pakhtunkhwa (KP) Province. In early 2009, the government of Pakistan launched a major military offensive against Islamist militants there and in the country's federally administered tribal areas. Fighting resulted in widespread damage to physical infrastructure and services, and approximately 3 million people were displaced. The offensive and lingering insecurity eroded what little trust citizens had in the state. A history of strained state-society relations, exacerbated by regional and ethnic tensions, made the task of restoring trust between the government and citizens of KP especially challenging.

A government-led postcrisis needs assessment supported by donor agencies identified the need to restore citizens' trust in the government as a priority in any development program in the area and as a key step in the peace-building process (ADB 2010). A multidonor trust fund was established in 2010 to respond to the needs assessment. The governance support project (GSP) is "one of the key instruments of the MDTF [multidonor trust fund] to support the reconstruction, rehabilitation, reforms, and other interventions needed to build peace and stability" (World Bank 2010). Its strategic focus is on enhancing citizens' trust.

Among other activities, the GSP is encouraging the use of citizen report cards and the implementation of a Right to Information (RTI) Law. The objective of the citizen report cards is to develop linkages between communities and civil society organizations. The World Bank's Social Development Department team collaborated with the World Bank's country team, the institute contracted by the project team to implement the citizen report cards, and the provincial Ombudsman's Office to ensure that they are effective in building citizens' trust. Specifically, the Social Development Department team helped to design the civic mobilization and interface components of the citizen report cards and implementation of the RTI Law, such as designing an awareness or civic mobilization campaign for disseminating results of the report cards to citizens and a campaign to improve awareness of the RTI Law and encourage citizens to exercise their rights under it.

Using the SA Framework to Inform Interventions in GSP

The analytical framework described in chapter 4 was used to inform these activities.

The project began by analyzing the macro context that is expected to mediate the effectiveness of SA interventions in KP according to the factors identified as important (chapter 3). This research was mostly desk based.

In the second step, keeping the macro contextual review in mind, the project carefully reviewed the drivers for each of the five components of SA identified by the framework—citizen action and state action as well as information, interface, and civic mobilization, which are more actionable elements—in order to inform the design of two interventions (an awareness campaign following the collection of citizen report card data and implementation of the RTI Law). Information on the relevant drivers was gathered in field research. For example, the fieldwork aimed to determine the existing state of each of the drivers within the information domain (for example, is information accessible to citizens, what sources of information are trustworthy for citizens, do citizens have information about existing interfaces?).

Fieldwork was conducted in three districts: Haripur, Swat, and Peshawar. In each district, two research sites were chosen: one urban and one rural. These districts were selected to capture the variation across KP with regard to the extent of violence endured, the types of customary institutions, and, to some extent, the involvement of CSOs in the area.[7] The data were collected through qualitative methods. Research started with a brief profiling exercise to collect basic information about the village or urban center, including availability and access to various services, basic structure of customary institutions, and intertribal relationships. At least two focus group discussions were carried out in each site with male and female residents. Wherever there was a marginalized group, a specific focus group was also conducted with representatives from it. In addition, two to three interviews were conducted at each site with customary leaders and other authority holders, members of professional or business associations, teachers, and other active members of the community. Five interviews were conducted at the district level with CSOs, government officials (from education, health, or sanitation departments), members of the national or provincial assemblies, and high-ranking bureaucrats. The findings from this field research are presented in the section on intervention strategy and will be published in more detail as a separate case study.

The proposed intervention design is based on the macro contextual review and the field research based on the SA framework. Throughout this process, the Social Development Department team collaborated with the GSP team. The findings were also presented at various times to the Implementation Support Unit, which the provincial government established to implement the GSP.

Mapping the Institutional Landscape Influencing the Intervention

This section presents results of the macro contextual mapping, describing the institutional landscape influencing the intervention, including the state and civil society actors.

State Actors

Pakistan is a federalist state with a significant degree of provincial autonomy. In the context of the case study, decision-making authority rests by and large with the KP provincial government. It is nonetheless essential to understand the broader country environment, where the state comes under heavy criticism by all stakeholders on account of corruption and lack of transparency. To a large extent, deficiencies in service delivery and poor governance are attributed to a lack of accountability. For more than half of its history, Pakistan has been ruled by the military, but even when multiparty elections have been held, the "long" route to accountability appears to have been almost absent. Political parties—prime actors in instituting public accountability—have failed to represent citizens' preferences and to translate them into a policy agenda (for reasons discussed below). They also have failed to hold the executive accountable on behalf of citizens.

Countrywide. Pakistan is divided into four provinces, two territories, and one capital territory. At present, the country has a parliamentary system, where the president is largely a ceremonial head of state, the prime minister is head of government, and there is a multiparty system. In 2013, for the first time, there was a peaceful transition from one democratic government to another.

Each province has a directly elected legislature, the provincial assembly. The provincial assembly elects a chief minister, who appoints cabinet ministers. A chief secretary coordinates and supervises the functions of the various departments of the provincial government, which are headed by department secretaries.

Gradually, electoral politics have become a competition for access to patronage. The outcome of elections often depends more on the influence in the locality and on community ties than on ideology or policy position. It also depends on a candidate's ability to mobilize financial resources (Waseem 2011). Politicians matter more than political parties in the political process. In such a context, politicians do not have strong incentives to make a concerted and unified effort to improve governance and public service delivery.

The judiciary has played an important role in providing a platform for civil society to voice its grievances to the state. It has also sided with citizens in demanding accountability from the government. Over the course of the last decade or so, the judiciary has involved itself in a wide range of issues, from the failure of the police to register a complaint to the controversial sale by the prime minister of a state-owned steel mill.

KP Province. Following the 2013 elections, a newly formed political party, Pakistan Tehrik-e-Insaf (PTI) came to power in KP Province on a platform that promised greater accountability. Provinces have the power to create specific institutions, and within a year of taking office, the PTI government took three important steps related to SA:

1. Promulgated an RTI Law and created an independent Information Commission; the Reform Implementation Cell is coordinating RTI implementation
2. Created the role of provincial ombudsman
3. Enacted the Right to Public Services (RTS) Act, which is now being implemented.

KP Ombudsman. The KP Ombudsman's Office was created in 2010 through an act of the KP provincial assembly. The postcrisis needs assessment had recommended the appointment of a provincial ombudsman to strengthen relations and trust between the state, communities, and civil society. While the primary objective in creating the role was to strengthen government's ability to address citizens' grievances against maladministration and to improve the government's accountability overall, it was also seen as a key step toward civic engagement. The KP Ombudsman's Office has a separate Child and Women Section.

The mandate of the Ombudsman's Office is to "investigate complaints arising out of maladministration of provincial government agencies and to provide free, fair, and expeditious relief to aggrieved persons, ensuring good governance and better service delivery through administrative accountability." Three areas lie outside of its jurisdiction: (a) services such as electricity and gas, which are within the purview of the federal government; (b) provincially administered tribal areas, such as the Malakand Division (as opposed to provincially administered "settled areas"); and (c) matters related to external affairs, the armed forces, or subjudice (contempt) in any court or tribunal.

Civil Society

The media are largely independent, although they are heavily regulated by the Pakistan Electronic Media Regulatory Authority. The real game-changer, however, has been the opening up and tremendous growth of electronic media in the last decade. The media have had a great impact in making society more aware of the country's political situation, as political issues are routinely discussed on electronic media and no longer considered off-limits.

On occasion, civil society in Pakistan has actively participated in state building. Its participation has taken the form of both street protests and peaceful demonstrations.[8] Less frequently—and much less effectively—civil society has also engaged with the state politically to voice its grievances, but it has not been able to build a coherent platform. The interests of civil society are varied and often mutually exclusive, and the necessary links to each other and especially to the state are lacking.

The primary reason for this lack of effectiveness has been restrictions on civil society. Freedom of association is guaranteed under Article 17 of Pakistan's constitution; however, this fundamental right has often been curtailed, abrogated, or subjected to restrictions. Military regimes and sometimes even democratic governments have used force against demonstrators, arrested numerous civil society leaders, and even orchestrated the killing of journalists. In the presence of vocal and violent groups, civil society groups that adopted peaceful methods of agitation were even more sidelined (Aslam 2010).

Some civil society groups have been able to remain relevant and active in political processes despite unfavorable circumstances. Pakistan's Human Rights Commission is one of the country's leading organizations fighting for human rights and democratic development. It has strenuously condemned the practices of the country's military and its political parties. It has earned the respect of the international community primarily through the profiles of its leaders, including Hina Jilani, Asma Jahangir, and I. A. Rehman, and their alliances with international civil society organizations. Similarly, lawyers' associations at the national, provincial, and sometimes district levels, along with journalists' associations, have remained vocal and engaged with the state to demand accountability.

Since the launch of the Lawyers' Movement—a broad-based movement that spanned two years (2007–09) and led to the ouster of the ruling dictator, General Pervez Musharraf—civil society has become more vibrant. In the two years the Lawyers' Movement was active, several CSOs, including student groups, emerged. While some of these disbanded once the movement ended, the long-term effects on the vibrancy of civil society remain.

Pakistan generally, and KP in particular, also have a large number of NGOs with narrowly defined mandates and small memberships. Their mandates vary widely, from addressing human rights violations and protecting the environment to rural development and education. Although the government does not give them guidelines or directly monitor their activities, NGOs must register with a government department. NGOs rely mostly on local or international donors for funding, because there is no government funding for NGOs. While most of them operate in KP, many are based in large cities, including Islamabad, Karachi, and Lahore. While civil society organizations command respect, Pakistanis tend to view NGOs as opportunistic as far as their activities and fundraising strategies are concerned.

SA Intervention Strategy in GSP

Tables 7.4 through 7.8 summarize the bottlenecks or opportunities for each of the five constitutive elements and suggest strategies for addressing them.

Table 7.4 Bottlenecks or Opportunities for State Action and Strategies for Addressing Them: Implications for the Intervention Design in Pakistan

Bottleneck or opportunity	Strategy
• *Intrinsic motivation.* Political interference blurs lines of accountability, destroys morale, and discourages initiative. For example, if a principal reprimands a teacher, the principal may be reprimanded by his or her superior if the teacher has links with higher levels of bureaucracy; a police department also reported a great deal of political interference by elected officials. Decisions on recruitment, promotions, and postings are influenced by patronage and not based solely on merit.	• Be mindful of the limits to horizontal accountability and the risks of elite capture in such a setting
• *Ability and resources.* State departments have limited resources, especially at the local level. Sometimes local elites pay for the day-to-day expenses of these departments (gasoline for police cars, office stationery). This practice makes officials compliant toward local elites.	• Be mindful of this practice even though it does not fall within the purview of social accountability activities and use other means to support capacity building in government departments and ensure that they have adequate resources
• *Official attitude.* Public servants behave—or are perceived to behave—as if they are superior to citizens and rule over citizens as opposed to serving the public. Since the perception of the quality of government services provided by a particular department is determined by the behavior of public servants, this phenomenon has negative implications. "A Pakistani police officer behaves like a villain. He considers his post as if it was left to him by his forefathers" (lawyer, Swat). "Personally, I feel that I am a servant of government. The problem lies with the perceptions of people. They think that we are superior, or even supreme" (police officer, Haripur).	• Support initiatives that strengthen professional norms and raise awareness among government officials of their responsibilities and the relationship of accountability with citizens • Involve government officials in the survey design and in the dissemination campaign relating to citizen report cards as well as awareness campaigns relating to right to information • Encourage government officials to accept and act on the survey results and boost their sense of civic responsibility

Next Steps

The results of the analysis were presented to the governance support project team, the implementation support unit of the GSP, as well as the Information Commission (including the information secretary) and the KP Ombudsman's Office (including the adviser to the ombudsman). Their implications for the design of the awareness campaign relating to citizen report cards and implementation of the RTI were discussed, and the final design and implementation will reflect them.

Table 7.5 Bottlenecks or Opportunities for Citizen Action and Strategies for Addressing Them: Implications for the Intervention Design in Pakistan

Bottleneck or opportunity	Strategy
• *Intrinsic motivation.* Citizens tend to be apathetic, feeling it is not their responsibility to hold government accountable. "Everyone is concerned with his own business. No one cares about the country, so who will question the state?" (male youth, focus group discussion, Haripur). "People do not have any collective sense, and they are not sincere with other Pakistanis. We think just for ourselves not for society or in a collective way" (community leaders, focus group discussion, Swat).	• Aim to inculcate a sense of civic responsibility; in an interview, one respondent expressed this need as follows: "Government needs to launch a social awareness campaign, so that people might feel the responsibility of caring for and using public property as if it were their own" (entrepreneur, Swat). • Build the capacity of citizens to take collective action. • *Longer term:* Undertake actions to effect change in the political system. Political parties need to organize themselves along ideological lines instead of relying exclusively on the political support of their members, so that they can effectively aggregate citizens' preferences. Capacity-building measures for political parties and parliamentary members, together with sustained engagement with these actors over time, can contribute to this goal. Citizens also need to realize that strong client relationships reinforce their dependence on specific persons and limit their choices in the long run.
• *Lack of legitimacy of nongovernmental organizations (NGOs).* Citizens distrust NGOs because of their lack of accountability to citizens and their dependence on foreign funding. "Most NGOs have a foreign agenda. They will do anything if they have a donor. You give them funds, and today they will talk about the environment, but tomorrow about something else" (focus group participant). They also lack legitimacy in the eyes of government officials: "I am not satisfied with NGOs, because they do not work with us in any sector. We ask them to do something, and they do something else" (chief coordination officer, Haripur).	

(continued next page)

Table 7.5 Bottlenecks or Opportunities for Citizen Action and Strategies for Addressing Them: Implications for the Intervention Design in Pakistan (continued)

Bottleneck or opportunity	Strategy
• *Efficacy and capacity for collective action.* Conflict has destroyed social networks, and rebuilding these networks will be a daunting task owing to lingering insecurity. As a consequence, existing networks cannot be relied on to coordinate collective action. A teacher in conflict-affected Swat explained, "The tradition of late night meetings in *hujras* [a public space where members of the community discuss social and political issues other] is finished. People have limited their dealings [with each other]." Similarly, in Peshawar, a participant in a male focus group discussion explained, "Following the violence there is lack of trust among people, and people do not welcome unknown people. Even mosques are locked because of thefts."	• Lead stronger efforts to encourage civic mobilization in conflict areas • Ensure that any effort to promote collective action adequately addresses citizens' concerns about security
• *Efficacy and capacity for collective action: role of media.* The media remain vibrant and have often partnered with citizen groups to demand accountability from the government. "We had repeated problems with the electrical transformer. WAPDA [the primary public energy producer] employees took it away for repairs, and we were without electricity for three weeks. Then the elders committee met with the SDO [sub-divisional officer, WAPDA] and threatened to report the matter to Geo TV and also block the road. It was repaired within three days" (male youth, focus group discussion, urban Haripur).	• Use media to disseminate information • Strengthen capacity of media to cover public issues and improve their investigative capabilities • Help media to improve outreach through a larger physical presence and train them on how to reach marginalized groups • Use media as a powerful partner in a pro-accountability coalition
• *Inclusiveness.* Women are highly marginalized and have a greater sense of apathy than men. They are not allowed to participate in collective action or, for that matter, in any public activity. As a result, they are not part of any informal or formal groups either in urban or rural areas: "Women are supposed to take care of the household. The head of the family represents them, so there is no need for them to be present on the committee" (male, focus group discussion, urban Haripur). The field research showed that women have little interest in politics or public affairs. Consequently, they do not seek out information on politics or other issues from the media. They are aware only of issues of accountability that have attracted a great deal of media coverage. For them, the television is only a source of entertainment.	• Ensure that special efforts are made specifically to mobilize women • Use different strategies to ensure that information reaches women

Table 7.6 Bottlenecks or Opportunities for Information and Strategies for Addressing Them: Implications for the Intervention Design in Pakistan

Bottleneck or opportunity	Strategy
• *Accessibility*. Citizens are unaware of their rights. The failure to know their rights is frequently cited as a reason that citizens experience ill treatment at the hands of government officials. Citizens have internalized their own ill treatment by public officials. Not knowing their rights, citizens tend to look to intermediaries for help. "If someone is illiterate or unknown to the police, he will be made to pay a bribe the first time he visits a police station. Someone who is educated or well-known can visit without any hesitation. He knows about his rights and the law, too" (community leader, focus group discussion, Swat).	• Undertake awareness campaigns with the specific aim of informing citizens of their rights, a need that respondents repeatedly expressed as important to improve accountability relations with the government: "Government has to start programs at the local level for the awareness of communities. When someone knows his legal rights, then he can ask for them" (male, focus group discussion, Haripur). "At the district (*tehsil*) level [the second tier of local government], programs should be launched to inform citizens about their rights. If they have some problem, then they should be advised about the direction they have to follow" (police officer, Haripur). • Frame information so that it emphasizes rights and entitlements, giving legitimacy to action. In addition to reporting aggregated perceptions of citizens on service delivery, the citizen report card should include information that is actionable, that is, it should suggest how citizens might use the information • Inform citizens about how to contact government in case they need similar information in the future • Ensure that information is disseminated through multiple channels, giving special attention to vulnerable groups (especially women). In Pakistan, electronic media are an effective way to share information, especially in urban areas. Street theater may be an effective tool in rural areas • Ensure that citizens get this information from trusted sources. In rural Khyber Pakhtunkhwa, citizens trust information disseminated through networks of tribal leaders. In general, citizens do not trust nongovernmental organizations (NGOs). Consequently, information disseminated through NGO-appointed "facilitators" who are not members of the community is not likely to be trusted

(continued next page)

Table 7.6 Bottlenecks or Opportunities for Information and Strategies for Addressing Them: Implications for the Intervention Design in Pakistan (*continued*)

Bottleneck or opportunity	Strategy
• *Awareness.* Citizens do not know whom to contact in the government, or how, for specific needs. "We do not have enough information. Most of us are illiterate, so we do not understand government functions" (male youth, focus group discussion, urban Haripur). For example, a Police Safety Commission has been established in Peshawar in response to complaints about police behavior. The commission is meant to hear complaints about misbehavior of police officials and react accordingly. Citizens do not know how to lodge a complaint, however. One of the participants in a focus group of male community members described the situation as follows: "The Police Safety Commission has a chairman and a secretary. Lots of complaints are made to this commission now, but only by people who know how to file complaints. There is lack of education in this area. Once the people are qualified in this area, these problems will be solved to a greater extent" (male, focus group discussion, rural Peshawar).	• Launch campaigns to disseminate information about agencies' mandates and processes as well as about the existing interfaces with the government (many departments have grievance redress mechanisms or complaint collection mechanisms) • Improve the capacity of citizens, individually or in groups, to communicate with the government by making them aware of how the government works and of the interfaces available to them and then train them in engaging with the government When asked what a successful information campaign regarding available avenues through which to communicate with the government should look like, a participant in the male focus group responded as follows: "Our people do not understand the media, neither newspapers nor radio. They are the people of *hujras*. Whether rich or poor, everyone has a *hujra* here. An information campaign should be such that all the people are gathered in the *hujra*. They are told about [the process of making a complaint], so when I hear about it, I can tell the next person. Then, tomorrow, if we want to make a complaint, we would know whom to call or which office to go to" (male, focus group discussion, Peshawar).

Table 7.7 Bottlenecks or Opportunities for Interface and Strategies for Addressing Them: Implications for the Intervention Design in Pakistan

Bottleneck or opportunity	Strategy
• *Legitimacy of existing interface.* Patron-client relationships represent the only interface available to citizens. Accordingly, citizens appeal to the government for personal favors, not for public goods. Political parties rely exclusively on the support of their members, not on ideology.	• Devise training programs for both citizens and political parties that emphasize rights and responsibilities, as well as the dangers of patron-client relationships. For citizens, incorporate this training into campaigns aimed at promoting an awareness of their rights

(*continued next page*)

Table 7.7 Bottlenecks or Opportunities for Interface and Strategies for Addressing Them: Implications for the Intervention Design in Pakistan (*continued*)

Bottleneck or opportunity	Strategy
• *Detrimental effect of violence on the credibility of the interface.* In addition to patrons (who could be elected officials, bureaucrats, and others within a community), citizens used to communicate with the government through tribal leaders. For instance, in rural Swat and Peshawar, citizens used them to communicate their demands to government officials. Violence brought an end to their mediating role, however. Many of them were uprooted, and, without them, citizens are unable to organize collective action.	• As violence subsides, revive former mediating roles, as citizens regard local leaders and elders as legitimate mediators • Ensure that, when these communication modes are revived, all members of the community, including women, are equally represented
• *Lack of information about the existing interface.* Citizens were not aware that interfaces are available to them to question government under the recently passed Right to Information (RTI) Law and Right to Services (RTS) Act or through the Ombudsman's Office, nor are they aware of their rights. Few respondents knew about the ombudsman or the RTI and RTS legislation. "The government should take steps to make the people aware of this bill [RTI] so that they can benefit from it. Once they know it, only then can it be practiced and become a good law" (focus group participant).	• Encourage government to launch a grassroots campaign to promote awareness of the interfaces available to citizens for demanding accountability

Table 7.8 Bottlenecks or Opportunities for Civic Mobilization and Strategies for Addressing Them: Implications for the Intervention Design in Pakistan

Bottleneck or opportunity	Strategy
• *Existence and capacity of mobilizers.* Neighborhood committees that are organic can be used as mobilizers. These committees represent all socioeconomic and religious groups in communities, with the notable exception of women. They have an impressive track record of collective action. They function better in some places (urban centers) than in others.	• Use neighborhood committees as effective mobilizers, for example, to encourage collective action by citizens and to boost their sense of responsibility to undertake action for the collective good (apathy is a key impediment to citizen action); in Haripur and rural parts of Peshawar, these committees were common • Use these committees to disseminate information

(continued next page)

Table 7.8 Bottlenecks or Opportunities for Civic Mobilization and Strategies for Addressing Them: Implications for the Intervention Design in Pakistan (continued)

Bottleneck or opportunity	Strategy
• *Legitimacy of mobilizers.* In most areas (other than some urban centers), there are few legitimate mobilizers. Otherwise, they are not readily identifiable. Nongovernmental organizations (NGOs) and their appointed "facilitators" are generally used as mobilizers in communities. They lack legitimacy, however, and are unable to mobilize citizens effectively. NGOs lack legitimacy in the eyes of citizens because of their poor performance and alleged corruption. They are not accountable to citizens, and they are dependent on foreign funding. "Most NGOs have a foreign agenda. They will do anything if they have a donor. You give them funds, and today they will talk about the environment, but tomorrow about something else" (focus group participant). "There is a lot of corruption in the NGO sector in Pakistan. The quality of their work is not good. Although they are provided funds, it is wasted on their employees' salaries and corruption" (male community member, focus group discussion, Peshawar). "I am not satisfied with NGOs, because they do not cooperate with us in any sector. We ask them something, and they do something else" (chief coordination officer, Haripur). Rural support programs have established community-based organizations, but, unfortunately, citizens have little trust in them, because they are believed to be under the control of elites. Because the government provides most of the funding for them, rural support programs are also considered "part" of government. The Pakistan Poverty Alleviation Fund, for example, was established by the government. "Tanzeem, a CBO [community-based organization] consists of 20 to 25 people. An NGO funds it. The members are from two or three households. They control the funds, and only they benefit, not the whole community" (political worker, Haripur). Other civil society organizations (CSOs) such as business and professional associations do not have much incentive to participate in activities for the benefit of the larger public. The only exceptions are lawyers' and journalists' associations, which could act as mobilizers for social accountability purposes. These associations are usually not active in rural areas, however. Tribal leaders and tribal networks could act as effective mobilizers, but the conflict has eroded their authority and effectiveness.	• Use mobilizers who are legitimate in the eyes of the community • Assess perceptions of a given NGO's legitimacy before using it for information dissemination and civic mobilization needs • In communities where legitimate mobilizers are not readily recognizable, identify actors who could potentially take the role, even if they do not perform this role at the time of the intervention • Train and equip tribal leaders and tribal networks to act as mobilizers. Doing so entails additional efforts and presents a different set of risks, however • Ensure that tribal networks in any given area are trusted and free of control of the elites. (This is less likely to be possible in Khyber Pakhtunkhwa than in other tribal areas, since tribal relationships are generally collaborative rather than hierarchical.)

(continued next page)

Table 7.8 Bottlenecks or Opportunities for Civic Mobilization and Strategies for Addressing Them: Implications for the Intervention Design in Pakistan *(continued)*

Bottleneck or opportunity	Strategy
• *Lack of mobilizers.* In areas prone to conflict, it is even more difficult to identify mobilizers, because of the lack of security and sometimes threats. "No single individual can show himself as a leader because these people were targeted more in the past" (focus group participant).	

Supporting State Legitimacy through SA: Local Governance Reforms in the Republic of Yemen

The Yemeni case study is based on the continuing dialogue on decentralization reforms. In the Republic of Yemen, one of the main factors behind the push for local governance is the desire to enhance engagement with citizens, bolster the legitimacy of the state, and strengthen its authority. In light of the wide range of intractable problems confronting the country, enhancing state legitimacy has been identified as an essential component in all future World Bank projects. For example, the guiding principles of the Interim Strategy Note (FY2013–14) focus on confidence-building measures, increased participation and inclusion, and greater government transparency and accountability. A National Dialogue Conference also identified strengthening an inclusive and accountable government with broad legitimacy in the eyes of its citizens as a prerequisite for the country's political development.

In this context, the World Bank is considering particular forms of local governance that address underlying sources of grievance and conflict and foster improved state-society relations and state legitimacy to support the government in implementing the reforms. The SA team in the Social Development Department contributed to this effort by identifying challenges and opportunities for SA within these local governance reforms.

Using the SA Framework to Inform Interventions in Local Governance Reform

The analytical framework described in chapter 4 informed this exercise. As a first step, the broader context that would mediate the effectiveness of SA interventions in the Republic of Yemen was studied. This research was mostly desk based. We also focused on political developments following the Arab Uprising and examined how the macro context has changed as a result of it. The following section on mapping the institutional landscape influencing the SA intervention in the Republic of Yemen briefly discusses the results of the macro contextual mapping.

Next, keeping the macro contextual review in mind, drivers of the five components that comprise SA were reviewed in order to determine the design of SA interventions in connection with local governance reforms. Field research collected information on the relevant drivers. For example, the data collected were designed to assess the state of each of the drivers within the civic mobilization sphere (for example, the existence, effectiveness, and legitimacy of mobilizers).

Fieldwork was conducted in six districts. Each location differed from the others in its social structure, the structure of tribal institutions, the presence or absence of marginalized groups, the relationships with the state, and the rural-urban divide. The locations were in both urban and rural areas:

- Urban: Sa'ana (lower-income neighborhoods) and Aden (residential neighborhoods)
- Rural: Al Jouba in Mareb,[9] Rural Taiz, Rural Hodeida, and Rural Dhamar.[10]

For each location, a community profile was drawn up, summarizing information about the basic social structure of the community and services. Focus groups were conducted with male and female participants and representatives of any marginalized groups in each community. Interviews were also conducted with elected officials (members of the local council), government officials, local customary leaders, and CSO members or community activists. In each community, two individuals from each category were interviewed.

Together, the information from the macro contextual review and the field research informed the proposed design of interventions. Throughout the process, the World Bank Social Development Department team collaborated with the World Bank country team in Middle East and North Africa region working on local governance reform in the Republic of Yemen.

Mapping the Institutional Landscape Influencing the Intervention

This section maps the institutional landscape influencing the intervention, focusing on state actors and civil society actors.

State Actors

In the Republic of Yemen, the tribe forms the basic unit of society. It regulates the lives of its members through customary laws. These laws regulate "public responsibility" such as the protection of persons, honor, and crime. They also define the code of conduct and rules in relation to personal matters such as marriage, divorce, and inheritance. Tribal leaders derive legitimacy by ensuring the adherence to customs and using various social sanctions for enforcement. For centuries, the tribe has been a decentralized sociopolitical organization that has presented itself as an alternative to the state.

Relations between the tribes and the state in the Republic of Yemen have influenced the structure of the state. The ascendancy of the tribe has meant that the state is just one actor among many in Yemeni society. The state operates through various groups, but primarily through tribal networks. Tribal leaders have assumed contradictory roles with respect to the state. On the one hand, they became part of the state's patronage network when they were brought into the formal system of the state as representatives of their communities. In exchange for their loyalty to the central government, they were awarded stipends, access to land, and other privileges (Al-Dawsari 2012). The state was therefore able to advance its agenda without having to make any effort at state building anywhere beyond the capital. On the other hand, these leaders have stood by their communities when particular tribal interests have been threatened (Romeo and El Mensi 2010).

Consequently, all institutions of the state are organized along tribal lines. Regional boundaries correspond to tribal territories. Political parties also represent tribal interests. Essentially, all actors within the state think of themselves as members of tribal institutions, and this thinking influences decision making.

Tribal patronage networks also undermine the establishment of a strong and functioning bureaucracy. Employees see their positions as sinecures in exchange for political loyalty, not as jobs requiring skills. There is a widely accepted culture of "job inheritance" in which a son of a government official is considered a legitimate replacement on the father's retirement. This has resulted in critical deficiency in the capacity of the bureaucracy to perform its basic functions. Many bureaucratic functions are subject to the discretion of tribal leaders. Consequently, society has no trust in the bureaucracy to implement any policies effectively.

At present, the Republic of Yemen is a unitary state divided into 21 governorates and 333 districts. Decentralization reforms have constantly resurfaced on the national political agenda, however. In addition to economic reasons, decentralization reforms are seen primarily as a means to address grievances in the south against perceived marginalization and dominance by the north (Romeo and El Mensi 2010).

The first meaningful attempt at decentralization came in 2000 with passage of a Local Authorities Law. Without changing the unitary structure of the state, the law opened the way for countrywide local elections in February 2001, which established local authorities in all of the country's governorates and districts. Under the law, the local authorities were to comprise elected local councils, appointed chief executives, and administrative executives—that is, devolved departments of the central administration based in local administrative units. In spite of the stated intention of making both the chief executives and administrative executives accountable to the elected councils, they were doubly subordinate to both central and local policy makers, and the strength of the vertical lines of command and accountability remain substantial obstacles to the ability of the councils to make and implement autonomous local policy and program choices (Mewes 2011; Romeo and El Mensi 2010).

Within their narrow mandate, local councils became increasingly vocal in demanding greater local autonomy, as evidenced by their participation in the annual National Conference of Local Authorities in the last decade.

Recognizing the limitations of the Local Authorities Law, in 2007, the president moved to establish genuine local government, accelerating the drafting and adoption of a National Decentralization Strategy. The strategy was implemented too slowly, however, and it floundered because it was associated too closely with former President Saleh's 2015 strategic vision.

The National Dialogue Conference held in early 2014 once again brought decentralization reform squarely into the spotlight, this time with a proposed federalist state structure. The National Dialogue Conference and the proposed reforms are discussed in more detail later in this chapter.

Citizen Actors

The northern and southern regions of the Republic of Yemen have different histories, resulting in divergent social structures and governance cultures. The former northern Arab Republic of Yemen and the southern People's Democratic Republic of Yemen were unified in 1990. In the north under colonial rule, before unification, the tribes and their leaders had effectively penetrated the state by virtue of their numbers in the bureaucracy, the military, and the legislature. This institutionalization of tribal authority changed the customary meaning of the term "sheik" from a religious to a political title. In the south, colonization minimized the role of the tribes in urban centers like Aden, but the tribe remained the primary unit of society elsewhere. At the time of unification, therefore, the north and south had completely different social structures.

Following unification, the social structure and governance system that prevailed in the north took hold in the south and led to confusion about identity and perceptions of injustice. Northern Yemenis tend to view themselves as the country's legitimate rulers. Southern Yemenis residing in Aden (urban Adenites), who consider themselves better educated and more liberal than their fellow citizens, were sidelined by the Socialist Party after independence. Their marginalization resulted in a gulf between northerners and southerners and a strong sense of injustice over certain groups benefiting more than others in the political system.

The issues that divide north from south persist and were an important item on the agenda of the National Dialogue Conference after the Arab Uprising. A special committee was formed to discuss these issues during the dialogue process.

Aside from the north-south divide, other groups have expressed discontent with the state's alleged bias toward them. The most visible sign of this discontent was the Huthi rebellion in the north, an insurgency by the Zaidi Shia sect that began in June 2004 with the express objective of defending the community against discrimination. Fighting has continued intermittently since (Salmoni, Loidolt, and Wells 2010).

While regional differences persist, there is a strong sense of national unity. The union of the two regions in 1990 was a dream come true for many citizens. Yemenis, including tribesmen, have a strong national identity (Wedeen 2009). Identity, however, is not tied to the concept of a sovereign state (Romeo and El Mensi 2010).

Arab Uprising and Recent Political Developments

Inspired by protests in Tunisia, youth and civil society in the Republic of Yemen took to the streets to call for regime change in January 2011. By then, President Ali Abdullah Saleh had ruled the country for more than three decades. Emboldened by the ouster of Mubarak in the Arab Republic of Egypt, the Yemeni movement was in full swing by late spring 2011. Various actors came together in a loose but forceful alliance, and members of the regime defected to join the protestors and opposition political parties. Huthi rebels in the north and Southern Movement activists also joined the alliance (Alley 2013). Yemenis called their uprising the "Change Movement of 2011" or sometimes simply "Change."

In response to the uprising and at the urging of the international community, on November 23, 2011, President Saleh agreed to a Gulf Cooperation Council initiative and a series of United Nations–backed implementation mechanisms. Under the initiative, Saleh agreed to transfer executive power to his deputy, Abd Al-Mansour Al-Hadi. After assuming the presidency, Al-Hadi, guided by the agreement, launched a National Dialogue Conference in order to lay the foundations of a new political order.

The National Dialogue brought political rivals to the table to chart a course for the country's future. The 465 delegates in attendance represented established political parties, newly formed political movements and youth, women, and CSOs. Nine working groups discussed issues such as southern secessionist demands, the Huthi insurgency, and governance. The dialogue ended in January 2014 with various suggestions on how to move forward.

One recommendation called for the creation of a decentralized federal system of government. Another emphasized the need to address the systematic marginalization of southern Yemenis. After the conclusion of the National Dialogue, progress has been made, especially with regard to greater federalization. It has been agreed that the Republic of Yemen will be transformed into a six-region federal system, with Sa'ana, the capital, and Aden, the former southern capital, given special status.

While several international observers considered the National Dialogue a success, there were some reservations. First, southern Yemeni groups rejected the results of the National Dialogue. The Southern Issue Working Group was unable to devise a plan for a new political system that would represent the south fairly. Second, the Huthi movement, which sent representatives to the National Dialogue, rejected its conclusions. One southern political leader resigned his membership in the dialogue, expressing frustration with the process.

Taking advantage of the current government's obsessive focus on the National Dialogue and the weakened state of the military, various armed groups have gained influence. The Huthi movement expanded its territorial control, and various tribal groupings expanded their influence in the northern highlands, gaining traction in areas previously known for greater degrees of state control. Two new armed entities also emerged: militias known as Ansar al-Sharia, which are affiliated with Al-Qaeda, and "popular committees," which formed to oppose Ansar. There have been repeated clashes between these armed groups (Alley 2013).

SA Intervention Strategy in Local Governance Reforms

Tables 7.9 through 7.13 summarize the bottlenecks or opportunities for the five constitutive elements and some strategies for addressing them.

Table 7.9 Bottlenecks or Opportunities for State Action and Strategies for Addressing Them: Implications for the Intervention Design in the Republic of Yemen

Bottleneck or opportunity	Strategy

• *Ability*. State authority is limited in rural areas. The security services are weaker and more divided than they were prior to 2011. Even under President Saleh, state forces enjoyed only limited writ outside main urban centers. Amid the insecurity that followed the events of 2011, a variety of armed nonstate actors have stepped in to fill the expanding void. Consequently, citizens have been forced to turn to these nonstate actors for conducting day-to-day business, even when many of them think that these institutions are authoritarian and self-serving. This sentiment was expressed in all areas where field research was conducted.
 	
    "In the absence of the government, we have no choice but to accept it [tribal authority]" (participant from a minority group, focus group discussion, Dhamar).
 	
    "Lack of security [and the situation of chaos] during the Change Movement forced many people to refer to tribal leaders" (civil society organization [CSO] member, Taiz).
 	
    The same respondent went on to say that these traditional institutions do not represent the community and are counterproductive to its development.
 	
    In urban areas, the prevalence of customary institutions is decreasing.
	• Begin to create links where state and tribal institutions can interact with each other in a productive way. Interactions within social accountability interventions and activities at the local level can help state actors to understand that tribal networks can account for more than state legitimation and to become partners in co-production. At the same time, it can allow tribal networks to build trust with state actors
	
	• Ensure that interventions target both tribal members and leaders, and not leaders exclusively, so that citizens can build or renew accountability relationships with the tribal leaders. This approach is critical, since engaging only with tribal leaders could increase their authority without improving their legitimacy with tribal members
	
	• Recognize that state building will depend to a large extent on how constructive these tribe-state relations and interactions are

(continued next page)

Table 7.9 Bottlenecks or Opportunities for State Action and Strategies for Addressing Them: Implications for the Intervention Design in the Republic of Yemen (*continued*)

Bottleneck or opportunity	Strategy
• *Capacity and incentives of the bureaucracy.* The phenomenon of job inheritance—where a son inherits a government job from his father after the father's retirement—is pervasive. As a result, government officials do not see these jobs as service but as their right. The fact that this phenomenon is accepted as legitimate exacerbates the problem. Many young respondents, however, spoke against this norm and understood that inheritance of government jobs within families is unfair and against the principles of merit.	• Support initiatives that strengthen professional norms and raise awareness among government officials of their responsibilities and the relationship of accountability with citizens

Table 7.10 Bottlenecks or Opportunities for Citizen Action and Strategies for Addressing Them: Implications for the Intervention Design in the Republic of Yemen

Bottleneck or opportunity	Strategy
• *Intrinsic motivation: concept of citizenship.* By and large, Yemenis attach greater importance to their tribal affiliations than to their relationship with the state. In other words, there is very little concept of a citizenship relationship with the state. However, the Change Movement has altered this understanding, at least in some instances. A new group of community activists is emerging at the local level, and they have a strong sense of a citizenship relationship with the state—that is, they think of themselves as citizens rather than as members of a tribal institution. Moreover, many citizens (including those from marginalized groups) are hopeful about the results of the process that the National Dialogue has started. Even though many think that they were not adequately represented, they still hope that the results will be legitimate, an indication that citizens are willing to forge or renew relationships with the state.	• Treat as a window of opportunity the willingness of citizens to forge a new citizenship relationship with the state that extends beyond their tribal affiliations • Focus on providing interfaces (tangible and virtual) where citizens can communicate with the government and make their expectations known, though much depends on how the government responds

(continued next page)

Table 7.10 Bottlenecks or Opportunities for Citizen Action and Strategies for Addressing Them: Implications for the Intervention Design in the Republic of Yemen (*continued*)

Bottleneck or opportunity	Strategy
• *Intrinsic motivation.* Since the "Change" of 2011, citizens are more motivated to take action to demand accountability from the government, particularly in connection with the provision of services such as electricity, school, health, and security. They have staged street protests, demonstrations, and marches, and they have agitated through the media. In many parts of the country, newly formed youth groups are attempting to coordinate collective projects. For example, in Hodeida, young men with different tribal affiliations have formed sports and cultural clubs, and they use theater to raise awareness in their communities about the rights and responsibilities of citizenship.	• Recognize that the greater the motivation of citizens to take collective action, the greater the likelihood they will participate in social accountability interventions • Harness this motivation quickly, as the longer the motivation persists without a tangible way of channeling it, the greater will be the resentment among these citizens
• *Capacity for collective action: relationships across groups.* Tribal affiliations are still strong, and they persist out of necessity, because tribal networks provide the only social safety net available. In some parts of the Republic of Yemen, citizens belonging to different tribes live in different neighborhoods. They prefer relying on members of their tribe for help and doing business with them. Collective action becomes difficult because consensus across groups is less possible owing to a lack of trust between tribes: "We all know each other, but for every tribe there is a border" (woman, focus group discussion, Mareb).	• Focus on creating opportunities for individuals with different affiliations to interact with each other and, especially, participate in activities with a common goal, because such interaction builds trust. Encouraging these interactions is generally difficult, because patterns of participation persist. Therefore, make extra effort to reach this goal • Be mindful of the risks, as, when interventions fail to promote relationships among groups, they tend to strengthen bonding capital, which may create greater discord
• *Inclusiveness.* Some groups, in particular, the landless, are marginalized. They have no role in local decision making and feel that they are inadequately represented. While some marginalized groups are vocal about their perception of injustices, others appear to have internalized society's attitude toward them. One of the participants in the discussion with members of a marginalized group expressed his resentment as follows: "We are now polishing the shoes of this country" [Polishing someone else's shoes is considered a demeaning task in Yemeni culture] (focus group discussion, Dhamar). Women are not included in the decision-making process at the local level, in either urban or rural areas. Nevertheless, following the Change Movement, participation of women in public life has increased.	• Identify marginalized groups in communities, because sometimes these groups are not even considered members of the community • Devise different strategies to reach marginalized groups and ensure that they are gender sensitive. Make special efforts to avoid reinforcing exclusionary patterns of participation

Table 7.11 Bottlenecks or Opportunities for Information and Strategies for Addressing Them: Implications for the Intervention Design in the Republic of Yemen

Bottleneck or opportunity	Strategy
• *Awareness.* The Change Movement has had a significant positive impact on citizens' understanding of their rights and responsibilities vis-à-vis the state. They now understand the accountability relationship with the government and know that it is their right to demand accountability from the government. "Following the events of 2011, most citizens have become aware of their right to demand accountability and transparency from officials" (civil society organization [CSO] member, Mareb). "Since 2011, people have started to question the government, in connection with the flow of funds, for example" (CSO member, Taiz). "Change made us understand our rights" (male focus group discussion, Dhamar).	• Build on the greater accessibility of information by providing channels through which citizens can express their demands to the government, for example, by equipping them with the knowledge of how government works and how they can communicate with the government • Ensure that state actors' understanding of accountability relationships is on par with those of citizens. This can be done through civic mobilization with the state. For example, providing them with information about citizens' expectations of them can help to motivate state officials to respond to citizen demands • Give greater credence to their understanding of relationships of accountability by providing citizens with information about the proper functions of government • Frame this information in terms of rights and entitlements, so that it gives legitimacy to action
• *Sources of information and their trustworthiness.* Yemenis in both urban and rural parts of the country rely on the media for information about public life. Reading newspapers, listening to radio, and watching news networks are popular, a development that some participants in focus groups attributed to the Change Movement. At the same time, however, some participants considered some newspapers and journalists as untrustworthy. The ability to identify trustworthy and untrustworthy sources indicates that citizens are shrewd in evaluating information. The Internet is emerging as a significant source of information, especially for young Yemenis. Many of them identified social networking sites such as Facebook as their source of information on political issues, among other things. Many participants confirmed that the Internet has played an important role in promoting an awareness of issues.	• Use newspapers and television to disseminate information • Strengthen capacity of the media to cover issues of public interest and improve investigative reporting • Expand the physical presence of the media to reach a larger audience • Train journalists on the means for reaching marginalized groups • Use the Internet and other information and communication technologies (ICTs) to disseminate information. Be cautious not to widen the digital divide and exclude the most vulnerable groups. Take stock of groups with no access to ICTs and ensure that information is generated through other sources • Be mindful of how the state uses the Internet and other ICTs and if and how it might attempt to curtail access

Table 7.12 Bottlenecks or Opportunities for Interface and Strategies for Addressing Them: Implications for the Intervention Design in the Republic of Yemen

Bottleneck or opportunity	Strategy
• *Existing interface: citizens' perceptions*. There is no interface between ordinary citizens and the state. In interviews, tribal leaders said that they have strong relationships with government and that citizens come to them whenever they need to communicate with the government (for example, to complain about public services). Nevertheless, in focus groups, citizens did not corroborate this assertion. Instead, they insisted that tribal leaders pursue their own interests, and they prefer not having to turn to them. When they need to communicate, most citizens do so through local council members (except in Mareb, where they communicate through the mayor). Government officials who were interviewed also agreed that the first line of communication is through a local council member. Council members do not have much authority, however. According to these members, "[We] carry these demands to higher government levels but do not receive any response from them" (local council member interview, Mareb).	• Consider using local council members as an effective interface if they are more autonomous or if they engage citizens more. Decentralization reforms provide the right vehicle
• *Existing interface: government's perception*. In some sites (Hodeida, Mareb, Sa'ana, Aden), government officials use tribal leaders as an interface between them and the citizens. For example, government officials consult with local customary leaders to identify communities' needs. Many government officials admitted that channeling funds to a community through local leaders is prevalent and convenient. They recognize, however, the issues of exclusiveness, the personal interests of local leaders, and the impact that these interests have on the distribution of public services. For example, a government official in Hodeida, expressed this as follows: "The negative effect [of having to go through customary leaders] is the pressure they put on us to give an undeserving person social security, only because he is related to them, or because he will do them a favor in return. As for the positive effect, they facilitate our work. For example, they help us reach a certain person or category" (government official, Hodeida). Elected officials in some places (Aden, Hodeida) said that local institutions and leaders are a hindrance and that they do not deal with these institutions at all: "They [local customary institutions] deepen the divide between the citizen and the state by imposing their repressive authority rather than embracing and cooperating with the state." "There is a contradiction [between the state and customary institutions]. The state works in accordance with the constitution and judicial and administrative departments. The customary institutions rule by custom and logic, not by law."	

Table 7.13 Bottlenecks or Opportunities for Civic Mobilization and Strategies for Addressing Them: Implications for the Intervention Design in the Republic of Yemen

Bottleneck or opportunity	Strategy
• *Effectiveness and legitimacy of mobilizers. Civil society organizations (CSOs)* are considered legitimate in almost all spheres. All participants in focus group discussions and interviews thought that CSOs are a positive force in society. Organizations established by the Social Fund for Development are also deemed legitimate by many citizens and representative of the communities' interest. "CSOs have proven their value in society by taking up its problems and concerns and consequently building good relations with the public" (government official, Dhamar).	• Use CSOs as effective mobilizers, but ensure that a CSO is deemed legitimate in any given community before relying on it for information dissemination and civic mobilization purposes
• *Effectiveness and legitimacy of mobilizers: younger community activists.* The Change Movement has given rise to a younger generation of community activists who participated in it. Since the movement has a good reputation among citizens, and its goals are perceived as just, these activists are also perceived as legitimate.	• Target the younger generation as mobilizers. Because they are members of their community, they are trusted and have access to all groups within their communities
• *Effectiveness and legitimacy of mobilizers: tribal leaders.* Tribal leaders are the other important actors in Yemeni society. Yemenis in both rural and urban areas do not perceive them to be legitimate, however. Many citizens suggested that traditional forms of authority can be fixated on empowering themselves. Some regard traditional rule as a form of power imposed on communities. Citizens do not want international organizations to go through tribal leaders to implement any development activities, primarily out of fear that these leaders will capture funds. Citizens expressed this fear clearly in interviews and discussions: "They [international donors] can build a better relationship with the community through information sessions for all groups in society, including marginalized and special needs people. These sessions would allow people to express their opinions and build better relations with the community" (CSO member, focus group discussion, Hodeida).	• Use tribal leaders as mobilizers, but only if you support them in acting as effective mobilizers. Using tribal leaders as mobilizers can be counterproductive because citizens do not perceive them to be legitimate. Nevertheless, discussions with community activists and others suggest that these institutions hold such an important place in society that they cannot be ignored. Supporting them in acting as effective mobilizers would provide an opportunity for these institutions to change as well. For example, a government official, who thinks that tribal leaders currently play a negative role in the community, suggested, "Community leaders and their sons are now educated, hold certificates, and hold various positions in the state, starting from army and security and ending in all aspects of the state. You can make this relationship positive if you know how to use it" (government official, Dhamar).

Concluding Discussion: The Role of Tribal Leaders and Tribal Institutions

The future of political and economic development in the Republic of Yemen depends to a large extent on the tribe-state relationship. Historical legacies have made this relationship increasingly complex. Tribal leaders who have been co-opted by the state have lost legitimacy in the eyes of their tribesmen. Even so, the absence of state institutions has forced citizens to refer to these leaders and tribal networks.

Given the impact that tribal leaders and institutions have on society, they have to be factored into any governance reforms. The challenge is to forge a constructive relationship between state and tribe and between tribal leaders and tribesmen. As the contextual review suggests, decentralization in the context of a federalist state and genuine local autonomy could help to turn tribal structures into assets for local governance and self-help in a process of endogenous development.

Designing an SA Intervention Strategy for the Village Investment Project: The Case of the Kyrgyz Republic

This case study focuses on a World Bank–financed village investment project (VIP) in the Kyrgyz Republic, applying the analytical framework to the design and interventions of an upcoming third phase. VIP is one of the World Bank's longest-running projects in the Kyrgyz Republic and has been implemented throughout the country. The first two iterations of the project, VIP1 and VIP2, focused on introducing and implementing community-driven development mechanisms and processes in local development agendas. Specifically, they incorporated community participation and the coordination of micro project activities into the work of local state and other service providers. The Community Development and Investment Agency (ARIS) is designing the third phase of the project with the goal of adjusting its design to fit the changing needs of the project and its beneficiaries. VIP3 aims to broaden its focus to foster more systematic and sustained engagement between beneficiaries and the local state. In order to do so, ARIS seeks to incorporate SA mechanisms and processes into VIP3's design.

Used as a prospective operational tool, the framework described in this report provides a road map for the design of an effective SA strategy in VIP3. As a first step, it was used to survey and map the institutions and actors shaping the accountability landscape in the Kyrgyz Republic (box 7.1).

BOX 7.1

Methodology for Data Collection

The case study uses three streams of data. First, data were collected from a desk review of existing SA activities and projects in the Kyrgyz Republic, including reports published by the Kyrgyz government and various international donors. Second, focus groups were conducted in the Kyrgyz *oblasts* (provinces) of Chui, Talas, and Osh between November 2013 and February 2014. More specifically, fieldwork was conducted in two villages or *aiyl okmotus* (AOs) within the same *raion* (administrative district) in each of these three *oblasts* (six villages in total). Four separate focus groups were used to collect empirical data: (a) local government officials; (b) nonelected local public servants; (c) community leaders, including heads of local civic associations, local NGOs, and CSOs; and (d) beneficiaries of development projects, including members of vulnerable groups. Third, data were collected in Bishkek and Osh through semi-structured interviews with government officials, political figures, leaders of political parties and organizations, project managers from leading donor agencies, NGO leaders, researchers, journalists, and other experts at the country level.

It also assisted in assessing the drivers of state action and citizen action to diagnose more accurately the SA context in the country. Finally, the analytic lens laid out in the framework, which identifies three intervention levers (information, interface, and civic mobilization), allows for the conceptualization and identification of relevant bottlenecks impeding SA and mitigating strategies to offset those obstacles.

Mapping the Institutional Landscape for VIP3

This section applies the framework presented in chapter 3 in order to map the institutional landscape for SA in the Kyrgyz Republic. Institutions in both the state sphere and the civil society sphere, which are relevant for the design of VIP3, are identified and described in figure 7.1.

State Actors

The Kyrgyz Republic has four tiers of governance, a legacy of the Soviet era. The first tier is the central government based in the capital, Bishkek. The second tier comprises seven provinces or *oblasts*: Batken, Chui, Jalal-Abad, Issyk Kul, Naryn, Osh, and Talas. The third tier consists of 47 *raions,* or

Figure 7.1 Landscape of Institutions Influencing a Social Accountability Intervention for VIP3 in the Kyrgyz Republic

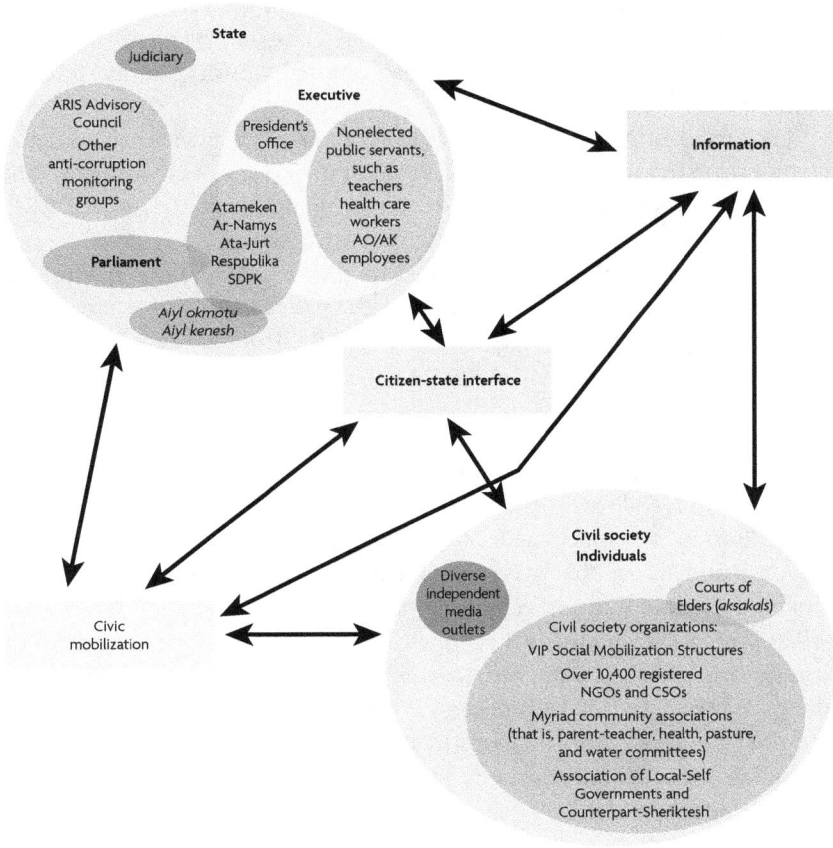

administrative districts. The fourth tier comprises 430 *aiyl keneshes*, or local governments, 21 towns, and 29 urban-type settlements.

As the result of governance reforms in 2009 and 2011, the influence of *oblast-* and *raion*-level administrators has diminished significantly, as both levels of government have witnessed reductions in the size of their budgets and their staff.

The President's Office. The country's most recent constitution, adopted in July 2010, transformed the Kyrgyz political system from a presidential democracy (established following the collapse of the Soviet system in the early 1990s) into a parliamentary one. In keeping with the constitutional provisions, the president, who is elected to a single six-year term, has veto power and the authority to appoint heads of some state agencies, including the prosecutor general, the head of the National Security Service, and the minister of foreign affairs.

The President's Office has the authority to monitor agencies that receive government funding and oversees ARIS and projects such as VIP3. The President's Office is therefore able to extend its support to the project. ARIS is an autonomous noncommercial legal entity, sometimes referred to as a government-owned NGO, co-founded by the presidential administration. ARIS enjoys the institutional support of the presidency. As such, it is able to elicit support for its projects, including VIP3, from various branches of the Kyrgyz government, including parliament, the court system, and local governments.

Parliament and the Supreme Council. The Kyrgyz parliament was established in 1991, following independence from the Soviet Union. It approves all ARIS projects. Under the Kyrgyz constitution, parliament has the right to form and direct the government cabinet, which bears chief responsibility for the country's economic and social development. Today, all ARIS projects, including VIP3, must be approved by parliament and its committees. ARIS is required to submit full project documentation to the parliament and its committees in hearings on projects. Parliament is required by law to ratify all loans from international financial institutions, including VIP3. As part of the process, it must consult with the following three committees:

- Committee on Agricultural Policy, Water Management, Environment, and Regional Development
- Committee on Foreign Relations
- Committee on Finance and Budgeting

ARIS's relationships with these committees depend on their political dynamics. ARIS generally enjoys productive relations with the Committee on Agricultural Policy and the Committee on Foreign Relations primarily because the pro-presidential party Social Democratic Party of Kyrgyzstan (SDPK), which has been supportive of ARIS and its projects, has a strong presence on both of these committees. According to ARIS representatives, ARIS's interactions with the Committee on Finance and

Budgeting have been strained because the committee has been chaired by a representative of Ata-Jurt, an opposition party that has been critical of foreign investors.

Judicial system and courts. Disputes related to VIP activities could be taken up in the courts. This is unlikely to happen, however, since many citizens do not see the courts as their primary option for resolving disputes. The country's judges are selected by an independent panel called the Council for the Selection of Judges, comprising government officials, judges, and NGO representatives. The powers assigned to the judiciary, however, are not sufficiently delineated, and political tensions have mounted as a result. Moreover, the council receives complaints and suggestions from citizens and groups of citizens, at least in theory. In practice, however, many citizens do not rely on the courts as their primary option for resolving disputes. Only 27.2 percent of court users do, while two-thirds prefer negotiations between parties (World Bank and SCO 2011).

Political parties. The current coalition government comprises three parties—Atameken, Ar-Namys, and SDPK—out of the five represented in parliament (Ata-Jurt and Respublika are the other two). SDPK, which is closely affiliated with the presidency, and Ar-Namys have both been supportive of ARIS projects, including VIP3. In contrast, Atameken and Ata-Jurt have been generally critical of foreign investors and World Bank–financed projects, including VIP3. Nevertheless, because of ARIS's backing from the President's Office and SDPK, the project implementation unit has received parliamentary approvals for its projects without much trouble.

Aiyl keneshes and aiyl okmotus. Aiyl keneshes (AKs) are the local governments operating at the regional level. Citizens elect their AK deputies to five-year terms. AKs are responsible for approving and monitoring local budgets, issuing legal documents to communities, and levying local taxes. AKs meet at least six times a year and hold annual assemblies of residents twice a year, where public records are disclosed.

Aiyl okmotus (AOs) are local administrations functioning at the village level, and they are accountable to their respective AKs. Both AKs and AOs are legal entities authorized to resolve issues independently as specified under their competencies. AKs and AOs played pivotal roles in the coordination of micro projects in VIP1 and VIP2. Under VIP3, AOs and AKs will be given greater responsibilities and a more structured role.

ARIS Advisory Council. In keeping with ARIS bylaws, ARIS is directly accountable to its Advisory Council, which comprises the following:

- Seven members who are delegated from central government agencies
- Seven members who are delegated from AOs
- Seven members who are representatives of NGOs.

The Advisory Council meets twice a year to discuss progress on ARIS-funded projects, including VIP3. Participating local governments and communities can submit their grievances, complaints, and suggestions about ARIS activities and VIP3 to members of the Advisory Council.

There are contrasting views on the importance of the Advisory Council. ARIS representatives see it as important in guiding ARIS, while other actors see it as only nominally important. In addition, although the ARIS website provides general information on the membership of the Advisory Council, further details about the workings of the council, including the minutes of its meetings, are generally not available to the public.

Civil Society Actors

The section describes the various types of organizations active in the Kyrgyz Republic that potentially could be harnessed to support SA interventions.

VIP social mobilization structures. VIP1 and VIP2 mobilized residents of each participating village (*aiyl*) under structures called village investment union executive committees (VICs) and local investment union executive committees (LICs). For VIP3, in villages where VICs and LICs already exist, the new project design will continue to engage these structures and strengthen their roles. In villages where VICs and LICs were not previously formed, new social mobilization structures will be established to engage with VIP3. The VICs operate at the village level and are responsible for identifying key community problems and micro projects to address these. By contrast, LICs operate over an entire AK area and function as a coordinating body among VICs from the same AK. LICs include community representatives from each VIC and members of the AK local government, including the *glava* (head) of the AO. They are responsible for preparing an AO investment strategy and the attendant AO investment plan, which outlines priority investments for the following year. LICs are also responsible for vetting and prioritizing investment proposals put forward by the VICs. In the first year, the community planning requirements are simple and culminate in the formulation of a basic "vision," supplemented by an investment plan.

All investment proposals and decisions at the village level are made on the basis of participatory planning, involving local stakeholders or their recognized representatives. During all phases of the project cycle, VIP3's social mobilization structures, either existing VICs or LICs or newly established ones, will work closely with local government officials and public servants.

NGOs and CSOs. The Kyrgyz Republic has a vibrant civil society and a high level of civic participation. The Ministry of Justice has registered 10,400 NGOs and CSOs that are active in various spheres of social life (including poverty reduction, human rights, religious freedoms, and empowerment of women and socially marginalized groups).

Within this diverse pool, two NGOs are particularly instrumental for VIP3: the Association of Local-Self Governments (ALSG) and Counterpart-Sheriktesh. Along with the President's Office, ALSG and Counterpart-Sheriktesh are founders of ARIS, and they have authority to inspect ARIS activities. Citizens, either individually or in groups, can turn to the ALSG and Counterpart-Sheriktesh to air their grievances and complaints about ARIS and VIP3. ALSG is well known among AOs. In fact, many AOs are members of the ASLG. Counterpart-Sheriktesh, however, is not known beyond the capital city.

Community associations. There are myriad community associations at the village level whose members typically take a keen interest—and often assume active roles—in VIP and its project committees. Parent-teacher committees, which exist in all secondary schools in the country, are particularly active community associations for VIP1 and VIP2, as many micro projects have focused on educational improvements and school infrastructure. There are also approximately 450 water user associations and more than 100 pasture committees in the Kyrgyz Republic, which contribute to an active civic presence in village life.

Courts of elders (aksakals). Courts of elders (*aksakals*) are formal organizations recognized under Kyrgyz law with jurisdiction over certain aspects of property, torts, and family law. These institutions handle minor legal matters delegated by local courts. Although recent studies show that the work of such courts produces mixed results, they nevertheless play important roles by applying traditional norms to reconcile disputes, including disputes relating to infrastructure such as those to be undertaken in VIP3. In cases when their rulings contradict national laws, disputing parties have the option to take the matter to state courts. Courts of *aksakals* provide expeditious adjudication in an environment where adjudication via more formal legal channels is difficult, costly, and inaccessible to many citizens. VIP3 can benefit from courts of *aksakals* in handling disputes within and among communities that arise as part of project activities.

Media outlets. The Kyrgyz Republic has the most vocal and critical mass media in the post-Soviet space, and it is ranked "partly free" in the 2013 Freedom House index. Citizens can use independent mass media outlets to air their grievances, including those related to donor initiatives such as the VIP3. The World Bank and ARIS organize press tours for local media outlets to raise public awareness about projects and increase transparency.

Drivers of State Action and Citizen Action for VIP3

After mapping the institutional landscape for SA, the second step of analysis, following the framework, is to identify the factors that drive or impede state or citizen action to assess the context and its receptivity to an SA intervention.

Regarded as the most open and democratic country in the Central Asia region, the Kyrgyz Republic is a particularly fertile environment for SA, and in general there is a high level of interest among both citizens and state actors. An effective SA intervention for the VIP3 can optimize this attitude and goodwill of the state toward engaging with citizens.

Drivers of state action for SA in the Kyrgyz Republic remain weak, however. Effective state action is hampered to a large extent by a lack of awareness on the part of the state about its role and responsibilities toward citizens. Effective state action is also impaired by its lack of capacity to resolve community problems effectively and meet citizens' needs. Moreover, formal or institutional incentives driving state action are weak. More often than not, motivation and incentives for action on the part of a local government depend on the personal character and integrity of the individual official. Both elected officials and civil servants often choose—at their own discretion—whether to engage with citizens or to neglect their public obligations. Elite capture and corruption aggravate the situation, creating further disincentives for effective engagement. Unfortunately, weak decentralization laws do not offer the necessary support for strong vertical accountability. Consequently, an SA intervention in VIP3 that strengthens drivers of state action is not only timely, but also pressing.

The positive drivers underlying citizen action in the Kyrgyz Republic are numerous and promising. Citizens have a strong motivation to forge strong links with their governing state bodies and officials. This state of affairs is in stark contrast to the role that citizens were permitted to assume under Soviet governance structures. As a result of the activities of various international donors and agencies, there is a resounding buzz around issues of SA in the country and their salience for citizens, even among remote and rural communities. In the Kyrgyz context, threats against action and the costs of taking action are less severe than in neighboring countries, although local elites continually undermine this through subversive tactics to secure their interests. Moreover, the capacity of individuals to organize collectively is high in the Kyrgyz Republic and has increased in recent years. Despite the awareness, relevance, and intrinsic motivation propelling citizen action in the Kyrgyz Republic, there is nevertheless a lack of knowledge of exactly how citizens can successfully effect social change. This perceived lack of efficacy may discourage citizen action. The positive experiences that citizens have with projects like VIP3 and their visible impacts on the community can gradually change perceptions, however.

SA Intervention Strategy in VIP3

VIP3 will seek to expand its reach in the country and to include even more beneficiaries by working with well-organized communities and local governments that successfully participated in VIP1 or VIP2 and by providing additional support to those that need more capacity training. In localities that previously participated in VIP1 or VIP2, VIP3 will continue to engage with existing VICs and LICs and to strengthen their roles. Nevertheless, VIP3 will provide particular encouragement to communities with weaker capacity. As part of its design, capacity training will be offered to AOs, both those participating in the project for the first time and those that had participated under VIP1 or VIP2. AOs will have the option of receiving this training, which includes facilitation on the creation of local development strategies. Moreover, for localities participating in the project for the first time, instead of establishing VICs and LICs, VIP3 will facilitate working groups composed of community beneficiaries and AO representatives. These working groups, which will be directly accountable to their respective AKs, will develop proposals for subprojects to be submitted to a competition at the AK level. Successful project proposals will then be submitted to a competition at the *oblast* level. ARIS will select the winners. Funds will be awarded based on the merits of the project proposal as well as the relevance of the project to the overall local development strategy.

Most notably, VIP3 seeks to integrate local government structures into the project better by strengthening SA mechanisms and processes. In order to incorporate an SA intervention successfully as part of VIP3's new design, the project must evaluate SA bottlenecks encountered in earlier iterations and devise a strategy to mitigate these shortcomings.

This section assesses the bottlenecks and the corresponding mitigating strategy to be considered in the design of an SA intervention for VIP3, as conceptualized according to the framework's three intervention levers: information, interface, and civic mobilization.

VIP1 and VIP2 cemented a strong civic mobilization lever in the project's first two iterations. VIP1 and VIP2 successfully introduced participatory mechanisms into local decision-making processes and initiated collaboration between beneficiaries and state actors around local development agendas. The project's early focus on civic mobilization was particularly critical at the project's onset given the recent collapse of Soviet rule, which left citizens disenfranchised. During the early phases of the state's transition from a highly centralized authority to a more decentralized one, VIP1 and VIP2 served as an important program for empowering citizens, enabling them to organize and take ownership of local development agendas.

The strategy for civic mobilization employed under VIP1 and VIP2 failed to establish a clear division of roles and responsibilities between citizen and state actors, however. Consequently, there is significant overlap of the roles and responsibilities that individuals assume when engaging and alternating between state and civic spheres. These blurred boundaries have had complex impacts on the accountability dynamics and relations between citizen and state actors. For example, it is not uncommon for residents who were associated with VIP1 and VIP2, either as ARIS employees or as VIC or LIC activists, to move into government positions at various levels. These vague boundaries can lead to elite capture of local development processes and business interests. It can also nurture the underpinnings of effective accountability, as elected officials originate from the very communities they represent, allowing them to work in the interests of their constituents (see chapters 3 and 5).

Today, VIP3's greatest challenge for SA is constructing a structured interface between beneficiaries and local state actors, which delineates clear roles and mandates for each. The role of interlocutors, such as local NGOs and CSOs, could be paramount in facilitating and monitoring this interface. The ongoing decentralization reforms in the Kyrgyz Republic are also working to unravel and better define the legal framework and mandate of local governments, which are currently in flux.

In an effort to mitigate its accountability bottlenecks, VIP3 should streamline and simplify the social mobilization process within the project and adopt a proactive information strategy. The information lever is critical, as citizen and state actors do not possess sufficient knowledge of their rights and obligations, especially in the face of evolving decentralization reforms. Training and information dissemination are vital components to be incorporated in VIP3's SA intervention.

Tables 7.14–7.16 explore further the bottlenecks or opportunities related to information, interface, and civic mobilization and corresponding mitigating strategies, which should be considered in the design of an SA intervention for VIP3.

Table 7.14 Bottlenecks or Opportunities for Information and Strategies for Addressing Them: Implications for Intervention Design in the Kyrgyz Republic

Bottleneck or opportunity	Strategy
• *Low level of awareness.* In many parts of the country, both citizens and public servants, including elected local government officials, report a low level of awareness as the primary obstacle in the way of greater accountability. Both citizen and state actors have limited knowledge of their rights and responsibilities. State actors are not fully aware of their obligations and responsibilities toward constituents, and citizens are not aware of their rights and the processes for holding officials accountable. Accurate and accessible information is especially important given the current decentralization reforms.	• Provide training on key topics to both citizens and state officials: legislation and legal rights and responsibilities, local budgeting processes, financial accounting and audits, tendering procedures, and dispute resolution and conflict prevention • Support decentralization reforms by providing training to clarify roles and responsibilities
• *Social exclusion.* For some beneficiaries, membership in a particular social group and the level of education affect access to information and public services. Some beneficiaries reported feeling that they have little voice in how the projects are run. Generally, women and members of ethnic minority groups report obstacles to accessing information. Some members of ethnic minority groups are simply afraid to participate in local government decision-making processes because of the lingering effects of the 2010 interethnic violence.	• Continue to ensure that micro project working groups are inclusive and representative of the community • Appoint a committee representative to serve as a special liaison to socially excluded populations • Consider the use of information and communication technology (ICT) and community radios to ensure the inclusiveness of information channels and dissemination to all segments of the population, especially vulnerable groups • Foster partnerships with the media for disseminating information on VIP3 projects, including budget information and grievance handling

(continued next page)

Table 7.14 Bottlenecks or Opportunities for Information and Strategies for Addressing Them: Implications for Intervention Design in the Kyrgyz Republic (*continued*)

Bottleneck or opportunity	Strategy
• *Elite capture.* In some *aiyl okmotus* (AOs), elite capture of local governments has emerged as an acute issue. Local elites seek to control critical information to avoid threats to power distribution. • *Corruption around access to information is a bottleneck.* In some cases, public servants, especially in local government, selectively share information with friends and relatives or sell it to well-connected community members.	• Formalize information channels. Currently, project information travels primarily through informal information channels, for example, by word of mouth. In an effort to formalize information flows and strengthen local government capacity, the Community Development and Investment Agency (ARIS) could support AOs in taking on the responsibility of disseminating public information. New information dissemination strategies should consider how AOs can build on existing informal networks to maximize impact and outreach
• *Migration flows and brain drain.* Migratory trends affect residents' access to information, because educated and skilled individuals leave for urban areas and other countries in search of economic opportunities. Kyrgyz villages are often stripped of skilled public administrators and community leaders who could otherwise facilitate information flows and communication.	• Nurture local leadership. As part of its social mobilization strategy, ARIS should nurture vocal, active, and trustworthy individuals who can serve as local leaders and assist in disseminating information. Often, the success or failure of a subproject depends on the personal drive and integrity of local leaders. Proper recruitment, training, and support of local leadership for VIP3 are crucial

Table 7.15 Bottlenecks or Opportunities for Interface and Strategies for Addressing Them: Implications for Intervention Design in the Kyrgyz Republic

Bottleneck or opportunity	Strategy
• *Blurred lines of authority.* In some *aiyl okmotus* (AOs), vague accountability relationships in the village investment project (VIP1 and VIP2) created parallel (albeit informal) governance structures and competing power dynamics at the local level. At times, village investment union executive committees (VICs) and local investment union executive committees (LICs) hold greater legitimacy as agents of social change than local governments do. However, unlike official local government bodies, VICs and LICs operate based on informal associations with no formal obligations to taxpayers or residents and local governments. Thus the mechanisms underlying the state-society interface in VIP1 and VIP2 were problematic from an accountability standpoint.	• Designate clear roles and responsibilities. Devise a clear and explicit mandate for state actors and social mobilization structures during the interface. Local government requires a clear and distinct set of responsibilities for which it can be held accountable. For example, consider augmenting its role in the organization and implementation of public hearings around different stages of the project cycle. Citizens need a clear set of processes to follow in order to exact accountability from officials. • Consider elaborating community monitoring schemes • Implement stricter and better-defined accountability measures for the Community Development and Investment Agency (ARIS) and support a conscious shift in its discourse toward accountability

(*continued next page*)

Table 7.15 Bottlenecks or Opportunities for Interface and Strategies for Addressing Them: Implications for Intervention Design in the Kyrgyz Republic (*continued*)

Bottleneck or opportunity	Strategy
• *Inadequate grievance redress mechanisms (GRMs).* The quality of GRMs or dispute resolution systems under the VIP1 and VIP2 varied across AOs and regions. In some cases, ARIS paid insufficient attention to dispute resolution mechanisms. In other cases, the weakness of dispute resolution mechanisms was due to preexisting conditions in those AOs. Corrupt courts and ineffective property rights protection exacerbate the situation.	• Support the information feedback loop by developing a comprehensive GRM • Support the role of the Kyrgyz Ombudsman's Office, ARIS Advisory Council, the Association of Local-Self Governments (ASLG), civil society, and courts of elders in grievance redress. Social mobilization structures could provide "front-end" support for a GRM through the formation of community monitoring groups • Consider using information and communication technology (ICT) and media for the GRM and formalize roles and responsibilities for AOs and AKs in this process
• *Lack of engaged interlocutors.* The record on engaging interlocutors in VIP1 and VIP2 is mixed. In some AOs, community members reported that they were insufficiently engaged by local nongovernmental organizations (NGOs) and civil society organizations (CSOs). In others, there were systematic consultations. Engaged and neutral interlocutors have an important role to play in facilitating interface, especially for mitigating corrupt or ineffective state leadership. Effective state-society interface is heavily dependent on the individual drive and character of local state officials and their personal willingness to engage with citizens.	• Foster partnerships. The presence of active NGOs and CSOs in the Kyrgyz Republic presents an untapped opportunity for facilitating interface. VIP3 should build broader coalitions through increased engagement with NGOs and CSOs. These interlocutors are also vital for sustained interface beyond the project ARIS is well positioned to create local partnerships with local community actors, as well as local and national state actors. Engaging ARIS in the creation of partnerships will also strengthen its accountability

Table 7.16 Bottlenecks or Opportunities for Civic Mobilization and Strategies for Addressing Them: Implications for Intervention Design in the Kyrgyz Republic

Bottleneck or opportunity	Strategy
• *Complex structures and processes.* Social mobilization strategies under the first and second phase of the village investment project (VIP) were successful insofar as they effectively garnered community support for village investment union executive committees (VICs) and local investment union executive committees (LICs). Nevertheless, in some *aiyl okmotus* (AOs), civic mobilization structures and processes appear to be overly complex, creating multiple layers and steps for decision making and information flow.	• Streamline the social mobilization process and mandate. Continue to support the social mobilization encouraged in VIP1 and VIP2, but in addition to their generalized functions, have the Community Development Investment Agency (ARIS) provide support to social mobilization structures (VICs, LICs, and working groups) in developing specialized tasks, such as community monitoring and information dissemination strategies

(continued next page)

Table 7.16 Bottlenecks or Opportunities for Civic Mobilization and Strategies for Addressing Them: Implications for Intervention Design in the Kyrgyz Republic (*continued*)

Bottleneck or opportunity	Strategy
• *Elite capture.* In some AOs, elite capture of local government bodies, VICs, and LICs inhibits effective collective civic mobilization. Wealthy and well-connected local residents use their positions in these community associations to defend their property and business interests. Moreover, membership in *aiyl keneshes* (AKs) and AOs, along with ties to local public service providers, allows local elites to control local tax policy (including land and property taxes) and the provision of public services. Transparent policy-making processes pose a threat to local power distribution, and elites are adverse to measures that would increase social accountability. They resort to a variety of means to block access to information, including kinship and neighborhood ties, peer pressure, and threats of retaliation. In some cases, elites use local bureaucracy to reward residents who cooperate with them and punish those who criticize local authorities.	• Factor in local power dynamics. Greater cognizance of the impacts that VIP has on the local political economy is needed, especially for better understanding the role of local elites. Local elites are not a homogeneous group, and alienating them can have adverse effects for VIP3. Powerful elites may serve as allies in furthering community interests. Alternatively, they may try to capture the project, undermining VIP3's objectives
• *Migration flows and brain drain.* Outmigration has had adverse effects on social mobilization. Local leaders, including members of VICs and LICs, move away, taking their knowledge and skill set with them.	• Nurture diverse leadership through VIP3's social mobilization structures, paying special attention to the involvement of youths
• *Priorities during the agricultural season.* During the agricultural season, residents in rural areas have little or no time for mobilizing.	• Adapt the project timeline to the agricultural season

Notes

1. However, in all four cases, the framework was finalized either after implementation (Sierra Leone) or after data collection had started or been completed (the other three cases). None of the projects was able to use the final framework from its inception since the case study process was enriching the design of the framework along the way. Consequently, some important elements of the final framework could not be analyzed with the level of depth and details that the framework warrants.

2. This fieldwork was financed by a Nordic Trust Fund Grant.
3. See United Nations (2013) for Sierra Leone's human development index values and rank changes.
4. Five representatives from each village were supposed to attend, including two men and two women in different age groups and the village's birth attendant. In practice, participation in the four meetings varied, and in some instances the payment of a travel stipend skewed representation.
5. As an example, in response to the problem of irregular clinic hours (contrary to government policy), one community planted a vegetable garden for the nurse in appreciation of the extra hours she worked. In return, the nurse agreed to keep the clinic open during official hours and to remain on call for emergencies. While the nurse's commitment was within the terms of her employment contract, in practice, the government was unable to ensure that she met her obligations.
6. The mammy queen is the female head of the community (see Cochran 2008).
7. Owing to security issues, the sample does not represent southern KP.
8. For example, in 1967, protests erupted in response to the Tashkent Declaration and continued until General Ayub resigned the presidency. Civil society also actively campaigned for Fatima Jinnah, who challenged Ayub in a bid for the presidency in 1965.
9. Sa'ada Governorate was chosen initially, but there was concern that its residents would be reticent without the presence of their customary leaders and that conducting focus group discussions in the presence of these leaders might not lead to candid discussions. Consequently, Mareb was chosen instead.
10. Amran Governorate, not Dhamar, was chosen initially. A sudden outbreak of violence in the governorate made field research dangerous, and Dhamar was chosen instead because it is structurally similar to Amran.

References

ADB (Asian Development Bank). 2010. "Post-Conflict Needs Assessment: Khyber Pakhtunkhwa and Federally Administered Tribal Areas." ADB, Manila, Philippines.

Al-Dawsari, N. 2012. "Tribal Governance and Stability in Yemen." Carnegie Endowment for International Peace, Washington, DC. http://carnegieendowment.org/files/yemen_tribal_governance.pdf.

Alley, A. L. 2013. "Assessing (In)security after the Arab Spring: The Case of Yemen." *PS: Political Science and Politics* 46 (4): 721–26. doi:10.1017/S1049096513001182.

Amnesty International. 2001. *At a Crossroads: Sierra Leone's Free Health Care Policy.* London: Amnesty International.

Aslam, G. 2010. "Dictatorship as a Bargaining Process: The Case of Pakistan." PhD thesis, George Mason University, Fairfax, VA.

Cochran, C. 2008. "Transitional Justice: Responding to Victims of Wartime Sexual Violence in Africa." *Journal of International Policy Solutions* 9 (Spring): 33–39.

Hall, M. 2012. "Peeling the Mango: Community Dynamics and Social Accountability in Efforts in Sierra Leone." Governance for Development blog, World Bank, Washington, DC.

Hall, M., N. Menzies, and M. Woolcock. 2014. "From HiPPOs to 'Best Fit' in Justice Reform: Experimentalism in Sierra Leone." In *International Rule of Law Movement: A Crisis of Legitimacy and the Way Forward*, edited by D. Marshall, ch. 8. Cambridge, MA: Harvard University Press.

IRCBP (Institutional Reform and Capacity-Building Program) Evaluations Unit. 2012. "Report on the 2011 Integrated National Public Services Survey: Public Services, Governance, and Social Dynamics." IRCBP, Freetown, Sierra Leone.

Mewes, K. 2011. "Decentralization in Yemen." In *Decentralization on the Example of the Yemeni Water Sector,* 85–115. New York: Springer.

Romeo, L. G., and M. El Mensi. 2010. "The Difficult Road to Local Autonomy in Yemen." In *Decentralization in Developing Countries: Global Perspectives on Obstacles to Fiscal Devolution,* 501–48. Cheltenham, U.K.: Edward Elgar.

Salmoni, B. A., B. Loidolt, and M. Wells. 2010. *Regime and Periphery in Northern Yemen: The Huthi Phenomenon.* Santa Monica, CA: Rand Corporation.

United Nations. 2013. *Human Development Report: The Rise of the South; Human Progress in a Diverse World.* New York: United Nations.

Waseem, M. 2011. *Patterns of Conflict in Pakistan: Implications for Policy.* Washington, DC: Brookings Institution Press.

Wedeen, L. 2009. *Peripheral Visions: Publics, Power, and Performance in Yemen.* Chicago, IL: University of Chicago Press.

World Bank. 2010. "Governance Support Project Program Document." World Bank, Washington, DC.

———. 2013. "Twenty Fragile States Make Progress on Millennium Development Goals." Press release, World Bank, Washington, DC. http://www.worldbank.org/en/news/press-release/2013/05/01/twenty-fragile-states-make-progress-on-millennium-development-goals.

World Bank and SCO (Swiss Cooperation Office). 2011. "Kyrgyz Republic Judicial System Diagnostic: Measuring Progress and Identifying Needs." World Bank, Washington, DC, May 17.

Zhou, Y. 2009. *Decentralization, Democracy, and Development: Recent Experience from Sierra Leone.* Washington, DC: World Bank.

Conclusion

This report provides an analytical framework for thinking about and operationalizing social accountability (SA) and unpacks the contextual drivers of SA effectiveness. It proposes a novel framing of SA into five constitutive elements—citizen action, state action, information, interface, and civic mobilization—and mines the evidence to build a framework to guide practitioners in assessing, in a systematic way, the contextual drivers that will support or hinder the effectiveness of SA approaches.

While the report provides a framework for specific issues, the analysis also has some overarching implications. It emphasizes that there are neither "best-practices" nor cookie-cutter approaches for reforms and actions that have a bearing on power relationships. Context does matter, and SA approaches need to be tailor-made. A contextual analysis needs to look deeply into the social and political environment for SA approaches. This includes elements as intangible (and thus difficult to measure) as the conceptions that individuals and groups hold of the state. It also needs to focus on a particular issue or problem, since SA approaches within the same locality will most likely differ depending on the issue at stake (land reform or teacher absenteeism, for instance).

The acknowledgment that "context matters" is not helpful for practitioners if it is not accompanied by a framework to guide their analysis. For this reason, the framework and the guiding tables developed in this report provide a way to analyze context systematically. In order to build this guiding framework, the report conceptualizes SA as the iterative interaction of five elements, going beyond the common acceptance of SA as a linear relationship that moves from information to citizen action to state action. Especially if SA approaches aim to have broad institutional impacts and to trigger both citizen and state action, they need to support not only information but also interface and civic mobilization.

The report offers five important messages.

First, although information is clearly instrumental to any SA approach, it should not be the sole area of focus for supporting and measuring SA. There is no doubt that information is crucial to any accountability relationship. However, the report challenges the common understanding that information leads citizens to demand accountability (citizen action), which in turn leads states to respond to citizen demand (state action). The accessibility of the information, its framing (supporting salience to citizens or the state on the issue, presenting the information in a novel way, or providing consistent messages to trigger action), and the level of trust that citizens or the state have in the information and its medium are essential drivers for citizen and state action. Yet information alone might not be sufficient to trigger state or citizen action in the absence of effective agents or organizations capable of mobilizing both state and citizen actors to engage in SA or a credible, representative, known, and accessible interface.

New information and communication technologies (ICTs) are a clear game-changer in the way citizens and states generate, use, and share information; how they coordinate for civic mobilization; and how they interact with government and public institutions through the digital citizen-state interface; yet they are not, on their own, a silver bullet for SA. They work best when they are embedded in SA institutions, processes, or systems and not stand-alone solutions: ICTs are a supplementary channel for information, participation, and collaboration, not a replacement. The design and implementation of ICTs also need to be user centric—that is, they need to give users more control, more choices, or more flexibility.

Second, the supply-demand dichotomy is unhelpful because it does not reflect the reality, since many SA approaches focus on building supportive pro-accountability networks across state and society. Although our framework conceptualizes SA into five distinct elements as a practical way to guide the assessment of contextual drivers for SA effectiveness, the report discusses in depth the fact that neither civil society nor the state is made up of monolithic homogeneous groups and that these categories frequently overlap. These overlaps and interactions offer opportunities for building and supporting coalitions across-the-board supporting stronger accountability.

The role of the state is crucial in SA approaches. The state provides (or hinders) the enabling environment for information and association, but can also actively support and even initiate SA approaches. Just as important, its level of (and capacity for) responsiveness to SA will determine the outcomes of SA initiatives.

Administrative, political, and social accountability can be distinguished for the sake of the analysis, but the links need to be acknowledged and leveraged. Many successful and innovative SA approaches build links between traditional institutions of administrative accountability and citizen engagement. Relationships between political and social accountability are complex, and they need to be acknowledged and managed, so that SA approaches reinforce, not displace, structures for political accountability.

Third, an instrumental view of SA as supportive of stronger service delivery is reductive of the potential of SA in driving deeper institutional changes. The range of potential outcomes of SA is wide: from benefits in the *state* (better governance), in *state-society relationships* (increased legitimacy), or in *society* (improved provision of public goods) and from *instrumental* (improved provision of public goods) to *institutional* (state building). Perspectives on whether SA "works" or not (a question with no generic answer) are partly determined by the value attributed to its outcomes. Unfortunately, impact evaluations, partly because they favor experimental and quasi-experimental methods, have been commissioned principally for SA's more measurable impacts on service delivery, which does not help to build the body of knowledge needed to understand the mechanisms through which SA initiatives are expected to have an impact.

An instrumental view of SA seems especially reductive in the context of fragile and conflict-affected situations (FCSs). Our case studies in FCS contexts show that there is growing interest and recognition of the potential role that SA approaches can play in rebuilding trust and mutual accountability between state and citizens.

Fourth, SA may not be effective in all contexts or for all issues, and it entails risks and trade-offs. When and how to support SA processes need to be assessed keeping this in mind, all the more so when the support is externally funded. SA processes do not automatically lead to positive outcomes. Numerous studies show the risks of instrumentalization or perversion of SA processes, leading to elite capture, tokenistic participation, apathy or disappointment, and even disengagement and retribution.

The trade-offs are difficult to assess, but they should always entail a cost-benefit analysis of the engagement from the citizens' perspective. There are many examples of SA accountability processes leading to exit or self-provision, not to stronger accountability. The availability of exit options acts as a particularly strong deterrent to collective action compared to the risks and transaction costs of engaging in efforts to exact accountability, especially for the poor. Furthermore, individuals or groups can support "public" interest or "special" interests, and this has clear implications for the type of results one can expect from specific SA interventions.

SA appears more likely to be effective where it builds on existing "organic" pressures for change and accountability, even where this approach appears to be only "second best." Discrete, donor-dependent SA interventions may bring about localized changes, but they may not be sustainable. Evidence finds that embedding SA interventions and principles in institutions, country systems, and all stages of the policy cycle works better. This is a far cry from applying SA "tools" across-the-board through external support and hoping that doing so will change complex power relations.

Finally, among the various operational implications stemming from this report, three are particularly important for external partners to take into account. First, since SA may entail a reconfiguration of social and political powers, SA approaches can sometimes be controversial. In some cases, external partners may not be in a position to engage in or support the whole gamut of SA approaches, and this should be acknowledged up front. Second, because SA involves changes in behavioral, social, and political processes, it is imperative to adopt an adaptive learning-by-doing attitude, for instance, by following a "problem-driven iterative adaptation" approach. This has implications for the approaches and methods used to measure results. Third, there are many cases of SA approaches achieving measurable and positive outcomes within a short time frame. Yet expectations of what SA can achieve in a given time period have to be realistic, and a long-term commitment to support sustainable SA approaches is needed. As mentioned in the report, there are limits to exclusively localized, information-led, "demand-side" interventions. In contrast, "strategic approaches" to SA that combine information access with an enabling environment for collective action can scale up and coordinate with government reforms to encourage public sector responsiveness to voice (Fox 2014).

This report's framework does not provide simple answers on whether and how SA leads to outcomes, but it does provide practitioners with a systematic way to assess context in order to design, implement, and monitor SA approaches.

The framework and guiding tables for unpacking contextual drivers are intended to support operationalization of the World Bank's corporate goal of "mainstreaming citizen engagement in World Bank Group operations" (World Bank 2014). The contextual drivers of citizen action, for example, can provide crucial understanding of how to motivate citizens to engage in World Bank operations. Similarly, knowledge about the impediments to information and mobilization, as highlighted in the report, can be integrated within a framework of citizen engagement.

The framework can be operationally applied at different levels of analysis to assess opportunities and challenges for SA from the country level, to the sector level, and down to a specific frontline service delivery unit. As such, it can support the following:

- Strategic, country-level, analytical, and engagement products such as systematic country diagnosis or development policy lending instruments, with the objective of providing information on the main elements that can support or hinder SA in the context of a particular country or sector. This is especially important to support a more encompassing use of SA approaches when working in challenging contexts such as FCSs.
- Sector and subsector analysis to determine the scope and likelihood that an SA engagement will improve the effectiveness of a select service (for example, curative health care or urban networked water supply) within a sector. For this purpose, the framework of this report is being teased out to map specific characteristics of both sector and context to the five constitutive elements of SA.
- Specific operations to assist task teams and country counterparts in critically assessing various entry points for social accountability work and their feasibility.
- Stronger monitoring and evaluation of Bank operations engaging citizens to improve governance and accountability, thus expanding and deepening our understanding of the mechanisms through which SA leads to outcomes. By ensuring proper documentation of cases through a combination of methods, with the right level of details, the framework should prompt efforts to document contextual factors that are often missing from program design and evaluation.

References

Fox, J. 2014. "Social Accountability: What Does the Evidence Really Say?" GPSA Working Paper 1, World Bank, Washington, DC, July.

World Bank. 2014. "Strategic Framework for Mainstreaming Citizen Engagement in World Bank Group Operations (Draft)." Draft from the Decision Meeting on July 8, World Bank Group, Washington, DC.

Social Accountability Approaches and Tools

Since the objectives of social accountability (SA) approaches and tools sometimes overlap, this appendix categorizes SA approaches and tools by primary objective area.

Transparency

Budget literacy campaigns are efforts—usually on the part of civil society, academics, or research institutes—to build citizen and civil society capacity to understand budgets in order to hold government accountable for budget commitments and to influence budget priorities.

Citizen charter is a document that informs citizens about their entitlements as users of a public service, the standards they can expect for a service (time frame and quality), the remedies available for failure to adhere to standards, and the procedures, costs, and charges of a service. The charters entitle users to an explanation (and in some cases compensation) if standards are not met. For more information, visit "Citizen Charter" on the Social Accountability E-Guide.

Data visualization is a method of finding and telling stories. The complexity of visualization can range from simple data to highly elaborate multidimensional data. There are two main approaches to data visualization. One is to visualize existing data (therefore, demystifying information). Another is to visualize data as they are generated and collected. The latter approach is useful when no or very little data are available, but information is needed for decision making and coordination in emergency response, service provision, and other development contexts.

Geo-mapping refers to a process of connecting data with a map and is one method for visualizing data into self-explanatory or understandable information. The World Bank's Mapping for Results, which shows the locations of World Bank–financed projects, is one example. Mapping for Results aims to achieve better monitoring of development impact, improve aid effectiveness and coordination, and enhance transparency and accountability by visualizing project location on a map.

Geo-tagging refers to a process of adding geographic identification meta-data (or geo-coordinates) to various media, including photographs, videos, websites, short message service (SMS, mobile telephone texts), quick response code (QR, a two-dimensional barcode), and rich site summary (RSS) feeds. In the context of social accountability, for example, geo-tagging allows recordings made at project sites using different media, such as pictures and videos, to be identified by location, and this information can be incorporated into a map (geo-mapping).

Independent budget analysis is a process whereby civil society stakeholders research, explain, monitor, and disseminate information about public expenditures and investments to influence the allocation of public funds through the budget. For more information, visit "Independent Budget Analysis" on the Social Accountability E-Guide.

Information campaigns are processes that provide citizens with information about government plans, projects, laws, activities, and services. A variety of approaches, public meetings, mass media, printed materials, public performances, information kiosks, websites, social media platforms, texting, and radio, among others, can be used. For more information, visit "Information Campaigns" on the Social Accountability E-Guide.

Open data refer to nonproprietary and machine-readable data that anyone is free to use, reuse, manipulate, and disseminate without legal or technical restrictions. While open data may originate from any source, *open government data* refer to data sets that governments generate, collect, and possess. As part of the concept, open government data ought to be released under a creative commons license, which allows sharing, distributing, adapting, and even making commercial use of the data, with only formal attribution required.

Public displays of information refer to the posting of government information, usually about projects or services, in public areas, such as on billboards or in government offices, schools, health centers, community centers, project sites, and other places where communities receive services or discuss government affairs.

Public reporting of expenditures refers to the public disclosure and dissemination of information about government expenditures to enable citizens to hold government accountable for its spending. For more information, visit "Public Reporting of Revenues and Expenditures" on the Social Accountability E-Guide.

Social media refer to a variety of online platforms that allow institutions and organizations, as well as individuals, to share information and establish two-way communications around relevant topics, including development. Currently, there are several types of social media platforms with different purposes: social networking (Facebook, MySpace, Twitter), document sharing (Scribd), video and film sharing (YouTube), photo sharing (Flickr), and blogs, among others.

Accountability

Citizen report cards are an instrument for assessing public services by the users (citizens) through client feedback surveys. Going beyond data collection, they are an instrument for exacting public accountability through extensive media coverage and civil society advocacy. For more information, visit "Citizen Report Card" on the Social Accountability E-Guide.

Citizens' juries are a group of selected members of a community who make recommendations or propose actions to decision makers after investigating a matter. Citizens' juries are a deliberative participatory instrument to supplement conventional democratic processes. For more information, visit "Citizens' Jury" on the Social Accountability E-Guide.

Community monitoring is a system of measuring, recording, collecting, and analyzing information and communicating and acting on that information to improve performance. It holds government institutions accountable, provides ongoing feedback, shares control over monitoring and evaluation, engages in identifying or taking corrective actions, and seeks to facilitate dialogue between citizens and project authorities.

Community scorecards are a community-based monitoring tool that assesses services, projects, and government performance by analyzing qualitative data obtained through focus group discussions with the community. It usually includes interface meetings between service providers and users to formulate an action plan to address any identified problems and shortcomings. For more information, visit "Community Scorecard" on the Social Accountability E-Guide.

Grievance redress mechanisms (or *complaints-handling mechanisms*) are a system by which queries or clarifications about the project are responded to, problems with implementation are resolved, and complaints and grievances are addressed efficiently and effectively. For more information, visit "Formal Grievance Redress Mechanisms" on the Social Accountability E-Guide.

Input tracking refers to monitoring the flow of physical assets and service inputs from central to local levels. It is also called input monitoring.

Integrity pacts are a transparency and accountability tool that allows participants and public officials to agree on rules to be applied to a specific procurement. They include an "honesty pledge," by which involved parties promise not to offer or demand bribes. Bidders agree not to collude in order to obtain the contract, and if they do obtain the contract, they must avoid abusive practices while executing it. For more information, visit "Integrity Pacts" on the Social Accountability E-Guide.

Participatory physical audit refers to community members taking part in the physical inspection of project sites, especially when there are not enough professional auditors to inspect all facilities. Citizens measure the quantity and quality of construction materials, infrastructure, and facilities.

Procurement monitoring, in the context of social accountability, refers to independent, third-party monitoring of procurement activities by citizens, communities, or civil society organizations to ensure that there are no leakages or violations of procurement rules. For more information, visit "Procurement Monitoring" on the Social Accountability E-Guide.

Public expenditure tracking surveys involve citizen groups in tracking the flow of public resources for the provision of public goods or services from origin to destination. They can help to detect bottlenecks, inefficiencies, or corruption. For more information, visit "Public Expenditure Tracking Survey" on the Social Accountability E-Guide.

Public hearings are formal community-level meetings where local officials and citizens have the opportunity to exchange information and opinions on community affairs. Public hearings are often one element of a social audit initiative. For more information, visit "Public Hearings" on the Social Accountability E-Guide.

Social audits (also called *social accounting*) are a monitoring process through which organizational or project information is collected, analyzed, and shared publicly in a participatory fashion. Community members conduct investigative work at the end of which findings are shared and discussed publicly. For more information, visit "Social Audit" on the Social Accountability E-Guide.

User management committees refer to consumer groups taking on long-term management roles to initiate, implement, operate, and maintain services. User management committees are for increasing participation as much as they are for accountability and financial controls.

Participation

Citizen-user membership in decision-making bodies is a way to ensure accountability by allowing people who can reflect users' interests to sit on committees that make decisions about project activities under implementation (project-level arrangement) or utility boards (sector-level arrangement). For more information, visit "Citizen/User Membership in Decision-Making Bodies" on the Social Accountability E-Guide.

Community contracting is when community groups are contracted for the provision of services or when community groups contract service providers or infrastructure builders. For more information, visit "Community Contracting" on the Social Accountability E-Guide.

Community management is when services are fully managed or owned by service users or communities. Consumers own the service directly (each customer owns a share) when they form cooperatives. For more information, visit "Community Management" on the Social Accountability E-Guide.

Community oversight is the monitoring of publicly funded construction projects by citizens, community-based organizations, or civil society organizations participating directly or indirectly in exacting accountability. It applies across all stages of the project cycle, although the focus is on the construction phase.

Participatory budgeting is a process through which citizens participate directly in budget formulation, decision making, and monitoring of budget execution. It creates a channel for citizens to give voice to their budget priorities. For more information, visit "Participatory Budgeting" on the Social Accountability E-Guide.

Participatory planning convenes a broad base of key stakeholders, on an iterative basis, in order to generate a diagnosis of the existing situation and develop appropriate strategies to solve jointly identified problems. Project components, objectives, and strategies are designed in collaboration with stakeholders. For more information, visit "Participatory Planning" on the Social Accountability E-Guide.

Reference

World Bank, Social Accountability E-Guide, https://saeguide.worldbank.org.

Results from Selected Meta-Analysis and Systematic Review of Social Accountability Evidence

Over the past five years, there has been increased concern about whether social accountability (SA) initiatives deliver the expected impacts. Various studies have attempted to assess the impact of such interventions along the dimensions highlighted in appendix A. These include the gamut of evaluative work: from randomized controlled trials to more qualitative or participatory approaches.

Although the base of evidence on interventions continues to be both relatively thin (though growing) and scattered, three lessons emerge clearly from the available literature: (a) contextual conditions matter for understanding why interventions have the impacts they do, (b) we need to expand the universe of impacts and trace them systematically, and (c) we need to pay closer attention to the mechanisms through which SA initiatives are expected to have impact. These three lessons are discussed in the rest of this appendix.

Highlights from the findings of some of these studies follow. The report itself provides a new way to aggregate the evidence related to contextual factors for SA effectiveness based on a review of the existing evidence.

Conventional Reviews

Fox (2014) highlights several issues with prevailing interpretations of the existing evidence to date. First, across the studies, evidence shows that information alone is not enough to spark community action and subsequent provider response. Second, community monitoring from below by itself is not enough to improve public services, mainly because it lacks bite. Rather, combined with other accountability mechanisms (for example, top-down accountability or sanctions with teeth), it can have the desired effects. Third, elite capture is a real problem in community-led programs, which are based on "induced" participation and programs that usually do not include mechanisms for accountability. Fox concludes from the evidence that we need to rethink some of our basic propositions of accountability work and move from a focus on "tactical" approaches to more "strategic" ones. Fox proposes a set of conceptual propositions that highlight some of the key issues: campaigns are more strategic than tactical interventions; targeted transparency is useful in mobilizing people; voices need representation as well as aggregation; institutional capacity is necessary for responsiveness, with accompanying incentives and sanctions; vertical accountability and links to electoral politics are essential; corruption and poor performance, if improved at one level, can simply shift to another level unless one thinks of accountabilities of scale and vertical integration of oversight; and, finally, an alliance of pro-accountability actors within the state to pro-accountability groups in society can overcome forces opposed to accountability through a "sandwich strategy."

McGee and Gaventa (2011) sum up the state of the evidence as follows: "Context is crucial. It determines which transparency and accountability objectives are feasible or desirable in the first place, and which initiatives are appropriate in pursuit of them. ... Impact depends not only on internal effectiveness, but also on the initiative's interaction with the context in which it unfolds." They note, however, six important explanatory variables. On the supply side, first, they find little evidence of impact of transparency and accountability initiatives in nondemocratic settings, but some impacts in emerging democracies and fragile settings. Essential freedoms of association, voice, or media enhance the prospects of impact. Second, a political environment that favors a balanced supply- and demand-side approach to accountability is critical to the success of a transparency and accountability initiative. Where the state is willing to adopt accountability provisions, these provisions need to be fully institutionalized and have teeth if they are to be useful. Champions inside the system can help citizen-led transparency and accountability initiatives to succeed, but may be constrained by systemic and institutional factors. Third, democratic space and committed state actors or political leadership may not be enough to bring about the desired changes. Also relevant are the broader political economy and prevailing legal frameworks and incentive structures within which political representatives and state functionaries operate. On the citizen side, four further factors emerge: (a) the importance of citizens' capabilities in understanding and analyzing information, which can be strengthened by active media; (b) prior experience with social-civic mobilization; (c) coalitions; and (d) intermediaries who can "translate" and communicate information. Transparency and accountability initiatives appear to gain traction from being linked to other civic mobilization strategies like litigation, electoral pressure, or protest movements and from invoking collective rather than, or besides, individual action. Citizens who were engaged upstream in formulating the policies are more likely to engage in monitoring them, and engagement in policy formulation can arguably increase accountability more than ex post monitoring. To understand the factors causing impact, one needs to look at both sides of the governance equation.

Joshi (2013) summarizes the impact of transparency and accountability initiatives in service delivery, finding that new accountability mechanisms have been effective in reaching their immediate goals: citizen report cards have been implemented and disseminated, community monitoring has been carried out, and information has been publicized. There is strong evidence of impact on public services in a range of cases. Mechanisms helping to expose corruption have had the clearest impact by bringing to light discrepancies between official accounts and the reality in practice. Initiatives have also been quite successful in increasing awareness of entitlements and empowering people to demand accountability, claim rights, and increase the practice of active citizenship. The evidence is more mixed, however, regarding the impact on the actual quality and accessibility of services themselves. Despite demands for accountability and exposure of corruption, experience suggests that direct social accountability mechanisms have little traction unless they are able to trigger traditional accountability and impose formal sanctions.

The main finding of this review is that the wide range and diversity of initiatives in the service delivery sector make it very difficult to establish conclusions about key factors that matter in achieving impact, even within similar initiatives. Most studies conclude that there is an urgent need to examine why certain transparency and accountability initiatives succeed and what factors seem to matter. The overarching lesson seems to be that context matters. Political economy factors, the nature and strength of civil society movements, the relative political strength of service providers (teachers' unions), the ability of cross-cutting coalitions to push reforms, the legal context, and an active media all appear to have contributed in varying degrees to the successful cases. Several studies highlight that citizen-led initiatives have impact when there is willingness from the public sector to support attempts to improve accountability. Most available evidence of impact is based on collective action rather than individual action. Social accountability mechanisms have impact when they can trigger traditional accountability mechanisms such as investigations, inspections, and audits. Information and transparency are a necessary, but not a sufficient, condition for desired outcomes to be realized. However, an active and independent media seem to be a critical part of several of the successful cases. Transparency and accountability initiatives without corresponding support for increasing the capacity to respond can lead to inaction and frustration on the part of providers.

Ringold et al. (2012) review the state of empirically generated knowledge about SA interactions in the area of human development, analyzing 15 rigorous impact evaluations carried out in developing and developed countries. The study stresses a particular difficulty of SA impact evaluations in human development sectors, since attributing causal links of SA tools to human development outcomes is challenging. Substantively, the evaluations demonstrate that asymmetries of information prevalent in the human development sectors make it difficult for individuals to assess the performance of providers without the assistance of social intermediaries. Citizens in most development contexts may be reluctant to challenge service providers, making direct oversight an ineffective accountability tool. Social intermediaries such as the media can serve as effective means of amplifying citizens' voice and holding providers more accountable. Context, such as the history of collective action and oversight in the human development sector, can be key and needs to be taken into account when planning evaluations of human development interventions.

Devarajan, Khemani, and Walton (2011) assess the state of SA evaluations and the substantive lessons learned for the Africa region. Among other issues, it examines the role of civil society actions in increasing state accountability for development. Examining those impact evaluations that foster civic mobilization for better service delivery, the authors find demonstrations of project effectiveness but underscore the need to pay particular attention to local context and initial conditions. There is little evidence of the spillover of the accountability processes introduced by SA interventions into communal practices, making sustainability of project achievements poorly understood. The study calls for technical support for locally grown accountability interventions that take local and national political and social realities into account on a more consistent basis.

Wong (2012) provides a meta-analysis of 17 robust impact evaluations of community-driven development interventions carried out by the World Bank. Two of the six areas of interest for this overview relate to SA processes and outcomes. One is the change in social capital (trust, collective action and association, and group and network dynamics), and the other is the change in perception of local governments by the population and popular participation in public decision making. In both cases (eight projects reportedly measure social capital outcomes, and five measure governance-related outcomes), results on the level and direction of change engendered by the project are reported to be mixed, with slightly more positive impacts on governance and no measurable impact on building up social capital and collective action. The study underscores the need for analytical work to examine the pathways of change and "unpack the black box of decision making" to understand better the workings of the observed outcome shifts.

Mansuri and Rao (2013) address the impacts of development interventions in the area of local participation primarily in the context of community-driven development and decentralization projects, thus analyzing a different universe than just SA interventions. They analyze about 400 assessments spanning from case studies to randomized controlled trial evaluations. They report evidence of elite capture of the benefits of participation at the communal level and stress the need for better contextualization of both interventions and analyses.

Bruns, Filmer, and Patrinos (2011) review broad accountability (not only social accountability) interventions intended to spur monitoring in education and find that information for accountability will work if information is understandable and if actors have some authority over decision making. Otherwise, the intervention will have no impact.

Gaventa and Barrett (2010) quantitatively summarize 100 qualitative case studies to find 30 cases in which citizen engagement was found to have made a difference to service delivery outcomes—however, not all cases were about accountability. Results indicate that 55 percent of those 153 outcomes were positive and 45 percent were negative. Negative results were associated with the failure of citizens to participate, due in part to fear of backlash against those who speak out and a sense of tokenism in the participation mechanism. The study finds context to be a critical component often overlooked by donors and thus leading to adverse outcomes.

The report underscores the need to overcome disciplinary barriers to create more context-responsive interventions.

Agarwal, Heltberg, and Diachok (2009) review the lessons from piloting and scaling up various social accountability interventions and find that, while the mechanisms can help to improve governance and development outcomes, they do not guarantee improvements in services. Overall they conclude that these are long-term processes, and a lot of how they unfold depends on the context in which they are located.

Rocha Menocal and Sharma (2008) trace the impact of citizen voice and transparency interventions across 90 donor interventions. Using a theory-of-change approach, they conclude that interventions are more likely to reach intermediate outcomes than final ones.

Goodwin and Maru (2014) examine the impacts of legal empowerment interventions. Legal empowerment efforts are defined broadly to include "those that seek to increase the capacity of people to exercise their rights and to participate in the processes of governing." Thus they include a range of social accountability interventions such as community monitoring, citizen scorecards, citizen audits, and right to information legislation. They also include general participatory interventions such as advocacy or identity registration as well as legal aid interventions such as the use of paralegals and alternate dispute resolution mechanisms that would not be considered SA by our definition. The review, examining 199 qualitative and quantitative studies, finds "substantial evidence on the impact of legal empowerment interventions." The most commonly reported impact is an increase in the agency of participants. They also point to evidence of behavior changes on the part of governments and other institutions. Most critically they find very few instances of negative impacts (97 percent of the studies identified at least one positive change). Of relevance is that this study uses the broadest definition of impact, including increases in legal knowledge, agency, ability to gain remedies, contributions to dignity, and social inclusion along with the usual outcomes, including reduced corruption, improved public services, and institutional changes.

Systematic Reviews

In addition to these conventional reviews, several recent systematic reviews have attempted to answer the question of whether and through what processes social accountability interventions might lead to impact.

Molina et al. (2013) recently completed (draft) meta-analysis of the impact of community monitoring initiatives (including information campaigns, community scorecards or citizen report cards, social audits, and grievance redress mechanisms) includes 10 completed evaluations and finds that the initiatives had a positive and significant effect on outcomes such as test scores and health status improvements as well as perceived satisfaction with the program. The interesting finding from this systematic review is that interventions with facilitated interaction between users and providers had a statistically significant treatment effect, pointing to the importance of interlocutors in the process. A significant but not surprising finding is that community participation is linked with program success—in other words, information interventions alone can fail to achieve their objectives if community participation is not triggered.

Lynch et al. (2013) offer a realist review of the evidence (seven studies) on whether interventions aimed at improving community accountability mechanisms and processes influenced *inclusive service delivery* and what factors affected accountability mechanisms. They find that the interventions surveyed had four common themes: (a) capacity development was a defining feature of all the interventions and was central to strengthening community accountability and promoting inclusive delivery; (b) all of the interventions had an empowerment element, either individual empowerment, community empowerment, or economic empowerment; (c) education, training, and access to information were central to reducing corruption; and (d) health outcomes were important in supporting effectiveness of interventions.[1] Interventions combined three generic types: social accountability (citizen report cards, social audits), process reforms (advocacy, engagement, or empowerment), or financial mechanisms (public expenditure tracking surveys). While the studies reviewed are robust in terms of methods (several report the results of randomized controlled trials), the diversity of interventions and the context-specific nature of findings suggest limited generalizability.

Westhorp et al. (2013) review the evidence from 159 studies on the "circumstances under which community accountability and empowerment interventions led to improved education outcomes." They identify 10 mechanisms through which accountability interventions might lead to improving education—eyes and ears, carrots and sticks, big brother is watching, the power to hire and fire, increasing community capacity, elder or council authority, increasing politician capacity, mutual accountability, mind the gap, and my children's future—and list 28 contextual features that provide an enabling environment. The mechanisms, combined with contextual features, could enable one to gauge the likelihood of particular interventions working in specific contexts. The authors, however, point to the tentative nature of these findings, the complexity of achieving educational outcomes, as well as the difficulties of unpacking accountability and empowerment.

Note

1. Because the seven interventions included in the review were of different types (from farmer field schools to cash transfers for youth) and reported different outcomes, no meta-analysis was done to assess whether interventions had impact.

References

Agarwal, S., R. Heltberg, and M. Diachok. 2009. "Scaling-up Social Accountability in World Bank Operations." World Bank, Washington, DC.

Bruns, B., D. Filmer, and H. Patrinos. 2011. *Making Schools Work: New Evidence on Accountability Reforms*. Washington, DC: World Bank.

Devarajan, S., S. Khemani, and W. Walton. 2011. "Civil Society, Public Action, and Accountability in Africa." Policy Research Working Paper 5733, World Bank, Washington, DC.

Fox, J. 2014. "Social Accountability: What Does the Evidence Really Say?" GPSA Working Paper 1, World Bank, Washington, DC, July.

Gaventa, J., and G. Barrett. 2010. "So What Difference Does It Make? Mapping the Outcomes of Citizen Engagement." IDS Working Paper 347, University of Sussex, Institute of Development Studies, Brighton, U.K. http://www.gsdrc.org /go/display&type=Document&id=3981&source=rss.

Goodwin, L., and V. Maru. 2014. "What Do We Know about Legal Empowerment? Mapping the Evidence." Working paper, Namati, Washington, DC.

Joshi, A. 2013. "The Impact of Social Accountability Initiatives on Improving the Delivery of Public Services: A Systematic Review of Four Intervention Types: Protocol." Unpublished mss., Institute of Development Studies, London.

Lynch, U., S. McGrellis, M. Dutschke, M. Anderson, P. Arnsberger, and G. Macdonald. 2013. "What Is the Evidence That the Establishment or Use of Community Accountability Mechanisms and Processes Improves Inclusive Service Delivery by Governments, Donors, and NGOs to Communities?"

University of London, Institute of Education, Social Science Research Unit, EPPI Centre, London.

Mansuri, G., and V. Rao. 2013. *Localizing Development: Does Participation Work?* Policy Research Report. Washington, DC: World Bank.

McGee, R., and J. Gaventa. 2011. "Shifting Power? Assessing the Impact of Transparency and Accountability Initiatives." IDS Working Paper 383, University of Sussex, Institute of Development Studies, Brighton, U.K. http://www.ids.ac.uk/files/dmfile/Wp383.pdf.

Molina, E., A. Pacheco, L. Gasparini, G. Cruces, and A. Rius. 2013. *Community Monitoring Interventions to Curb Corruption and Increase Access to Quality in Service Delivery in Low- and Middle-income Countries: A Systematic Review.* Oslo: Campbell Collaboration.

Ringold, D., A. Holla, M. Koziol, and S. Srinivasan. 2012. *Citizens and Service Delivery: Assessing the Use of Social Accountability Approaches in Human Development.* Directions in Development. Washington, DC: World Bank. http://www.odi.org.uk/sites/odi.org.uk/files/odi-assets/events-documents/4871.pdf.

Rocha Menocal, A., and B. Sharma. 2008. *Joint Evaluation of Citizens' Voice and Accountability: Synthesis Report.* London: Department for International Development. http://www.odi.org.uk/sites/odi.org.uk/files/odi-assets/publications-opinion-files/3425.pdf.

Westhorp, G., W. Walker, N. Overbeeke, P. Rogers, G. Brice, and D. Ball. 2013. *Community Accountability, Empowerment, and Education Outcomes in Low- and Middle-Income Countries: A Realist Review.* Systematic Review. London: University of London, Institute of Education, Social Science Research Unit, EPPI Centre.

Wong, S. 2012. "What Have Been the Impacts of World Bank CDD Programs? CDD Impact Evaluation Review and Operational and Research Implications." World Bank, Washington, DC.

Selected Methods to Measure the Impact of Social Accountability

Table C.1 Selected Methods to Measure the Impact of Social Accountability

Approaches	Methods	Main characteristics and purposes
Action-reflection and action research	Participatory action research	• Contributing to the identification of reflection on and further refinement of ongoing interventions
Case based	Naturalistic, ground theory, ethnography, configurations, qualitative comparative analysis, within-case analysis, and simulations and network analysis	• Comparing combinations of causal factors across and within cases • Providing analytic generalization under certain conditions based on a theory and identifying clusters or subsets of causes that will make similar causal inferences
Cost-effectiveness and value for money	Improved results-based management, rating and weighting, trend analysis, and cost-benefit analysis or social return on investment	• Measuring and comparing the value that programs generate with the money spent to justify and demonstrate their investment worthiness
Experimental	Randomized controlled trials, quasi-experiments, natural experiments, before-and-after comparison, with-and-without comparison, difference-in-difference, regression discontinuity, and propensity score matching	• Producing statistical evidence of cause-and-effect relationships • Producing counterfactuals

(continued next page)

Table C.1 Selected Methods to Measure the Impact of Social Accountability (*continued*)

Approaches	Methods	Main characteristics and purposes
Mapping	Network mapping and social network analysis	• Identifying key stakeholders, bottlenecks in the flow of information or those who are isolated from knowledge flow, opportunities for better flow of information and influences, and key points of influence to be targeted for change
	Outcome mapping	• Assessing the intervention's contributions to the achievement of outcomes with focuses on changes in the behavior, relationships, or actions of direct partners for an intervention
Narrative	Group interviews, stakeholder interviews, focus groups, community interviews, in-depth interviews, narrative analysis, and most significant change	• Bridging the gap between "cause" and "effect" through understanding change from the perspective and interpretation of stakeholders
Participatory	Participatory monitoring and evaluation, participatory or democratic evaluation, empowerment evaluation, participatory rural appraisal, participatory learning and action, and collective action research	• Providing validation for participants that their actions and experienced effects are caused by an intervention and getting them to adopt, customize, and commit to a development goal or objective
Statistical	Statistical modeling, longitudinal studies, and econometrics	• Providing correlation between cause and effect or between variables and identifying the influences of usually isolated multiple causes on a single effect
Synthesis	Meta-analysis, narrative synthesis, and realist-based synthesis	• Accumulating and aggregating within a number of perspectives to provide analytic generalization
Theory based	Theory of change, process tracing or process evaluation, contribution analysis, impact pathways, realist evaluation, and congruence analysis	• Identifying or confirming the causal processes or chains • Bridging the gap between data and interpretation of the data or the gap between causes and effects
Other	Indexes and rankings	• Comparing status through a system of rating

Sources: Gaventa and McGee 2003; Roche and Kelly 2012; Stern et al. 2012.

References

Gaventa, J., and R. McGee. 2003. "The Impact of Transparency and Accountability Initiatives." *Development Policy Review* 31 (S1): S3–S28.

Roche, C., and L. Kelly. 2012. "The Evaluation of Politics and the Politics of Evaluation." Background Paper 1, University of Birmingham, Development Leadership Program, Birmingham, U.K.

Stern, E., N. Stame, J. Mayne, K. Forss, R. Davis, and B. Befani. 2012. "Broadening the Range of Methods for Impact Evaluations: Report of a Study Commissioned by the Department for International Development." Department for International Development, London.

Using Causal Chains to Recast the Evidence and Identify Contextual Drivers for Social Accountability

Rather than restricting our review of the evidence to "what works and what does not," we used reverse engineering to translate selected social accountability (SA) impact evaluations into attributed "causal chains."[1] For each of the selected cases, we carefully laid out some explicit (tested) hypotheses and some implicit (untested) mechanisms or change paths.

We focused on experimental and quasi-experimental impact evaluations—a choice that proved useful for investigating causality, despite the limitations of experimental methods in SA evaluations. As explained in chapter 2, most of these cases tend to be information based, for the very reason that the methods considered most "rigorous" to date are concerned primarily with information. So it was a fairly simple matter to aggregate findings on the factors that will make information conducive to action (figure D.1).

Translating impact evaluations into causal chains is useful for better understanding SA interventions. It helps to suggest indicative questions useful for examining SA assumptions critically and unpacking some possible factors contributing to SA outcomes. Our aggregation of the evidence from quasi-experimental impact evaluations showed that, for example, a task team should ask the following questions when disseminating information on a specific issue to support SA:

- Is the information on the issue significant enough for citizens to care?
- Does the information demonstrate a causal relationship between state action—or inaction—and outcomes?
- Are citizens likely to trust the source of the information and the setting in which it is disseminated?

Figure D.1 An Example of the Use of Causal Chain to Retrofit an Impact Evaluation

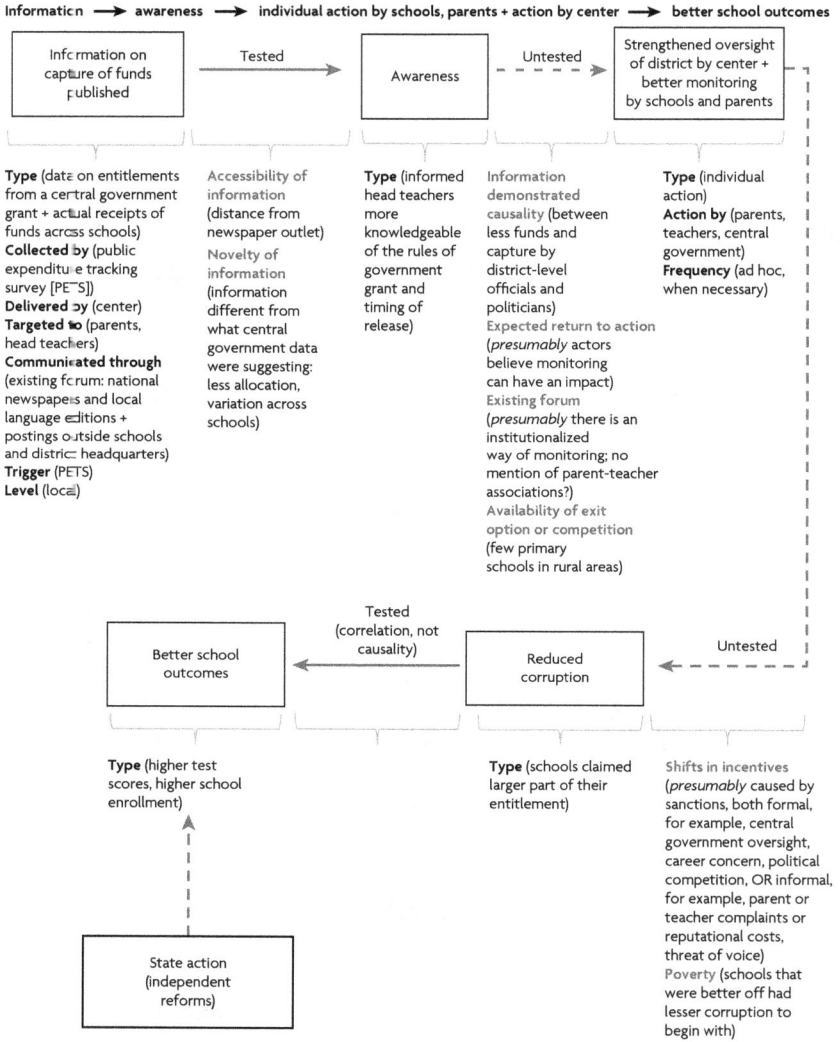

Information ⟶ awareness ⟶ individual action by schools, parents + action by center ⟶ better school outcomes

| Information on capture of funds published | Tested | Awareness | Untested | Strengthened oversight of district by center + better monitoring by schools and parents |

Type (data on entitlements from a central government grant + actual receipts of funds across schools)
Collected by (public expenditure tracking survey [PETS])
Delivered by (center)
Targeted to (parents, head teachers)
Communicated through (existing forum: national newspapers and local language editions + postings outside schools and district headquarters)
Trigger (PETS)
Level (local)

Accessibility of information (distance from newspaper outlet)
Novelty of information (information different from what central government data were suggesting: less allocation, variation across schools)

Type (informed head teachers more knowledgeable of the rules of government grant and timing of release)

Information demonstrated causality (between less funds and capture by district-level officials and politicians)
Expected return to action (*presumably* actors believe monitoring can have an impact)
Existing forum (*presumably* there is an institutionalized way of monitoring; no mention of parent-teacher associations?)
Availability of exit option or competition (few primary schools in rural areas)

Type (individual action)
Action by (parents, teachers, central government)
Frequency (ad hoc, when necessary)

| Better school outcomes | Tested (correlation, not causality) | Reduced corruption | Untested |

Type (higher test scores, higher school enrollment)

Type (schools claimed larger part of their entitlement)

Shifts in incentives (*presumably* caused by sanctions, both formal, for example, central government oversight, career concern, political competition, OR informal, for example, parent or teacher complaints or reputational costs, threat of voice)
Poverty (schools that were better off had lesser corruption to begin with)

| State action (independent reforms) |

Sources: Björkman 2004; Hubbard 2007; Reinikka and Svensson 2004, 2005.

Further, it is essential in SA design to examine contextual factors and to identify the stage of an intervention at which they will most influence success or failure. For example, although we know that elite capture, information asymmetry, a broken social contract, and unresponsive states all get in the way of success, we have little or no evidence to help us to pinpoint the stage of an intervention at which they become insuperable obstacles—something a causal chain approach can support.

Yet even an attempt to generalize the causal link most tested by quasi-experimental impact evaluation—from information to citizen action—proved difficult to capture generically. Hence, although the causal chain shown in figure D.2 compellingly accounts for the contexts of a particular intervention, it cannot be generalized.

Some assumptions in the chain that seem intuitive, such as the premise that novelty makes information more likely to trigger action (Is it *new* information?), do not always hold. For instance, two studies show that the level, frequency, and consistency of information can influence citizen behavior (Keefer and Khemani 2011; Pandey, Goyal, and Sundararaman 2009).

In addition, citizen action in various contexts may not follow a single sequence. For instance, the salience of a problem (Do I care?) may be so great in a given context that it drives in parallel (rather than in sequence) both individual awareness of the citizen's role (Do I believe my own individual action will have an impact?) and the capacity of individuals to form collective demand (Do I expect fellow community members to join me in taking action to affect change?). Causal chains, being linear, lack the flexibility to reflect such contextually variant causal trajectories.

Finally, information leading to action does not exhaust the SA agenda (a point stressed in chapter 2). Focusing on quasi-experimental impact evaluation restricted our analysis to moments of "induced" SA—state and donor interventions—as opposed to organic movements and spaces and to time frames considerably shorter than those necessary for complex social changes. And because most quasi-experimental impact evaluations emphasize service delivery outcomes, other potential outcomes tend to disappear from view (explaining, perhaps, why the factors that induce them have never been tested). Ultimately we enriched our preliminary analysis based on quasi-experimental impact evaluation with a much wider range of sources.

Figure D.2 Causal Chain for an Information-Focused Social Accountability Intervention

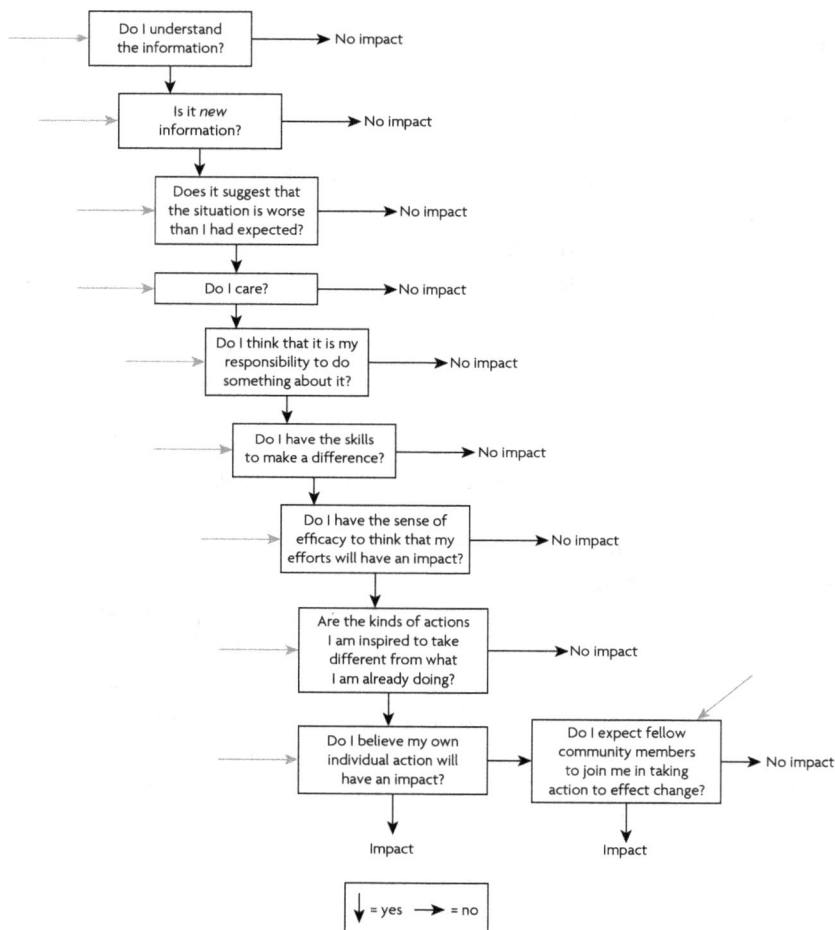

Source: Leberman, Posner, and Tsai 2013.

Note

1. This appendix draws on Majumdar (2013), which uses data from experimental or quasi-experimental impact evaluation in the education sector, together with relevant information, case studies, and qualitative work associated with each impact evaluation to embed and contextualize these interventions.

References

Björkman, M. 2004. "Public Funding in the Educational Sector and Its Effect on Test Scores." IIES Working Paper, Institute for International Economic Studies, Stockholm University.

Hubbard, P. 2007. "Putting the Power of Transparency in Context: Information's Role in Reducing Corruption in Uganda's Education Sector." Working Paper 136, Center for Global Development, Washington, DC. http://www.cgdev.org /files/15050_file_Uganda.pdf.

Keefer, P., and S. Khemani. 2011. "Mass Media and Public Services: The Effects of Radio Access on Public Education in Benin." Policy Research Working Paper 5559, World Bank, Washington, DC.

Lieberman, E., D. N. Posner, and L. Tsai. 2013. "Does Information Lead to More Active Citizenship? Evidence from an Education Intervention in Rural Kenya." Political Science Department Research Paper 2013-2, Massachusetts Institute of Technology, Cambridge, MA.

Majumdar, S. 2013. "Impact of Social Accountability Interventions: Evidence Mapping." Background paper prepared for this book, World Bank, Social Development Department, Washington, DC.

Pandey, P., S. Goyal, and V. Sundararaman. 2009. "Community Participation in Public Schools: The Impact of Public Information Campaign in Three Indian States." *Education Economics* 17 (3): 355–75.

Reinikka, R., and J. Svensson. 2004. "Local Capture: Evidence from a Central Government Transfer Program in Uganda." *Quarterly Journal of Economics* 119 (2, May): 679–705.

———. 2005. "Fighting Corruption to Improve Schooling: Evidence from a Newspaper Campaign in Uganda." *Journal of the European Economic Association* 3 (2-3): 259–67.